The Family Court without a Lawyer

A Handbook for Litigants in Person

Lucy Reed

First edition published May 2011 (Revised and reprinted April 2013)

Second edition published May 2014

Third edition published August 2017

ISBN 978-0-9935836-1-2

Bath Publishing Limited
27 Charmouth Road, Bath
BA1 3LJ
Tel: 01225 577810

email: info@bathpublishing.co.uk

www.bathpublishing.co.uk

Bath Publishing is a company registered in England: 5209173

Registered Office: As above

Foreword to the 3rd Edition by Sir James Munby

President of the Family Division

I am delighted to be able to welcome and applaud the latest edition of this important, and for litigants in person in the Family Court, absolutely invaluable book. Written by an author who has vast practical experience of what really goes on in family courts, this Handbook will continue to serve as a trusty, reliable and up-to-date guide and companion to those who find themselves on their own in court and without the assistance of a lawyer.

This latest edition could not be more timely, as the long-term impacts of LASPO on the administration of justice in the family courts become daily more and more apparent. As Mr Justice Cobb said in his Foreword to the last edition, and I could not agree more:

> "Now, more than ever, does the obligation fall on those of us working in the family courts to assist litigants in person to achieve the best outcome; this is plainly in their interests, but it is in the interests of justice as a whole. Initiatives across Government and the voluntary sector have gone some way to aid those facing courts on their own; this book makes a huge contribution to those endeavours."

The Family Justice Council has done valuable work in providing user-friendly literature for litigants in person, but otherwise the work thus far undertaken by Government – whether the Ministry of Justice, Her Majesty's Courts and Tribunals Service or the Family Procedure Rule Committee – has been sadly inadequate. So it is to the voluntary sector and to practitioners such as Lucy Reed that we must continue to look.

The truth is that we face a massive challenge. At present our practices and procedures are designed for – assume – a family justice system where the typical litigant has legal representation, whereas the reality is that, across vast swathes of the family justice system, the typical litigant now has no legal representation. The consequence is that practices, procedures and rules designed for lawyers are largely inaccessible – truth be told, unintelligible – to litigants in person. The Family Procedure Rules are a monument to a certain traditional style of legal drafting but are no more useful or intelligible to the litigant than the Tax statutes are to the taxpayer. And most court forms are little better.

The fact that this handbook is as long as it necessarily has to be if it is to achieve our author's objectives is no criticism of her but rather an indictment of the unnecessarily over-complicated 'system' which her readers are condemned to navigate.

In time these serious blots on our system will be remedied, but in the meantime the need for books such as this will only increase. And given the traditional snail's pace of legal reform in this country I foresee the need for many further editions from our author before we reach the promised land. In an ideal world we would not need a book like this but that world exists only at the end of the rainbow. So we will always need books like this. My hope is that, in due course, as our processes are simplified, our author will be able to produce a correspondingly shorter text. In the meantime I can only hope that she continues her good work. I look forward to the next, and to many further, editions.

James Munby

8 August 2017

Foreword to the 2nd Edition by Mr Justice Cobb

The timely publication of the second edition of this invaluable book coincides with the most significant reforms of family justice for a generation. The launch of the Family Court, supported by innovative and radical transformation of the processes of public family law and private family law, and wider access for the media to its hearings and judgments, combine to effect a fundamental break with the past.

The reforms have, in some measure, been incubating for decades. But two factors more than any others have stimulated reform at this stage – the report and recommendations of the Family Justice Review panel (November 2011), and the implementation of the Legal Aid Sentencing and Punishment of Offenders Act 2012 (LASPO 2012) (which came into force in April 2013). These drivers have compelled change in substantive family law, and in the systems and processes of family justice; in each case the architects of change recognised the inevitable increase in the numbers of litigants in person seeking to access the family courts. In one material respect (namely the promotion of dispute resolution away from the courts, through mediation and otherwise), these drivers for change had common cause.

Inevitably, the processes of family justice have had to flex to accommodate the higher numbers of litigants accessing the court without lawyers. The Child Arrangements Programme [PD12B FPR 2010] in private law has been designed with specific consideration to the needs both of the unrepresented litigant and the judges conducting their cases; the associated PD12J ('Child Arrangements & Contact Order: Domestic Violence and Harm') has been drafted with the same pen. Lawyers steeped in practices of the family courts are adapting to what the President of the Family Division has described as the 'cultural revolution'.

But what do these reforms mean to those who face the prospect of the Family Court without the benefit of legal advice? Their needs are no less great; they continue to cross the threshold of the Family Court at a time of crisis in their lives – many are vulnerable and ill-prepared to handle the process. Now, more than ever, does the obligation fall on those of us working in the family courts to assist litigants in person to achieve the best outcome; this is plainly in their interests, but it is in the interests of justice as a whole. Initiatives across Government and the voluntary sector have gone some way to aid those facing courts on their own; this book makes a huge contribution to those endeavours.

In this second edition, Lucy Reed has outlined and discussed the changed landscape of family justice. She has covered the new material with great clarity, and has updated the explanations of key elements of family law – its substance and procedures – in this single volume which is written with obvious understanding of the standpoint of the unrepresented litigant; the text is clear and accessible. It is likely to be an ever-more useful reference point for litigants in person, for their families, and for their McKenzie Friends; for those who have representation, this will equally provide a useful handbook.

'The Family Court without a Lawyer' is a unique and invaluable companion for those who find themselves navigating the Family Court as litigants in person. I am confident that this work, in its new edition, will be ever more widely used and appreciated.

Mr Justice Cobb

May 2014

Bar Pro Bono Unit

The author and publisher are donating 5% of book revenue to the Bar Pro Bono Unit.

The Bar Pro Bono Unit is a national charity which enables pro bono advice and representation from volunteer barristers for those who cannot afford to pay for such help and are unable to obtain legal aid. The Unit team is passionate about increasing access to justice and aim to ensure that in each case the barrister is of the same expertise and experience as would be expected in a privately funded case. The panel of pre-volunteered barristers has expanded to over 2,000 with over 250 QCs.

www.nofamilylawyer.co.uk

Working versions of many of the documents and templates available in the Toolkit & Resources section of this book are available to download on our website - www.nofamilylawyer.co.uk.

Introduction

Finding yourself caught up in a court case in the Family Court is a daunting prospect at the best of times. And the period after your relationship has broken down is not the best of times. For the uninitiated finding your way through the law and the jargon to make some kind of sense of what is happening to your life can be almost impossible. Expecting people in the throes of a relationship breakdown or family crisis to be able to link in to the alien processes that are now controlling their lives is a tall order. These are emotional times and rational thinking and objectivity is going to be pretty difficult.

Navigating through this stage of your life without a lawyer can be even more unnerving, and can leave many people feeling doubly vulnerable, disempowered and defensive. As a litigant in person (for that is what you are if you are left to manage a family court case without the help of a lawyer) these are not qualities you want to radiate or base your handling of your case upon if you want a good outcome. At these most difficult of times you need to be well informed, calm and objective and focused on how to interact with your ex and the justice system in a productive way. Any lawyer worth their salt will tell your ex and you that it is far better to avoid coming to court if you can. There are alternatives to court for most families (around 90% of separating couples manage it), and the umbrella term 'Dispute Resolution' or 'DR' is used to describe the range of assisted methods of dealing with disputes after family breakdown (see Chapter 2). Many people say that if they had known how difficult court proceedings would have been they would have tried other methods to avoid it - this book should give you a handle on how things can unfold where families turn to the court system. It is not the easy option.

This book recognises two things: firstly, that not everyone will be able to access a lawyer and secondly, that with the right information a litigant in person (or LiP) need not be at a significant disadvantage. There is no pretence in this book that in some cases you would not be much better off with a lawyer if you had the choice, but increasingly getting 'lawyered up' is not an option for ordinary people in ordinary jobs with ordinary incomes. So if you are going to have to go it alone, do a little reading and research early on, keep cool and keep practical.

So this book is a starting point for litigants in person. It's not a substitute for a lawyer or for legal advice but it is written from the perspective of a lawyer who works day in and day out in the Family Court, and who has seen litigants in person variously 'crash and burn' or 'win the day' (although any experienced family lawyer will tell you it's less about 'winning' than it is about finding an outcome that works). In it you will find explanations of the law and of how the system works that you can understand without a law degree, and tips for how to conduct yourself and your case so as to give yourself the best shot at achieving a good outcome. I hope that it will help to demystify the court process and cut through complicated terminology, which can be a source of fear for most non-lawyers. Language is power and understanding the language of the court gives you a bit of that power back.

There will also be something in this book, I hope, for those who have a busy solicitor who never seems to have quite enough time to explain things at your pace - you won't be alone if this describes your situation. Some of the things that are perplexing you about what on earth is going on may be explained in this book.

This book may also be helpful for those around you: your bewildered family who want to support you but don't really understand what's going on, your McKenzie friend or perhaps an advice worker who is not that familiar with the ins and outs of family cases. Even if you never go to court it may be helpful to understand what it would be like and some of the reasons why lawyers and friends or family with first-hand experience may be urging you to try and avoid it if you can.

I wrote this book for a number of reasons:

As a barrister representing parties in family cases week on week, I often see LiPs with perfectly good cases doing themselves a disservice, all for want of a little balanced information and guidance. A lack of advice shouldn't affect the outcome of a case but sometimes it does. And it can lead to the court making the 'wrong' decision (although as readers will discover there is very rarely anything as clear cut as one single 'right' answer).

Fairness is important to me. In my day job I represent clients of all backgrounds: husbands and wives, mothers and fathers, children and their guardians, social services, those accused of violence or abuse and those who are victims of it. What I want most of all at the end of the week is to feel that I have played a positive part in helping broken families to achieve a release from the court system so that they can get on with their new lives, so that they can come to terms with the past and move on to the future. The system is far from perfect but what most of us working within it are aiming for is justice, and if that is to make sense at all it must be something that everyone is able to access. I hope that with this book I can spread a little of my experience more widely and contribute towards making justice for families more widely accessible.

LiPs clog up the courts - insensitive of me to say so perhaps, but true nonetheless.

And in the current economic climate there are more LiPs than ever. Since I wrote the first edition of this book the Government has withdrawn legal aid cover for most of the types of cases that are dealt with in it. When people running their own cases don't have a clue what they are supposed to be doing, don't know when they are fighting a losing battle or aren't able to be selective about which battles to fight and which to walk away from, hearings take longer and cases get postponed. The problem is not a lack of information (the internet in particular is a fantastic free resource) but the filtering of it: having the tools to work out what information is valuable, reliable and helpful is essential if you are to avoid being distracted from getting your life back on track.

This book has no agenda other than that which is set out above, but be aware that there is an enormous amount of information out there that needs to be treated with caution. Consider whether you want to sort out the problems within your family and your life or whether you want to become part of a wider campaign against the family justice system as an outlet for your bitter and frustrated feelings. If your aim is the former and you want to survive this time, coming out of it with self respect and knowing you have done your best to get a good outcome, then this book has something to offer you. If you are attracted by the latter, you may be looking in the wrong place.

My clients often find it reassuring to know that their lawyer has some experience of the realities of family life and of what they are going through, and in the same way you may want to have a mental picture of who is writing this book. I come from a pretty ordinary but loving family, and went to an ordinary school. I am mum to two young boys. Thankfully I am happily married (to an American), but relationship breakdown has affected my wider family. It is close in my memory how difficult even the 'easiest' of relationship breakdowns can be and how many people they can affect. In our house, although we share things as best we can, for the time being I am the breadwinner and my husband is the main carer. And the Cab Rank Rule (the rule which says barristers must not turn away clients who want to instruct them) means that as a barrister I represent mums, dads, partners and kids in pretty much equal measure. Some are wholly reasonable and well intentioned, some are malicious, and some are just idiotic. I don't see any of those characteristics as exclusive to men or to women and I give them all the best guidance and help I can. The same applies to this book.

Whatever circumstances have brought you to this book I wish you the best with the future. Remember, there is life after family breakdown and life after litigation.

Lucy Reed, Family Barrister

Contents

18. International Issues, Relocation & Abduction

19. When Things Go Wrong - Enforcing & Changing Child Arrangements Orders

PART 7: TOOLKIT & RESOURCES

PART 1: UNDERSTANDING THE SYSTEM

1.   Getting The Most Out Of This Book

1.1   Introduction

This book isn't an invitation or encouragement to go to court, but is intended to be a useful starting point for those who, for whatever reason, are having to navigate the Family Court without the benefit of a lawyer. It will not give you all the answers you need in every circumstance but it should give you a frame of reference so you can understand what is happening and what approach you should take. Handling your own court case can be like stepping into a totally alien world, where you don't understand the language and everyone is playing a game but they haven't told you the rules - your future and your family is not a game, but you do need to understand the basic rules before you can participate effectively.

This book is not the same as getting legal advice. It is an attempt to give you sound guidance about how things work generally - but each case is different, so whilst this book may be a reasonable alternative to legal advice where you cannot afford a lawyer it is not a substitute for it. I've had to strike a balance between being clear and precise about what the law says and providing too much detail which can be confusing and can make matters worse. The book covers the things that litigants in person are most likely to come up against but it doesn't (and can't) cover all possible eventualities or scenarios.

I hope this book will equip you with the tools to go away and research more specific information or seek more detailed advice from a range of sources. Use this book in tandem with the internet. It should make you feel a little more self-confident when you step into the court building. There is a lot of information in this book, but do not feel you have to know it all off by heart or even that you need to read every chapter, or read them in any particular order. Try to operate according to the following:

- Do not get too hung up on procedure - Family Courts are really quite flexible and will allow a certain amount of leeway to a LiP who uses the wrong form or who doesn't know all the jargon. You don't need to memorise everything in this book about the court process, but knowing roughly what process you need to follow should allow you to focus on the important part of your case - the facts and the outcome. Similarly, don't waste your time trying to score technical points against your ex (it certainly won't help and it may even do your case harm). Don't expect the law to tell you the answer - in most cases the only law that matters will be either s25 of the Matrimonial Causes Act 1973 or s1 of the Children Act 1989. All either of those will tell you is what factors the court has to consider before it makes a decision. In essence the court has to consider everything that is relevant, weigh it up and do what it thinks is fairest, and where children are involved what is in the best interests of the child or children. Acts of Parliament don't tell either the Judge or you what the outcome should be. Judges have a very wide discretion to make decisions.

- Be wary of case law - case law (judgments given in other cases) can tell you what other courts have done in other cases, but as the facts of each case are a little bit different, what the court has done in one case does not necessarily apply to your case. It can be hard to draw the right conclusion from case law if you are not experienced or if you do not have access to the full range of cases, and it is easy to misunderstand what the case law is telling the Judge to do. If in doubt, go back to first principles - s25 Matrimonial Causes Act 1973 or s1 Children Act 1989. Some of the most useful and important cases are listed in the Table of Cases in the Toolkit & Resources, and are noted throughout the book.

- Research thoroughly but don't overdo it. Do not come to court with twenty different judgments - you won't be able to remember what they say, the Judge won't have time to read them, and they will distract you and the court from the real issues. Do give some consideration to how reliable your source is. If you are looking up the law on the internet check that it is up to date. If you are relying on a case, check that there is no other case saying the exact opposite. Keep reminding yourself of the checklists in the statutes and make sure you haven't gone off on a wild goose chase.

- Seek advice when you need it. Everyone benefits from a reality check from a fresh pair of eyes once in a while, even if it's not a lawyer (Chapter 4 gives you some more suggestions. See also the rules on confidentiality in Chapter 11). Lawyers and Judges do this too when they can't see the wood for the trees. It's no failing to acknowledge this may be helpful to you too. If you are getting bogged down consider what other sources of support and guidance you can access.

This book is written to be useful for a range of people and perspectives - mums, dads, husbands, wives, partners, wider family members. There is lots of information available that focuses on things from one perspective or the other, and in particular a lot of material that focuses on things from a 'Father's rights' or dad's perspective. There is value in that type of material, but this book takes a broader approach - if you understand your case from all angles and all perspectives you will run it more effectively, regardless of what your own particular angle is. One of the first things that young lawyers learn is that, to be as effective and as persuasive as possible in court proceedings, you need to understand all the arguments *for* your position or view, AND all the arguments *against* it. You need to go around the back of the case, imagine you are the lawyer for your ex, identify the weaknesses in your own position and deal with them - very few cases are completely black and white. This book will help you (whoever you are) see your case in the round, in the way that the Judge will when coming to the case. That should benefit men and women equally. Rights-based guidance - guidance that is focussing on *your rights* and *why you are right* - can cause you to miss crucial considerations, and can leave you unprepared, unsuccessful and unhappy. If you are involved in a dispute that has got bad enough to go to court you need to be prepared to *genuinely* consider whether your ex might have a point, and whether you need to change your position or behaviour - your behaviour is the only thing in your control. This book is about finding practical ways of achieving your goals. It isn't meant to be a manifesto or critique of the system. This book is not legal advice and should not be treated as such.

1.2   How this book is put together

The book is divided into seven parts:

- Part 1 explains the basics of how the court and legal system fit together.

- Part 2 gives you some general practical guidance about courts and court procedure and tips on how to manage your case.

- Parts 3, 4 and 5 each deal with a particular type of case, starting with an overview of the law in that area and then a more practical look at how that type of case works.

- Part 6 deals with some of the things that come up later on in a case.

- Part 7 is your toolkit.

The book will give you the most benefit if you use it in conjunction with the numerous resources available freely on the internet. But it is not essential: the core of what you are likely to need is contained in this book, and for many readers some of it will not be needed at all. All websites referred to in the book are listed in the Part 7, Internet Resources chapter and specific links will be contained on the website associated with this book. Although I have only included websites that I think are likely to be reliable, it is up to you to make sure that those websites are still up to date, and to form a judgment about their contents.

This book does not always regurgitate the precise wording of the law because it is meant to be a manageable and easy to use guide for non-lawyers. Often the law is rephrased or summarised. Where I have used an exact phrase or term that comes directly from the law this is in **bold**. References to the piece of law that is being described are at the end of the sentence in question [in square brackets like this] so that if that particular piece of law comes up in your case you can look up the exact wording using the internet (you might not always need to do this).

Any forms referred to are available for download on the Justice website (or collection from your local court office). They can usually be completed on your computer and printed (but not saved). It is better to fill in a draft by hand and only type in your final answers when you are sure you are ready to finalise and print. Always print 3 copies of everything.

This book tries not to use too much legal jargon. Any legal words or abbreviations are explained in the Jargon Buster in the Toolkit & Resources.

I look at families with an open mind and whilst I recognise that certain scenarios often occur along gender lines, I try not to make assumptions about people's gender roles. I use 'he' and 'she' interchangeably in this book because Judges, lawyers, caring parents and breadwinners can be male or female, although in fact they do not fulfil these roles in equal numbers. Sometimes I describe a scenario where people are occupying 'traditional' gender roles, but even if I do not spell it out each time you can assume that if the man and woman were in each other's shoes the outcome and approach should be the same.

The information in this book covers the law in England & Wales, although there are some minor distinctions between English and Welsh law which are not covered. It does not apply to Scotland or Northern Ireland where the law is different.

The information in this book is as up to date as possible at the time of going to print. Updating information may be available online from time to time at www.nofamilylawyer.co.uk or on my blog Pink Tape.

2. Family Breakdown - Do We Have To Sort Things Out Through The Court?

2.1 So much to think about and sort out!

It is difficult to think straight when you are in the middle of a family or relationship breakdown. Apart from the emotional upset that a split will bring there will be a number of practical ramifications such as where you will live, what the living, schooling and contact arrangements will be for any children you have, how you will divide up your property and possessions, and notifying various agencies of your change of circumstances so they can adjust your benefits. Over time you may be able to sort out all these things between yourselves or you may need some professional help, possibly from a mediator or a lawyer. There is a useful 'Breaking Up Survival Guide' (and lots of other useful information) on the Advicenow website, which is a good place to start.

If you are reading this book you are probably past the point of trying to salvage your relationship, but if not, consider whether relationship counselling might help.

If you are sure your relationship is over, you may be able to make a complete clean break once you have sorted out the practicalities. But if you have kids the chances are that you will be better off trying to find a civilised way of relating to your ex to enable you to both remain involved in parenting your children. This is easier for some people than for others, and whilst it often does get easier with time some people are never able to find a constructive way of communicating. Be aware from the outset of the potential of unresolved disputes to fester and to damage the potential to work together in the future. If you can avoid going to court your chances of keeping things civil are generally much better. Simply shutting your ex out of your life is only rarely realistic when you have kids - you need to face up to the reality that your relationship as parents has to continue, albeit in a different way. If you have been the victim of violence or abuse this may affect the practicalities of co-parenting - see Chapters 21 and 22. The Sorting Out Separation, Parent Connection and the One Plus One websites provide lots of really helpful resources to help you adapt and find ways of co-parenting and to find your feet, to and to understand what you need to do to make things as easy as possible for the kids. There are lots more useful websites listed in the resources section at the back of this book.

2.2   Sorting out finances and benefits

If one of you leaves the family home you may need to consider making temporary arrangements to keep the finances ticking over, particularly if you are a one income family.

If you are receiving any benefits like income support, child tax credits or housing benefit you may be entitled to more if your partner has left the home or even if you are living separately but still under the same roof. Investigate this promptly as you may only be able to backdate any increased claim for three months.

If you are not receiving any benefits check whether you are now eligible because you are living alone. You might qualify for housing benefit or council tax benefit or for child tax credits even if you didn't before.

If you have been left without access to the family finances you might need to sort out your own bank account and get your benefits or wages transferred over or direct debits stopped or moved. These things take time so get on to it promptly.

Remember, even if you are no longer living at home, the house is still a joint asset and you may need to sell it. Letting it fall into disrepair or letting charges accrue on your mortgage account will mean less in the pot for both of you.

So, whether you are a breadwinner or a home maker it is in both of your interests to maintain and insure your home and to keep up mortgage payments on it until you can sort out a permanent solution if you can, even if you are the one who has left. If you can't, try to agree a way forward with your ex and importantly with the mortgage company. Do this BEFORE you fall into arrears. Many mortgage companies will be flexible and will allow you a payment holiday or will transfer to interest only until you can sort things out, but they will be less flexible if you and your ex have a poor payment record.

You may need to sort out child maintenance. You can do this by agreement between you or through the Child Maintenance Service (previously the Child Support Agency). You can work out a suitable figure for Child Support by going to the Child Maintenance Options website and using the calculator. The easiest thing to do is to make arrangements between you at the rate the calculator gives you. Since April 2010 if you are in receipt of benefits and child support through the CSA/CMS it will not affect the amount of benefits you get.

You may find the divorce and separation micro site run by Money Advice Service (the consumer financial education body), helpful.

2.3   Domestic violence or abuse
Victim

If you are the victim of domestic violence or abuse you may need help to pro-tect yourself or your children from your partner, either to get him or her out of the property or to keep him or her out. The court can make an injunction order called a non-molestation order to stop your ex harassing you or being violent or abusive to you, or an occupation order to keep him or her out of the house. If this type of order is broken by your partner the Police can arrest him or her.

If you are on a low income you will probably be eligible for legal aid to do this. If not you may be able to get help from domestic violence organisations (or through a solicitor if you are able to pay).

If you have to deal with this kind of application yourself see Chapters 21 & 22.

Accused

If you have been accused of domestic violence or abuse you may find that this has implications for you in terms of housing and contact with your children.

If your ex has applied for an injunction against you saying that you should not harass or be violent towards him or her, you won't qualify for legal aid (unless you are also able to qualify as a victim of abuse yourself). You are slightly more likely to be able to get legal aid if you are at risk of being forced to leave your home and you have nowhere else to go or if you have been the victim of domes-tic violence yourself, but only if you are on a low income.

Support

If you are worried about your violent or abusive behaviour or want to change it there are organisations that can help. Your local social services may be able to point you in the right direction or you could try the Respect website.

If you are struggling with your alcohol intake, drug use or feeling very low or mentally unwell, there are lots of agencies that can help. For some people these problems are the cause of a relationship breakdown, for others the consequence: either way the time after separation can be difficult and if you are finding it hard to cope you are in company with many others. There are some contact details and basic information for national organisations and support services listed in the Internet Resources section in the Toolkit & Resources but you may find it most useful to look for local support groups and services, and your GP can often be very helpful and supportive in finding and referring you to them.

2.4   Will I need to go to court?

Not every relationship breakdown leads to court. In fact most do not. This book is primarily for people who have already reached the stage where the alternatives seem to have been unsuccessful, but it is always worth re-evaluating whether there is some alternative way to resolve your dispute or sort out your situation. There is an increasing understanding and emphasis on finding ways to avoid court, but the reality is that some families are unable to sort out their issues without some assistance from a court.

If you need to go to court you need to go to court - it is no reflection on you or your family if you find that to be the case. But do give some thought to the information below - don't disregard it just because things seem dire, or because a court case has already been started.

'Alternative Dispute Resolution' or ADR describes ways of sorting out disputes apart from the 'traditional' route of court. ADR comes in many forms and has many names - sometimes it is called 'non court dispute resolution', NCDR, or just DR. You might want to consider the following options to help you through this time, and (if you can) discuss them with your ex:

- Mediation is probably the form of alternative dispute resolution that is useful in the broadest range of cases, and is the option that is most widely available. Mediation is where someone who is impartial helps both of you to agree what should happen without giving you legal advice. Any agreement you reach is non-binding. You cannot be forced to attend mediation but you will not be permitted to make an application to the court until you have at least considered whether mediation might be suitable by attending a 'Mediation Information and Advice Meeting' (MIAM) (see Chapter 8 which explains what you must do and when). There are exceptions to this requirement, for example in case of emergency, but they are limited.

- Collaborative Law is a way of reaching agreement without going to court. Each of you will meet face to face with your own lawyer, trained in the collaborative approach, to try and agree what should happen. You will each have your own advice but your lawyers will try to work constructively to find a solution with you. If you cannot reach an agreement through collaborative law and need to go to court, you will both need to instruct fresh lawyers.

- Round Table Discussions is a way of describing meetings between parties and their lawyers as in Collaborative Law but usually involving both solicitors and barristers. This may not be cost effective unless your assets are relatively sizeable. You can, however, retain your lawyer in any court proceedings that follow.

- Arbitration is a process that parties agree to enter into alongside legal advice. The parties agree that the arbitrator will make a decision on their case which will be legally binding. Family arbitration is a relatively recent innovation and can be used to resolve financial disputes, and has only recently been extended to cover disputes about children. It is an attractive option if there is a particular need for privacy (for example if there is press interest in the family) or in order to avoid court delay (a particular problem in London), but it is realistically only likely to be accessible and economical for families at the wealthier end of the scale, as the parties must be able pay their legal costs, the costs of the arbitrator and in financial cases the costs of obtaining an order approving the arbitrators award. More information is available from the Institute of Family Law Arbitrators Website.

- Private FDR is a process whereby a lawyer, who is often also a part time Judge, will hold a 'hearing' that operates just as a 'Financial Dispute Resolution' hearing would operate in the court process, with the Judge giving a view about the strengths and weaknesses of the positions taken, so that the issues can be narrowed and (hopefully) the parties can negotiate a settlement. Although it is non-binding, it otherwise has the same attractions as arbitration, and is probably also only suitable for couples with relatively substantial wealth, as the parties would be paying privately for their own lawyers and the private 'Judge'.

- There are a range of other novel legal services out there to help you sort things out as smoothly as possible, such as Intelligent Divorce. This is a fixed fee service which supports couples (together or separately) to gather all the financial information they will need for advice from a barrister about the likely outcome at court, which they can use to help reach an agreement. Check the credentials of any such service before paying.

Many solicitors' firms will be able to help you access this kind of help, or will even be able to provide it themselves. You might want to consider visiting a solicitor (or instructing a barrister directly) to give you some one-off preliminary advice about your situation and guidance about how you might approach managing the practicalities of separation. They should be able to guide you as to which option is right for you. Mediation is not for everyone. You may not be able to face sitting in the same room as your ex, and of course you cannot reach an agreement where only one party is willing to agree. However, some Alternative Dispute Resolution methods like mediation are likely to be cheaper and less draining than going to court - if they are successful. Some services, particularly mediation relating to children, may be available for free in your area (or may be funded by legal aid), but you may well have to pay for others. Legal aid is available for mediation, so if you are on a low income you will probably be able to attend a MIAM (and any subsequent mediation) for free. Even if you are not on a low income yourself, if your ex is eligible for mediation legal aid your attendance at a MIAM will be covered by legal aid.

3.   Family Courts

3.1   Types of courts

In England and Wales there are a number of different types of courts:

- Magistrates Court - deals with more minor criminal matters and many family matters. Used to deal with many family matters as the 'Family Proceedings Court', but this has been taken over by the Family Court from April 2014.

- County Court - deals with non-criminal matters (called 'civil' law). Used to deal with most kinds of family law, but this has been taken over by the Family Court from April 2014.

- **The Family Court - since April 2014 almost all family cases are dealt with in a new 'Family Court'. Some more complex cases are dealt with in the Family Division of the High Court. The Family Court sits in court buildings up and down the country and is made up of Judges and Lay Justices (Magistrates), some of whom will also work in the Magistrates and County Courts. The Family Court has its own rules: the Family Procedure Rules.**

- Crown Court - deals with more serious criminal matters with a Judge and jury. Does not deal with family cases, but in cases involving crimes such as child abuse, the outcome in the Crown Court may affect any related family case or vice versa.

- High Court - deals with all sorts of cases, and is divided into separate divisions: Family Division, Queen's Bench Division and Chancery Division. A Judge in the High Court has greater powers in family cases than a Judge or Lay Justices in the Family Court or County Court. The High Court deals with some family appeals.

- Court of Appeal - only deals with appeals, including appeals from the Family Court.

- Supreme Court - the highest appellate court in England & Wales and deals with appeals from the Court of Appeal (The Supreme Court was created in 2009 to replace the House of Lords Appellate Committee, the difference being that the Supreme Court is separate from and independent of Parliament).

This book is mainly concerned with family cases that will take place in the Family Court. If your case is in the Family Division of the High Court or an Appeal Court you are likely to benefit from legal representation and guidance more specific than this book can provide.

Lay Justices

Lay Justices (often referred to as Magistrates, JPs or Justices of the Peace) usually hear cases as a panel of three (sometimes two). Lay Justices are not legally qualified and are part time and unpaid, but they are assisted by a qualified Legal Adviser who will sit in court with them and advise them about the law before they make a decision. This arrangement can sometimes mean that the case takes a little longer to deal with than a case dealt with by a Judge, because the Justices have to discuss the case after they have heard the evidence, and take legal advice from the adviser before agreeing and writing out the reasons for their decision. This means that they can be more inflexible about procedure and do not tend to be so creative about finding solutions as a Judge who is confident handling the law.

Some straightforward things can be dealt with just by the Legal Adviser, but others have to be dealt with by a bench of Lay Justices. If there is an issue which is in dispute it has to be dealt with by the Justices.

Because Lay Justices are just local people rather than professional lawyers it is often said that they are more representative of the people they are making decisions about. Although there are attempts to make Lay Justices more representative of the population, the reality is that Lay Justices often come from very different backgrounds to the families who they are making decisions about. This is also true of Judges, although diversity is improving.

The Family Court does not have entirely separate buildings, so Family Court hearings might take place in the Magistrates Court building or the County or Crown Court building (just to confuse you!). Cases which are being dealt with by a Judge will probably be heard in the County Court building but you should always check the court order.

There are some types of case that are considered too complex for Lay Justices to deal with and will be dealt with by a Judge.

An appeal from a decision made by Lay Justices will be dealt with by a Judge.

Most of the references in this book to the 'court' or the 'Judge' can be read as applying to Lay Justices. You can assume this is the case unless the book says otherwise.

Judges

There are two levels of Judge in the Family Court: District Judge and Circuit Judge. A Deputy District Judge is simply the name for a part time District Judge (and a Deputy High Court Judge likewise).

A Circuit Judge is more senior than a District Judge and will decide appeals from a District Judge or Lay Justices.

A decision will usually be made at the start of the case about what level of Judge should deal with the case depending on the issues.

A Recorder is the name for a part time Judge of Circuit Judge level (I've no idea why!).

An appeal from a Circuit Judge (or Recorder) will be dealt with by the High Court (or in certain types of cases the Court of Appeal).

Judges and Lay Justices in the Family Court must apply the law as interpreted by higher ranks of Judges in other cases. This is called following a precedent (or *stare decisis* if you like Latin).

3.2 CAFCASS

CAFCASS is the Children and Families Court Advisory and Support Service and it provides social workers to advise the court about what is in the best interests of children who are the subject of a court case. CAFCASS is independent of social services, and falls under the Ministry of Justice.

In disputes between parents the court may ask CAFCASS to write a report or carry out other work to help the family, or to help the court reach a decision. Where the case is very complex a CAFCASS Officer may be asked to act as a Guardian for the child (this is a role within the court case only, and is not the same as a 'legal guardian' - see Chapter 17 for more). In cases where social services want to take a child into care CAFCASS are always asked to provide a Guardian for the child and advise the court throughout about what is in the best interests of the child, and whether or not social services' plans for the child are right for him or her.

CAFCASS has experienced fluctuating difficulties in meeting the demands placed upon it by the court system for a number of years, and at times, particularly after the increase in court work after the Baby Peter case, there have been long delays in getting cases allocated to a worker and in getting reports. At the time this book was published things have improved, but there has been a shift in emphasis to try and reduce the level of demand for CAFCASS reports (called 'proportionate working').

CAFCASS often attend court at the start of a case concerning children, to see if they can help the parents reach an agreement, or to advise the court on what help they can provide. You should expect to see a CAFCASS Officer at the first hearing in any case involving children. At some courts this will involve the CAF-CASS Officer sitting in court with the Judge / Justices and advising them; in others it will involve the CAFCASS Officer meeting with both parents (separately or together) and sometimes the children before going into court (whether children come to court varies between courts but in any event is only if they are old enough - not usually before they are nine years old); in some courts there will be a combination of the two. In some courts parents are invited to meet with a CAFCASS officer at their offices prior to the day of the hearing.

CAFCASS also perform routine basic checks on parties with the help of the Police and social services at the very start of cases involving children. They are expected to try and speak by telephone to each parent before the first hearing to ask them about whether there are any safeguarding issues, such as domestic violence or drug abuse.

4. Lawyers, Legal Advice, Representation & Support

4.1   Introduction

This book cannot be a substitute for a lawyer or legal advice but it can help you find your way around. If you are reading this book you may never have instructed a lawyer before, perhaps because you cannot afford one or perhaps because you are not sure whether you need to.

This chapter tells you about the sorts of legal help that might be available and makes some suggestions about different ways of funding them.

There are several different types of lawyers:

- Solicitors;

- Barristers;

- Legal Executives;

- There are often other non-qualified individuals working at solicitors' firms, and these are often referred to as Paralegals. 'Paralegal' is NOT a legal qualification, although some paralegals may be very experienced and some may be part qualified lawyers who cannot find a lawyer post. Many solicitors' firms will also have trainees who have a legal degree but are not yet fully qualified. A trainee barrister is called a pupil. An advocate is just a label for the sort of lawyer who does the talking for you in court - often but not always a barrister.

Each different type of lawyer is subject to regulation and some form of professional conduct requirements. Although the specifics vary, all lawyers have a duty to act in the client's best interests and upon their instructions, as well as a duty to assist the court and to further the interests of justice. Lawyers must not mislead the court in order to protect their client or advance their case. A lawyer who does not behave according to their code of conduct may be the subject of a complaint to their regulator and this can lead to them being disciplined or struck off, meaning they would be unable to work as a lawyer. This should give you some reassurance as a litigant in person in your dealings with an opposing lawyer.

I've used the term lawyer to describe lawyers who are properly qualified, but in fact there is nothing to stop anybody calling themselves an 'expert' or even a 'lawyer'. However, it is a criminal offence to pretend to be a 'barrister' or 'solicitor' without being fully qualified and authorised. If someone just calls themselves a 'lawyer' you need to check what sort of lawyer they are and whether they are authorised to practice to make sure they are what the label suggests.

You can find out more about different types of lawyers on the Legal Choices website.

4.2 Cases where you really ought to get legal advice

As a rule of thumb if your case involves any of the following features it is advisable to seek some basic legal advice even if you can't afford full representation.

In cases about children

- Where social services are threatening to remove the child from home e.g. into foster care (you will probably be entitled to legal aid in this scenario), or where your child has already been removed by social services,

- Where there are allegations of non-accidental injury of a child the case is about and who you are caring for, or where it is said you might have caused the injuries,

- Where there are allegations of sexual or physical abuse of a child in your care, or where it is said you are responsible,

- Where there is an international element such as an application to move permanently abroad or a risk of abduction abroad,

- Where a child was conceived through some form of assisted conception.

In cases about finances

- Where it is said by you or by another party in the case that another person or a business owns a share in the house or property that is being divided by the court,

- Where there is a valuable business and its value is in dispute,

- Where there are foreign assets or issues about foreign law,

- Where a party is bankrupt or might be about to go bankrupt,

- Where the mortgage company is trying to repossess the house - get housing advice urgently,

- Where the other party is about to dispose of the assets or money (for example by giving things away, withdrawing the funds, selling the house for less than it is worth to a friend or re-mortgaging),

- Where there are pension issues.

Generally

- Where a party cannot be found, is avoiding service or ignoring court orders,

- Where another party is mentally unwell or incapable of handling the case,

- Where there are more than two parties to the case,

- Where a hearing lasting more than two days has been listed,

- Where the Judge or the lawyers are talking about the 'Inherent Jurisdiction' (see Chapter 5) or about transferring the case to the High Court,

- Where you want to make an appeal (act quickly - time limits are usually 21 days).

4.3   Solicitors

Solicitors operate up and down the country, often from high street offices, and are usually your first stop if you need a lawyer. Historically a client would instruct a solicitor, who would in turn instruct a barrister if necessary. In some circumstances it is now possible to bypass the solicitor and instruct a barrister directly under the Direct Access Scheme (also called Public Access - see below), but this is usually not appropriate in family cases (you can find out more about Direct Access by looking at the Legal Services Board or Bar Council websites).

A solicitor will run a case for you (technically they will 'conduct the litigation'), and this involves filling in the forms, issuing applications and lodging documents with the court, being the first point of contact for your case, sending and receiving correspondence about the case and liaising with the court etc.

Some solicitors will also represent you in court. Sometimes though, your solicitor will suggest that a barrister is instructed to act for you at court. This might be because the solicitor you have instructed chooses not to undertake advocacy work, because they have another commitment on the day of your hearing, or because the case requires a particular expertise in advocacy or an area of law that they do not have (or because a barrister is cheaper).

Sometimes solicitors will be prepared to work for you on an as and when basis, carrying out specific tasks as and when you need their help or advice, rather than conducting the case throughout and receiving and responding to correspondence. They may offer fixed fee packages for specific pieces of work or stages of a case.

Nowadays many solicitors who deal with family work will do only family work, but in some small High Street firms a single solicitor will undertake a range of types of law (housing, conveyancing, wills, family, commercial etc) with no particular expertise in any. Check before instructing - most solicitors now have informative websites with information about each lawyer in the firm. You should try and find a solicitor who is a member of Resolution, or if the case is about children, a firm where someone is on the Law Society Children Panel.

4.4   Barristers

A barrister is a specialist type of lawyer whose main role is to represent a client at court through advocacy and negotiation, and to advise the client either in writing or face to face.

Barristers do not usually conduct litigation or handle client money (barristers have only been allowed to conduct litigation since January 2014 so this is not yet an established way of working for them). This often makes them more cost effective than solicitors because they don't need the administrative backup to handle funds and to deal with urgent correspondence, unlike solicitors.

Most family barristers spend the majority of their working week in court as advocates, whereas solicitors by their nature must spend a considerable proportion of their week dealing with paperwork. This means that a barrister may be a sensible choice where your case requires skilful advocacy (although some solicitors are also very experienced and skilful advocates).

Barristers can now accept instructions to advise or represent you directly without the assistance of a solicitor, but because they cannot usually conduct litigation this will often not be the best way of doing things in family cases.

Like solicitors, barristers are now becoming increasingly specialised in the areas of law within which they practice. Most family lawyers nowadays specialise in that field and do not undertake work in other fields. Your solicitor will usually instruct a barrister who has experience in the field of family law.

4.5   Direct access barristers

If you are thinking of instructing a barrister *instead* of a solicitor ('direct access') you can find a list of qualified barristers on the Direct Access Portal website and information about instructing barristers directly on the Bar Council website. There are also other searchable online directories.

The important thing to remember about instructing a barrister this way is that it can be more cost effective because it cuts out the need to pay for two lawyers. This means that in effect you carry out the role of solicitor, continuing to act as a litigant in person for the purposes of sending and receiving correspondence or dealing with the court or the other party or their solicitor (although you might instruct a barrister to give you guidance from time to time about correspondence or developments).

Instructing a barrister directly in this way is most likely to be appropriate if you want the barrister to carry out a review of the papers and the case and give you some advice on your prospects and what you should do next. They might do this in writing or by meeting with you to advise you face to face (this is called a conference).

Some barristers will agree to represent clients at a hearing without a solicitor also being involved, but this is unusual. If you want to instruct a barrister in this way you will need to make sure that you make enquiries and arrangements well in advance because most barristers will want to consider the papers before confirming whether or not they think it is appropriate to take on the case as representative rather than just adviser.

Now that barristers are allowed to conduct litigation it may be that they will start to offer a wider range of services that includes some administrative support and conduct of litigation, but it is unclear at the time of writing how this will develop.

The Bar Standards Board Guidance on Public Access gives you an idea of what a barrister can do when instructed directly:

> *'5. What a barrister can do on your behalf:*
>
> *Some examples of work which a barrister is allowed to do:*
>
>   *a) A barrister may appear on your behalf at court.*
>
>   *b) A barrister may give you legal advice.*
>
>   *c) A barrister may draft legal documents for you.....*
>
>   *d) A barrister may advise you on the formal steps which need to be taken in proceedings before a court or other organisation and draft formal documents for use in those proceedings.*

e) *A barrister may draft and send letters for you. A barrister can assist you with drafting letters if your case goes to court but the letters will need to be sent out in your name.*

f) *If a witness statement from you is required in proceedings, a barrister may prepare that statement from what you tell him or her. A barrister may also help to prepare witness statements from another person based on the information which that person has provided.*

g) *Where a case requires an expert witness (for example, a surveyor...), a barrister may advise you on the choice of a suitable expert and may draft a letter of instruction which you can then send to the expert as a letter from you on your own notepaper.*

h) *Barristers can negotiate on your behalf and can attend employment, Police or investigative hearings where appropriate.'*

The following are examples of work that a barrister may do, but only if they have been authorised to conduct litigation:

a) File proceedings on your behalf with the court or file other applications, or take other formal steps in court or other proceedings. (If the barrister has not been authorised to conduct litigation, you will have to send the documents to the court, although the barrister could help prepare them for you.),

b) Instruct an expert witness on your behalf.

A barrister is not allowed to handle a client's money (by comparison, solicitors can hold client money in the firm's trust account), except when they are being paid for work done of course.

4.6   Legal Executives

Legal Executives specialise in a particular area of law, which means the everyday work of a Legal Executive is similar to that of a solicitor.

Some are trained and qualified as Legal Executive Advocates, which means that they can represent clients in the Family Court. They cannot represent clients in other courts. They would normally instruct a barrister to represent you in a higher court or if they weren't qualified as advocates.

4.7   Regulation & complaints

Each type of lawyer is regulated by a different organisation:

- Solicitors are regulated by the Solicitors Regulation Authority.

- Barristers are regulated by the Bar Standards Board.

- Legal Executives are regulated by ILEX Professional Standards (IPS).

The Legal Services Board is the overarching regulator for all types of lawyers (they are concerned more with how professions operate as a whole than individual complaints).

The Legal Services Ombudsman deals with consumer complaints about all types of lawyers (but only where the complaint is about your own lawyer, not someone else's).

In the first instance regulators usually require you to complain to the chambers or firm of the lawyer you have a complaint about.

4.8　Finding a lawyer

The Law Society, the Bar Council and ILEX publish details of practicing Solicitors, Barristers and Legal Executives respectively. You can use these to check that the lawyer you want to instruct is a qualified lawyer in good standing (see also Legal Choices site).

You can also find information about whether you might be able to get legal aid on the gov.uk website, and about what local legal aid providers are near you on the Justice Website.

Local knowledge can be important, particularly in divorce cases where you may need to consider the value of your home or you may need to sell it - ask friends and family which local firms they would recommend and look in local papers for adverts.

Details of solicitors who are members of Resolution can be found on their website.

Your local court will not advertise solicitors or barristers but may have leaflets telling you about local Law Clinics or free advice and support services in your community.

4.9　Choosing a lawyer

It is important to make sure that, whichever lawyer or firm you instruct to help you with your case, they are experienced in dealing with family cases. You don't necessarily need a fully qualified solicitor or barrister to handle your case - what you need is somebody who deals with family cases day in day out and knows what they are doing. For example, a junior solicitor at a reputable firm may be all you need.

Before you instruct a lawyer check if they are a member of Resolution, if they are on the Children Panel, and if they provide or have links with any mediation or alternative dispute resolution organisations (most specialist family barristers are also members of the Family Law Bar Association).

Resolution members must adhere to a code of practice concerning family cases so if you instruct a lawyer who is a member of Resolution you can be relatively confident that they will approach your case in a sensitive, constructive and cost-efficient way and that they will try to resolve matters for you by agreement if possible.

4.10   Paying for a lawyer

You may be eligible for public funding (or 'Legal Aid') from the Legal Aid Agency, usually depending on your finances. It is always worth checking if you can obtain legal aid - do not assume that you cannot just because you are working. Although your income may rule you out, you may qualify for legal aid with a small contribution from you towards it. The rules on income are relaxed for applications for protective injunctions .

You usually have to consider or attempt mediation before being granted public funding (and before being allowed to make an application to court). There are exceptions to this, for example if the other party refuses to cooperate or if you have been subjected to domestic abuse. These are set out in Chapter 8. If you are on a low income you should be able to get legal aid to pay for mediation even if you cannot get it for a court case.

If you are not eligible for public funding you will probably have to pay any legal expenses yourself. Some companies offer financial products to help you pay the costs of a case where you are seeking to recover money or assets (e.g. on divorce or separation). If you want to instruct a solicitor enquire about any products that they can recommend or what flexibility they can provide in terms of payment arrangements. A few solicitors will offer a 'Sears-Tooth' arrangement in financial cases, which means the client signs over any sum awarded to the solicitor, to cover their costs when the case is over, leaving the balance for the client. This is quite a high risk for a solicitor and will only usually be offered if the assets are significant and the prospects good. It won't be suitable for cases concerning children. You can find out more about Sears-Tooth agreements on the Marilyn Stowe Blog.

In 2013 the law was changed to allow the courts to make a legal services order (LSO) in financial cases after divorce (see s22ZA Matrimonial Causes Act 1973). LSOs are court orders requiring one person to pay an amount over to cover some or all of the likely legal costs of the other person at the start of the case. This type of order might be made where one person is in a significantly more vulnerable position financially, and would otherwise be prevented from being able to pursue a court case because they could not raise the funds to pay a law-yer. The orders will usually only be made where the paying party has sufficient available funds to make the payment, and they will be a last resort when all else has been tried and failed. As these sorts of orders are new it is difficult to predict how often they will be made, but they are likely to be quite rare and only really made in cases involving quite wealthy couples where one person has a high income and control of the assets and the other has little independent income. There is more information about LSOs in Chapters 12 to 14.

If you don't think you can afford to instruct a lawyer throughout your case, con-sider whether you can afford some one-off advice (from a solicitor or a barrister) without asking a solicitor to handle all the paperwork and correspondence. Or consider whether or not you would like to direct limited funds towards the costs of an advocate at any hearing, rather than using up all your resources getting to a final hearing with the help of a solicitor and then having to represent yourself at the hearing. Discuss this with any solicitor you are thinking of instructing. Most solicitors will not charge you for this kind of discussion before you take the plunge and instruct them, and a good solicitor will try and find creative ways to balance your budget with the needs of the case. Different solutions will be right for different people - it will depend on how much paperwork there is, how complicated the preparation for any hearing is likely to be or whether there are any difficult legal points. Be wary of saving all your funds to hire a barrister for the trial - you could find that your barrister is not able to achieve the results you would like, and that your funds could have been better spent on getting some good advice on how to run and prepare the case so it is ready for the trial. It often pays to get some advice at the outset to set you on the right track even if you can't keep it up all the way through.

Do your homework before choosing a lawyer - there are lots of different servic-es and fee structures available to suit different pockets and different cases. Be realistic about what help you will need. If you are going to end up going back to your solicitor every five minutes for help you may want to try and find an arrangement that involves a ceiling on your costs.

A word about 'as and when' help from a lawyer: don't confuse help with advice. If you instruct a lawyer from time to time to carry out a specific task, they will carry out the task you have set, but the lawyer is probably in no position to give you advice. There is no substitute for paying a lawyer to sit down with you, go through the case properly, and to advise you on what steps you *should* be taking. For example, a solicitor may, at your request, send a letter making a proposal for settlement of your case to the other lawyer. But the proposal might be one which is very unlikely to be accepted. If they have all the information about the case your lawyer may be able to give you some *advice* about what would be the best proposal to make in your letter, giving you the best chance of achieving a settlement. Be clear with your lawyer what you want them to do - you are not achieving value for money by paying a solicitor to make a proposal on your behalf that does not hold water.

You may see 'as and when' help referred to as 'unbundled services'. This way of offering legal services is quite new, and the higher courts have not yet really clarified how they will approach this sort of arrangement if things go wrong. This means the potential risks are difficult to assess - for you or a solicitor you want to instruct.

4.11   Can I get legal aid? How do I go about it?

Legal aid is not available for every type of family law issue. The sort of family law issue which is within the scope of the legal aid scheme is set out below. If your issue is on this list you may still have to pass other tests to get legal aid. These are dealt with below.

- For a Mediation Information and Advice Meeting (MIAM) or mediation itself, depending on your finances and the other person's finances (see http://www.familymediationcouncil.org.uk/family-mediation/assessment-meeting-miam/);

- Advice / representation for private family law matters e.g. divorce, dissolution of civil partnership, property, finance and children matters ONLY IF:

    - there is evidence of domestic violence or abuse; OR

    - there is evidence of child abuse;

- Domestic violence injunctions for victim of domestic abuse;

- Forced marriage victims or potential victims;

- If the local authority has brought a case to court asking the court for orders about your child or a child you have parental responsibility for;

- Sometimes if the local authority has brought a case to court asking the court for orders about a child you do not have parental responsibility for (for example if the child lives with you or you are asking for the child to live with you, or if you are accused of hurting a child);

- To stop children being removed from the UK or to get them returned if they have been unlawfully removed;

- To enforce European Union and international agreements about children and maintenance;

- For an appeal or an application to discharge a care or placement order, or an application for leave to oppose an adoption - ONLY IF your case is strong enough and you are on a low income;

- Where children are parties to a court case (care cases or complicated private disputes) the child is entitled to legal aid.

In almost all the examples above you can only get legal aid if your case is strong enough AND you are on a low income. The only exception is cases where the local authority has brought a case to court asking the court for orders about your child or a child you have parental responsibility for when you are entitled to legal aid regardless of your income or the strength of your case.

This is just a rough guide. It is always sensible to ask a legal aid lawyer whether or not you are eligible before spending money on a lawyer or going it alone. There are very strict rules about the proof that you have to show to qualify for legal aid in these cases.

Non-means and non-merits tested

Some sorts of legal aid are non-means tested. This means it doesn't matter how much money you earn or have in the bank. In most cases though you can only get legal aid if you are on a low income (domestic violence injunctions are an exception).

Most sorts of legal aid are only available if the case is strong enough to justify it. However in a few categories legal aid is available automatically.

If you are a parent who is involved in public law (care) proceedings (that is where social services make an application to court asking for orders about your children and sometimes asking for them to be removed from your care, see Chapter 16) you are automatically entitled to legal aid and you should go and find a family legal aid solicitor as soon as possible.

If you have parental responsibility for a child that is not your own child (this would usually be where there is a child arrangements order saying a child lives with you) you are also entitled to legal aid in any care proceedings about that child.

Means tested

Some sorts of legal aid are means-tested. This means they are only available if you are on a low income.

This book does not deal with the means-test - visit the CAB AdviceGuide website for up to date information about the income and capital limits and to see if your income or capital prevents you from getting legal aid. Just to give you a rough idea, at the time this book was published you would not qualify for legal aid if your gross monthly income (excluding certain benefits) is over £2,657 or you have savings of more than £8,000. If you own your own home this is taken into account as capital, but generally your mortgage will be deducted. Sometimes if your income is on the borderline you can get legal aid if you make a monthly contribution to it. The income limit of £2,657 is dis-applied for applications for a protective injunction.

To start the process of applying for legal aid go to: www.gov.uk/check-legal-aid, which gives you all the details for applying online or by phone and what to do if it's urgent.

The following assumes that you are financially eligible for legal aid.

Domestic violence injunction

If you are applying for a domestic violence injunction (a non-molestation order - see Part 5) you may be entitled to legal aid to make that application. Although you will need evidence to put before the court to obtain an injunction (usually in the form of a witness statement from you) you do not need to satisfy the very strict evidence requirements set out below in order to get legal aid. If you obtain an injunction that will then be evidence you can use to satisfy the legal aid evidence requirements if you are involved in any case about the children or divorce that starts within the next five years (see below).

Cases about children or money

If you are involved in any other kind of family case (e.g. dispute about where a child should live or contact with their other parent, financial proceedings after divorce) legal aid is not available, except in very limited circumstances. You will only be eligible for legal aid if one of the following applies:

- You have evidence that you are the victim of domestic abuse or are applying for an injunction to protect you or your child as a result of such domestic abuse, or

- You have evidence that you are protecting your child from child abuse from the other person in the case, or

- In cases of child abduction.

You will also have to satisfy a merits test, which means that the Legal Aid Agency will look at how strong your case is when making decisions about funding. A very weak case is unlikely to get funding.

Domestic abuse

If you are the victim of domestic abuse by your ex (or the person who the dispute is with), legal aid is available subject to your financial eligibility and strength of your case.

Except in care proceedings where legal aid is automatic, if you want legal aid you will have to be able to produce evidence of the domestic abuse or risk of abuse before you can apply, and that evidence must be through **one** of the following documents. It's a long list but you do only have to get one of these pieces of evidence before you can apply. A previous rule that evidence could not be more than two years old has now been somewhat relaxed for some sorts of evidence, by replacing the two year cut off with a five year cut off (at the time of writing there are reports that this five year rule will be scrapped, but no changes have yet been made).

Types of evidence (domestic abuse)

The regulations that define what evidence does and does not count are really difficult to work through, and do get tweaked from time to time. I've set out what they said at the time this book was published, based on the Legal Aid Agency Guidance and the Regulations, which were updated in May 2016 after a court case decided they needed to be updated. Any legal aid lawyer will be able to tell you if there have been significant changes to these requirements since publication. The evidence must show domestic violence against you (not some other person) by the other person in the case. However, in cases of sexual offences, the victim is not named and so it is okay to submit evidence which doesn't have your name on it as victim.

a) **a relevant conviction for a domestic violence offence.** The law says that a conviction is 'spent' and can be disregarded for most purposes after a period of time. How long depends on the type and length of sentence. You can find out if a conviction is likely to be spent on the Your Rights website. You can rely on an unspent conviction regardless of how old it is, OR a spent conviction as long as it is not more than five years old. You can find a list of relevant domestic violence offences on the gov. uk website (https://www.gov.uk/government/publications/domestic-violence-and-child-abuse-offences). You'll need proof of the conviction and the date of it from the court, the CPS or Police. The evidence must identify you as the victim of the offence. You might be able to make an application under 'Clare's Law' for information about your ex's previous convictions - ask at your local Police Station;

b) **a relevant police caution for a domestic violence offence against you** (but the caution must have been given within the last five years before the date you make your application);

c) **evidence of relevant criminal proceedings for a domestic violence offence against you which have not concluded** (if the Police have charged your ex with an offence but it's awaiting trial they or the Crown Prosecution Service should be able to confirm this in writing for you);

d) **a relevant protective injunction** (Protective injunctions is a catch all description for a range of injunctions, which includes non-molestation orders and orders under the Protection from Harassment Act, covered in Chapters 21 & 22). The injunction must be in force or must have been granted not more than five years before the date of your application for legal aid. Even if your injunction ends or is discharged it will still count as long as it was first granted in the last five years;

e) **an undertaking** (Undertakings are described more in Chapters 21 & 22 and are usually given as a result of an application for an injunction). The undertaking must be by the person who you are in dispute with in your family case, must have been given within the last five years before the date of your application and importantly you cannot use it as evidence to get legal aid if you gave a cross undertaking (if both of you made promises not to behave in a certain way). Cross undertakings are explained in Chapters 21 & 22 but if you don't know what one is you probably haven't given one!;

ea) evidence that the other person is on relevant **police bail for a domestic violence offence**. If the bail ends and the other person is not charged you will need to submit a replacement piece of evidence;

f) **a letter from a member of a MARAC** [Multi Agency Risk Assessment Conference] confirming that you were referred to the conference as a victim of domestic violence and that the conference put in place a plan to protect you from a risk of harm by the other person in the five years before your application;

g) **a copy of a finding of fact that there has been domestic violence** by the other person in the case against you, made by a court in the United Kingdom. The finding of fact decision must be not more than five years old at the date of your application;

h) **a letter or report from a health professional**. This might be from someone like your GP, community psychiatric nurse, your or midwife or health visitor. It must confirm that they or another health professional has examined you in person within the five years before the date of your application and that you had injuries or a condition consistent with being a victim of domestic violence and they have no reason to think that this wasn't caused by domestic violence (this might cause a problem if you lied about how you got the injuries at the time). The person writing the letter must be someone who has access to your medical records and the letter must confirm that;

i) **a letter from a UK social services department** confirming that you have been assessed within the five years before the date of your application as being a victim of domestic violence by the other person or that you were at risk of domestic violence from them. Instead of a letter you can provide a copy of the assessment report if you have it;

j) **a letter or report from a domestic violence support organisation in the UK** confirming that at some point in the five years before your application for legal aid is made you spent 24 hours or more in a domestic violence refuge. The letter or report must state the dates you were there and must confirm that you were there because of allegations by you of domestic violence;

k) **a letter or report from a domestic violence support organisation in the UK** confirming that at some point in the five years before your application for legal aid is made you were **turned away from a refuge**

because it was full. It must state the date you were refused admission;

l) **a letter or report from a health professional** with access to your medical records, or from either the person who made or the person **who received a referral for specialist support or assistance for victims of domestic violence or people at risk of it**, which was made within the five years before your application for legal aid;

m) **a domestic violence protection notice or order** against the other person to protect you at some point made in the five years before your legal aid application. These are sometimes called 'go notices / go orders' (see Chapter 21);

n) evidence of **a court order binding over the other person** in connection with a domestic violence offence against you, which is in force or which was granted in the five years before your legal aid application;

o) **Financial Abuse**. Following a challenge in a court case in 2016 the Legal Aid Agency will now consider granting legal aid where you can show domestic violence in the form of financial abuse. The evidence should show that the behaviour is done with the intention to gain power and control. There are no specific pieces of evidence that you must provide, but this is likely to be things like bank or credit card statements, text messages, emails or diary entries, or a letter from a domestic violence support organisation. In some cases if there are no documents showing financial abuse you may need to make a statement setting out in writing what financial abuse you suffered and why there are no documents to prove it.

The legal aid for private family matters section of the Justice website also provides template letters that you can ask one of the people named above to complete in order to obtain the necessary evidence.

If you are the victim of domestic violence or abuse by your ex you may also qualify for legal aid to deal with your finances on divorce if you can satisfy the evidence tests set out above (and the usual means and merits tests).

Child protection

If you are applying to the court to obtain orders that are intended to protect a child from abuse (or want to resist an application made by a person from whom the children are at risk of abuse) you may be eligible for legal aid subject to your financial eligibility and strength of your case.

If you want legal aid you will have to be able to produce evidence of the risk of abuse before you can apply, and that evidence must be through **one** of the following documents showing the other person in the case is a risk. It's a long list but you do only have to get one of these pieces of evidence before you can apply. For some categories of document there is a two year cut off that applies (unlike for domestic violence offences where the cut off is usually five years), so if your evidence is more than two years old you may need to look at one of the categories that does not have a cut off. The two years runs back from the date you make your legal aid application.

You can find a list of things that count as 'relevant child abuse offences' on the gov.uk website (https://www.gov.uk/government/publications/domestic-vio-lence-and-child-abuse-offences).

Types of evidence (child protection)

a) **a relevant conviction for a child abuse offence**. The law says that a conviction is 'spent' and can be disregarded for most purposes after a period of time. How long depends on the type and length of sentence. You can find out if a conviction is likely to be spent on the Your Rights website. You can rely on any unspent conviction regardless of how long ago the conviction was, OR any spent conviction as long as the conviction was not more than two years before your application for legal aid. The conviction can relate to any child. You'll need proof of the conviction and the date of it from the court, the CPS or Police;

b) **a relevant police caution for a child abuse offence** given at some point in the two years before your application for legal aid. The caution can relate to any child;

c) **evidence of relevant criminal proceedings for a child abuse offence which have not concluded**. This only applies where the person accused has actually been charged with an offence;

d) **a protective injunction against the other person made in order to protect the child in the case**, which is either in force or which was grant-ed at some point in the two years before your application for legal aid. A relevant injunction is something like a non-molestation order or an occupation order - but it must be made to protect the child (it can be made to protect you as well);

e) a copy of a **finding of fact**, made in proceedings in the UK at some point in the two years before your application for legal aid, saying that the other person abused a child;

ea) evidence that the other person is **on bail for a child abuse offence**. If the bail ends and the other person is not charged you will need to submit a replacement piece of evidence;

f) a letter from a social services department in the UK confirming that **the child was assessed as having been a victim of child abuse by the other person, or that the child was at risk from them**. The assessment must be not more than two years old at the date of the legal aid application. Instead of a letter you can just use a copy of the assessment itself;

g) a letter from a social services department in the UK confirming that at some point in the two years before your legal aid application was made **there was a child protection plan in place** to protect the child from abuse or a risk of abuse by the other person. Again a copy of the plan itself will do;

h) **an application for a protective injunction (see d) above) made at the same time as an application for a prohibited steps order** against the other person which has not been dealt with at the time of the application. This enables you to get legal aid in order to bring an urgent application to protect a child from abuse or harm by the other person.

The 'Legal aid for private family matters' section of the Justice website also provides template letters that you can ask one of the people named above to complete in order to obtain the necessary evidence.

Can I get legal aid if allegations are made against me?

Unfortunately, if you are someone who has had allegations of domestic violence or abuse or child abuse made *against you* there is no legal aid available (unless of course you are able to satisfy the requirements above because you have also been the victim of domestic abuse or you are applying yourself for orders to protect a child).

Before the general election in 2017 Parliament was considering a change to the law that would mean that if you are accused of domestic abuse and do not have a lawyer, you will not be allowed to question your accuser yourself, and the court may appoint a lawyer to ask questions for you, at the court's expense. This would not be the same as being fully represented, as the lawyer would only be involved in the questioning of that witness, and you would still have to represent yourself through the other parts of the case. It is likely that similar changes will be contained in a fresh bill put forward by the new Parliament but the detail might change as it goes through Parliament, or it might not get passed at all.

Child abduction

If your case relates to abduction of a child out of the UK or is a matter which will be dealt with in the High Court you may qualify for legal aid, subject to means and merits tests.

To access legal aid you must telephone the Civil Legal Aid helpline (0345 345 4 345) or fill in the online form on the gov.uk website (https://www.gov.uk/civ-il-legal-advice). If the matter is urgent you can go directly to a legal aid solicitor.

You cannot get legal aid to pay for advice or representation by a barrister through public access, but if you instruct a solicitor they will be able to instruct a barrister for you under legal aid if the case requires it.

Exceptional legal aid

Legal aid can theoretically be granted in cases which are normally not covered in exceptional circumstances. Under s10 Legal Aid Sentencing and Punishment of Offenders Act 2012 (LASPO) exceptional funding can be granted where a refusal of funding would breach the Applicant's human rights. These applications are unlikely to succeed in a 'run of the mill' case, difficult to complete without a lawyer and very often are unsuccessful. If you think your case might fall within this category you should try and find a legal aid lawyer to help you complete the application. You may need to try several firms before you find one willing to help you.

4.12 Paying court fees

If you are eligible for legal aid your solicitor will pay the court fees for you and claim them back through the Legal Aid Agency.

If you instruct a solicitor they will pass the court fees on to you to pay.

If you are a litigant in person you will need to pay your own court fees to start an application unless you qualify for help with fees because you are on benefits or low income (see Chapter 8).

4.13 Free legal advice - Law Centres

There may be a Law Centre local to you that can provide free legal advice. Most do not cover family law. Check your local centre to find out if they cover family cases and whether you need to make an appointment.

Law Centres are struggling to survive and many are closing. All are very busy and you may find it difficult to get an appointment or to get urgent help. They might be able to point you in the direction of other local services.

There may be other local projects or advice surgeries run by law students at local universities or law colleges or by local solicitors firms.

4.14 Free generalist advice

Your local Citizens' Advice Bureau or advice centre may be able to help. They probably will not be able to give legal advice and may not deal with Family Court work, but they might be able to point you in the direction of other local services. Check to see what their appointment system is.

4.15 Free legal advice - pro bono

Legal aid may be free at the point of access (although it is not 'free' in the sense that you may have to pay a contribution or repay your legal aid costs at some point), but lawyers are still paid for the work they have done.

Many lawyers give a portion of their time helping clients for free and (because lawyers can't resist a bit of Latin!) this is called 'pro bono' work.

Lawyers generally take part in pro bono work through a particular organisation or scheme and so you will need to approach a pro bono organisation or agency rather than simply identifying a solicitor or barrister you like and asking them to work for free.

National pro bono organisations that provide free representation (mainly through barristers) include:

- Bar Pro Bono Unit;

- Free Representation Unit (not family);

- There may be other local services, often run by law students at local universities or law colleges or by local solicitors' firms. These are more likely though to provide advice rather than actual representation at a hearing.

You usually need to be referred to this type of organisation by a solicitor or Citizens' Advice Bureau or your MP or to apply directly by filling in a form explaining your case and your financial circumstances. There may be a delay in getting a decision or finding representation and most organisations cannot guarantee to help. They will probably only be able to offer you a limited amount of help by way of representation at a single hearing rather than running advice or ongoing case management. They will probably not take on the job of a solicitor and so court documents will continue to be sent to you as a Litigant in Person and any correspondence will usually be directly between you and the other party (or their solicitor).

4.16   Helplines

There are a number of organisations that run helplines that may be able to give you some general guidance, although this will probably not involve advice from a lawyer. Some of these are listed in the Internet Resources section of the Toolkit & Resources.

4.17   Non-legal support and assistance - McKenzie friends

A 'McKenzie friend' is the term used in courts for somebody who provides quiet support and assistance to a litigant in person whilst they are in court. They might for example take notes or help the litigant in person find a particular document or remind them quietly of the points they wanted to make but might have forgotten. Importantly they are also a source of confidence and moral support. They might also be involved in any discussions that you have with the other lawyer outside court.

A McKenzie friend is not allowed to speak in court, unless the Judge makes an exception. A McKenzie friend is not allowed to conduct litigation (to run your case) unless the Judge makes an exception. You must tell the court if you want your McKenzie friend to do these things for you. If they do this without permission they are committing a criminal offence.

Although the other person in the case is entitled to object to the person you have chosen to come into court with you, it is now common for the courts to allow you to have a McKenzie friend, but still very uncommon for them to be granted rights of audience (to be allowed to speak and represent you) or the right to conduct litigation. Read the McKenzie Friend Guidance for more information about this (in the Resources section). Some courts will ask your McKenzie friend to provide a CV or fill in a form before letting them come into court with you.

A McKenzie friend can be somebody you are friends with or perhaps an extended family member. It is important that they are someone who can understand your situation but who is not too close to be objective and who will not get angry or over-emotional. They should be able to help you to make decisions and keep on track even when your own judgement is clouded by anger or hurt. Often it is really hard for close family members to do this, and objections may be raised to a family member being involved as a McKenzie friend, so as a rule of thumb it's often better to try first to think of a friend who is not known to the other party and who is not likely to be controversial to act as your McKenzie friend.

There are a number of organisations who can provide McKenzie friends. They will not be legal advisers but may have experience of their own court case or of being a McKenzie friend before. Some courts have a Personal Support Unit (PSU). PSUs can provide a volunteer to help you in many practical ways. They cannot give legal advice or represent you but they can:

- Listen to clients tell the story of what has happened so far as well as what their current worries are;

- Prompt clients to order their thoughts;

- Tidy paperwork into a rational order and index it;

- Help clients to find out which forms they need to fill in, to complete them if they know what they want to say, and to take the paperwork to the appropriate customer service desk or court office;

- Help people find their way around court or tribunal buildings and offices;

- Assist in discussions with court or tribunal staff;

- Go into court or tribunal hearings with clients;

- Signpost clients to free legal advice or representation, or to access relevant advice online.

Other organisations may bring with them their own agenda and particular view of the Family Court, so do make sure you find out about them and the organisation before you involve them. A McKenzie friend who is determined to see injustice or to argue every technical point on offer just to score a point may not do your case any good at all and may distract you and the Judge from the real issues.

A McKenzie friend is allowed to see the case papers but must not pass them on to anybody else or discuss them with anybody else who is not involved in the case. It is important that you make sure your McKenzie friend understands this because it will be you who gets into trouble if documents or information are circulated more widely (see Chapter 11).

4.18 Paying for help from non-lawyers

There are a number of internet-based commercial organisations providing guidance and drafting services, and paid-for McKenzie friends. These types of services are not technically legal services and are not provided by barristers or solicitors (anyone can call themselves a lawyer). There is no problem with using these services as long as you understand the limitations and risk associated with this type of service: you are not getting expert legal advice and you will not have the protection of the legal regulators and Ombudsman, and there is no requirement for them to hold indemnity insurance. You should check whether they have insurance and are registered for data protection purposes. You may find that particular organisations or the individuals working for them lack the judgment and objectivity you need. This may be a false economy - you may find that solicitors offer fixed fee packages that are quite competitive and a direct access barrister may be able to advise or represent you for a reasonable fixed fee. To give you some sort of benchmark, a barrister or solicitor representing a parent at a first hearing in a dispute about contact with a child under legal aid will usually be paid a fixed fee of about £205 (incl VAT), and £150 (incl VAT) for a conference. It's very variable, but charging Mckenzie friends typically charge between £200 and £350 plus travel time for attending this sort of hearing - and that is for supporting you in court rather than full representation. Although many lawyers will charge privately paying clients more than legal aid rates, this will depend upon complexity and the seniority of the lawyer you instruct - it is quite acceptable to ask if you can instruct a lawyer at the equivalent of legal aid rates. You need to decide what's the best use of your money by comparing options.

In the last couple of years the rules about how lawyers can organise their businesses have changed to allow them to work together more easily with non-lawyers in 'Alternative Business Structures'. This means that in future you will be able to access legal advice in a different way than is possible now, because big businesses who sell other things are starting to provide legal services as part of what they do (for example supermarkets who have already started to provide things like insurance and banking services). It's difficult to know until it happens how this might change things, but if you do decide to use a new kind of service do ask about the qualifications of the person handling your case and about their expertise in family law.

4.19 Mediation and arbitration providers

There are organisations and individuals who offer family mediation around the country. Mediation can be a cost effective alternative to going to court and is something you can try even if a court case has been started.

Mediation is voluntary, so it does require both people involved in a dispute to agree to give it a try. Depending on what type of dispute you are involved in you may still need to ask the court to confirm any agreement you reach with a court order, but if you have agreed everything this is usually a relatively straightforward paper exercise.

A mediator is an impartial person who will help you work through disputes to try and find solutions that you can both live to accept.

Even if you can't get legal aid for a court case you may qualify for legal aid to mediate, and some mediators offer reduced fees for those on a low income who do not qualify for legal aid. See Family Mediation Council (FMC) website for further information.

Most family mediators are trained and accredited by a member of a body that is a member of the FMC. They will usually display their accreditation logo on their website or publicity material. The following organisations are members of the FMC: the ADR Group, the College of Mediators, the Family Mediators Association, The Law Society, National Family Mediation, Resolution.

You can find out more about mediation on the websites of any of the FMC member organisations listed above.

You can locate a mediator through the family mediation helpline on the justice website (although this will only bring up mediators who carry out mediation under legal aid).

Arbitration is relatively new in family law, and now covers cases involving both financial matters and children.

Arbitration is often confused with mediation but it is quite different. Just like mediation, arbitration is voluntary, but once you are signed up the arbitrator will make a decision for you both, just like a Judge would, and that decision is enforceable through the courts (whereas in mediation either party can say 'stop' at any time, and the only decisions taken are those that both of you agree).

You can find a family arbitrator via the Institute of Family Law Arbitrators (IFLA) website. Legal aid is not available.

4.20 Other sorts of advice

Sometimes it is sensible to try and get some advice from some other sort of specialist apart from a lawyer. For example, if you or your spouse or civil partner are getting divorced or dissolving your partnership and one or other of you has a large pension you may want to think about independent financial advice before making decisions (see the helpful article by barrister Rhys Taylor on my blog Pink Tape: Pensions on divorce for litigants in person, August 2016).

In some cases it might be sensible to take tax advice before making decisions about moving assets between you and your spouse.

5.   Law

5.1   Introduction

Although this might be an over-simplistic summary for other purposes, in this book it might be helpful for you to think of the law as coming in three main types:

- Acts of Parliament or 'Statutes' and often referred to as 'black letter law' or 'Primary Legislation';

- Secondary (or 'delegated') Legislation. The main form of Secondary Legislation is Statutory Instruments (SIs). They are often used to implement the detail of an Act of Parliament, to bring it into force or to create procedural or regulatory rules or to deal with technical details;

- The common law. This is the bit of the law that is not created by Parliament but which is described by Judges in their judgments.

The principles set out in the judgments of Appeal Courts have to be followed by all the lower courts (they are *binding* on less senior Judges). This is called the doctrine of Precedent (or *stare decisis* in Latin) and the judgments are also called case law or authorities.

Authorities are used to help the court, the parties and their lawyers to work out how the law should apply to their particular case. Working out whether or not a legal principle contained in one judgment can be applied to your case is a tricky task and easy to get wrong.

There are two bits to a judgment: the *'ratio'* (the principle the case decides) and *'obiter'* remarks (these are comments which are not directly relevant to the thing the Judge had to decide). It is only the *ratio* that is binding on other courts, although they may consider parts of a judgment which are *obiter*. It is important to realise that not every case you read about in the newspapers or that you can find published online will have any status as a precedent.

5.2   Inherent Jurisdiction

Generally the courts have only the powers specifically given to them by Parliament through statute. For example the Senior Courts Act 1981 tells Judges broadly what they can and cannot do. When a Judge or lawyer says that 'the court is a creature of statute' this is what they mean - they have to do what the law says, and they can only do what the law permits.

However, in a limited category of cases, the High Court (and any Judge sitting as a High Court Judge) has an additional power called 'Inherent Jurisdiction', which means in essence they have powers to make orders that are not specifically contained in any Act of Parliament. If Parliament has not given the lower courts the power to make an order to deal with a particularly unusual problem, the High Court may have Inherent Jurisdiction to make an order. An example of this is an order relating to medical treatment of adults who cannot make their own decisions, or children whose parents and doctors cannot agree (this type of case is dealt with either in the Court of Protection or the High Court) or the court's wardship powers, which can be used where the Children Act or other pieces of statute law do not provide a mechanism to ensure that a child's best interests are protected. The inherent jurisdiction comes from the Crown, and you can think of it as existing in areas that Parliament has not touched. It can't be used to do something contrary to law made by Parliament - it can only fill in the gaps.

Readers of this book are unlikely to need to deal with the Inherent Jurisdiction, but it is helpful to understand roughly what it is in case it is ever mentioned. If it is you probably need a lawyer.

5.3   Relevant Statutes

There are two main pieces of Statute that apply to family law:

- The Children Act 1989;

- The Matrimonial Causes Act 1973 (The Civil Partnerships Act 2004 is the equivalent for same sex couples).

In addition you might encounter some of the following:

- The Married Women's Property Act 1882;

- The Adoption and Children Act 2002;

- The Child Abduction & Custody Act 1985 (which incorporates The Hague Convention on Child Abduction into English Law);

- The Child Support Act 1991;

- The Children and Families Act 2014;

- The Family Law Act 1986;

- The Family Law Act 1996;

- The Human Fertilisation and Embryology Act 2008;

- The Human Rights Act 1998;

- The Inheritance (Provision for Family and Dependants) Act 1973;

- The Marriage (Same Sex Couples) Act 2013;

- The Mental Capacity Act 2003;

- The Protection from Harassment Act 1997;

- The Trusts of Land and Appointment of Trustees Act 1996.

If your case has an international element there may be European Regulations that govern things like whether a case should proceed in the UK or in a court abroad, and arrangements for recognizing orders made in one country in another. See Chapter 18 Jurisdiction.

Each of the Children Act 1989 [CA] and the Matrimonial Causes Act [MCA], and the Civil Partnerships Act 2004 [CPA] give the court a range of powers and set out a checklist of the things that a court has to consider before making an order. In most family cases the law gives the Judge a very wide discretion to choose what order to make, rather than providing a set answer. This is why case law is very important because it tells us how different Judges have made decisions according to the facts of a given case, and how they have interpreted the limited guidance that the law gives them. On the other hand it's important not to over-emphasise the value of case law because most decisions are based on a unique sets of facts and do not always provide principles that are easy to apply to other cases. The most important feature in your case will always be the unique facts surrounding your family, not what the court has decided in respect of someone else's family.

Below follows a summary of the Acts referred to above. Some of them are dealt with in more detail later on in the book. The summaries only cover the bits that are likely to be relevant to the topics in this book.

5.4   Summary of the Acts

The Children Act 1989

The CA gives the court the power to make a range of orders about children. Whenever the court considers making an order under the CA it must only do so where it considers that making an order is better than making none at all (the 'no order principle') and the most important thing for it to consider is the best interests of the child (the 'paramountcy principle'). The court must consider the welfare checklist in s1 of the CA when deciding what the best interests of the child are. The CA is mainly dealt with in Part 4.

The Married Women's Property Act 1882

The MWPA has been largely repealed and what is left in force is largely redundant, as the court has very wide powers under the Matrimonial Causes Act 1973. You almost certainly won't need to worry about this Act at all unless you are seeking an order for the sale of your home before the court case has finished (see Chapter 12).

The Adoption and Children Act 2002

The Adoption and Children Act 2002 deals mainly with placement for adoption and adoption. It is structured in a similar way to the CA in that it has a welfare checklist that the court must consider before making orders.

The Matrimonial Causes Act 1973

The MCA gives the court a range of powers to divide up property and deal with financial matters when spouses divorce or separate. The court can order the sale or transfer of property, decide who owns what proportion of a property or asset and adjust that ownership as appropriate, share pensions and order maintenance or a lump sum to be paid from one party to another.

The Child Abduction & Custody Act 1985

The Child Abduction & Custody Act 1985 makes the Hague Convention on child abduction into UK law. Many countries have signed up to this Convention, and if a child is wrongfully removed to a country which has signed up to the Convention (or is kept there wrongfully) the Convention tells the court it must send the child back to its home country for the court there to decide on his future (unless certain limited exceptions apply). Where the abduction is to Europe there are European Regulations which also apply.

The Child Support Act 1991

Deals with child maintenance, giving responsibility to the Child Maintenance Service rather than the court in most cases.

The Children and Families Act 2014

This act amends the Children Act but as it came into force just before this book went to print I've mentioned it here. You will need to check any version of the Children Act you read is the updated version.

The Civil Partnerships Act 2004

The CPA gives almost identical powers to the court when dealing with separating Civil Partners as it has when dealing with separating spouses under the MCA.

The Family Law Act 1986

This act sets out when the courts in England & Wales have power to make orders relating to children when there is a connection to another part of the UK (Scotland, Northern Ireland) or where a foreign court might have jurisdiction.

The Family Law Act 1996

Part IV of the FLA 1996 allows the court to make injunctions called 'non-molestation orders' where a party has been violent or abusive or harassing (often described as 'restraining orders' on TV or in newspapers). The court can also make an occupation order which says who can and cannot live in the family home. Under this piece of law the court can make orders about who pays the outgoings on your home and transfer a joint tenancy if you live in council or housing association property, depending on the type of tenancy (see Chapters 15, 21 and 22).

Sometimes if you are unable to apply for an order under the Family Law Act 1996 you can use the Protection from Harassment Act 1997 which gives the court similar powers to make an injunction - this is often called a restraining order or harassment order.

The Human Fertilisation and Embryology Act 2008

This act deals with children conceived through assisted conception and the legal identity of their parents.

The Human Rights Act 1998

The Human Rights Act 1998 brings the European Convention on Human Rights into UK law. The rights which most often arise in family courts are the right to private and family life (article 8), right to a fair trial (article 6), right to freedom of expression (article 10), and right to freedom from discrimination (article 14).

Some human rights are absolute rights - they have to be met (for example the right to a fair trial). Others, including the right to private and family life, are not absolute rights. These rights must be balanced against other people's human rights, and as a result sometimes your rights must give way to someone else's, most often a child's. They are best thought of as principles to guide the court's approach about these really important rights rather than hard and fast rules.

The Marriage (Same Sex Couples) Act 2013

This act makes same sex marriage legal.

The Mental Capacity Act 2003

Defines when a person is incapable to act on their own behalf in a court case, for example if they are suffering from a mental illness that prevents them from making decisions.

The Protection from Harassment Act 1997

Allows the court to make injunctions in cases of harassment. Usually not necessary in family cases as the FLA 1996 gives the court more flexible powers.

The Trusts of Land and Appointment of Trustees Act 1996

Allows the court to make orders about properties owned by former cohabiting couples, deciding what shares they own and ordering sale of the property.

5.5   Court rules

Court rules are a type of secondary legislation called a Statutory Instrument. The court rules in family cases are mostly contained in one set of rules called the Family Procedure Rules 2010 (FPR). The court rules are revised frequently, sometimes with several statutory instruments in one year. It is important that you check that any copy of the rules you want to refer to is an up to date (revised) version. The Ministry of Justice publish the up to date rules on their website (justice.gov.uk).

A few bits of the FPR just say that the Civil Procedure Rules (CPR) apply. The CPR are the main non-family rules. You can find these online in updated form also on the Justice website.

Finally, the court rules are supplemented by Practice Directions (PDs), which must be followed. The PDs are also available on the Justice website.

Some of the most important pieces of law and rules are reproduced at the end of this book for ease of reference.

6. Reality Check - Your Case In Context

6.1 Introduction

Although many families manage to get through separation without coming to court, yours will not be the only family going through this experience. There will be many others who will be experiencing the anxiety, the frustration and the bewilderment. For some the family justice system will meet their expectations, for others it will not. Not all will leave with what they consider to be a 'good' outcome, some will leave feeling victorious or vindicated, whilst others will leave disappointed and angry. What family lawyers regularly observe is the large number of cases where both 'sides' leave exhausted, deflated, frustrated and disillusioned.

You need to know that the family justice system is facing a number of problems that will affect your case. Your family is one of many. Your problems, however awful they are for you, are probably far from the worst that the Family Court has to deal with. You need to see your experience of the family justice system in this context.

The Family Court continues to experience a sustained and significant increase in demand, particularly in child protection cases.

The Family Court has faced austerity cuts, closures and lay-offs just like other parts of the public sector.

The rates of pay for lawyers representing people through legal aid have been cut and some solicitors' firms have stopped doing this work. Most types of family cases covered in this book won't qualify for legal aid at all and it will usually only be *victims* of domestic abuse or those who are seeking orders to protect children themselves from abuse who are able to get their representation paid for by the state, along with parents of children involved in care proceedings (see Chapter 4).

CAFCASS has been under sustained pressure for a number of years and inspections by regulators have not always been positive. Its priority in recent years has been public law cases (where social services have taken parents to court) and in response it has developed a working model known as 'proportionate working' which focuses on risk assessment.

Social Services are in a similar position with cuts and enormous pressure on resources.

The Official Solicitor, who represents parents who lack capacity to instruct solicitors themselves because of mental health or learning difficulties, often has a waiting list.

Add up all these things and what you get is delay. The family court system is faced with more work than it can manage, with fewer resources than it needs and delay is the end result. And this is likely to remain the case for the foreseeable future. All families and all children are important, but you must face the reality that your case is probably nowhere near the top of the list.

All of this is really to caution you to be realistic, to help you understand why court is not going to be a miraculous overnight solution to your conflict, to urge you to be patient and to reassure you that the courts and the people working in them are not insensitive to the issues you face, but are simply trying to do the best they can to share the resources of the court equally between all the families in similar predicaments.

6.2   Family Procedure Rules

The courts are always trying to find ways to streamline and make the process more efficient and effective. The Family Procedure Rules 2010 were introduced in 2011 as part of this process. They introduced new rules to help Judges manage cases, and an overriding objective of enabling the court to **deal with cases justly, having regard to any welfare issues involved** [rule 1.1]. The rule says that **dealing with a case justly includes, so far as is practicable**:

- **ensuring that it is dealt with expeditiously and fairly;**

- **dealing with the case in ways which are proportionate to the nature, importance and complexity of the issues;**

- **ensuring that the parties are on an equal footing;**

- **saving expense; and**

- **allotting to it an appropriate share of the court's resources, while taking into account the need to allot resources to other cases.**

At the heart of these new rules is the goal of making the Family Courts work better. The court must apply the overriding objective to everything it does, as must the parties and lawyers. Rule 1.4 tells the court that in particular it must promote the overriding objective by actively managing cases. This includes:

- encouraging the parties to co-operate with each other in the conduct of the proceedings;

- setting timetables or otherwise controlling the progress of the case;

- identifying at an early stage -

  - the issues; and

  - who should be a party to the proceedings;

- deciding promptly -

  - which issues need full investigation and hearing and which do not; and

  - the procedure to be followed in the case;

- deciding the order in which issues are to be resolved;

- controlling the use of expert evidence;

- encouraging the parties to use an alternative dispute resolution procedure if the court considers that appropriate and facilitating the use of such procedure;

- helping the parties to settle the whole or part of the case;

- considering whether the likely benefits of taking a particular step justify the cost of taking it;

- dealing with as many aspects of the case as it can on the same occasion;

- dealing with the case without the parties needing to attend at court;

- making use of technology; and

- giving directions to ensure that the case proceeds quickly and efficiently.

In addition, the FPR bring in a number of specific changes which are designed to clamp down on wastage of court time or of public funds and private resources. They are dealt with in Chapter 8.

Courts are therefore careful about allocating time and resources to a particular case. Your case will be no exception.

6.3   Popular myths

There are some popular misconceptions about the Family Court that often colour people's view of the court system and affect how they approach things. It's important to have a realistic understanding of how things work if you are going to give yourself the best chance of achieving your goals, and so this short chapter aims to dispel or explain some of the urban myths about the Family Court and family law right from the off.

The first popular misconception though is that court is the answer. There are lots of other alternatives that may well work better for many cases. Some of these are summarised in Chapter 2. If you have exhausted or discounted all other options you may find that, particularly where children are concerned, court is a pretty blunt tool with which to tackle a very delicate problem - relationships.

Do not delude yourself that victory (whatever *that* is) will make things any easier or reduce the scope for tension between you and your ex.

The court cannot make people agree, make them like one another, make them fundamentally different or more responsible and it cannot police private conversations in peoples' homes. The court cannot micro-manage contact or hold your hands forever, and relying on the court is no substitute for communication between you. Your relationship as a couple may be over but you are still linked together as parents.

The court has limited powers to enforce its orders, or at least is often hampered in using those powers against the parents children are living with, because anything they do may have an undesirable knock on effect on the children. Two illustrative examples may explain the problems:

- If the kids are living with mum, who looks after them when she is locked up for a 'short, sharp shock'?

- What happens to the kids' relationship with daddy when they find out (as they inevitably do) that daddy asked the Judge to send mummy to prison?

Do not believe everything you read in the papers or on the internet. The internet is a fantastic resource but it is not always reliable: it may be out of date, or skewed because of a particular agenda or just because it is written by someone who does not properly understand the law. Some of the websites listed in the resources section of this book are maintained by Government departments or other official bodies independent of the government. Others are run by charities or campaigning groups that are large enough to be reasonably reliable in check- ing and updating their information. There are any number of smaller organi- sations and campaigning groups that you may find offer useful resources and support to you, but who may provide information that fits in with their particular ethos or world view. Read it, learn from it, but do not expect it to be complete or unbiased. You will do better if you can try and see the arguments from both sides of the fence - if you can anticipate the weaknesses in your position you can deal with them effectively. Websites that are focused on criticising the system or one particular group of people (women, Fathers etc) are unlikely to give you the balanced insight you need in the long run.

Do not forget that family courts are private and although reporters can usually come into the court room the media are not allowed to report cases without per- mission. This means that generally speaking the cases that are reported are not representative of what happens day in day out in the courts. They are reported because they are unusual or extraordinary, because they break new legal ground or because the process has gone very wrong and there has been, or might have been, a miscarriage of justice or because of some celebrity angle or salacious storyline. Most cases are far more humdrum, although every bit as important to those involved in them. When journalists report cases they often condense cases to the point where the legal significance is obscured or the facts distorted. And they do not and cannot report everything. Particularly where cases are reported anonymously you are almost inevitably getting only the tip of the iceberg, and often the journalist may have had to rely on snippets of information given to them by one party, and perhaps from listening to part of the hearing - but they will not have seen the documents. News reporting of cases can be informative but it is rarely a full representation of what has really happened. It is more com- mon now than in the past for the full judgment to be published by the court in an anonymised form, where a case has hit the press - see Chapter 11.

Contrary to the views of some, the courts do not routinely or intentionally dis- criminate against men but it can often seem this way because many Fathers are disadvantaged by the fact that the children live with their Mother, perhaps be- cause they have taken the main responsibility for childcare during the relation- ship, and the court is not very good at redressing the power imbalance that can stem from this. Similarly, in families where the parents adopt the traditional roles of male breadwinner and stay at home (or part time hours) mum, the father may find that his own housing and capital needs are at the back of the queue when it comes to trying to finance two homes where before only one was needed. Where children live with their Father, non-resident Mothers experience similar problems. Delay makes things worse for everyone and the family courts are very oversubscribed. This is why you should consider whether alternatives to court may be more effective.

If you are a parent with care of a child however, you should not kid yourself that the court will just let you stop your children from seeing their other parent without very good reason. The court will expect there to be contact even if it is inconvenient or emotionally difficult for you and the Court of Appeal tells Judges that they must exhaust all options before giving up on contact.

Court proceedings are not good for kids. For that matter they are not good for adults. Consider them as a last resort.

Remember also that whilst you have a right to bring an application, you have no right to your day in court per se: it is up to the court how your application is dealt with and how much court time and public money is spent on your private dispute. You have no right to air your grievances just to make you feel better - the court will hear evidence only about disputes that it can resolve by making orders i.e. sorting out the finances and making arrangements for the kids. The court is not in the business of ruling on who has been the biggest idiot, the worst love rat or workshy good-for-nothing just so you can post it on Facebook as a victory or feel vindicated that the divorce was all your ex's fault.

There are many popular misconceptions that are widely held by members of the public. Hopefully as you read through this book most of those will be dispelled. But below are a few of the most common misunderstandings and myths that regularly have to be explained by lawyers at the first meeting, or which can complicate relationships and the process of sorting things out if they are left unchallenged.

6.4   Common law man and wife

There is no such thing. Just because you have lived together as if you were married doesn't necessarily mean you are entitled to stay in the house, or to a share of it - you are particularly vulnerable if the house is only in your partner's name. Cohabiting doesn't give you the same rights as you would have if you had married. You should read Chapter 15.

6.5   Millionaire divorcees

There is a lot in the media about the wives of very rich men walking away with vast fortunes on divorce. If you are reading this book you are probably not in their social circle and your own divorce will have a very different outcome.

For most families the court has to make a rough and ready estimation of what is in the pot and try to do its best to be fair to both parties, putting the needs of the kids first.

Where there is enough to go around the court will use equality as a starting point. But often there isn't enough and so something has to give - equality may have to go out of the window. Husbands in such cases often come out of divorce with less than half the assets because the court has to prioritise by putting a roof over the kids heads (along with their mum as carer - the reverse will apply if dad is caring for the children).

Where there are no kids the situation may be very different.

6.6   The ostrich approach

It won't go away so get your head out of the sand.

If you ignore an application to the court by your ex you run the risk of getting all sorts of grief - for example if you just ignore orders and don't provide the information requested or don't come to court, your ex could ask the court to make an order to punish you by prison or a fine if you carry on ignoring the court. Or the court can make decisions about what should happen to your assets and home, what maintenance you should pay, or that you should pay your ex's costs. If you haven't participated you won't be able to complain later that these orders are unfair.

If you are finding it all impossible to understand, at the very least go to the hearing and explain that to the Judge. Ask for clear instructions about what you need to do for next time. Judges don't like ostriches but they will do their best to help you participate if you attend and ask.

6.7   Earning or paying for a right to contact

A Father does not have to prove himself or earn a right to contact. The starting point is that there should be contact of some kind. A child is entitled to a relationship with both parents unless there is a very good reason why it cannot happen. Being unable to pay maintenance is not one of them.

As far as the law is concerned there is no connection between whether an absent parent is paying maintenance and his / her entitlement to contact with their child. The child is entitled to expect to be maintained and to have a fulfilling relationship with both parents, but the fact that a parent fails in one respect does not affect the other. You will not get very far refusing contact because no maintenance has been paid. Equally, you cannot purchase a right to contact with your child, nor will you get very far by threatening to stop maintenance in order to get contact. The court will take a very dim view of this type of behaviour.

6.8   Right to contact with children

Parents and children have a right to family life, which usually (but not always) includes contact with children, but as with most human rights, these are not absolute rights and they have to be balanced with other people's rights.

It is often said that it is the *child's right* to have contact with his family not the parents' right. What this really means is that children are not a possession and that a parent has no automatic right to contact where that is in conflict with the child's own human rights or needs.

In short, there has to be a very good reason for there to be no contact at all (for example a history of serious violence or a serious risk that the contact will harm the child somehow), and there will need to be good reasons for contact to be restricted (how, where, how often, how long etc) but it is rare for there to be no contact at all.

The amount and type of contact will depend on what is practical and what will be best for the child, not on any notion of being entitled to 50% of the child's time.

The question of whether a child should have overnight contact, or should live with both parents on an alternating basis is not one which has a standard answer - it will depend on the circumstances and what is right for that child. The courts do not operate on the basis that any particular arrangement is always appropriate or always better than another, although there are some arrangements that seem to work well for many children.

6.9   Innocent until proven guilty - interim protection

Yes, what you've seen on the telly is correct as far as it goes - you are presumed innocent. However, this does not mean that the court can ignore allegations of harmful conduct or risk until they are proved. In the period between allegations of violence or abuse being raised and the court making a decision about whether the allegations are true, the court will probably need to treat them *as if they might be true*, just in case. This is a temporary measure whilst evidence is gathered but it can be lengthy and frustrating.

Sometimes contact must be stopped, managed or restricted while allegations are being dealt with. If you are the person who has had allegations made against you it can seem like the presumption of innocence has been abandoned.

Once the court has gathered and heard all the evidence it will make a proper decision about whether the allegations were true and make longer term plans.

For further information, see Chapters 16 and 17.

6.10 Prosecution for perjury or suing for defamation

You cannot sue for defamation (libel or slander) in relation to things said in the course of court proceedings.

A Judge saying that he does not accept one person's evidence or prefers another's is not enough to amount to evidence of perjury - people can give genuine but different accounts of the same events without deliberately lying. They can be wrong, mistaken, or they may misinterpret or misremember. It is up to the authorities to prosecute for perjury, which is a criminal offence. It is highly unlikely that they would do this even if the Judge decided that someone had deliberately lied in a family court hearing.

In any event, you would not achieve anything useful by pursuing such actions so it is best to simply disregard them at the outset.

The court can punish a person for contempt of court if they sign a court document with a false statement of truth on it, but this is likely to be very rare.

When parents are involved in a dispute *between themselves* about their children or finances they are entitled to refuse to answer questions so as not to incriminate themselves. This does not apply in cases brought by a Local Authority (care proceedings) where the dispute is between the parents and the state.

PART 2: PUTTING IT INTO PRACTICE

7.   What To Expect At Court

7.1   Introduction

Going to court is stressful at the best of times, more so without a lawyer to explain things to you. You will probably feel a lot better though, if you have a rough idea of what might be going on around you at court and how the hearing will proceed, and if you prepare yourself well.

7.2   Preparing yourself

If you are really nervous it might help to settle your nerves if you come for a visit to the court building on a day in advance of the hearing - at least then you don't need to worry about getting lost on the morning of the hearing. You probably won't be able to sit in on a family hearing as they are held in private but there will probably be other kinds of case you can sit in on so you can get a feel for things. If you aren't able to visit the court before the hearing take a look at the short videos associated with this book on YouTube (search nofamilylawyer).

Leave plenty of time to get to court the first time - aim to arrive half an hour before the hearing is listed (unless the order specifically says you must get there earlier - often the court will ask you to come 45 minutes or an hour early). Make sure you have written down the address before you leave and make sure you know whether you are going to the County Court or the Magistrates Court building, as the Family Court could be located in either. Do not rely on the bus or taxi driver or a passer-by to know the difference. They will inevitably direct you to the wrong court! Some courts sit at more than one location so make sure you check the venue for every hearing. The Justice website has the address and links to a map of every court. Don't go to the Crown Court by mistake - they are often (but not always!) in a separate building and only deal with criminal matters.

Most courts do not have dedicated parking. Check out the parking situation before you leave and bring enough change for any meters.

Check your bus or train routes in advance and allow plenty of time to make your way from the station. You don't want to arrive late and in a flap.

Don't bring anything sharp to court. It will be confiscated by security. Expect to be patted down by security and to have to empty your pockets, and to show the inside of your bag. This is routine.

If you are running late or can't attend through illness do your best to get a message to the Judge through the court office or perhaps by ringing another lawyer involved in the case who can pass on the message.

Bring a snack if you get flaky mid-morning. You may be there some time.

Bring more than one pen and some paper to write on.

Bring your mobile phone. Turn it onto silent before you go into court. Make sure you know how to do this.

Bring any documents that you might want to rely on - if other parties have not seen them bring at least 3 copies and hand them to the usher when you sign in. Bring any bundle that has been prepared.

Bring a copy of the order telling you what time to arrive. This should contain the case number and address.

Don't get in a flap about what to wear. You do not need to dress as if you were going to a wedding or funeral. Just make sure you are clean, presentable, and comfortable and don't wear anything too distracting - don't dress to impress or try to look super fabulous to show your ex what she or he is missing. It can give the wrong impression. You just want to look sensible and measured even if you feel like a wreck on the inside.

Do not bring everyone and their dog to court for moral support. Having a whole gaggle of people at court can raise the temperature, increase the chance there will be a scene, and is likely to result in you being coiled like a spring by the time you get into court. You need time for quiet contemplation before you go into court. Fiercely loyal friends who want to help you fight your corner are well meaning but they may make things more difficult. By all means bring a friend or family member, but make sure it is someone you can trust to keep their temper and not mouth off and show you in a bad light. Remember that anything said in temper outside court is likely to be reported to the Judge and it will not look good. You need to find someone who is both loyal and diplomatic. Do not bring the kids unless absolutely unavoidable (or unless the court has ordered them to attend - this doesn't happen often). They will distract you from what you need to focus on, and they will pick up on your stress and upset. If you do have to bring the kids, bring a friend to babysit them whilst you are in court as they probably won't be allowed into the courtroom. If you are at court to deal with a dispute about contact, think about how you will deal with an approach by your ex to say hello to them. You can avoid a difficult confrontation by giving your friend a fiver and asking her to go to a café nearby with the kids.

Assume that the case might take all day even if it is listed for 30 minutes. Courts often block list cases, meaning that they tell several families to come to court at the same time as you and simply deal with the cases as they become ready to see the Judge. This works fine when as expected a few people don't show up and a few more cases agree things and are dealt with very quickly, but if everybody attends and wants to argue their point before the Judge and the list is very busy you can end up waiting for a long time. If you have kids make sure you have a back-up plan to get the kids collected from school just in case. If you are working make sure your boss knows you might be all day. If you are in the car put enough time on your parking ticket to make sure you are not running out to top up every five minutes. Phone parking apps can be handy, because you can renew your parking without leaving the building if things are running late.

7.3   Court building

In most courts there is a list of cases on the wall somewhere near the entrance, or a security / reception desk where they keep a list of cases so you can check where you need to go to. In family cases, often the name is not listed and this is why you need to remember to bring your case number. This will be printed on all the documents you get from the court. Sometimes they will have a list of cases which identifies the case by the surname of the person who made the application or sometimes by the surname of the child so if they can't find your case using your own name try your ex's name or the child's surname.

Some courts are well equipped with lots of private rooms for people to use. Others are not and you may find it difficult to find anywhere very private. If you have experienced domestic abuse and are worried about being confronted by your ex ask the court staff if they can find you a private room or sit within eye range of the signing in desk. You may be able to ring in advance of your hearing to arrange a private room (there is usually a box to tick on the application or response form - but it is a good idea to check before the hearing to make sure it has actually been arranged).

There is usually a coffee machine at court. Sometimes there is a café. Often they accept cash only. Bring change.

7.4   Before the hearing

Try and be at court half an hour before the listed time for the hearing (or earlier if the order says so). Sign in as soon as you arrive and make sure that court staff know where you are.

You might want a friend or supporter to come into court for moral support or to remind you of the things you want to say to the Judge. This is called a McKenzie friend and is dealt with in Chapter 4. If you are going to be asking for your McKenzie friend to come in with you let the court staff know as soon as you arrive so that your ex can be given advance warning and things don't get delayed. At some courts your friend may be asked to complete a short form telling the Judge who they are. Don't be surprised if your case is not called in before the Judge straight away or if the Judge does not deal with the cases in the order they are written on the list. You will be called into court when the Judge is ready.

Judges usually sit (hear cases) from 10.00am to 4.00pm or 4.30pm with an hour or so to break for lunch around 1.00pm. They will sit longer if necessary, for example if the case is urgent. Some Judges are more flexible than others.

Expect to be approached by the lawyer for your ex (if they have one) before you go into court. This is perfectly normal. They are just trying to introduce themselves and see if anything can be agreed, or at least to make sure everybody agrees what isn't agreed! Your instinct may be that you don't want to talk to your ex's lawyer in case they trick you, but a brief chat before you go into court can be helpful to everyone and any lawyer has a duty to a litigant in person not to mislead them and not to mislead the court. You do not have to commit yourself to anything outside court, but you may get a valuable insight into what is going to be said in court from a pre-hearing chat, which is far better than hearing something for the first time in court and having to think up a response on the spot.

If you have had to come to court because your ex is being unreasonable, there is a good chance that they will have been advised that this is the case by their lawyer when they arrived at court and you may find that you are able to negotiate with their lawyer where previously progress has not been possible. It is always worth a try when a new lawyer is on board - sometimes legal advice results in a change of position. If it doesn't work you are no worse off.

If there is a lawyer involved in the case, you are likely to be handed a document of some sort, probably summarising the case and explaining what your ex's position is. Take it. Read it. It will obviously explain the case from their client's perspective and may set out 'facts' that you don't agree with, but it may also contain inaccuracies based on genuine mistakes which you can correct either by pointing them out before you go into court or to the Judge. Don't be afraid to say to the Judge if you have not been given enough time to read it - ask for your case to be put further back in the list to give you a few minutes to look at it properly before you speak to the Judge.

This is a good opportunity to make sure that everybody has all the necessary documents. If you have brought something to court with you to show the Judge but your ex and their lawyer have not seen it, you should hand them a copy as soon as you can (directly or via the usher if easier). You should hand in any documents to the usher on the reception desk or to whoever has identified themselves as dealing with your particular Judge on that day.

7.5   The court room

Most court rooms are not as you would imagine from watching the telly. Most family hearings will be heard in the Judge's chambers (office). A typical chambers will have a large desk with a few books on it that the Judge sits at, and a row of tables opposite it, or sometimes around in a horseshoe shape so that everyone can sit facing or looking at the Judge (so depending on the layout you might be sat with your ex along the desk to your left or right, or opposite you). Everyone is at the same level and there are no raised benches or docks. The witness 'box' is often a separate small table and chair with a glass of water on it. The Judge might have a computer.

Some court rooms are more old-fashioned and the Judge will sit on a slightly higher level, separated from everyone else by a high bench. There will be a proper witness box. Sitting in front of the Judge in this type of court room will usually be a member of court staff who will introduce the case, assist the Judge when necessary and will carry on quietly doing administrative work whilst the case continues. You are more likely to be in a court room like this if your case is being dealt with by a Circuit Judge.

In some courts you may see microphones. These usually do not amplify anything, but record what is being said. There is sometimes no audio recording in the Magistrates Court buildings, although the Magistrates' Legal Adviser must take a handwritten note of what is said.

If the case is being heard by Lay Justices (Magistrates) the layout will usually be similar to a Judge's chambers, with everybody sitting at plain desks arranged in rows or in a horseshoe shape. The Lay Justices will sit in a row together, with the Chairperson in the middle. To one side there is usually a separate desk at which the Legal Adviser will sit. He or she will introduce the case, manage the hearing and give the Lay Justices legal advice throughout the hearing.

Different courts have different seating arrangements, so just ask where you are expected to sit if you are unsure. In some courts the parties themselves will sit behind their lawyers, but if you are acting in person you will probably be asked to sit in the same row as the lawyers, as you are your own representative. If you have a hearing or visual impairment or need to be able to get up and move around ask the Judge if you can sit somewhere you can hear / see better or where you can get out of your seat easily. Many courts have a hearing loop system - let the court staff know in advance so they can set you up.

Water is usually available in courtrooms. Ask if you don't have any within reach.

Turn your phone off before you go into court.

If somebody is in court and you are not sure who they are just ask. Sometimes trainees sit in to see how things are done - they will have been told that they must keep matters confidential, but you are entitled to object if you are uncomfortable with them being in court.

Nobody will wear wigs and gowns in court. The court staff sometimes wear plain black gowns so you can work out who they are. The lawyers usually wear suits.

7.6   The hearing itself

What to call the Judge

Do not get too worked up about how to address the Judge. Most are pretty relaxed about it and have been called any number of things, not all of them printable. As long as you are polite and respectful you should not have a problem. If there is a lawyer they will most likely speak first so you can copy what they call the Judge. The correct forms of address are as follows:

- District Judge, Deputy District Judge or Lay Justices: 'Sir' or 'Madam' (some people call Lay Justices 'Your Worship' - they don't seem to mind this but it's not required!);

- Circuit Judge or Recorder (including Deputy): 'Your Honour';

- Any other Judge: 'My Lord'.

What to call the other lawyers

You could call them any of the following (Not 'that shark my wife has hired'):

- My wife's / husband's lawyer;

- Mr Smith;

- Lawyer for the (Respondent / Applicant / Child (as appropriate).

You might hear the Judge referring to counsel for so and so. Counsel just means barrister.

Everybody has to stand up when the Judge or Lay Justices come into the room and when they leave the room (if you have restricted mobility the Judge won't mind if you don't - just let the court staff know or explain to the Judge).

If you are in a proper court room with a bench and a witness box you may be expected to stand up when speaking (although most Judges are happy for you to do what makes you feel most comfortable if you don't have a lawyer). You don't need to stand up whilst someone else is talking. You can either take your cue from the other lawyer as to whether you need to stand up or just ask the Judge - she won't mind.

If you need more time

The right to a fair trial includes a right to equality of arms (the idea that there will be a level playing field), and a right of effective access to justice. These are particularly relevant to the litigant in person who may require more time to understand, prepare and respond to issues raised and documents produced, and a more flexible approach to their handling of the case.

If you have been given new documents or information or are just not quite ready do not be afraid to ask for more time. You can ask for the hearing to be put to the back of the list, or if it is really necessary for the hearing to be adjourned (put off) until another day. If you have been given new material or there has been a change of position it may be fair for you to have a chance to respond in writing or with more evidence, and for you to have an opportunity to study the documents before responding.

If you need to ask for an adjournment and it is not agreed by the other lawyers you should mention that you are concerned that your right to a fair trial may be affected and that as a litigant in person you need time to consider and respond. You could mention the overriding objective (see Chapter 8).

Do not cry 'breach of human rights!' at every possible opportunity. It is a weapon to be used selectively. A gentle and polite reminder of Article 6 (Right to a fair trial) and why you are in difficulty is usually enough.

Remember that litigants in person only qualify for a slightly more flexible approach insofar as they are disadvantaged by not having a lawyer. The right to a fair trial is something that everyone is entitled to rely on whether they have a lawyer or not, but the more competent and together you are the less you can rely upon the need for *special* assistance or *leeway as a litigant in person*.

A typical hearing will involve the following sequence of events:

- Introductions - who is in court and who they represent.

- If there is a disagreement about a McKenzie friend the Judge will usually deal with this first.

- Opening - a brief introduction to the case and what everyone is here for today. If there have been case summaries prepared and the Judge has read the papers, or if the Judge has dealt with the case before this may be very brief or skipped altogether. At this point the Judge or any lawyer will often check that the court has the up to date papers - this is your chance to check that he has yours (and that your ex or his/her lawyer has them too). Do check, even if you have handed something into the usher that morning - court staff are very busy and documents often go astray.

- If everyone involved agrees what needs to happen next in the case, the Judge will proceed to make a directions order. Occasionally the Judge will disagree with what the parties have agreed should happen and may make a different order.

- Evidence - (only in some hearings):

  - Each witness will give their 'evidence in chief' (their own account based upon their witness statement) and will then be subject to 'cross examination' (questions from the other lawyers or parties). The Judge may ask some questions of the witness. The evidence given by witnesses will help the Judge to decide things like what has happened in the past, what the truth is about their finances (for example), and what is likely to happen in the future.

  - If there is any evidence from a social worker, CAFCASS officer or expert witness the court will usually decide when to hear their evidence, but it often makes sense to hear their evidence first.

  - Once any professional or expert witnesses have been dealt with, the Applicant will usually give evidence, followed by any of the Applicant's other witnesses.

  - The Respondent will usually go next, followed by any of the Respondent's other witnesses.

  - The order might be swapped around if the evidence mainly relates to allegations made by one party against the other. If this is the case, the person making the allegations should usually go first so the person the allegations are about has a chance to hear the accusations before responding.

- The Judge will hear closing speeches (submissions) from the parties, Respondent first, Applicant second. The submissions are a party's chance to put forward legal arguments and explain why their position is the one that should be accepted by the Judge, and why their evidence is the more reliable or accurate.

- The Judge will give a judgment - this may be immediately ('*extempore*'), after a short break or it may be 'handed down' on another day. Occasionally, judgment is handed down by email, but usually only if this is agreed.

- Once judgment has been given the Judge will hear any argument about costs (rare) or any application for permission to appeal.

Some Judges will say very little whilst the case is being presented to them. Others will be constantly asking questions to lawyers and witnesses, some will even ask a represented party direct questions, bypassing their lawyer. Some will make clear their views from the start, but others will be very difficult to read. Often a Judge will ask difficult or challenging questions of a lawyer or a witness - this does not necessarily mean that they disagree with them, simply that they are testing their evidence or arguments to check that they stand up to scrutiny.

7.7   When might the Judge hear evidence?

It is important not to have unrealistic expectations of what the Judge might do at a hearing. Judges do have powers to be quite proactive in managing cases but if there is a real dispute between you they might not be able to deal with the case properly at a first hearing or in a very short time slot.

If your hearing is listed for 30 minutes or an hour and is called a 'directions hearing', 'conciliation appointment', 'review hearing', 'pre-trial review', 'first hearing dispute resolution appointment' (FHDRA), 'first directions appointment' or 'financial dispute resolution hearing', it is not intended to be a hearing at which evidence will be given (although the Judge has the power to hear brief evidence if appropriate this is unlikely to happen without notice to everyone involved and where the court has a long list of other cases to deal with).

Some issues need to be sorted out before a case can get to final hearing because the court needs to decide the factual basis before working out what to do next. In this type of case, the court will list a fact-finding hearing to deal only with these disputes of fact. For example,

- Where there are allegations of physical violence between the parents that are not accepted as true

- Where there are allegations of physical or other abuse to the child that are not accepted as true

Occasionally, the court will list a hearing with a long enough time estimate to hear some evidence because an urgent short term decision to be made even though the case is not ready for a final hearing - for example where there is a dispute about what school a child should attend and it is almost the start of term, or where there is a dispute about taking a child on holiday and the final hearing could not happen until after the date for the holiday. At this type of hearing the court will usually hear only quite limited evidence, and only in relation to the point that cannot wait. This is called a contested interim hearing.

The main time when the court will hear evidence is at a final hearing. The court will allow long enough for all the witnesses to give their evidence, for both parties to have their say and for him to make a decision. Particularly in children cases a hearing intended to be a final hearing can turn out to be a contested interim hearing because the court cannot finish the case off there and then.

8.   General Procedure

8.1   Introduction

The Family Court has by its nature to be flexible because of the variety of cases it deals with and the very different circumstances and needs of the families affected, but there are still quite a lot of rules about how people must make and deal with applications and how the court must deal with them. These are mainly contained in the Family Procedure Rules 2010 (FPR) and the Practice Directions (PDs) which go with it. The FPR and the PDs are published on the Justice website, and should include any amendments.

There are a few types of family case where the rules are mainly in another set of rules called the Civil Procedure Rules (CPR). The cases where you may need to look at the CPR are in relation to enforcement of some orders (see Chapter 23) and 'ToLATA' cases (see Chapter 15).

Because the rules deal with so many potential scenarios and types of case you will not need to worry about most of them - so don't panic! This chapter will tell you a bit about how the court procedure generally operates, and about the main points to note in the FPR.

8.2   The overriding objective

The FPR start by saying that everything the court does must be aimed at dealing with cases **justly, having regard to any welfare issues involved** [see Part 1 FPR]. This is the overriding objective. The rules say that this means that everyone must do the best they can to ensure that:

a) the case is dealt with **expeditiously and fairly**; and

b) **in ways which are proportionate to the nature, importance and complexity of the issues;**

The court must also

c) **ensure that the parties are on an equal footing;**

d) **save expense;** and

e) **allot to the case an appropriate share of the court's resources, while taking into account the need to allot resources to other cases.**

The rules tell the court that it must always have the overriding objective in mind, that it must be proactive in managing cases in order to make sure the objective is achieved and that everybody must help the court with this. Rule 1.4 and Part 4 of the rules give more detail about how the court can and should try to achieve this.

You should bear in mind the ethos of the overriding objective when approaching your case. It will help you to understand what is expected of you and it might sometimes be a tool you can use to help you persuade the court to do something or to let you do something.

The best thing you can do though is to follow these simple rules. If you do you will be more or less on the right track:

- Give as much warning as possible (to the court and to anyone else in the case) of any application or step you are planning to take

- Send a copy of all documents you want to rely on to the court and to anyone else involved in the case

- Pay attention to dates and deadlines in orders. If you can't meet them apply for an extension of time before time runs out. Likewise, if you can't attend a hearing ask promptly for it to be re-fixed.

- Respond to letters or requests promptly.

If ever you find yourself on the wrong side of the rules or miss a deadline, act promptly to put it right and if necessary refer to the overriding objective - for example the need for the court to ensure you are on an equal footing to a represented party, or to ensure that the case is dealt with fairly bearing in mind you are trying to manage as a litigant in person.

8.3   Before making an application - considering mediation

It should go without saying that court is not the best way to resolve family disputes, and if it can be avoided it probably should be. The court will generally expect you to have at least thought about whether or not you can sort things out without going to court *before* you make an application and can stop an application from proceeding if that hasn't happened.

Nobody can *make* you go to mediation, but in April 2014 the law changed to say that before making an application to the Family Court the Applicant **must** *find out about mediation* through attending a Mediation Information and Assessment Meeting (a MIAM) - unless they qualify for an exemption. A mediator will invite both parties to a dispute to attend a MIAM, usually separately, but if the other person fails to respond or does not attend then the matter can proceed to court. When an application is made the person making it must complete form FM1 containing either:

- Confirmation from a mediator that they have been to a MIAM, or

- Confirmation from a mediator that mediation is not suitable, or

- Confirmation from the person applying that they are exempt from attending a MIAM;

A mediator can only confirm mediation is not suitable if:

- mediation is not suitable because the other person is not willing to attend a MIAM; or

- mediation is not suitable because the other person failed to attend a MIAM; or

- mediation is not suitable for some other reason.

Alternatively, you can claim exemption from attending a MIAM without confirmation from a mediator if:

- There is evidence of domestic violence (the evidence must be something on the list in PD3A);

- The case would concern a child and either that child or a child she lives with is under a Child Protection Plan or is subject to a child protection enquiry;

- The application must be brought urgently because of a risk to life, liberty or physical safety of the person applying or his family or home and any delay would cause a risk of harm or of abduction of that child or unreasonable hardship to the person making the application. See below for a fuller definition of 'urgent';

- The person applying has or is attending mediation about the issues in the application or there is a relevant and recent MIAM exemption that can be applied (check the rules if you think this applies to you, this is a rough summary FPR r3.8(1)(d));

- The person applying is bankrupt;

- The person applying doesn't have an address for the other person;

- The application is of a sort that would be made without telling the other person (without notice);

- One of the people involved has a disability that requires certain facilities, the person applying has contacted all the family mediators in their area (up to a maximum of three) and none of them can provide those facilities;

- One of the parties is in prison or on bail or subject to a licence with conditions that prevents them from having contact with the other person;

- Where one of the parties is habitually resident abroad;

- The child might be a party to the case (usually only applicable in complex cases or where an older child wishes to be represented);

- The person applying has contacted all the family mediators in their area (up to a maximum of 3) and none of them can provide a MIAM within fifteen working days.

If you have not complied with the MIAM requirements and don't qualify for an exemption the court may refuse to issue your application or you may be asked by the court at the first hearing to go back and do it and this will slow things down.

Broadly speaking, the rules about MIAMS apply to the following types of case:

- Applications for orders about children, except where there are emergency applications or applications made by a Local Authority (social services).

- Applications about finances on divorce or finances for children

The MIAMs requirements don't apply to:

- Applications for non-molestation orders (domestic violence injunctions - see Chapter 22);

- Disputes between cohabiting couples about the ownership or sale of their former home (ToLATA - see Chapter 15) - although in these cases mediation may be a good idea, and the court may still expect you to consider it;

- Applications that are for a consent order (i.e. you both agree the court should approve an order you or your lawyers have drawn up);

- Applications to enforce an earlier order of the court that has been broken;

The rules about MIAMS are set out in more detail in FPR Rule 3 and Practice Direction 3A.

Legal aid is available for attendance at a MIAM, so if you are on a low income you will probably be able to attend a MIAM for free. And if your ex is eligible for a free MIAM you will also qualify.

8.4 Making an application

A person who wants to ask the court to make an order must make an application. They are called the Applicant (occasionally they are called the Claimant). The person who is responding to the application is called the Respondent (occasionally the Defendant).

Sometimes when both of you make different or opposing applications (called cross-applications) you can end up being both an Applicant and Respondent. This can be a bit confusing; usually the court will just call the person who made the earliest application the Applicant, and the other the Respondent. Sometimes lawyers and Judges will fall back on referring to you as 'mother' and 'father' or 'husband' and 'wife' (where appropriate) to avoid confusion - it's a bit impersonal sounding but it can help stop mix ups.

There are two types of application:

- Applications which start a case e.g. an application for a child arrangements order.

- Applications which relate to a case that is already running e.g. an application for direction about a child arrangements application or for an interim order or hearing. Lawyers call this an application made 'within proceedings'.

An application must usually be made in writing, and on the correct form, although occasionally where a case is already running you can make an application orally at a hearing or the Judge will say you do not need to formally apply in writing (see Chapters 17, 20 and 22 for more detail of when this may be the case). There is guidance throughout the book about what type of form to use in particular types of cases. This chapter covers rules and forms that apply to all types of cases. Practice Direction 5A sets out what form you should use, but it's a bit longwinded, so you may need to ask the court staff. Court staff are usually very helpful if you are unsure what type of form you need, which bits you need to fill in or what you need to attach, but they cannot give you legal advice. Some will be more helpful than others and although they may be very familiar with the procedures none of them are legally trained.

When an application is issued (see below) it must usually be provided in triplicate (three copies - one for you, one for the court and one for the other party, with extra copies if there are more parties), and there will be a fee (except for an application for a domestic violence injunction where there is no fee).

If you are on a low income you may qualify to pay a reduced fee or no fee (sometimes called 'help with fees' or 'fee remission'), and if you are on certain benefits you will automatically get fee remission. These are: Income-based JSA or ESA, Income Support, Universal Credit (gross annual earnings less than £6,000) or State Pension Credit. You can apply for fee remission online at www.gov.uk/help-with-court-fees. When you apply for Help with Fees the court service will check directly with the Department of Work and Pensions whether you receive the qualifying benefits and will check whether your income makes them eligible for help with fees. The online service will generate a reference number, for example, HWF-A73-L8T which you will be asked to write on your main application form. The process works by self-assessment, but in some cases you may be asked to provide paperwork such as bank statements and payslips or benefit documentation.

Check what time your court office is open until - lots of court counters are now only open until 2pm. You might be able to issue an application outside these times if it is something that requires an urgent hearing (i.e. a hearing that day) and if you have made a prior arrangement by telephone.

When an application is filed (sent to the court) and any fee has been paid the court will check it is in order, give it a case number (unless it is an application within a case that is already running and which has its own case number) and issue it. You can tell an application has been issued because it will have the court seal on it (the court seal is a circular stamp that has the name of the court and a crest on it) and a case number.

What is 'urgent'?

Anything that involves your children is likely to be something you consider urgent. However, the court will not treat everything as urgent just because it is *important* to you - every family case is important - something is only 'urgent' for the court's purposes if it genuinely cannot wait.

You can see above that 'urgent' has a particular definition if you are asking to skip the MIAM requirement (a risk to life, liberty or physical safety of the person applying or his family or home and any delay would cause a risk of harm or of abduction of that child or unreasonable hardship to the person making the application). PD12B says that 'urgent' means:

'Where an order is sought as a matter of urgency, an application may be made to the Court for an emergency order without the requirement for the Applicant to have attended at a MIAM. The categories of urgent application justifying such an exemption are set out in rule 3.8(c) FPR and include cases in which:

(1) There is a risk to the life, liberty, or the physical safety of the prospective applicant or his or her family, or his or her home;

(2) Any delay caused by attending a MIAM would cause:

   (1) risk of harm to the child;

   (2) A risk of unlawful removal of a child from the United Kingdom or a risk of unlawful retention of a child who is currently outside England and Wales;

   (3) significant risk of a miscarriage of justice;

   (4) Unreasonable hardship to the prospective applicant;

   (5) Irretrievable problems in dealing with the dispute (including the irretrievable loss of significant evidence).

(3) There is a significant risk that in the period necessary to schedule and attend a MIAM, proceedings relating to the dispute will be brought in another state in which a valid claim to jurisdiction may exist, such that a court in that other State would be seised of the dispute before a court in England and Wales.' [PD12B pa 12]

PD12B only applies to cases about children but it is a useful guide to what sorts of things the court will class as 'urgent' in any sort of case. Leaflet CB8 gives more information (Justice website).

What is 'without notice'?

A without notice hearing is one which is held before telling the other person about the application to court. It is only appropriate where an order needs to be put in place before the other person finds out, usually because if they know in advance it will defeat the object of going to court, because they've been 'tipped off'. PD12B gives a useful definition of when a without notice application can be made:

> *Without Notice Orders should be made only exceptionally, and where:*
>
> *(1) If the applicant were to give notice to the respondent(s) this would enable the respondent(s) to take steps to defeat the purpose of the injunction; cases where the application is brought without notice in order to conceal the step from the respondent(s) are very rare indeed; or*
>
> *(2) The case is one of exceptional urgency; that is to say, that there has been literally no time to give notice (either by telephone, text or e-mail or otherwise) before the injunction is required to prevent the threatened wrongful act; or*
>
> *(3) If the applicant gives notice to the respondent(s), this would be likely to expose the applicant or relevant child to unnecessary risk of physical or emotional harm.*

If you make an application without notice you must say in writing why it is necessary and the court will arrange a hearing that the other person can attend soon after the first hearing, so that they can have their say. Leaflet CB2 'Urgent Hearings and Those Without Notice in Relation to Child Arrangements' gives more information (Justice website).

8.5 Swearing documents

Some applications need to be sworn or to attach a sworn statement called an affidavit. If you are not religious you can affirm (this is a solemn but non-religious promise to the court).

If at any stage you need to swear an affidavit (most likely in connection with a divorce) you can take it to the court office and they will take your oath and witness it for free (solicitors or notaries will charge).

These days most documents are just signed by you with a statement of truth, and you don't usually need to formally swear them and have them witnessed, but in divorce and certain other cases you may still need to do this.

8.6 Service of an application

Depending on the type of application you may be expected to serve a sealed copy of the documents on the other party (i.e. send them to the other person in the case) or the court may do it for you - check when you go to court to issue. Usually a person is served by the documents being sent to them in the post. Two days after posting the court will consider them 'served'. If you are the person who has to serve the documents you usually have to fill in a certificate of service form to confirm that they have been posted. The court staff will give this to you.

Sometimes the rules say it isn't good enough to serve by post and the documents have to be handed to the person (called personal service). You should ask the court to do this.

There are rules about how much notice (advance warning) you need to give to the other party of your application before the court can deal with it. Depending on the type of application you are making this will be anything from two days to 14 days: two days for non-molestation / occupation order applications [Rule 10.3 FPR], but check Practice Direction 12C for applications about children, as the times can vary. In matrimonial and financial proceedings the court will tell you the date you have to take certain steps by.

If the court has made an order without the other person knowing about it they will need to be served with the application and order within 48 hours. Again, you should ask the court to do this.

Where the rules say there must be a certain number of days' notice this means complete days (called 'Clear' days by lawyers) between the date of service and the date of the hearing. For example:

- You must give two days' notice. This means two clear days.

- You serve an application on a Friday (or you post it on a Wednesday and it is assumed to be served two days later on the Friday).

- Saturday and Sunday don't count because they are not working days.

- Monday and Tuesday are days one and two respectively (unless Monday is a Bank Holiday), and so the hearing could not be before Wednesday (Thursday if a bank holiday week).

If your case is urgent you must ask the court to agree to a shorter gap between service and hearing. (On your application you must ask for 'an order abridging time for service'). Point this out to the court staff when you issue your application so they will deal with it quickly.

8.7   If the court thinks the application or response is hopeless

If the court thinks that the application is completely hopeless or that it is asking for something the court just can't order, the Judge can strike out the case [Rule 4.4 FPR]. Striking out means getting rid of. The court would not do this if the case just looked weak but might succeed; it would only be allowed to strike out a case if it really had no hope of succeeding. The court can do the same for a response to an application, and can strike out the response, leaving the application undefended. Again, this would only happen with a hopeless rather than a weak response. This is an unusual step to take in a family case.

8.8   Serving and receiving documents during the case

If at any stage in your case you want to rely on new material or evidence you must make sure that:

- you provide a copy of it (serve it) as soon as possible to the other party (or their solicitor if they have one);

- you let them see the original if they ask (and always have it to hand at court just in case);

- you send a copy to the court (filing);

- you ask whoever is preparing the bundle and the index to include your document in the index and the bundle.

8.9   Communicating with the other person

If the other person involved in the case has a lawyer you should generally communicate with them rather than with the party individually (unless invited to do otherwise. If there are allegations of harassment it is almost always wiser to ignore invitations from your ex and still communicate with the lawyer. This way you can't be accused of anything you haven't done).

Any other lawyer in the case has a professional duty to assist the court and not to mislead you. In addition most solicitors will be members of Resolution, and most barristers will be members of the Family Law Bar Association, both of which have an ethos of courteous communication and avoiding inflaming disputes. You will generally find that if you are polite and respectful to solicitors and barristers they will behave similarly to you, albeit that they may not have the warmest manner, and they have to act based on what their client tells them. Even though they will almost certainly not admit that their client's position is unreasonable to you, they are likely to be privately advising their client honestly of the weaknesses in their case.

You might receive a letter which says 'Without Prejudice' or 'without prejudice save as to costs' at the top. This means that it is a letter which is intended to be closed correspondence not seen by the Judge. This type of letter is sent (usually in financial proceedings) where a party wants to make a proposal to settle the case which is not the same as the position they are putting forward to the court. This might be perhaps because they recognise there is some weakness in the case or simply because they want to resolve things by dispute and they are prepared to compromise if they can do this without the costs of a full hearing. So usually when you see the words 'without prejudice' this means 'we'd like to make a deal'.

A 'without prejudice' letter is a deal offered that is not intended to prejudice the case run in court if it does not result in a deal. Therefore this kind of letter must not be shown to the Judge because it might affect her view about the case. If it is shown to the Judge by mistake, that Judge might have to stop hearing the case (recuse him/herself - see Chapter 25) and a whole new hearing would have to be started.

8.10   Applications - Part 18 & Part 19

There are two main pathways for making applications, which are described in Part 18 and Part 19 FPR. It is quite difficult to explain when you should use Part 18 and when you should use Part 19. There is some general guidance below, but if you are unsure you should ask court staff whether your application should be under Part 18 or Part 19.

Use Part 18 if you are applying for permission to start a case, if you want to apply for a non-molestation order or occupation order or for applications to have a Guardian appointed or if you want interim maintenance or an injunction to stop your ex disposing of your assets. Use Part 18 for applications within a case that has already been started, or where your case has finished but something happens that means you need the court to look at it again.

Use Part 19 for applications for anything that doesn't seem to fall under Part 18 and doesn't have a set form, and for applications for permission to appeal.

If you do have to make an application under Part 18 or Part 19 those parts of the rules will tell you how the application will be dealt with and what you should expect. Each rule has its own Practice Direction [PDs 18A and 19A] which gives more information.

8.11 What if one of the parties doesn't do something they should have?

If the court orders a party to do something (like send a document to the court or the other party, or give an explanation of something) and they don't do it in time the court can impose sanctions, for example by saying that the person can't continue with their application, or by saying they have to pay costs. You can ask the court to lift the sanction but you have to produce evidence showing there was a good reason for the failure and deal with the things listed at Rule 4.6 FPR (If the sanction is a costs order you can't use this rule - you have to appeal it instead. See Rule 4.5(2) FPR, Chapter 25).

8.12 What if one of the parties wasn't at court for a hearing when the order was made?

The court can still carry on even if someone doesn't show up at court. The court does need to be happy that everybody knows about the hearing, but can go on and make orders or dismiss an application [see Rule 27.4 FPR for more detail].

If the court does go ahead without everybody at court and makes an order or dismisses the application, the person who was not at court can apply to have the order set aside [Rule 27.5 FPR]. (Note that this is different from the set aside applications described in Chapter 25).

You can also apply to have an order set aside if it was made without you being told about the hearing (without notice), for example where a non-molestation order has been made and you knew nothing about it until you were served with the order. But you have to apply back to the court within seven days of being served with the order.

8.13 If you can't make a hearing - adjournments

It is really important that if you find you cannot get to a hearing (for example because you are ill or your car breaks down) you do your best to let the court and the other party know that you can't come and you would like the hearing to be rearranged. If you miss a hearing by mistake it is really important that you find out quickly what took place at the hearing, and if necessary let the court know why you weren't at court, and that you make an application to set aside the order made under Part 18.

If you know you are not going to be able to make a hearing through illness or an unavoidable appointment (such as surgery) or because you are abroad, and you wish to postpone the hearing to a date when you can make it, you should take the following steps:

- Write to the court as soon as you are aware of the problem, explaining that you are applying for an adjournment (in Children matters use form C2, otherwise a letter will be sufficient). Your form or letter should be clearly marked with the name of the Judge if known, the case number and the hearing date that is causing the problem. You should explain why you can't come, why you can't rearrange AND provide documentary evidence of the difficulty. This might be flight tickets or booking confirmation, medical note or letter from your GP, or hospital appointment letter. You should also state, if possible, when you WILL be better / available to come to court so that the court can consider the length of the possible delay.

- It is important to ensure that any medical evidence actually shows that you cannot attend court - the fact that you are unwell or find court anxiety inducing does not necessarily mean you are not fit to attend court. Ideally any letter from a medical practitioner should be based upon a recent examination of you and should give details of the condition you are suffering from and why it prevents you from coming to court.

- You must send your application to the other person in the case. If the other person is represented their lawyer is likely to agree to an adjournment if you have provided evidence that you really can't come to court, to avoid a wasted hearing, so it is always worth checking before you apply to the court if the other party will agree in advance.

If you do not apply for an adjournment or if you do not supply proper evidence that shows you really cannot make it the court may well carry on and make decisions in your absence.

If you know you have appointments or commitments coming up that you cannot move, and you know the court is going to be fixing a hearing around that period it is always sensible to let the court know - either at the hearing where the Judge is considering future dates, or by writing to the court and others in the case.

8.14 Witness statements and evidence

The main source of written evidence in court will be witness statements, with documents attached. In financial cases you have to file your evidence in a set form called Form E.

There are specific rules in cases about children and in financial cases about when you can produce and rely on evidence. In general if you want to rely on any evidence that the court has not already ordered you to provide you must ask for permission. If there is any objection raised by the other party to the court considering something on which you want to rely, you should ask the court to deal with this first, at the start of any hearing.

Remember that whenever the court orders you to prepare or get a document it will usually order that you file it and serve it. Filing a document means sending it to the court. Serving it means sending it to everyone else in the case via their lawyers, or directly to them if they do not have a lawyer. The court will generally not serve documents on other parties for you. It is up to you to make sure that the documents you want to rely on have been provided to everyone and they have had a chance to see and think about them. If they are surprised by them at the last minute and things have to be postponed because they are not ready to deal with them this will be at best frustrating, and at worst could result in you having to pay any legal costs that have been wasted (this is unlikely but it is possible).

The same goes in reverse. Any document that somebody else wants to rely upon at court should be sent to you or given to you in advance of the hearing. If it is not you may want to ask the Judge for a short time to read it properly. If you are given a really big pile of documents that you simply can't digest on the day you might want to ask the court to adjourn, reminding the court that you are a litigant in person and that it is more difficult for you (you could refer to the overriding objective). Alternatively, the Judge might be able to put your case back down the list and call you back later that day instead, which would avoid a long delay. What you ask for and what the Judge will do will depend on the urgency of the case and how busy the court is.

There are some documents that are commonly produced at the last minute. These are case summaries or position statements prepared by lawyers for use at that particular hearing. These are typically a couple of pages long and summarise the history or a party's view of the case for the court, to bring them right up to date. The court will not usually be too worried about these being produced the day before the hearing or even brought to court on the day because they help speed things up.

Sometimes evidence is only available very late and has to be brought to court on the day and the court (and other lawyers) will usually take a reasonable view about this. For example, if a letter from your GP or a valuation of your pension has been asked for well in advance, but only arrives on your doormat on the day of the hearing, you are unlikely to be criticised if you bring it with you. You might well be criticised if you have delayed letting the other person or their lawyer see it though.

Don't forget that with most types of cases you will only be able to rely on evidence where you have first obtained permission from the court to file and serve it. If you want to file a witness statement from yourself or someone else who has witnessed a particular event you should ask the court to make a direction allowing you to do so. Remember to make clear if you plan to file a witness statement from someone apart from yourself so that the order can say you are allowed to file 'any evidence upon which you seek to rely' rather than just 'a witness statement', otherwise the lawyer for your ex might object when you send them more than one statement.

PD 22A describes what form a witness statement must take. A template of what a witness statement should look like is set out in the Forms, Templates & Useful Documents section in the Toolkit & Resources. PD 22A is quite detailed: don't get too worried about the minute detail of what it says. Do your best to follow the format and put the information in a logical and clear order. If an objection is raised to the format of your witness statements you can ask the court for permission to rely on them, explaining that you are a litigant in person and have done your best.

Do not hold documents back in order to gain a tactical advantage by ambushing or surprising someone at the last minute or by tricking them into saying something you can prove isn't true. If you do you may well find the court will not allow you to use the documents that you have held back, or that the case will have to be postponed and you will have to pay the costs. Anything you want the court to consider must be shown to the other parties in the case sufficiently early for them to be able to properly consider it and to take advice on it.

If you have documents that belong to someone else (including your ex's post) you must return the originals immediately. You cannot wait until they have tripped up and said something that is contradicted by the documents you have. Even if you are worried that something will be hidden or that papers will be destroyed it may be unlawful to take or copy material that belongs to your ex and that is confidential. The case of *Tchenguiz v Imerman; Imerman v Imerman* [2010] EWCA Civ 908 confirmed this. Material does not have to be in a locked cupboard or a password protected computer to be confidential, and can be confidential even though you are married and living in the same house. Each of you is entitled to a life separate and distinct from your shared matrimonial life, but there will be some matters as to which confidentiality does not apply, for example a bank statement being left openly lying about in a common part of the house but it will all depend on the circumstances so you must be very careful. The court will usually order the return and/or destruction of confidential material.

8.15 Bundles

A bundle is an indexed file of the relevant court papers. PD 27A sets out who is responsible for putting together the index and bundle for the hearing. Broadly speaking, if there is a lawyer involved the lawyer will do it. If there are no lawyers you may submit a bundle of your own but it must be structured in the way described in the practice direction. In some cases about children the court may prepare a bundle if there are no lawyers. You could ask the Judge to arrange this in your case if you think this would be helpful. It is sometimes necessary to ask for permission to include certain documents in the bundle, as the Practice Direction places limits on what should go in.

The general rule in PD27A is that all the papers that make up the bundle must not exceed 350 pages (approximately one fat lever arch file full) and that the court's permission must be sought for more documents to be included in the bundle. It is important that only documents that are actually going to help the Judge are included - the danger is that if too much material is included the really important stuff will get forgotten. But, if for some reason there is a need for more than 350 pages to be in the bundle you (or the solicitor preparing the bundle) will need make sure that the court approves in advance, usually at the previous hearing.

8.16 Experts

In some cases it will be necessary for the court to hear expert evidence - some examples of the sorts of experts that are sometimes instructed are where:

- there is an adult medical issue that affects capacity to care for a child, capacity to work or financial need;

- a child had a significant medical issue that affects their care and accommodation needs;

- there is a need for a specialist risk assessment;

- there are concerns about someone's mental health or functioning;

- there are concerns about a child's psychological or emotional wellbeing or where there is alienation from a parent;

- there is a dispute about the value of a business or property;

- there are concerns about drug or alcohol misuse and drug testing is required;

- there is an issue about paternity and DNA testing is required.

Experts are not the 'norm' - they are the exception rather than the rule and their evidence cannot be relied upon unless you have permission to instruct an expert. In cases concerning children you need to have the permission of the court *before* the expert is instructed. In most cases it is not easy to get permission. If the court can manage without an expert it will do so - and it should be obvious that in some cases the cost of an expert outweighs the size of the issue at stake (for example the costs of valuing a very small fledgling business when there are other far more substantial assets available to meet the family's needs). The court rules are very clear that experts can only be permitted where their instruction is *'necessary'*. Prior to 2013 the rules said expert evidence had to be 'reasonably required' but the 'necessary' test is tougher.

An expert means an *independent* expert (i.e. someone with no prior involvement in the case or with the parties), and they will usually be instructed jointly by the parties through an agreed letter of instruction. If there are no lawyers the court might draft the letter of instruction to ensure it covers all the relevant points and to avoid difficulties about the wording. It usually falls to the parties to each pay a share of the costs of the expert evidence.

If you consider that an expert is necessary in your case you will need to make an application promptly, following the instructions in Part 25 and the relevant Practice Direction [PD25D for financial cases, PD25C for children cases]. In reality you are most likely to be thinking about an expert because the Judge or CAFCASS have identified that there is an issue that they need assistance with. In those circumstances they may take the lead in identifying an expert and sorting out the letter.

There are some template letters of instruction on the Law Society website. They will need some adaptation to suit your circumstances but are a useful starting point. There are some template questions for children cases in Annex A to PD25C. However, you can ask the court to prepare the letter of instruction if it is something you don't think you can manage or if you think you will be unable to agree it with the other person in the case.

8.17 Special measures for vulnerable parties

If someone involved in the family court as a party or a witness is fearful or intimidated, for example because someone else involved in the case has been physically or sexually abusive or threatening, they can ask the court to take special measures to help them take part or to give their evidence. Special measures include appearing over a video link from another room in the court building or another building entirely, or arranging a screen so that a vulnerable witness does not have to see the person they are fearful of.

Court staff can also sometimes arrange separate waiting areas or for you to access or exit the court via a separate exit.

All of these arrangements will need to be made in advance of the hearing date, because not all court rooms or court buildings have the necessary facilities. If you are asking for the court to arrange a screen or a video link you will usually need to ask the Judge to approve this as appropriate.

Witnesses who have a difficulty communicating or understanding things may need an intermediary or foreign language / sign language interpreter. The court can arrange this but again, arrangements need to be made in advance. This book doesn't give any further information about that because if you are reading this book you probably don't need an interpreter or an intermediary.

8.18   Can I see the court file?

FPR r29.12(3) says that: *'a party to any family proceedings...their legal representative...may have a search made for, and may inspect, and obtain a copy of, any document filed or lodged in the court office in those proceedings'* unless the court directs otherwise. This doesn't cover everything that may be on the court file, for example it doesn't cover the Judge's own notes, but it would enable you to get a copy of a document you were missing that you couldn't get off the other party - and probably includes getting a copy of correspondence or documents sent directly to the court by the other party without copying you in.

Sometimes court staff will refuse to allow people to obtain copy documents from the file - refer them to FPR r29.12(3).

With only very limited exceptions, non-parties are not entitled to see the file or obtain copy documents.

9. Evidence

9.1   Introduction

Courts make decisions based upon evidence. The law gives a Judge a framework but at the end of the day a Judge has to do the best she can to understand what the facts are relating to each child, each couple, or each family. She does this through evidence.

There are a number of different types of evidence. In a Family Court setting the most common types of evidence are:

- Written witness statements, setting out what has happened in the past and what a person says will or should happen in the future. Occasionally there is a set form for written evidence, such as the Form E Financial Statement in financial proceedings;

- Oral evidence, when a person attends court and gives evidence in front of the Judge, so their written evidence can be challenged, explained or tested. The Judge takes account not just of what is said, but also of how it is said, of what is not said, and of the body language and demeanour of the witness in the witness box and generally;

- Reports (and oral evidence) from experts or professionals (e.g. social worker, CAFCASS or psychologist). This type of evidence is opinion evidence, rather than factual evidence, although sometimes a professional / expert will need to give evidence about what they have seen or observed as well as what their view is;

- Drug or alcohol test results;

- Police logs or hospital records;

- Letters or reports from your GP or counsellor about treatment, therapy or any condition;

- Medical records;

- Photographic evidence.

9.2   Written and oral evidence

If you want to rely upon the evidence of a particular person (that is if you want the Judge to take it into account) you will need to produce a written witness statement which confirms at the bottom that the statement is true, and is signed. A letter may be accepted but it is better to use the template the Forms, Templates & Useful Documents section in the Toolkit & Resources. PD 22A to the FPR sets out in detail what format a witness statement should take and the template is modelled on this. Some courts provide templates for witness statements which you may be expected to use.

Unless everybody in the case agrees that the statement is true you will need to make sure that the witness who has written the statement can come to court to give oral evidence and be asked questions. You may still be allowed to rely on a written witness statement if they are not at court, but even if the Judge permits this she will attach much less weight to it (this means it will not help you very much, particularly if it is contradicted by another witness who has come to court).

Of course, most of the time the main and only witnesses will be you and your ex-partner and the Judge will not want to hear evidence from lots of family and friends about their opinions. Most people *can* produce a handful of friends who will tell the Judge that they are a fantastic parent and the other one is a useless rat (even if this is not entirely true), so this doesn't really help the Judge to get to the bottom of things. You need to focus only on witnesses who can help you prove a fact that is necessary to your case (for example that a particular event did or did not take place). And when you are writing documents for your own case you should try to avoid running down your ex unless it is essential to your case.

If a witness doesn't have first-hand knowledge of what's in their statement this is called 'hearsay'. Hearsay is what someone else has told you has happened. Hearsay evidence may not be allowed, and if it is allowed it won't be given very much weight. If there is a witness who was actually there and can give a first-hand account the court is likely to pay more attention to that. The general rule is that if there is a witness who can give a direct account that is the person who should be called to give evidence. Some examples of what is and isn't hearsay are:

- where a doctor gives evidence that he has seen a bruise on a patient, this is not hearsay. He has seen it with his own eyes;

- if the doctor went on to say that this was how the bruise was caused, this would be hearsay (or opinion);

- if the doctor gives evidence that the person with the bruise reported at the time that it was caused by their partner, that isn't hearsay - he was there when the account was given. The doctor would not be giving evidence about how the bruise was actually caused but about what the person who had the bruise said about it at the time (this might help the court decide if the person has said that innocent injuries were caused by violence).

Usually the court will not be very interested in a witness statement or letter which simply tells the court that you are a good mum or dad and that you love your children very much, or that you are a hard worker while your ex is lazy, or which is a general character reference. This is because it is ultimately the Judge's responsibility to assess your parenting, and if the Judge needs guidance about your parenting skills or your relationship with the child she will get those by asking social services or CAFCASS to help (see Chapter 17). Although people often find it surprising, in financial cases, how people behave towards each other and how much effort they put into a relationship are not usually very relevant (see Chapter 14). Letters from professionals involved with the family, for example school teachers, nursery staff or health visitors, about what they have seen may be more helpful, but they are often wary of getting involved in disputes of this kind when they still have to deal with both parents. GPs are usually willing to provide a letter describing what is recorded in their patient's medical records and basic factual information.

Other types of evidence which are sometimes used or which parents sometimes want to rely upon are:

- Video or sound recordings;

- Text messages and voicemail;

- Printouts from internet sites like Facebook;

- Expert reports not ordered by the court;

- Lie detector tests;

- Print or internet news articles;

- Letters from the children or the children to give evidence at court.

9.3   Audio or video recordings

This type of evidence is usually recordings of police interviews (children are often video interviewed, adults usually on tape), or very occasionally of 999 calls. In most cases the court will not want to see or hear the actual recording and will arrange for a transcript to be prepared (unless a child's body language is going to be particularly important).

Other than this, video and audio recordings are not usually admitted (other than the odd voicemail - see below) and are not often as relevant as people seem to think they are.

The court may take a dim view of you recording a child saying something about things which the court is being asked to decide, telling tales on the other parent or being asked questions (obviously this does not include normal day to day snapshots). It is likely to result in concern that you have coached a child at some point before the recording started and of course it is impossible to prove that this has not happened. For this reason a tape of a child saying they want to live with you can be more harmful than helpful.

A tape recording of your other half being abusive or making some threat is similarly open to suggestions of editing, being taken out of context or being a pre-meditated recording of a set up. It may well not take matters any further and can give a poor impression. An extreme example of how making recordings can backfire can be found in *M v F (Covert Recording of Children)* [2016] EWFC 29.

9.4   Text messages and voicemail

These may be considered by the court but you will be expected to produce the whole exchange and call log for the period rather than isolated messages. Even if the messages were really one way rather than an exchange a call log may still be necessary in order to prove that this is the case.

If your phone can only keep a certain number of messages or wipes them after a certain number of days you must be careful to download any messages, or photocopy them, or to record them in full in writing, logging the number, date and time for each. It is helpful if you can get someone independent to view the messages and to sign to confirm your record is accurate.

The court will usually consider the written records of text messages and call logs, but you must make sure that the phone is made available for inspection by the other party's solicitor on request, and that you bring it to court for the Judge to see if necessary.

Similar points apply to viber, whatsapp and other social media messaging apps.

There is no point in producing a voicemail message that is inaudible - it is likely to be disregarded if there is any question over what is being said.

9.5   Facebook

Information from Facebook and similar sites, apps or platforms can be relevant, but it does bring its own problems and risks.

You will need full printouts of whatever it is you are relying on. It is sensible to keep date stamped electronic versions in case their veracity is challenged.

Do NOT log in to anyone else's Facebook account to get information, even if you know the password from before you split - you may be committing an offence.

Be aware that once you start making allegations about something said on Facebook, your own Facebook account will be subject to scrutiny. Only do it if you are squeaky clean yourself AND the information is really relevant and cannot be obtained from any other source.

Be aware of the risk of a Facebook war between your friends and theirs. It can be very unpleasant.

Some of the things that can be demonstrated by Facebook are:

- somebody has a lifestyle that is far more luxurious than is consistent with their financial disclosure (but consider how much of Facebook is bragging as opposed to reality?).

- that a person is smoking, drinking or using drugs or living a party lifestyle (but consider if you can prove that they are doing it more than once, or if you can actually do more than raise a suspicion or draw an inference).

- that a person has done something during contact that they have promised not to do.

- that a parent has been trying to contact and / or influence a child via Facebook.

- that a parent has been discussing private details of a case about the children with their friends or local community, and spreading rumours or wrong information (see Chapter 11).

- that a person has been making threats or harassing someone via Facebook, by themselves or a friend (sometimes people do this with a false account and it is then very difficult to prove who is actually doing it).

9.6   Reports

You MUST have the permission of the court before a child is examined or seen by an expert for the purposes of a report to the court. The court is unlikely to grant permission after the fact - you must get the permission FIRST.

9.7   Lie detectors

These are not used in the Family Courts in England & Wales.

9.8   News articles (print or internet)

There are all sorts of material in the press about miscarriages of justice or particular stories of a parent's battle for contact, or a particular divorce settlement. But much of it is incomplete, inaccurate or just plain misleading because the press are quite restricted in what they can publish. If you want to rely upon a particular case that has been in the news find out the name and go and look it up on BAILII. Read the judgment. If the case really says what the press reports suggest you can rely on the full judgment not a newspaper clipping.

Sometimes a Local or National Paper or website might carry an article about one of the parties to a case which will be relevant. Typically this might be about the success of a local business run by one of the parties, which will be relevant to the value of it. But be aware that such pieces may be as much about good PR as they are about objective fact. Just because your ex is trumpeting all about his fantastic new venture to the local rag does not necessarily mean that his business is worth anything. Do not let yourself be taken on a wild goose chase - is there anything else available which helps you get a more reliable grip on what the business might be worth or how it is doing?

9.9   Letters and children's evidence

Children rarely give evidence in family cases, and these cases are usually confined to cases where it cannot be avoided such as cases where really serious allegations are being made by the child about abuse or harm. Even in those cases usually children are interviewed by the Police and the video produced as evidence. If a child has been video interviewed and the video evidence is going to be presented to the court this is a pretty good indication that you need a lawyer, whichever parent you are.

Parents often come to court with a letter or drawing from the child. Invariably the other parent will say it was coached or dictated. The Judge will usually look at it, but its weight as proof of what a child wants may well be limited. It may be seen by the court as more important as an indicator of how much pressure the child is under to please one or both of his parents. In reality it probably won't sway the court either way unless it is something that has been produced by an older child and has been written unprompted and come into the case via an independent person such as the Guardian, CAFCASS officer, school teacher or social worker. And of course, in a case about children, even if a letter is accepted as an accurate record of a child's wishes, those wishes are just one of many things the Judge has to take into account.

9.10 Challenging evidence

If you do not accept the evidence produced by the other party or the evidence of an expert, you are entitled to challenge it by asking the witness to come to court at the trial and by asking them questions (this is called cross examination).

You must make sure to tell the court and the other party or their solicitor if you want to challenge a particular piece of evidence, and ask for the relevant witness to be made available on the day of the trial.

If the witness is an expert or a social worker or CAFCASS officer you should ask the court to order them to attend, otherwise they may not be able to come on the day. If the expert is not available on the day of the hearing you may need to ask the court to adjourn the hearing to a day when they can come.

Cross examining a witness is important because if a witness's evidence is not challenged, the court will treat it as true and correct and it will not be any good for you to say at the end that it is wrong or untrue. Only if it is challenged by cross examination does the Judge have to decide whether or not to accept it. She can accept some or part of the evidence.

There are some tips on giving evidence and how to ask questions of another witness in Chapter 10.

9.11 Do I have to answer that? Self-incrimination

In private law proceedings (disputes between you and an ex) you cannot be made to give evidence and are entitled to refuse to answer questions so as not to incriminate yourself [s98 CA]. Obviously in most cases you would need to give evidence to make out your case, but there are occasions where you could be asked a tricky question that might tend to incriminate you - if this is the case you can decline to answer. This does not apply in public law cases (cases started by social services) where you could be told you have to give evidence.

10. Managing And Running Your Case

10.1 Legal research

You may well never need to look up the original law when dealing with your case because it is generally not as technically complex as many areas of law. But if you do want to look up a piece of law, the information below may be useful. You will also find some of the most commonly used bits of law set out in various chapters of this book and in the Key Law section in the Toolkit & Resources.

The first rule of searching on the internet is: learn what a Boolean search is. You will get MUCH better search results if you use the search functions properly and you will save time, headaches and mistakes. (For more information on Boolean searches, see for example http://websearch.about.com/od/2/g/boolean.htm or just google 'what is a Boolean search?').

Statute

All recent Acts of Parliament are now available free of charge on the internet. You can find most legislation from about 1990 onwards online at legislation.gov.uk.

It is extremely important that you check any online source to make sure that the version of the legislation you are looking at is up to date, or that you know which bits have been amended. Most sources publish the law as it was originally passed by Parliament and you may find that you need to check section by section to see if the original version has been changed. Legislation.gov.uk is not always up to date.

You should also check that the law that you are looking at is actually in force. There are pieces of law that have never been brought into force, but which have not been repealed. Some Acts of Parliament say when they will commence, others say that they may be brought into force by an order. In these cases you may need to find the Statutory Instrument that brings some or all of the Act into force. Check on www.legislation.gov.uk or in an up to date text book in a law library - the statutory instrument or Act which amends the law will be there even if the law it is amending hasn't been updated.

Be aware that some small campaigning organisations do publish the text or summaries of the law on their websites. These websites may be useful for many things, but are often run by amateurs and volunteers who update the site as and when they have the time and inclination, and are therefore not necessarily accurate or up to date. If you want to ensure you have a printout of the correct and current law, go to www.legislation.gov.uk and check the updating notes.

The most reliable and most straightforward way to check the up to date law is to buy a textbook containing the up to date version of it. A list of sources is included later in this chapter.

Case law

Every published case is given a unique reference, called a 'neutral citation number' which will look something like this; [2011] EWCA Civ 123 (for Court of Appeal) or [2008] EWHC 123 (Fam) (for High Court Family Division) or [2016] EWFC B123 (for Family Court). You can use this to search for a case and to check that the one you have is the one everyone else has too.

You may also see other types of citation that tell you where to find not just the transcript of a Judgment but in which Law Reports it has been published. They will look like this:

> [YEAR] 1 FLR 123 (FLR is Family Law Reports)

> [YEAR] FCR 123 (FCR is Family Court Reports)

> [YEAR] WLR 123 (Weekly Law Reports)

> [YEAR] TLR 123 (Times Law Reports) etc

The number before the acronym for the Law Report tells you the volume number, and the number after it tells you the page number. In most cases a print out from one of the websites listed below is quite adequate, but if you need to you may be able to locate these print versions of judgments in University or Law Libraries.

There are subscription services such as Lexis and Lawtel that lawyers use to get easy access to judgments, but you will almost certainly not need these - and they are expensive.

10.2 Resources

Legislation

www.legislation.gov.uk (National Archives)

> Contains all primary and secondary legislation from 1988 onwards and many statutes from prior to that date.

> Includes new legislation as soon as it is passed through Parliament.

> Statutes are shown in their original and revised form (i.e. incorporating

amendments) BUT there are long delays in getting amendments updated - often if a piece of law has been amended in the last couple of years the amendments will not have been added and the site will show a message saying something like this:

> *'Changes to legislation: There are outstanding changes not yet made by the legislation.gov.uk editorial team to Children Act 1989. Those changes will be listed when you open the content using the Table of Contents below. Any changes that have already been made by the team appear in the content and are referenced with annotations.'*

You will be able to find the new piece of law that says there is an amendment to the old one, but it can be a pain to cross reference all the law and amendments to work out what the current version says!

For changes made after 2002 each Statute is marked to show whether amendments have been incorporated or if they are outstanding. If changes are not incorporated there are links to the changes so you can look up what they are.

Statutory instruments are not in revised form so you need to trace back over any amendments to work out what the current version of the law is. The only Statutory Instrument that you are likely to need is the Family Procedure Rules 2010.

Justice website: www.justice.gov.uk

The up to date FPR are available along with all the associated PDs on the Justice website at www.justice.gov.uk (search under Procedure Rules).

Parliament: www.parliament.uk

Text of bills passing through Parliament and official records of debates in both houses (Hansard).

Case law

British and Irish Legal Information Institute: www.bailii.org

Most important judgments are now available for free online at BAILII. It isn't enormously user friendly, but try using the advanced search function. If you are looking for a case with only initials instead of names, try searching for the name of the Judge and date, or use keywords of 'family' or 'children' to sift out family from non-family cases or by using the neutral citation number (click 'case law', then 'find case by citation').

Wherever possible this book gives the neutral citation number for a case so that you can type it straight into BAILII. But even if you only have a reference to a set of law reports to go by you can still type this into BAILII.

Sometimes the neutral citation doesn't bring up a judgment even though the case is on BAILII - if this happens use a keyword such as the name of the Judge or court location.

Family Law Week: www.familylawweek.co.uk

Free source of judgments, articles and commentary on family law.

Family Law: www.familylaw.co.uk

Free source of judgments, articles and commentary on family law.

House of Lords: www.publications.parliament.uk/pa/ld/ldjudgmt.htm

Archive of judgments before formation of the Supreme Court in July 2009.

Supreme Court: www.supremecourt.gov.uk/decided-cases/index.html

Judgments of the Supreme Court since its formation in July 2009.

Judiciary of England & Wales: www.judiciary.gov.uk

Some judgments (all judgments on this site will also be on BAILII which is easier to search) and a range of guidance, templates etc on the Family Court Guide pages.

Search engine: e.g. www.google.co.uk

Occasionally a judgment or summary of a case will be published somewhere on the internet that you might not expect, such as on a barrister or solicitor's website. If you can't find it elsewhere, try google (use .co.uk not .com).

Textbooks

Hershman & Macfarlane Children Act Handbook (republished each year - now Bloomsbury Press). Around £50.

10.3 Managing your paperwork

When you are dealing with a court case you can quickly amass a vast stack of paperwork. It's important to be able to find what you need quickly and the key to this is to organise your papers. I would suggest using some version of the system below, but do whatever works for you.

- Put everything in a large ring-binder (don't bother with the small ones) and use file dividers to separate things - don't bother with one for each document, just use one for each category of document and put the documents in each category in chronological order.

- If your green credentials will allow it avoid printing everything double sided. You might not think it would make a difference, but I promise you will find things much more easily if everything is single sided. And don't staple each individual document in your file - it stops the pages turning.

- Splash out on another file when yours is full. This avoids you having to sort through your papers when the file bursts its seams and everything goes up in the air and comes down in a heap.

- Have a separate section for each of the following, and file them in date order (you can put them in reverse date order if you like to see the most recent thing on the top but if you do it so the most recent document is last, your filing system will more closely resemble any court bundle that solicitors prepare for a hearing, which will save you time and stress):

    - On top, keep a running note of calls to the court or to the other side, who you spoke to, what was said etc. If you are keeping a running note or diary of contact or other events you might want to keep these records on top of your file too.

    - Applications and orders.

    - Correspondence with the court.

    - Correspondence between yourself and the other party / parties or their solicitors.

    - Witness statements or position statements.

    - Expert reports.

    - Legal research and legal submissions.

- Anything else.

- If there is a bundle, prepared by the other person's lawyer or by the court you can use this as a base for organizing your documents.

I would suggest avoiding putting everything in plastic sleeves. You need to be able to get to all your documents and don't want to be scrabbling around trying to get things out of slippery sleeves when the Judge is asking to see a particular document. If your papers are methodically organised you won't need sleeves.

10.4 Preparing for a hearing where the court is going to hear evidence

If you are representing yourself at a hearing you will need to know where all the important documents are in your papers so that you can cross-examine the witnesses you want to challenge effectively, and answer any questions the Judge asks you.

First, make sure that if there is an official bundle you have a copy of it, and that you have sorted your papers into the right order to match the index and number them accordingly. Usually, the court will order a party with a solicitor to prepare the bundle and index so that everybody has the same page references and can be sure that they are all referring to the right document [PD 27A].

If there are any documents that you want to refer to or rely on you must make sure that everybody involved has a copy before the hearing starts. If it is a long hearing, the lawyer for the other party will probably be expected by the court to make up a bundle of all relevant documents. You should ask the lawyer preparing the bundle to include these documents in it. If they don't agree, raise it with the Judge at the start of the hearing. Take copies with you if you have not circulated them beforehand. If you cannot take copies and court staff will not photocopy them (assume that they won't), you should try and ensure that all the lawyers have seen the extra documents before the hearing starts.

Use different coloured post it notes to identify statements by different people. But don't go mad - if you have a sea of post it notes you won't find anything. Don't allow frantic application of post it notes or highlighter to become a substitute for carefully reading and absorbing documents.

Similarly, don't underline absolutely everything on the page or it becomes meaningless. It's better to use a highlighter than underline with a biro as you can still read what's written clearly and you can photocopy the document without your private scribbling being seen by everyone else in the case.

Draw up a 'Case Theory' for a final hearing. This is a lawyer's trick. You need to distil your whole case and your position into no more than half a page. You should be left with the most important issues and the roughest sketch of the picture you want to paint to the court by the end of the trial. Imagine how you will present your case in your closing speech. Work back from there. What do you have to prove or show to be able to make your arguments stand up? This document is your guiding document. You can change it as you go along but you need to keep it in mind at all times. It will help you to avoid becoming side-tracked.

10.5 Cross examination

The most effective cross examination is often polite cross examination. Being aggressive and confrontational can be effective when used by experienced lawyers at the right time, but lawyers know that it can simply result in the witness putting up all their defences and you get nowhere. Be nice and they may leave their guard slightly down. If your questions are the right questions you won't need to be rude.

Being aggressive and confrontational or upsetting a witness can lose the sympathy of the Judge. Consider what damage it might do to your case if the Judge thinks that you have bullied your ex in the witness box or have been aggressive to a professional. The Judge is watching what you do, what you say and your body language, whether you are giving evidence or testing it (and they have a very clear view of all of those things from where they sit in court). If you are unsure if a question is appropriate or how to ask a particular question, ask the Judge.

When you are preparing your questioning make sure you keep checking back to your case theory - are you asking questions that will help you build up the right picture and prove the points you need to prove? If you are going to be asking the court to make a finding that your ex has hidden assets, are you asking the right probing questions to raise enough suspicion in the mind of the Judge? You will not be able to make submissions at the end of a case about things you have not raised by cross-examining the other party or in your own evidence. If there are points that you want the Judge to agree with, and you know your ex does not agree, you have to 'put' them in cross-examination (this means you have to ask them as questions), even if you know they will just disagree. It might seem pointless but you need to do this. The point is they have to have an opportunity to agree, disagree or explain.

Write down the questions you want to ask the witness. Group them under headings or topics so that you can make your points in a logical order. Be prepared to change tack depending on what answers you get. Often the welfare checklist or s25 factors are a useful way to approach this (depending on what type of case you are dealing with). Try to think of questions that box in the person being asked ('closed' or 'leading' questions that require a yes or no answer or that point the witness in a particular direction), rather than questions that let them tell the story their way ('open' questions). Break it down into teeny steps. Each question should only be about one single thing and not a series, for example:

- DON'T ASK: 'On 24 July you went to Mrs Smith's home and kicked down the door, didn't you?' (That's two questions)

- DO ASK: 1. 'Did you go to Mrs Smith's home on 24 July?'

- AND THEN 2: 'And when you got there you kicked down the door, didn't you?' (ask the second question even if the answer to the first question is 'No')

Try to stick to facts rather than opinion, and try not to just run down your ex.

Try to tie what you are asking to things that are written down in the paperwork. If there is a particular document you will need to use to ask a particular question, jot down the page reference next to the question so you don't have to go looking for it and then lose your train of thought.

The Practice Direction relating to domestic abuse and violence [PD12J] suggests that in cases where there are allegations of violence or abuse by one of the adults against the other it may be appropriate for the court to ask the parties to identify their questions in advance, or even for the Judge or Lay Justices to assist by asking questions on their behalf. The court will be alert to the fact that it can be difficult for both parties asking questions of one another directly when there is this sort of background, particularly where the questions are about the abuse itself.

10.6 Cross-examining professional witnesses

The starting point is that the Judge must follow the guidance of professionals unless there is a good reason not to do so. This means that if the recommendation of CAFCASS, a social worker or other expert is against you the cross examination is really important - it is your main chance to undermine their recommendation and free the Judge to reach a different conclusion.

Judges will not discount the evidence of a professional witness very lightly. It is very hard to prove that a professional is incompetent or malicious or biased, so do not pin all your hopes on this. What can sometimes be done is to show that there is a mistake, misunderstanding or an omission and most good professionals - if questioned politely - will accept that there is room for different views about a case, or will accept if they have made an error about something. But they are entitled to disagree with you. Ask yourself:

- Have they investigated the case fairly and fully? Have they read all the papers (most reports have a list of what has been read) or were they missing important information when they formed a view?

- Have they met with both parties at home? Have they seen the child with both parents? Have they seen the child alone? If not, why not? Have they seen one party many more times than the other?

- Have they considered all the factors in the welfare checklist or have they forgotten to weigh something important into the balance.

- Have they misunderstood something important or have they wrongly reported something that you said to them?

- Have they based their recommendation on wrong facts or on the basis of allegations that haven't been proved?

- Have they approached the case with an open mind?

- Have they fully thought through all the possible solutions to the case? For example, where both of you have made applications for sole care, could a shared arrangement be a solution? Could the case be better resolved by taking a staged approach rather than making an unsatisfactory final order now? Could the case benefit from more expert input? Are there more creative ways of sorting out a problem with contact than have been considered in the report? Suggest all these things to them and ask them to clarify their own recommendations and why other things won't work or aren't suggested.

Focus your questioning on those types of issues, along with putting the alternative view to the witness. Think about suggesting other alternative ways of moving the case forward to the professional that they might not have thought of.

10.7 Your own evidence

The evidence you give before you are asked questions by any other party or their lawyer is called your evidence in chief. If you are going to be giving evidence and you are acting without a lawyer the Judge may ask you some questions to help you along with your evidence in chief, but you might want to make a short list of the things you need to cover in your evidence so you don't forget anything. The Judge is likely to ask you if there is anything else you would like to say to the court, and this is when you can make sure you have gone through all the important points. Increasingly, the courts are treating your written statement as your evidence in chief. This means that the only spoken evidence you will be able to give is in response to questions by the other party or their lawyer - so, particularly if the court has said that 'witness statements will stand as evidence in chief' it is important to make your witness statement contains everything you need to say.

Any other party will be entitled to ask you questions, through their lawyer if they have one or directly if not. As set out in paragraph 28 of PD12J if they don't have a lawyer the Judge may help them with their questions. If you are a victim of domestic abuse and you would find answering questions asked directly by your ex difficult you should raise this with the court and ask for the court to consider making adjustments for you. For example, the Judge might ask questions on behalf of your ex or you may be able to give evidence from behind a screen or by video link from another room. You should ask about these things when your trial date is fixed rather than on the day that a hearing is due to take place.

If you are being asked questions by a lawyer or your ex it is a good idea to look at the Judge when you answer – it will help you pace your answer so that the Judge can keep up with taking a note, and it will be less anxiety provoking than looking at your questioner. Keep calm, speak slowly, answer questions straightforwardly and keep to the point. If you don't understand a question, if you don't know the answer, if can't remember or if your mind goes blank and you need a question repeating – say so. Don't answer a question unless you are sure you understand what is being asked.

10.8 Submissions

The person whose application it is or the person making the allegations usually makes their submissions (legal speech) first. This gives the person responding to the application the chance to hear everything before responding. If you are the person who has to go first you must try to predict what will be said by the other party or their lawyer in response and deal with it head on. Your chance to reply to things you haven't covered afterwards will be limited. The Judge will tell you which order things will go in.

Write down some short notes of the points you think you might make to the Judge once the evidence is finished (your 'submissions'). As previously noted it is a good idea to have an outline of this at the start but not a script - be prepared to adapt what you are going to say depending on how the case goes. Your case theory should be a good starting point for your submissions, modified according to what seems realistic and strongest in the light of the evidence.

If your case is about money you could try and address each of the points in s25 MCA 1973, and you might want to focus on those parts of s25 which are likely to be the most important in your case (perhaps financial needs and resources).

If your case is about children you could try and address each of the points in the welfare checklist. Again, you might want to focus on those parts of the checklist that are most likely to be the most important in your case.

If you know that there is a particular piece of case law that the other party or their lawyer is going to rely on think about what you want to say about why that case is different from yours, or why it doesn't apply to the circumstances in your case, or why it might mean something different from what the other party says. If there is another case that you think says something different prepare to summarise why that is, and highlight the most important paragraph so you can read it to the Judge. Bring a copy to give to the Judge and the other lawyer.

Think about what you would say if you were the lawyer for the other party. What are the weaknesses in your case? Don't ignore them - they will be highlighted to the Judge by the other lawyer or your ex. Make sure that you give an answer to points they are likely to make.

Two simple examples are given below.

Example 1

- Your application is for your children to live with you:

- The fact that the children repeatedly say that they want to live with you is a strong point in your favour, particularly if they are older children, but the fact that you have one bedroom for you and four children to live in might be a weakness.

- Obviously you must remind the Judge of the children's wishes and feelings, and that these are important, but you must also tackle the problem head on. Tell the Judge how you are going to deal with the accommodation problem (what will the sleeping arrangements be, how long until you get rehoused) and why the plus points outweigh the negatives (for example, by comparing the alternatives - if teenage children are likely to rebel or walk out if forced to remain with the other parent, say so).

Example 2

- In a financial application on divorce your case is that your ex should provide a lump sum of a certain amount so you can clear debts and rehouse.

- It might be easy to prove that you need the amount you are requesting but the real issue might be whether or not your ex can actually raise the money.

- Make sure that you cover both why you need the money and how it is practical and fair for the ex to find the money. You might make points about her ability to borrow the money (bearing in mind things like income or the amount of equity in the house), or about the fact that her lifestyle suggests she has some money hidden away.

11. Privacy And The Media In Family Cases

11.1 Introduction

There are strict and complicated rules about what information can be published about your family case. The law at the moment is partly contained in court rules [Rule 12 FPR and Practice Directions 12G, 12I, 27B and 27C], and partly contained in statute law [mainly s12 Administration of Justice Act 1960 (AJA) and s97 CA].

There are stricter rules for cases about children, or involving children, than for cases which do not really involve children.

There are four main issues about which people are often confused (this includes lawyers!):

- Who can come into court?

- Who can see the papers?

- Who can be told what is in the papers or what evidence has been given?

- What counts as 'publishing'?

11.2 Who can come into court?

The starting point is that all family cases are heard in private [Rule 27 FPR].

Applications for non-molestation orders and occupation orders are heard in private unless the court says otherwise [Rule 10.5 FPR].

The only exceptions are:

- In the main part of a divorce which is usually in open court (the bit concerning money will be private);

- In applications for somebody to be committed to prison for contempt of court (for example by breaching an order) which is usually held in open court;

- When the court makes certain orders it has to pronounce them in open court even if the hearing has been in private. This includes Decrees of divorce or dissolution of civil partnership, committal orders and non-molestation orders.

When a case is heard in private the general public are not allowed into court, and the only people who can come into court are:

- The parties (where a child is formally made a party they usually do not come to court hearings unless they are old enough to give instructions to a solicitor (although increasingly they may meet with the Judge separately on occasion), and the court has given permission for them to attend in order to give their solicitor instructions, to hear what is being said or to give evidence - these are all very rare even for teenagers)

- The parties' lawyers (usually a barrister or solicitor, sometimes a barrister and a solicitor or someone from the solicitors' office who is there to take a note)

- A McKenzie friend (see below)

- The Judge and court staff (including sometimes somebody who is shadowing the Judge or who is assessing them)

- Any CAFCASS officer or social worker involved in the case

- A witness (usually only whilst they are giving their evidence)

- Occasionally one of the lawyers will have someone work shadowing them (you might hear them being called a pupil or trainee), and this is usually permitted with the agreement of the parties

- Sometimes a person who has suffered domestic violence or who has a learning difficulty or mental health problem might ask for a support worker to come into court and this is usually permitted

- The press (this means someone holding a press card), although they rarely attend court. The press are not allowed to attend hearings that are for the purposes of dispute resolution, such as an FDR (see Chapter 14) or an FHDRA (see Chapter 17).

Family members, partners and friends are not usually allowed into court unless they fall into one of the categories above.

Children must be left outside, although a Judge may sometimes allow a baby or very small child into court if they are quiet or it cannot be avoided. If the child is at all likely to understand what is being said this is very unlikely to be allowed.

McKenzie friends are now generally permitted into court unless an objection is raised and the court is persuaded it is a valid objection. There is more information about McKenzie friends in Chapter 4.

The court can hear applications by individuals to be allowed to come into court, or from the parties for an individual or the press in general to be excluded [FPR Rule 27.11].

Hearings in the Court of Appeal and Supreme Court are generally open to the public and anyone can attend (unless the court orders that the case must be held in private). Where the case concerns children the parties will usually be referred to by letters rather than their full names or the court will order that the press do not publish the full names of the parties or child.

Occasionally a Judge will sit in open court, which means that anyone may attend and that anyone may report what has been said in court. In such cases, which are rare, the Judge will usually make an order saying that the family must remain anonymous or restricting certain information that cannot be published.

11.3   Who can see the papers?

Where no children are involved

In cases which are just about money or property and which don't involve children, the financial information that is disclosed and other documents in the case should only be used for the purposes of the proceedings. You must not use the information that has been disclosed for some other purpose and you must treat it as private. Reporters are normally allowed into court, but they are not entitled to see the papers that are referred to in court unless they apply for permission and the Judge agrees, and you should not show them papers unless everybody in the case agrees [PD 27B]. This may change, and in future it may be that journalists are permitted to see some case papers so they understand what is going on, even though they may not be able to report everything in them. If you are unsure it may be worth checking the up to date Practice Directions to Part 27 FPR on the Justice website.

Children involved

Cases involving children are very different. Rules 12.73 - 12.75 FPR and Practice Direction 12G set out the rules in cases under the CA or any other case which is **wholly or mainly** about the **maintenance or upbringing** of a child. This could include some applications under the FLA or for financial orders under the MCA as well as those under Schedule 1 CA (see Chapters 13, 21 and 22).

Obviously you must be able to show the papers to any legal adviser or any person who is helping you in the preparation of your case. This would include (for example) an advice worker who is not a lawyer, and a McKenzie friend. You are allowed to communicate information about the case to someone else in order **to obtain support, advice or assistance in the conduct of the proceedings** but the discussion must be **confidential**. This might include for example a supportive partner who is helping you prepare for the hearing even if they will not be coming into court. It does not mean that you can show all the documents to everyone in your family or all of your friends or that you should let anybody keep copies of them. The person you show the information to must understand that the information is confidential and mustn't be used for any other purpose or passed on. Do not share information about the case with friends who might think it is a good idea to drum up support for you by telling people in your friendship group about how awful your ex is being in court on Facebook. This will not help anyone.

You can communicate information in order to participate in mediation or alternative dispute resolution.

You are allowed to show the papers to a healthcare professional including a doctor or therapist in order to obtain counselling or healthcare for yourself or a child in the case.

You are allowed to pass the papers on to complaints or regulatory bodies in order to make a complaint about the Judge, a lawyer, the court system or some professional in the case (an expert, social worker or CAFCASS for example) or a complaint about the law, policy or procedure applying to your type of case.

You are allowed to pass papers to all these people only for that purpose and they must not pass them on to anyone else or use them for anything else. So, for example, if you pass papers to a McKenzie friend, they cannot then pass them to the press or publish information in the documents on the internet.

You can show the papers to your MP if it is for the purpose of confidential advice, assistance and support or to make a complaint.

Making a complaint is not the same as running a campaign to get the law changed. The rules about complaints don't cover you passing information about the case in order for it to be publicised.

You cannot show the papers to the press unless the court has given you permission.

You cannot show the papers to an expert that you want to ask to prepare a report unless the court has given you permission to instruct them and to show them the papers.

You cannot show the papers to anyone else except as described in the list above.

Judgments of the court are also private unless the court says it's ok. Sometimes the court will give permission for the judgment to be published in an anonymous form with letters instead of names. If it does give this permission it will be on condition that the child (and usually the parties) remain anonymous. This could mean that you would not be able to publish the judgment as 'my case' because that would identify the child.

If you are not sure what you can and cannot do - ask the Judge before doing anything.

11.4 Who can be told what is in the papers or what evidence has been given?

In cases not involving children

See paragraph 11.3 above.

In cases involving children

You can tell people what is in the court papers or what evidence has been given in the same way that you can show them the documents (to get advice, support or assistance in preparing your case, to make a complaint, to get therapy etc.).

Neither the parties nor the press nor any other person is allowed to publish what has been said in evidence, or in court generally, or the contents of a judgment unless the court specifically gives permission.

11.5 What counts as 'publishing'?

'Publishing' includes communicating information to *any* person. It does not just mean publishing something in a newspaper or book, or to make it available to the public generally. It includes (for example) putting something on Facebook (even if your privacy settings mean it is not entirely public) or other social media like twitter, on website advice or discussion forums (even if they are members only) and on blogs or websites. It could even include sending a text message to friends.

Because the definition of publishing is very wide, this means you must be very careful not to publish something unless the rules allow you to, or the Judge has given you permission. This does not mean that the court will necessarily refuse permission if you ask - the important thing is to ask first.

s12 AJA 1960 says that, apart from the cases described above where the rules give you permission to communicate the information (and hearings held in open court), then telling or showing anyone outside the case anything that falls into the following categories is not allowed by anyone. Things that cannot be published without permission include:

- Accounts of what has gone on in front of the Judge sitting in private,

- The publication of documents such as affidavits, witness statements, reports, position statements, skeleton arguments or other documents filed in the proceedings, transcripts or notes of the evidence or submissions, and transcripts or notes of the judgment.

- Extracts or quotations from such documents.

- The publication of summaries (see the judgment of Munby J at paragraph 66 in *Re: B (A Child) (Disclosure)* [2004] EWHC 411 (Fam)).

In addition s97 CA says that you cannot publish any information that might identify the child as being involved in a case or the address of their school.

- The definition of 'publication' in s97 is slightly different: you can tell individuals that you have made an application about your daughter but you cannot publish to the public 'at large' or 'any section of it'. This means that you cannot post about the case to all your friends on Facebook because they are a section of the public.

- s97 applies only until the case has ended but s12 AJA continues indefinitely (*Clayton v Clayton* [2006] EWCA Civ 878). So even though you will eventually be able to publish information about the fact that your family has been involved in a case you will not be able to tell the full story unless the court gives permission.

- s97 applies even where a case is heard in open court.

It should be fairly obvious that lots of people publish things that are in breach of these two pieces of law. Even though it may seem as if these laws are regularly flouted you should think about the impact upon your child of information being published (what if their friends see information about the case and they get teased at school?) and the impact upon your case of the court knowing that you have breached your child's privacy and disregarded the law.

11.6 What happens if someone publishes or discloses information that they shouldn't have?

If you publish something in breach of s12 AJA 1960 you will be in contempt of court and if an application is made by the other party you could be at risk of committal to prison or a fine in the same way as if you had broken a court order.

This kind of punishment is very rare, and generally won't happen unless the court has first warned you of the consequences of publishing something you shouldn't by making an injunction order saying you must not publish information and by attaching a penal notice to the order (a penal notice is a written warning saying that if you break the order you could be sent to prison or fined). But if the court were to find that you had deliberately published something you shouldn't you could be fined or sent to prison for up to two years.

Breaking s97 CA is a criminal offence rather than a contempt of court. It does not require you to be warned first or any penal notice to be attached.

Obviously, it is better if at all possible, not to put yourself even at risk of this kind of penalty or conviction - **if in doubt ask the court for permission to do what you want to do** [application on form C2, Part 18 FPR]. **Seek legal advice if possible and do not rely on the advice of any press representatives you meet at court or elsewhere, or on anyone without legal qualifications - they may not understand the law themselves.**

You should consider the impact upon the children or the other person in the case of information being published. If the court thinks that allowing publication of the information would be harmful to the child it is unlikely to agree to it. If you were to publish information without permission the court might take the view that you were putting your own wishes before the child's needs. It could actively damage your case rather than helping it.

11.7 Will the court make exceptions about what information can be published or passed on?

In individual cases the court may relax or tighten the rules - for example if there is commercially sensitive information being given in evidence in financial proceedings the court can decide not to allow the media in and / or could order the parties not to tell anyone the information. In some cases the court might make an order saying that certain information *can* be published or passed on where the rules wouldn't normally allow this (for example in a case about children which raises a point of public interest or where inaccurate information is already in the public domain). The court will make its decisions with the welfare of the children in mind, and will try to balance the children's or parents' rights to privacy with their rights to free speech [see Practice Directions 12I, 27B and 27C in particular]. In January 2014 the President of the Family Division published Guidance about when it will permit anonymised judgments to be published, and that guidance can be found on the FLBA Guidance Locator and Judiciary website.

It is important to remember that publishing information is still not allowed even if it is anonymised so if you do want to publish anonymised information about your case you must still ask for permission.

11.8   Possible future changes

In 2014 the President of the Family Division, Sir James Munby, proposed further reforms in this area but to date no further changes have been made. It is possible that further guidance will be published in the future, but it is likely to relate to what the press can have access to and when and how judgments should be published rather than being a complete change to the basic law in this area. Check The Transparency Project website for further updates on this area.

PART 3: DIVORCE, SEPARATION & FINANCES

12. The Law On Ending A Marriage Or Civil Partnership & Financial Matters

12.1 Introduction

Divorce law is largely contained in the Matrimonial Causes Act 1973 (MCA). There are two parts to a divorce:

- The divorce itself (this is called the 'matrimonial proceedings' or 'application', and is the bit that turns you into ex-husband and ex-wife);

- Financial order proceedings (this used to be called Ancillary Relief or 'AR'). The court's power to make orders about financial arrangements depends upon there being a divorce underway - you cannot ask the court to formalise arrangements about finances until a divorce application has been issued, although this doesn't stop you starting to discuss finances or agreeing them between yourselves.

A spouse (husband / wife) can obtain a divorce by issuing an application for divorce (formerly called a petition – but you may still hear it being called a petition). If granted the court will issue a Decree Nisi (a provisional order), but a divorce is not made final until the court grants a Decree Absolute. The court can also make orders of judicial separation (a legally recognised form of separation usually used where there are religious objections to a divorce) or nullity (where a marriage is declared invalid) but these are quite unusual and not dealt with in this book (you can read about nullity in s11-13 MCA).

You can start to sort out the finances as soon as you separate but nothing is binding until the court has approved it, and the court cannot approve anything until the divorce application has been issued.

12.2 Divorce

You must have been married for at least a year in order to get divorced. Although it has been talked about for years we don't have 'no fault divorce' in England & Wales. You need to apply for divorce on one of a list of specified grounds. The court must be satisfied that the relationship has irretrievably broken down before it can grant a divorce. It can be satisfied on one of the following possible grounds:

- Adultery

- Behaviour

- Desertion for two years*

- Separation of two years* (only if both consent)

- Separation of five years*

    *this means continuous years immediately before the application was issued.

There are rules about habitual residence (where you and your other half live and are based) that you must meet before the courts in this country can deal with your divorce. Guidance on this is contained in the notes to the Divorce Application (Form D8). If you both live in this country there will not usually be an issue but see Chapter 18 on Jurisdiction for more detail.

12.3   Ending a same sex marriage

The rules for same sex couples who are divorcing are identical to those for heterosexual couples, with one exception: a divorce can only be granted on grounds of adultery if the adultery is with someone of the *opposite* sex. As it is comparatively rare for divorce to be granted on grounds of adultery, and there are less contentious ways to secure a divorce, this is unlikely to have much practical impact. There is also a minor difference in nullity cases: unlike heterosexual couples, same sex couples cannot annul their marriage for non-consummation.

12.4   Civil partnership

A civil partnership can be brought to an end either by converting it to a marriage or by dissolution (equivalent to divorce). Like marriage a civil partnership can also be brought to an end by annulment (nullity), and civil partners can ask for an order of formal separation.

Ending a civil partnership by converting it to a marriage

As a result of the Marriage (Same Sex Couples) Act 2013, civil partners are able to convert their civil partnership into a marriage.

Ending a civil partnership by dissolution

The ending of civil partnerships by dissolution are covered by the Civil Partnership Act 2004 (CPA).

Although it is a separate piece of law it largely mirrors the Matrimonial Causes Act 1973, and in essence everything said above for divorce goes for civil partnership apart from the following:

- You won't see the words 'petition', or 'Decree' being used in civil partner-ship cases. Because civil partnerships are a more modern development they have always used more modern terms like 'application' and 'order'.

- Civil partners are not 'spouses'.

- A civil partnership cannot be dissolved on the grounds of adultery. All the other grounds apply (behaviour, separation and desertion).

Where I've referred to the terminology applicable to married couples you can read it as applying to civil partners too unless I've said otherwise. References are given below to both the relevant sections in the MCA and their equivalent in the CPA.

12.5   Financial remedies and financial orders (Ancillary Relief)

The law on financial matters when couples divorce is contained in sections 21-40B of the MCA [s72 & Schedules 5 -7 CPA].

The court can make the following orders:

- Order for sale of a property

- Order for transfer of a property

- Order for a chargeback

- Order for payment of a lump sum (immediate or deferred)

- Order for spousal maintenance (this is called 'periodical payments' in the MCA 1973 - sometimes lawyers abbreviate it to PPs. PPs may be capital-ised into a lump sum, which can be for a fixed period of time, which can be extendable or non-renewable, or for as long as both parties are alive (called 'joint lives'). The court can order the PPs to be secured against other property)

- Pension sharing (and other pension orders)

The law says that any order for periodical payments stops as soon as the person receiving them remarries. The law also says that if you have not made an appli-cation for financial orders before you remarry you cannot apply for any orders at all. This would not stop the other party applying to the court if the remarried person had all the assets in their name [s28 MCA 1973].

The court can also make orders in favour of children but these are relatively uncommon (most often they arise in relation to the costs of private education or where one parent is so wealthy that the normal child maintenance rules don't apply) and unlikely to be relevant to families who cannot afford legal representation, so they are not dealt with in this book.

The court can also make orders for maintenance whilst it is considering the case. This is called 'maintenance pending suit' or 'interim maintenance'.

The court can also make orders (injunctions) to stop the other party from hiding or spending or disposing of money that they don't want their ex to get hold of or the court to know about. Section 37 of the MCA 1973 [Paragraphs 74-75 Schedule 5 CPA] says that the court can make an order preventing the other party from disposing of property, transferring it abroad or doing anything else with it in order to defeat your claim for a financial remedy.

- Defeating a claim for a financial remedy means doing something which would stop you getting an order, or which would mean you would end up with less than you would have done.

- Under s37 if the other party has *already* disposed of some property to someone else in order to defeat the claim the court can sometimes set aside that sale or transaction.

- If the property in question was disposed of less than three years before the application and it has had the effect of disadvantaging the Applicant in their financial remedy application, the court will presume the property has been disposed of deliberately to make it more difficult to get a financial remedy - and then it is up to the person who has disposed of the property to show that there is an innocent explanation [s37(5) MCA].

- If the person who now has the property paid good money and didn't know or had no reason to believe that the transaction was intended to frustrate the financial remedy process the court can't set the transaction aside [s37(4)].

None of the orders described above can be made before a divorce application has been issued. If a party wants to seek an urgent injunction to stop money being spent or hidden they must start a divorce at the same time if they have not already.

12.6 Orders the court can't make

People are often surprised to hear that the court cannot do the following things:

- Transfer credit card or other debt from one person's name to another, even if it has arisen from joint spending in the course of the marriage;

- Order one party to pay off debts in another party's name, although the court can take into account debts one person is left with when deciding how to divide up other money or property, and can order a lump sum or maintenance to be paid over which can be used for that purpose;

- Order a party to pay child maintenance (except in very limited circumstances - as described below);

- Do anything about re-possession proceedings;

- Transfer a tenancy with a private landlord.

The court is only allowed to deal with maintenance for children in very limited circumstances:

- If the parent who would pay maintenance is earning above the maximum amount of income dealt with by the Child Maintenance Service (CMS) (currently £3,000 per week).

- If the other parent is not required for some other reason to pay child support via the CMS, for example because they live abroad, you may be able to make a claim within your financial proceedings, although there may be practical difficulties in pursuing a claim against someone who does not live here.

- The court can make an order for a parent to pay a child's school fees under the MCA.

- The court can make an order for a parent to pay **expenses attributable to a child's disability**.

- When it makes a financial order after divorce the court can make an order about child maintenance if both parties agree it should, but after a year either party can apply back to the CMS if they think the amount is wrong.

- The CMS took over from the Child Support Agency in all cases where applications are first made after 25 November 2013.

It was previously thought that the court could not order the sale of a property until the final decision at the end of the case. Following a case in the High Court in October 2015 it is now possible in some circumstances for the court to order sale of a property under the MWPA or ToLATA, and to order vacant possession by terminating the other party's rights of occupation of the property under FLA. See *BR v VT* [2015] EWHC 2727 (Fam) (it's a technical decision so it is worth googling some commentary for an easier explanation of this).

12.7 How the court makes decisions

s25A of the MCA [Schedule 5 Paragraph 23 & Paragraph 59 CPA] tells the Judge that when she decides to make an order she must consider whether or not it is possible to **terminate the financial obligations of each party as soon after the grant of Decree** (divorce order) **as is just and reasonable**. When the court makes a maintenance order it must be only for long enough to enable the person receiving them to **adjust without undue hardship to the termination of their financial dependence on the other party** i.e. to get back on their feet. Together these are known as a 'Clean Break'. This means cutting as many of the financial links between the parties as soon as this can be achieved, both property and income. This is not always possible (particularly if there are children) but it is a legal goal. Child maintenance obligations carry on regardless of any clean break in respect of other financial matters.

Section 25 [Schedule 5 Paragraph 21 CPA] is the most important part of the MCA to know about. It tells the court how to decide on how to use its powers. Section 25 tells the court that it must look at **all the circumstances**, but it must focus on the following:

- **Welfare of the children**

- **Income, earning capacity, property and other financial resources which each of the parties to the marriage has or is likely to have in the fore-seeable future**

- **Financial needs, obligations and responsibilities which each of the parties to the marriage has or is likely to have in the foreseeable future**

- **The standard of living enjoyed by the family before the breakdown of the marriage**

- **The age of each party to the marriage and the duration of the marriage**

- **Any physical or mental disability of either of the parties to the marriage**

- **The contributions which each of the parties has made or is likely in the foreseeable future to make to the welfare of the family, including any** contribution by looking after the home or caring for the family

- **The conduct of each of the parties, if that conduct is such that it would in the opinion of the court be inequitable to disregard it.**

- **The value to each of the parties to the marriage of any benefit which, by reason of the dissolution or annulment of the marriage, that party will lose the chance of acquiring**

It can be difficult for lawyers - let alone litigants in person - to work out what this means in practice and in cold hard cash, because there are so many variables and no formula. The Family Justice Council and Advice Now have each written some really useful guidance which discusses the criteria above and how they might apply in practice. These guides include useful case studies as examples and they are well worth reading. Below is a summary of what each of the factors in s25 covers.

Welfare of children

The **welfare** of any **child of the family** is the **first consideration** the court must think about. Lots of other things will be relevant, but the children are always the top consideration.

A 'child of the family' is any child who has been a part of your household during the marriage and who has been treated as part of the family, even though they may not be your own biological child.

Once a child is 18 they stop being the first consideration, but they may still be relevant because often children continue to be a financial burden on their parents after this age, especially if at university, and the court will bear these ongoing parental obligations in mind when working out what a party needs or can afford.

Income, earning capacity, property and other financial resources which each of the parties to the marriage has or is likely to have in the foreseeable future

If you or your ex are expecting a bonus or pay-out, likely to inherit or working for an employer which is considering redundancies these are all things which will be relevant.

Financial resources can include things that you (or your ex) do not own or earn but have or could have available to you (or them), for example a new partner's income, support from parents, a place to stay that is provided rent free or at below the market rate by friends or family, or benefits you could be entitled to. It could also include your capacity to obtain credit or a loan.

The court will consider whether or not a party is meeting their earning potential bearing in mind their care responsibilities, health, skills etc.

Financial needs, obligations and responsibilities which each of the parties to the marriage has or is likely to have in the foreseeable future

The most important need each party has is to house themselves (and any children) in either rented or owned accommodation. In most cases this is the main practical problem - how to find enough money to house the family in two homes.

Apart from the obvious things like rent, council tax, food bills, petrol, credit card bills this could include money owed to friends, sick or elderly adult family members one party has to support or care for, adult children who are still at university or still to some extent dependent.

Money which has been lent by family or friends on an informal basis or payments a party feels they ought in fairness to make to repay for support in previous years has to be considered but it might not be very important in the grand scheme of things if there are other bills or debts that need to be dealt with and which are payable by law.

The standard of living enjoyed by the family before the breakdown of the marriage

It is not uncommon that couples have been living beyond their means. Even if they haven't, the basic economics of running two households mean that it is unlikely that either party can expect to maintain the same standard of living as before. In practice therefore this factor is not often terribly relevant, unless it is in order to make the point that an ex must be hiding assets or income because what they say they earned or are earning simply does not match up with the money that was available in the course of the marriage.

The age of each party to the marriage and the duration of the marriage

Age is important because it gives the court an idea of what prospects a party has of re-establishing a career, improving their income, building a pension or saving for retirement.

The length of the marriage is most important when thinking about what part of the assets now owned have been created during it.

In a short marriage without children the court might treat assets you brought into the marriage as your own. The longer a marriage the more likely the court is to think that it is fair to treat everything you both own as available to divide between you - including income if during the course of your marriage your decisions as a couple about who would work and who would care for the children have meant one of you is left with a reduced earning capacity.

If you lived together before you got married the court is likely to look at the whole period of your relationship when thinking about whether it is a 'long marriage'.

Any physical or mental disability of either of the parties to the marriage

Obviously any disability may impact on the ability to earn, to manage finances, accommodation needs and cost of living generally, and life expectancy.

The contributions which each of the parties has made or is likely in the foreseeable future to make to the welfare of the family, including any contribution by looking after the home or caring for the family

The court will generally take the view that non-financial contributions are of broadly equivalent value to those of the breadwinner.

If one party is going to be left with a reduced earning capacity and smaller pension because they are going to continue to be responsible for the care of the children for years to come this is likely to be relevant.

The chances are though, that if you can't afford a lawyer contributions are not going to be that relevant to your case, which will probably be more about needs and practicality.

The conduct of each of the parties, if that conduct is such that it would in the opinion of the court be inequitable to disregard it

This part of s25 is worded quite differently to the others: the other parts always have to be considered in each case. Conduct (bad behaviour) is only considered if the court takes the view that it should not be ignored. Many many cases involve one partner who has had affairs, or who has been violent, or who has been unpleasant to live with. These things do not really help the courts to work out how to sort out the finances, and the court could very easily become distracted by parties trying to prove that one was more badly behaved than the other, when it should really be focusing on how to fairly meet both parties' and any children's basic practical needs, and so for these purposes bad behaviour is usually put to one side, even if it is quite serious.

If you want to rely upon conduct to argue that the court should give your ex less of the assets you will probably have an uphill struggle. You may find that the Judge asks you to confirm whether or not this is really your position and you could end up having to pay any extra costs arising from this approach.

The value to each of the parties to the marriage of any benefit which, by reason of the dissolution or annulment of the marriage, that party will lose the chance of acquiring

For example widow's pension, inheritance, health insurance.

The parties may reach an agreement between themselves but it will not be legally binding upon them until it is formally approved by the court. If the parties both ask the court to approve a financial agreement it will usually do so. See Chapter 25 under the heading 'Set aside'.

A financial order is a once and for all resolution of the financial ties between the parties. Once the court has approved an order for financial remedies neither party can come back to court again to sort out something they have forgotten, to change something or to ask for more. The only exceptions to this are that the court can vary maintenance payments, extend maintenance orders or convert maintenance payments into a lump sum, described below and that an order might be changed if it is appealed or set aside (see Chapter 25).

A court can say that an order for spousal maintenance is for a fixed period, for 'joint lives' (as long as both are alive) or until a certain thing happens (usually until the person receiving money remarries or cohabits with a new partner or until the youngest child is 18 or has finished university). If the court gives a fixed end date the person receiving the maintenance can apply to have that time extended as long as they apply before the order expires, but they would need to show a good reason for this. The court can decide to say when it makes the order that the person receiving the maintenance should not be able to come back and ask for the order to be extended, but the court probably wouldn't do this if there are very young children [s28(1A) MCA].

If a court orders a person to pay spousal maintenance to the other party, either of them can come back to court later on to ask the court to vary the amount of the order, sometimes to extend the order, or to capitalise it (pay it off in one or more lump sums) [s31 MCA, Part 11 of Schedule 5 CPA]. Usually the person asking for the change would need to show some change in circumstances and justify the change they are seeking and if asking for more money they would need to be able to demonstrate an ability to pay.

Chapter 13 contains more information about how the divorce procedure works and Chapter 14 contains more detail and more information about the practicalities of sorting out the finances.

13. Getting Divorced, Dissolving Or Converting Your Civil Partnership

13.1   Introduction

In essence the law about ending civil partnerships is the same as the law for ending marriages, although, just to keep you on your toes, some things are given different names in the case of civil partnership:

- The parties to a marriage are sometimes called 'spouses', the parties to a civil partnership are just called civil partners. This chapter uses the word 'partner' to refer to husbands, wives and civil partners.

- Spouses get *divorced*, but civil partners *dissolve* their partnership. This chapter uses the word 'divorce' to refer to divorce and dissolving civil partnerships.

- The orders that bring about the end of a marriage are called *decree nisi* and *decree absolute*, but in civil partnership dissolution cases they are called the *conditional order* and *final order*.

- This chapter (and this book) is going to use the terminology that relates to marriage rather than civil partnership because there are they are the terms most readers of this book will have to get to grips with. The process relating to civil partners is almost exactly the same as for married couples, but where there are differences I will say so.

- In both marriage and civil partnership cases the person who starts the divorce or dissolution process is the Petitioner or Applicant. The other person is the Respondent.

The basic legal framework is set out at Chapter 12 and you should read this first.

In order to get divorced one of you needs to issue a divorce application at a Family Court. You should check on the Justice website which is the nearest court office to you that accepts this sort of application. Alternatively you can ring your local Family Court office and check.

13.2   Conversion from civil partnership to marriage

Same sex marriage has only been legal since March 2014 - people who became civil partners before then can now convert their partnership into a marriage. You can convert your civil partnership for a modest fee at a register office or licensed wedding venue, with or without a ceremony. Details are on the www. gov.uk website.

At the point the civil partnership becomes a marriage the civil partnership will cease to exist and the marriage will be treated as having started on the date the civil partnership was entered into i.e. the marriage will be back-dated. You will get a marriage certificate which shows the date of your original civil partnership.

13.3 Making an application to the court to end your marriage or civil partnership

If you both agree the relationship is over, it is often sensible to agree which of you will issue the application, and there is usually no disadvantage to agreeing to let your other half issue if they prefer. If your other half has a solicitor, it is probably practically much easier to let them issue the application and agree to pay half the costs - you both have an interest in getting that part of things sorted out.

Divorce applications (you may still see them called divorce petitions in some places) are made on Form D8. Form D8 can be downloaded from the Justice website. (Note: these forms have changed from 7 August 2017, so do make sure that you use the up to date version (although you can still use the old ones until 4 September 2017)). The information below gives a little bit of guidance, but you should read the supporting notes that go with the form very carefully because they are very helpful. Please fill in your form carefully and accurately - it is likely to be rejected by the Judge if things are not completed or if there is a discrepancy, for example if the names on the form do not match exactly with those on the marriage certificate.

You will need to issue your divorce application by post to one of the 11 regional Divorce Units rather than your local Family Court (unless an urgent hearing is needed). You can go to your local court to issue an application if there is a counter service in operation, but it will still be sent to the regional divorce unit for processing. Use the Court and Tribunal Finder on the gov.uk website to find your regional unit.

NB: At the time of writing an online pilot has just been launched, which runs until 28 July 2017 in certain courts. You will need to check the HMCTS website to see whether or not this pilot is available in your area or whether it has been rolled out nationwide. The process does still require you to print out the completed forms and send them to a court (see Practice Direction 36D).

13.4   Jurisdiction

Jurisdiction just means the court is allowed to make the order. You need to complete the boxes on the application about jurisdiction very carefully. You need to make sure that you tick the correct box in 5.1 or 5.2 or your application is likely to get rejected. For example, typically, where you are both established in England or Wales you will be able to tick the box in 5.1 that says 'The Petitioner and Respondent are both habitually resident in England and Wales', and most people will be able to tick one of the options in 5.1. If you cannot tick a box in 5.1 you will need to look at 5.2. If you married or live abroad or are foreign nationals the English / Welsh courts may not have jurisdiction. See Chapter 18 on jurisdiction.

13.5   Grounds

Separation for two years

If you have been separated for two years and you both agree you should divorce, one of you should complete the form D8, making sure you tick the two years separation box in Part 5. The other party will need to confirm their consent at a later stage. If they don't the application will not be able to proceed.

Separation for five years

If you have been separated for five years, one of you should complete form D8 making sure you tick the five years separation box in Part 5. The other party will not need to confirm their consent but would be entitled to disagree if they say that you have not actually lived apart for five years.

Adultery

If you want to apply on the grounds of adultery, you should complete form D8 making sure you tick the adultery box in Part 5, giving details in Part 6. You can name the person that your partner has committed adultery with or simply say the adultery was with 'a person unknown' or 'a person whom the Applicant does not wish to name'.

- Note that you can *divorce* on the grounds of adultery but you cannot *dissolve a civil partnership on grounds of adultery*. Also, a same sex marriage can only be ended on grounds of adultery if the adultery is between a man and a woman, although if one spouse has had an extra-marital affair with a person of the same sex this would probably count as 'unreasonable behaviour' (see below).

- Be mindful of the fact that there are easier and less contentious ways to get a divorce, and that if your partner does not accept they have been adulterous you will have to prove it, including the physical act of adultery. If you name the person your partner has had an affair with they will become a Co-Respondent, that is a person involved in the case and entitled to have their say. There is really no advantage to this type of application and it is generally to be avoided at all costs. One alternative is to apply on the grounds of unreasonable behaviour (see below) and to include in Part 6 a statement that the Respondent has been involved in an inappropriate relationship with another person.

Desertion

This is unusual, but if required fill in D8, tick the desertion box in Part 5, and in Part 6 set out when you last lived together, when you last saw or heard from your partner, and when you last received financial support from them.

Behaviour

The most commonly used route to a divorce is an application on the ground of unreasonable behaviour. Unless your divorce is based on separation, desertion or adultery one of you will have to issue an application setting out what unreasonable behaviour the other has been responsible for that has led to the breakdown of the relationship. This can be upsetting, but in reality it does not much matter who starts the process, the outcome is the same either way and any decision the court has to later make about sorting out your finances will not be affected by the application or what is said in it.

It is important to remember that (apart from two or five years separation cases) there is no such thing as faultless divorce in England & Wales and the court simply cannot grant a divorce without a certain amount of criticism being made by one party of the other. Of course this is all a bit surreal and a divorce may end up being granted on the basis of one parties' fault where both are in some respects to blame - but there is nothing to be gained by making a point of whose fault it is. It will simply delay things and put you at risk of extra legal costs.

It is possible to agree to each issue an application (this is called cross applying) and ask the court to make cross orders but frankly this is unnecessarily expensive and you have more important things to focus on.

If your other half is delaying getting things going you may need to issue the application yourself.

For a behaviour application it is important to tick the box that says that 'the Respondent has behaved in such a way that the Petitioner cannot reasonably be expected to live with her / him' and to set out in Part 6 where it says 'Statement of Case' a list of examples of the kind of behaviour that means that you cannot any longer be expected to live together. This might include things like:

- Since approximately DATE the Respondent and Petitioner have ceased socialising together, have no common interests and effectively live separate lives;

- The Respondent and Petitioner frequently argue about the same issue which they have been unable to resolve. This causes the Petitioner distress;

- The Respondent refuses to let the Petitioner go out to work and denigrates her in front of the children;

- The Respondent drinks alcohol to excess and when drunk is regularly verbally abusive to the Petitioner;

- On DATE the Respondent and the Petitioner had an argument and the Respondent damaged the door by kicking it. The Respondent was fearful for her safety and the Police were called;

- The Respondent and the Petitioner have since approximately DATE slept in separate rooms and the Respondent refuses to be physically intimate with the Petitioner and have been living separate lives;

- The Respondent is addicted to gambling and has sold the family's television and the children's playstation in order to pay gambling debts;

- The Respondent refuses to discuss finances with the Petitioner and the Petitioner has recently discovered that she has run up large credit card debts and re-mortgaged the family home;

- The Petitioner is aware that the Respondent has been involved in an inappropriate relationship with a fe/male that the Petitioner does not wish to name.

The above are just examples and may not apply in your case (hopefully they don't all apply!), but they should give you some idea of the kinds of things that might be included. You do not need to list every awful thing your partner has ever done, but you do need to put in enough information to be sure that the grounds for a divorce are made out. It is generally a good idea to include a few examples of the kinds of behaviour you have experienced, but they do not necessarily need to be very serious when taken individually. There is, therefore, usually no need to make very serious allegations that your other half is likely to challenge or be upset about in order to get your divorce. Particularly if you have children or finances to sort out, be wary of chucking all possible criticisms into your application if they are not necessary - it just raises the temperature and can have a knock on effect on the speed of the divorce and negotiations about other things.

It is important to remember that if you have continued to live together for six months after the last incident of unreasonable behaviour the court may not grant your divorce, because it may be an indication that the marriage has not irretrievably broken down as a result of the incidents in the application. Therefore, if you've been living together but separately (perhaps because you are broke and stuck there whilst waiting to sell the house) it will be important to explain this when you get to the next step, of applying for your decree nisi.

You must make sure when you fill in your application that you fill in the section headed 'Prayer' by ticking any box you think might possibly apply. If in doubt tick it, with the obvious exception that if there aren't any children you don't need to tick the boxes about children and if neither of you owns a house you don't need to tick the property adjustment order box. This is to protect your position for later on in case the court has to sort out the finances. But nothing will happen about the finances unless you later ask the court to proceed with an application for a financial order by filling in a Form A. This is dealt with in the next chapter.

13.6 Responding to an application

Once an application has been issued it must be served on the Respondent (and any Co-Respondent). The court will serve the application for you but you must ask them to do this when you issue the application. Once this is done the Respondent has seven days from when they received the application to file an acknowledgement of service form, which will be sent to them by the court. If they complete this saying that they agree that the divorce should be granted, the divorce will proceed as undefended which means that it can be processed more quickly. The court will send you a photocopy of the acknowledgement of service [PD 6A para 10.1].

If the Respondent returns the acknowledgement of service saying that they do not agree with the divorce or the contents of the application, or if they file an answer or cross application the case will proceed as 'defended' which will take longer. The Respondent must file an answer (form D8B) within 21 days of the deadline for the acknowledgement of service. An answer is a document setting out why the divorce shouldn't be granted. There is no need to file an answer if the only thing that you don't agree about is who should pay the costs.

If the acknowledgement of service is not returned the Petitioner will need to ask the court bailiff to serve the application personally on the Respondent, or to deem service (to accept that the Petitioner has had the documents even if they have not confirmed it) or dispense with service. You may need to provide evidence that your partner has received the application, for example if they have told you they have, you could swear an affidavit saying this, or you could attach a letter or photocopy of a text they have sent you (for example: 'got your bloody court documents in the post, chucked em in the bin!' would probably do the job). If you have problems with service you will need to look at FPR Rule 6.15-6.20 and Practice Direction 6A paragraphs 10-14 and make an application.

13.7 Next steps

Once service has been sorted out and the time for filing an acknowledgement of service has passed, the case can proceed [see FPR 7.19].

If your application is undefended (i.e. the acknowledgement has been filed saying the divorce is agreed to or no acknowledgement has been filed) the Petitioner must file an affidavit in form D80 (there are several versions of D80 depending on the type of divorce, so choose the appropriate form from the Justice website) asking for directions for the case to proceed.

If your application was on grounds of two years separation with consent but no acknowledgement has been filed you might need to apply to amend your application to rely on a different ground because you don't have the consent you need on the acknowledgment.

If the application is defended (i.e. the acknowledgement of service says the divorce isn't agreed) either party can make the application by completing a form D80 'Statement in support' as soon as the time for filing an answer has run out (even if an answer hasn't actually been filed).

The application must explain if there have been any changes to the information in the original application on D8 and say what they are [Rule 7.19(3)].

13.8 Undefended applications

Once the application has been filed the Judge will look at the papers and decide if the divorce should be granted. If the Judge is happy that everything is in order he will issue a certificate telling the parties when the Decree Nisi will be pronounced (you don't need to attend unless you want to challenge it). If the Judge is not happy with something, the court will list a Case Management Hearing or make directions. Judges quite often send an application back because of a minor technical mistake on the form, so check everything - and in particular make sure that you have ticked all necessary boxes and identified the signature of the other party.

13.9 Defended applications

The court will list the matter for a Case Management Hearing. At the Case Management Hearing the Judge will make sure the case is ready for trial and set a date for trial when the court will hear the evidence and decide if the case is proven. The trial will be in open court. A party who defends an application that is granted is likely to have to pay the legal costs of the party who successfully proves their application. If the Petitioner is successful the court will pronounce the Decree Nisi.

13.10 Decree Absolute (Final orders)

There is a procedure for asking for the Decree Nisi to be set aside or rescinded but this is not set out in this book [but see FPR Part 7 Chapter 4].

At least six weeks must pass after the grant of the Decree Nisi before you can apply for the final order [s1(5) MCA as amended by SI or s39 CPA]. After this period the Petitioner must give notice that they want the order finalised by filling in Form D36.

The Respondent can apply for the order to be made final if the Petitioner has not asked for it to be made final and three months have passed after the Petitioner's six weeks are up [s9(2) MCA or s40 CPA].

The order will be finalised unless there is some procedural irregularity or one of a number of other unusual factors apply.

If there has been a delay of more than 12 months between the Decree Nisi and the application for it to be finalised, the Petitioner will also have to explain in writing why there has been a delay, confirming that the parties have not lived together since the Decree Nisi (or if they have what the dates are), whether any child has been born to any female partner / spouse since the Decree Nisi / conditional order.

13.11 Reasons to rush

- Your ex has threatened to hide or dispose of assets that you think you might be entitled to a share of. You need to act quickly and may need to ask the court to make an injunction stopping this (see Chapter 12). The court cannot make an injunction of this kind until the application has been issued (it doesn't have to have been finalized, just issued).

- You are desperate for income in the short term and you need to ask the court for interim maintenance (see Chapter 12). The court cannot make an order of this kind until the application has been issued.

- You want to remarry. Be aware that remarriage or cohabitation may impact upon your financial settlement (see Chapter 12).

13.12 Reasons to delay

There are two main reasons why you may not want your divorce to be finalised:

- Your ex has a substantial pension and is elderly or in poor health. Whilst you remain married (until Decree Absolute) you are likely to be entitled to a partner's pension on their death. If you have divorced and your ex dies before the finances are sorted (for example before the court has ordered that you should get a share of the pension), the pension will be lost.

- Your family home is in your other half's sole name. You will be able to obtain some limited protection from the home being sold from under you by registering your matrimonial home rights with the Land Registry (visit their website), but if your divorce is finalised before the finances are sorted out your matrimonial homes rights protection will lapse.

13.13 Can I change back to my maiden name?

You can do what you like! There is nothing in the law that says you had to use your partner's name in the first place, and there is nothing to say you can't change it back.

You do need to make sure that you let your bank and other organisations know about your change of name, and they may have some paperwork for you to fill in in order to change your account.

Although you can carry on using different names for different purposes, you may want to amend your driving licence and passport if you are likely to want to use it as ID (e.g. for credit or car hire etc) - if it doesn't match you might have a practical problem.

14. Finances For Divorcing Couples Or Civil Partners

14.1 Introduction

The law governing financial arrangements on divorce or on the dissolution of civil partnerships is contained in the Matrimonial Causes Act 1973 (MCA) and Civil Partnerships Act 2004 (CPA). It is set out at Chapter 12. Unless stated, arrangements for civil partners are the same as for married couples, so you can treat references in this chapter to 'divorce' as including civil partnership. I'm going use the word 'partner' throughout this chapter, to refer to both spouses and civil partners.

The legal situation for couples who have never been married or civil partners is different from that faced by married couples or civil partners and is dealt with in Chapter 15.

This chapter deals with the practicalities of the financial part of a divorce or dissolution, which is called the financial order or financial remedy proceedings (sometimes called by its old-fashioned name Ancillary Relief or AR). I'm going to refer to this type of case as 'financial proceedings'. The rules about financial applications are mainly contained in Part 9 of the FPR but the overriding objective and other case management powers of the court will also be important.

This chapter deals firstly with settling finances by agreement, secondly with the procedure that financial proceedings follow, and lastly with what the MCA says about how finances should be untangled and assets divided up. It also deals with some issues that commonly come up and the types of thing I often have to explain to a client the first time I meet them.

Don't forget that the court cannot do anything about the financial situation until the divorce itself has been started. And don't forget that if you are planning to remarry it is important to wait until you have started any application for financial orders. Otherwise you may not be able to bring a claim at all [s28 MCA 1973].

14.2 Sorting out the finances by agreement

Sorting things out before you come to court

You must have attended a Mediation Information and Assessment Meeting before starting a financial application. There are exceptions to this rule. Further details of what is required are set out in Chapter 8.

If you do manage to sort things out through mediation or between yourselves without coming to court you should still think about asking the court to approve the arrangement and make it into a court order so that neither of you can back out (see below for more on that). In fact there are some things that you can't do without a court order (sharing pensions for example). The mediator will usually draw up a record of what you have agreed to do that you can ask a lawyer to convert into a court order, or which you can ask the court to approve.

The court will usually approve a consent order on paper without the need to come to court. This involves you both filling in some fairly straightforward forms which are available from the Justice website (form D81 on the Justice website). You will still need to have your divorce itself underway before you can ask the court to approve any financial order though. Sometimes if an agreement you've reached looks on paper as if it might be unfair the Judge will ask for an explanation in writing or ask you to come to court for a quick hearing to reassure the Judge that you both understand what the court is about to approve.

The court will also be highly likely to approve any agreement you reach through family arbitration (see www.ifla.org.uk), but in reality if you are reading this book arbitration is not likely to be cost effective for you.

Benefits of settling (agreeing)

There are a number of reasons why it is a good idea to settle if at all possible, rather than going to court or to a full trial. These include:

- It will probably be less stressful,

- It will probably be quicker,

- It will probably be less unpleasant or acrimonious, particularly important where children are involved. The benefits of being able to say that mummy and daddy have agreed what should happen are not measurable in financial terms.

- It will probably be less costly. At each stage of the proceedings the costs being incurred climb more steeply. The cost of paying for lawyers between Financial Dispute Resolution Hearing and trial (see below) will jump steeply, and most of those costs will have been incurred before the parties walk through the door on the morning of the hearing.

- There will probably be a broader range of options. The parties can agree to include things in the order that a Judge could not impose, for example recitals about child maintenance, or undertakings about things that will be done by one party or the other (a recital is a record contained on a court order about what has been agreed or that explains the background to the making of the order for future reference - but it is not binding like an actual court order).

- You may have the ability to leverage issues that the Judge would disregard. There are some things that can form a part of your negotiations outside court and that can be offered by one party in return for a concession from the other that would not be relevant for a Judge. This might include, for example, agreements to continue to maintain a Mother-in-law, to keep up a particular health insurance policy or to continue to make available some other perk or assistance.

When can I settle?

In short, you can settle at any time - and the sooner the better. The sooner you settle the sooner you can get on with your life and can avoid mounting legal costs - even if it is just your ex who is paying for a lawyer or who is publicly funded, this can affect you because it means their ability to meet their own living costs is depleted and this might affect the outcome if the Judge has to decide things.

Parties can agree things at any stage, at court or in between hearings. If you are able to sort things out either directly with your partner or through their solicitor, the court can be asked to approve what has been agreed without another hearing. (It is important to get any agreement approved by the court for the reasons set out at the end of this chapter). If your partner has a lawyer, the lawyer will be able to draw up a record of what has been agreed to present to the Judge. This will usually take the form of a consent order. If neither of you have a lawyer it is probably a good idea to write to the court saying what you have agreed and asking the court to make the agreement into an order (form D81). You could agree who is going to write the letter and get the other person to sign it. The Judge might still want you to come to court to clarify what you have agreed and sort out anything you have forgotten.

I recommend that at an early stage you spend some time reading the Advice Now and Family Justice Council guides to financial remedy proceedings. They include an explanation of the way a court would look at things, and give some case studies which will help you to think about what sort of settlement might be suitable in your type of circumstances, and this should help you to think of sensible proposals that you might make to your ex. You could share the guides with your ex too.

14.3 Starting financial proceedings

Once a divorce application has been issued (and the MIAM requirements have been complied with), either party can issue a Form A, which sets the process for financial proceedings in motion. There are a number of boxes to tick on a Form A. If you are the person issuing the Form A you should tick all the boxes that apply to you and any you are not sure about (if you don't have children you obviously don't need to tick any boxes relating to children, and if there isn't a house or land you don't need to tick the box about property). This keeps your options open and avoids any technical arguments down the line.

Once there is a decree nisi in the divorce the court can make final financial orders but they will not take effect until the final order in the divorce.

Once a Form A has been issued the court process will swing into action. The court process generally involves up to three stages, the idea being always to try and resolve matters before getting to the final stage:

- First Directions Appointment (FDA)

- Financial Dispute Resolution Hearing (FDR)

- Final hearing (trial)

14.4 Legal services orders and maintenance pending suit

If you are unable to afford the costs of a lawyer but consider that your ex has sufficient surplus income or available capital to be able to assist you with these costs you may apply for a legal services order [s22ZA of the MCA], which would require them to pay you a sum or sums to cover your legal expenses. This is primarily aimed at the sort of case where there is plenty of money around, but where one party has no access to it and might be prevented from pursuing a valid claim if they don't have a lawyer. If you think you fall into this category consider making an application at the same time you start financial proceedings so that the court can consider it before the case proceeds further. Read FPR r9.7 and PD9 pa 12 if you think your case falls into this category and follow the procedure set out in Part 18. It is important that you provide evidence that shows why your case meets the criteria set out in s22ZA of the Act, in particular that you cannot fund legal advice or representation through a loan or some other mechanism.

If your ex is the sole earner in the family and you have been unable to agree on any holding arrangements for covering your outgoings you may need to make an application for 'maintenance pending suit' (or MPS). Maintenance is a regular amount of money paid by the other person to meet your income needs, and 'pending suit' just means a temporary order whilst the final decision on the longer term arrangements is awaited. Again, this sort of application is usually made at the start of the financial proceedings, although it can be made at any stage if circumstances change. PD9 makes clear that you can combine both an application for a LSO and MPS in the same application / documentation. As with an order relating to your legal expenses you will need to provide evidence about your short term needs. You must use the Part 18 procedure.

14.5 Disposal of assets

Occasionally it is necessary to start divorce / dissolution and financial proceedings in a rush because when a relationship breaks down one person threatens to dispose of or hide assets, or behaves so as to make the other suspect that this is what they are planning. The court can make an order to prevent this and in certain circumstances can set aside (undo) a disposal of an asset - if it has been done with the intention of defeating or frustrating a claim by the ex (i.e. it has been sold or given away to prevent the ex from getting their hands on it).

If you are in this situation you may need to make an application at the outset of the case. If there is a risk that telling the other person you plan to ask for an order will tip them off, it may be appropriate to make the application without telling the other person of it first. You must provide evidence of any threat or of why you think that they are planning to get rid of an asset, either by selling, giving it away, putting it in someone else's name, hiding it or sending it abroad AND of why you need to come to court without telling the other person first (what do you think they would do if they knew?). FPR r9.6 tells you to use the Part 18 procedure.

14.6 Before the First Directions Appointment

Before the FDA the court will have issued standard directions requiring each party to:

- file and serve a Statement of Issues, Chronology and any questions (see Part 7 of this book),

- fill in Form E and send a copy to the court and the other party,

- confirm whether or not they are ready to treat the FDA as an FDR i.e. roll stage 1 and stage 2 up together.

A Chronology should include:

- the dates of marriage, separation, application for divorce, and conditional and final matrimonial orders (if applicable),

- date of birth of parties and any children,

- date of purchase of any home or property (if relevant), and

- any other key dates (such as date of redundancy).

A concise Statement of Issues should include the things that the parties need the court to work out for them because they aren't agreed, such as:

- What are the parties' real incomes and earning capacities?

- How much does each party need to rehouse?

- Should the family home be sold?

- Should one party pay the other one maintenance and how much should it be and for how long should it be paid?

- Should one party pay the other party a lump sum and if so how much?

- Should a party's pension be shared and if so how much?

- Should there be a clean break (explained below)?

14.7   Disclosure and Form E

Both parties to a divorce have what lawyers call a 'rolling duty of full and frank disclosure'. This means that the court will expect you to show the other party all documents which might affect the outcome of the case, whether they are helpful to you or not. The duty of full and frank disclosure means that you must fill in your Form E honestly and completely, and that you must ensure it is correct before you swear to its truth.

The duty of full and frank disclosure is not just limited to documents - there might be something important that you know about but which is not in a document (for example if you have spent the money in the savings account or if you are going to get a big bonus or be made redundant). If this is the case you must tell the other party (or their lawyer) and the court. It is best to do this in writing.

The duty of full and frank disclosure lasts throughout the case - this is the 'rolling' bit. If something important changes or comes to light after you have filed your Form E you must update it. If the court directs that you should answer further questions about your finances you must answer fully and frankly.

The duty of full and frank disclosure also applies to documents that are helpful to your case. You cannot hold them back in order to surprise the other party or try and catch them out. If you are going to rely on a document at any trial you must disclose it (show it) at the start or as soon as you have it.

If you have documents belonging to the other party you must also disclose these as soon as possible, you must give the originals back and you must not keep copies. If they are relevant the other party will have a duty to disclose them to you.

If you do not comply with your duty of full and frank disclosure you can be penalised by the court in costs or the court might draw adverse inferences (this means they might work on the basis you are hiding something and treat you as if you have more funds and assets than you have disclosed).

Form E is a lengthy form in which each party must disclose all their financial information. Although it may not look like it, Form E is a type of witness statement, so it is important to be accurate - it is the core of your evidence in the case. There will be a substantial amount of information to attach to it and it is important to be thorough. You should attach the following:

- 12 months bank and building society statements. If you know there is likely to be an issue going back further it may be sensible to include more. Allow enough time to order duplicate copies if you do not have them to hand. There will be a small fee from your bank. You are expected to do what is necessary in order to get 12 months of statements and failing to order them will only result in delay. Include statements for every account held even if the balance is negligible, and if you have closed an account provide statements up to and including closure;

- 6-12 months credit card statements. Although this is not a required attachment to Form E, it is sometimes necessary and is often asked for by lawyers at the FDA. If you are saying that there is credit card debt accrued during your relationship on things for the family's benefit, and you want this to be taken into account or an order that helps you pay it back, it is worth disclosing those credit card statements at the start;

- Documents relating to any loan if you are saying that it should be treated as a joint debt;

- Mortgage statement including details of any arrears or repayment arrangements;

- Any recent valuations on the home (or any other property you own);

- Policy documents relating to any endowment or other policy with a cash value;

- Proof of any other assets owned (share certificates, premium bonds etc.);

- P60 and last 3 months wage slips (I'd suggest providing more if your last 3 months are not representative - for example if they are distorted by a large Christmas bonus or an unusual amount of overtime);

- Evidence of entitlement to any benefits received;

- Most recent accounts for any business you run, or, if not available, the last tax return;

- Evidence of mortgage capacity (or lack of it) if this is likely to be an issue;

- Evidence that your employment is coming to an end or is likely to do so through redundancy or a fixed term contract (contract, redundancy notice etc.);

- Transfer value for any pension you hold (you will have to ask your pension provider for this, and they have to give you one free valuation per year. Ask promptly - they are often slow. If you have not received a response by the time you file your Form E, attach your letter of request instead and update the form when it arrives).

It is quite a chore getting all this together but it is far easier to do it properly the first time than have to keep going back and filling in the gaps. If you have not done it properly, it might be thought or said that you are trying to hide something and although this may not be true it is NOT an impression you want to create. If you have no real assets or income, or less than your ex would like to think you have, make full disclosure so that it can be seen to be so as early as possible. A poorly completed Form E can breed suspicion on the part of exes and lawyers alike and this means cases can become unnecessarily drawn out, bitter and expensive. This is particularly so where the main earner is self-employed and income is not straightforwardly set out on a pay slip. Remember that if your ex has a lawyer, that lawyer has a duty to ensure that their client gets a fair deal, and cannot simply ignore gaps in your disclosure. As a rule of thumb it is best to try and knock these issues on the head as soon as possible by disclosing whatever is likely to lay an issue to rest rather than the bare minimum that is required.

Because in a court case you and your ex have to disclose this information under the duty of full and frank disclosure, neither of you is allowed to use the material for any purpose apart from the court case itself. If you are worried about misuse of disclosure you should bring this to the court's attention.

14.8 Questionnaires

If disclosure is incomplete or something is unclear from the Form E, parties are entitled to ask questions to the other party. These are usually exchanged before the First Directions Appointment and if possible it is a good idea to answer them before you come to court so that things are not held up. If this is not possible or you object to the questions being asked the Judge will decide which questions should be allowed.

The types of questions that might be asked could involve:

- An explanation of particular transactions on bank statements,

- Confirmation of the value of a policy or asset,

- The whereabouts of particular funds or assets that do not appear on the form E,

- Missing documents,

- Attempts to find work, what bonus is expected,

- Explanation or breakdown of figures provided (see Part 7 of this book).

14.9 Other useful information

If you are owner-occupiers of your home and there is likely to be an issue about how you can both afford to rehouse, it is often helpful if you can come to court ready with information about your mortgage capacity (or lack of it), and the price of local property (rented and to buy) which would be suitable for you or for your ex.

The other party may not bring this with them on the first occasion, but it may be something that you can ask the court to direct for the next hearing.

14.10 At the First Directions Appointment (FDA)

The court will make directions to ensure that when the case next comes back to court the matter can proceed to FDR stage and hopefully can be resolved by agreement.

If both parties agree that they have all the information that is necessary, the court may treat the FDA as an FDR (see below). It is increasingly common for a Judge to treat the first hearing as an FDR even where the parties are not really in agreement to this, in order to save on wasted expense both for the parties, the Legal Aid Agency and the court. If this happens the Judge will excuse herself from any further dealings with the case (or should be asked by the parties to excuse herself).

The types of directions that are likely to be made are:

- For the completion of Questionnaires. The court will usually delete any questions that are disproportionate or irrelevant (for example if the amount and detail of questions is over the top considering the size of the assets in the case, or if the answer is unlikely to make much difference to the outcome) and allow for three or four weeks for the answers to these questions to be provided.

- For valuation of any property. If the parties cannot agree on the value of a property it will usually need to be valued. Often it is sufficient to ask a local estate agent to carry out a 'market appraisal' for free, rather than instruct a surveyor to carry out a full valuation. The parties will usually have to pay half of the costs of a valuation. If you cannot agree on a valuer, the court will make directions about this. Often this will be that one party is to provide a list of estate agents they are happy with and the other is to pick one off the list. There are a number of mechanisms the court uses to sort these issues out - as a last resort the Judge will simply name someone herself.

- For the provision of information about mortgage capacity and housing costs.

- For the provision of any other information that appears to be outstanding. For example if one party says that they cannot work because of an injury and the other party does not accept this is true there may need to be medical evidence either from the GP or consultant or from an independent expert.

- Listing the matter for an FDR. Occasionally, it is obvious that the parties are not going to be able to agree matters or the sums in dispute are so small that it does not make sense to waste time with an FDR. In these cases the court will simply skip the FDR and list the case for a trial.

14.11 Financial Dispute Resolution Hearing (FDR)

An FDR is a Judge-led attempt to resolve a financial dispute by agreement. The Judge will (should) adopt a much more hands on approach than would normally be the case. Whereas Judges are generally quite careful not to express their views before they have heard a case fully (so as to ensure that the parties can both feel that the case has not been pre-judged), at an FDR the whole point is for the Judge to express a provisional view in order to help the parties see where the case might go if it ends up at trial. For this reason a Judge who has dealt with an FDR will not be allowed to deal with the trial, as it is important for the trial Judge to come to the case without any pre-conceptions or fixed ideas.

At the FDR the Judge will usually hear briefly from each party about what the issues are and what they each say is the correct outcome before giving a view about what she might do if she was hearing the case at trial.

The Judge might say that one or other party is being unrealistic, or that both are asking for orders that the court is unlikely to order bearing in mind the law. She may suggest a way of resolving things that the parties have not thought of or give a view about the size of a lump sum or the percentage of a pension share. Often the Judge will send the parties outside for further negotiation having heard what she has said. This may be repeated several times until either the parties reach agreement or it becomes clear that they simply cannot agree.

If the matter is agreed the court will proceed in one of three ways:

- By making an order on the spot, or

- (If the wording needs a bit more careful thought) by approving 'heads of agreement' until the lawyer for the other party can draft a full order (heads of agreement is a written summary of what has been agreed and will be binding on the parties from its approval by the Judge), or

- By allowing the parties time to draft a full order at court and approving that before they leave.

The court cannot impose any solution on the parties at an FDR and so if the matter is not agreed the Judge will make directions for trial, which may include:

- Directions for the filing of any further evidence or documents including any expert evidence (unlikely where the assets are modest),

- Fixing a date for the trial and a time estimate,

- Making directions for the filing of position statements or other documents to help the court,

- Ordering a party who is legally represented to take responsibility for making up a bundle for the use of the court and the parties,

- Clarifying which witnesses will be expected to give evidence at the trial,

- Ordering that a different Judge should deal with the trial.

The Judge may also record things that you have agreed on and what your positions are on certain issues, so that the Judge dealing with matters next time knows what she does and does not need to deal with.

If at the final hearing you are likely to want to refer the Judge to financial documents - things like bank or credit card statements - you should ask the Judge to direct that those documents are included in the bundle, as PD 27A (Bundles) say this sort of document must be specifically approved by the Judge to go in the bundle. If it isn't in the bundle the Judge won't see it and you won't be able to ask a question about it or show the Judge a particular transaction.

Some issues make a case more complex and are likely to prevent resolution of a case at FDR stage. If they are present in your case you may want to consider seeking legal advice:

- If one party suggests that a third party (someone apart from you or your partner) has a share in a property or is owed a substantial amount of money by one or both of you that must be repaid, or if there is a property in someone else's name that one of you says is really owned by the other,

- If there are or are said to be substantial assets abroad,

- If there are trusts,

- If there has been an agreement about the finances that one of you now wants to stick to but the other one does not,

- If one of you is, has recently been or is likely to be made bankrupt,

- If there are pensions of any real size.

These sorts of issues can make the legal situation more complicated, the outcome less predictable and the costs higher - these are important risk factors when you are thinking about whether or not to accept an offer to settle. You have to try and be a little bit commercially minded and continually assess whether carrying on is worth the risks. Could you end up worse off than you are if you forge ahead refusing all proposals to settle?

14.12 Trial

At the trial the Judge will usually hear evidence from both parties.

It is relatively uncommon for the Judge to hear evidence from anybody else in a financial case, but this may be permitted if relevant.

Where necessary the Judge may hear evidence from an expert (if permission has been given previously), for example on the valuation of a property or business.

At an FDR the only people who can make a decision are the parties. At trial the Judge will make the decision. The Judge may make the orders requested by one or other party or may make orders that neither has asked for or is happy with.

Usually the parties will each pay for their own legal expenses and will not be able to recover them from the other party even if the Judge agrees with their case. However, if a party has adopted an untenable position and has caused legal expenses to be incurred for no good reason there is a possibility that they will be ordered to pay some or all of their partner's legal costs. There is more information about costs in Chapter 24.

14.13 Equality - why can't I just have half?

The court has to look at all the financial information you have both provided and think about the s25 factors (see Chapter 12) in order to decide how to divide the money and assets. It is difficult if you are not a lawyer to try and work out what this will mean in practice, and many people believe that they are entitled to half of everything. Unfortunately it isn't that straightforward.

In the last decade the Supreme Court (previously the House of Lords) has dealt with several big divorce cases. Although they all related to cases involving very large amounts of wealth these cases do give some guidance about how the court should try and approach the s25 factors described above. This guidance can be summarised by saying that the court will try to divide the money and property equally IF IT CAN, bearing in mind how much money there is to go around and what everybody needs. Unless you are very wealthy the focus will be on practical and fair solutions rather than making sure you get back every penny you put into a relationship or exactly half of the money or property. Generally speaking, in a case involving an average family with a modest house and regular incomes, the court will not be interested in whether one person says they have worked harder, brought in more money or made more effort in the marriage, and will not base its decisions about the assets on these things (see *White v White* [2000] UKHL 54 and *Miller v MacFarlane* [2009] EWHC 891 (Fam)).

In a similar vein, even if you have contributed more than half of the money to the relationship (whether by income or home or inheritance) this does not necessarily mean that you will be able to recover that intact. The court will bear that in mind, but it will also have to think about the practical needs of both parties and any children.

14.14 A word about splitting the contents of your home

Looked at objectively there are probably more important things to sort out than who gets to keep the flat-screen or the knackered old washing machine, although if you are cash-strapped having to replace the basics can be a challenge.

The court can make orders about who should keep the contents of your home but be aware that most Judges will be very reluctant to waste court time on this level of detail and the result of putting a list of disputed items in front of a weary Judge at the end of a long hearing can be pretty unpredictable (you might as well draw straws!). The court will not spend a long time on this kind of thing because it has other families with really urgent and serious issues it has to deal with (and it has to comply with the overriding objective). So there are two things to remember:

If you can agree on nothing else try and sort out between you how to deal with the contents of the home. Avoid having to involve the court if at all possible. You might want to:

- Each produce a list of what you want and see what you can and can't agree;

- Where there are two of something agree you keep one each (sofas, beds, tellys);

- Keep things you brought into the relationship with you;

- Draw lots or go around the house picking an item in turn;

- Agree that whoever keeps the house keeps the bulk of the contents;

- Agree to sell everything, but be aware the second hand sale value will not be enough to replace everything new;

- If there are important items that you want to keep (sentimental value, heirlooms etc or essential items that you really cannot afford to replace in your new home) then identify these and try and reach agreement on these specific items first;

- Agree to sort this out through mediation.

If you cannot agree all the contents and you are going to ask the court to deal with the issue, don't leave it till the last minute. Prepare a clear list of items you want but which are not agreed, and a summary of how the rest has been split and make sure the Judge is told as early as possible that this will need to be decided. List 'contents' in any statement of issues prepared for the court.

Don't let the issue of contents distract you from the bigger picture. In a year, two years' time you will not care who got to keep the good saucepans or the Yucca plant. More importantly don't let it eat up valuable court time or the attention of the Judge, when there are more important things you need to focus the Judge's mind on.

14.15 Dealing with non-disclosure

Dealing with an ex who is hiding his assets or the true extent of his income from the court is quite difficult to deal with if they are self-employed. It is quite hard to unpick all of this, and you may have to try and interpret your ex's business accounts and tax returns. You might find the best way to tackle this type of issue is to focus on whether you can demonstrate that your ex's lifestyle is inconsistent with the poverty he says he is living in. What do his bank statements show (foreign holidays, cashpoint withdrawals, luxury items)? Do they show regular spending that simply couldn't be sustained on the income he says he has? Do they suggest there are other accounts that haven't been disclosed? Do they show payments for things you don't understand (credit cards, policies etc)? If your ex has secured credit how has he been able to do this (loan or mortgage applications often state a wholly different level of income than is on Form E!)?

Primarily you need to use the questionnaire process to help you with this aspect of your case, and to get you enough material to be able to demonstrate to the Judge at the trial that things are not as they seem. Use your knowledge of how the business used to work to put your questions together. Some examples are given at the rear of the book in the Forms, Templates & Useful Documents section in the Toolkit & Resources.

14.16 Private detective?

People often seem to think that hiring a private detective to find out all the dirty secrets of your ex is a necessary part of divorce, or that a private detective will put them at an advantage in the court process. They are wrong.

There are three reasons why you might want to hire a private detective to nose around your partner's affairs: to find out about infidelity, to prove infidelity, to find out more about someone's finances.

The first is really a personal matter and if you are reading this book you probably already know the worst. As for the second two reasons, here are a few things to think about.

Why do you need to prove infidelity?

If you have read Chapter 13 you will know that you can get divorced whether or not there has been adultery. All that is necessary is that the relationship has broken down irretrievably due to your spouse's unreasonable conduct. Alternatively you can divorce on the grounds of two years separation by agreement or five years separation without. Of course, you can get divorced on grounds of adultery but that's probably the most unpleasant route to take.

If you do apply for divorce on grounds of adultery you are likely to have to prove the actual adultery in order to get your divorce. This means you would need *evidence*. However, the grounds of divorce almost never have any bearing upon the financial settlement that the court will order. There is no financial advantage in securing a divorce on grounds of adultery as compared to (say) unreasonable behaviour). Proving your partner is an adulterer will not affect the financial division. And it might not even make you feel better in the long run.

It is therefore a waste of your money to hire a private detective to prove adultery. Occasionally I have seen evidence from a private detective clearly demonstrate that someone is living a lifestyle way out of kilter with their supposed income, but generally speaking there is a risk that taking this course will cost money you can ill afford for no gain or that it will just result in very unpleasant levels of tension between you.

Finding the money

What *might* be worth doing is hiring a private detective to find out more about your partner's finances. However, when the court is involved there is a strict process of disclosure where both parties have to give full information about their finances which is described above. It's usually more cost effective to work with that court process in the first instance. The advantage of waiting to see what information is given voluntarily is that you will have more information to work with as a starting point.

Be realistic about what a private detective could achieve. The direct financial information that a private detective can lawfully gather is going to be relatively limited (public sources such as electoral roll etc), and is unlikely to tell you anything you don't already know. You MUST make sure your private detective is acting lawfully. Private detectives are unregulated, the court will probably not allow you to rely on anything that has been unlawfully obtained, and you could end up in difficulties with the authorities. A private detective might be able to carry out surveillance to prove a point about someone who is living a lifestyle that is totally out of kilter with what is showing on their Form E, but it is a real gamble, particularly since you would have to get the court's permission to rely on any material you do obtain via that route.

In my experience hiring a private detective is a distraction at best and an expensive disappointment at worst. If you have enough money to spend on a private detective you should seriously consider whether it would be better spent getting some legal advice.

You will not be able to recover the costs of hiring the private detective.

Social media evidence

It may be that you can see from social media or online activity that your ex's disclosed finances don't appear to match their lifestyle. If you wish to rely on evidence from facebook or some other social media platform you will need to ensure the following:

- You obtain any information lawfully (i.e. by viewing something that is publicly available or properly accessible to you as a 'friend', not by logging in using their password or using their device when they are logged in)

- You screenshot any relevant information (showing the URL bar and the full context) which should keep a timestamp in the filename

- You must be able to demonstrate the account is operated by your ex

- You do not distort the true picture by very selective download of only certain information

- You disclose it at the time - you might wish to ask questions about apparent discrepancies between a particular screenshot and an answer to a question

I would say that in my experience this sort of material is often not as helpful as it might appear at first blush. Lots of people go out in their posh clothes and best jewellery for a party once in a while but it does not necessarily prove they are living a lavish lifestyle that is inconsistent with their stated income. And lots of people make jokes or brag on social media, so what they say may not be true at all. Ask yourself - is this really going to get me anywhere or will it just make me look a bit like a stalker?

14.17 Maintenance

The court can order maintenance at whatever amount and frequency it thinks is appropriate, and it can order maintenance to last until a particular date or event, or to carry on until one party dies (a joint lives order). If it includes an end date it can say that the term cannot be extended, or that it can be extended if an application is made before it ends. It can order the amount to change on particular trigger events or dates (for example once the youngest child is at school when the parent caring might be expected to increase their income and need less financial support). Any maintenance order ends automatically if the person who is being paid remarries.

It's important to realise that maintenance payments are not automatic and will depend on a combination of things (all those factors in section 25), in particular the needs and resources of both of you. In *SS v NS (Spousal Maintenance)* [2014] EWHC 4183 (Fam) [2015] 2 FLR 1124 the Judge sets out some guidelines for thinking about whether maintenance should be paid and if so for how long. Translated into plain English the main points are:

- Maintenance should be paid if a relationship has caused financial need (for example if someone has given up work to care for the child of both parties) but not to cover need that arises for some other reason (for example if someone has had to give up work because they've gone on to have a child by someone else).

- The amount should usually be based on need.

- The court will aim to have an end date for the maintenance sooner rather than later unless that can't happen without 'undue hardship'. People should be expected to work towards independence.

- The court should probably prefer an order with an end date that can be extended on application than a 'joint lives' order.

- If choosing between a term that can be extended or one that cannot the court should normally make a decision that protects the financially weaker person.

- Your lifestyle when together is a factor but it isn't the only thing or the most important thing - and the more time that passes the less important it becomes.

- The Judge has to stand back and look at the amount payable and ask if it is a fair proportion of the income of the person who is paying.

Either party can apply to vary (up or down), to discharge or to extend the term of a maintenance order (except obviously you can't apply to extend a non-extendable order). Usually a person making such an application will need to show some change of circumstances to justify their application. It is also possible to apply for capitalisation of maintenance, which means a calculation of all the maintenance likely to be due in future is made and a lump sum or series of lump sums paid instead so the person can invest the capital to produce an income in future.

14.18 Common practical solutions

Housing your family in two homes instead of one on the same overall income is going to be more of a struggle. If one of you is left caring for the children they may end up entitled to more benefits but generally speaking both of you are going to have to get used to the idea of a lower standard of living than in the past. This is basic maths.

If you had enough money to go around with some to spare it would be easy to split everything you have in half and go your separate ways. But in the real world this is often impossible or impractical. It is sometimes not possible to get your half of the assets out of the home that the children are living in because it can't be sold and the parent left living in it can't raise a mortgage big enough to buy you out. So you have to find another way.

In this type of case the court might make an order for the house to be transferred to the person left living in the house, and an order for the other person to have a charge on the property (secured just like a mortgage) for a fixed sum or percentage that has to be paid out by a particular date, when the house is sold, when the children get to a particular age (perhaps at a time when you think that the caring parent will be in a position to be earning properly again, or in some cases not until the kids are 18 or have finished university) or sometimes if the partner remaining in the property remarries or cohabits. This type of order is sometimes called a *Mesher* order by lawyers and Judges. There are some interesting articles about the pros and cons of *Mesher* orders on Marilyn Stowe's family law blog (www.marilynstowe.co.uk). The Advice Now and FJC guides also explain a bit about this issue.

If the court thinks that a partner who is looking after the children needs a certain amount of spousal maintenance to keep meeting the outgoings on their home, the court can make an order for the amount of maintenance that would add up with the child maintenance to just the right amount overall, and can say that it will adjust as the child maintenance goes up or down. Or the court can say that some of the maintenance can be paid directly to the mortgage company and that the amount of maintenance can go up and down with the mortgage payment due each month.

The court cannot change a debt from one party's name to another, but if there is enough money available (or if the court is satisfied that the person paying will be able to borrow enough money and that it is fair to expect them to do this), it can order a lump sum to be paid which can be used to pay off the debt or purchase a particular item that is needed. The court might say this is money that the person paying can find from their own savings or accounts, or from selling something in their name or if the home is going to be sold the court can adjust the amount of money paid out to each of the parties to give one party a bit more or less. Of course all of this depends on there being some money available to split between you.

If you don't own your own home the court can make an order transferring a housing association or local authority tenancy from both of your names to one name, or from one to the other. Sometimes it is necessary to ask the court to make an order so that both of you can ask to be rehoused, as it can cause difficulties if you give up your tenancy voluntarily. If either of you wants the court to make an order to transfer the tenancy to or from your name you must apply under Schedule 7 FLA 1996, which is dealt with in Chapter 15 on cohabitation. If you have been married the court cannot make an order transferring the tenancy until it has made a Decree Nisi.

14.19 We had an agreement - now my ex doesn't want to stick to it (or now I don't want to stick to it!)

There are several types of 'nuptial' agreement:

*   Pre-nuptial agreement which is an agreement made before marrying

about what will happen if you ever split up;

- Post-nuptial agreement which is an agreement made during the marriage about what will happen if you ever split up;

- An agreement reached between you at around the time you split up (separation agreement);

- An agreement reached at court and approved by the Judge but not converted into an order.

Pre-nuptial and post-nuptial agreements are the subject of lots of newspaper articles, but are not dealt with in this book in any length because they are usually only relevant to parties who are wealthy enough to afford lawyers. In short though, the court does not have to uphold pre- or post-nuptial agreements, but the fact that the parties have entered into one is very likely to be an important factor when the Judge looks at all the circumstances and s25 MCA 1973.

In 2010 the Supreme Court gave some guidance on nuptial agreements in the case of *Radmacher v Granatino* [2010] UKSC 42. It said that:

'The court should give effect to a nuptial agreement that is freely entered into by each party with a full appreciation of its implications unless in the circumstances prevailing it would not be fair to hold the parties to their agreement.' [Paragraph 75 of the judgment]

This applies to all the four types of agreements listed above.

If you have reached an agreement between yourselves at some point and one of you wants to stick to it but the other has changed their mind this is called an *Edgar* agreement (named after *Edgar v Edgar* [1980] EWCA Civ 2). Although the *Radmacher* case tells us that the court will probably uphold the agreement unless there is a very good reason not to, the fact that you have reached an agreement cannot stop either of you later changing your mind and applying to the court. The kinds of things that might make the court agree to order something different from the agreement are:

- If there was undue influence (pressure or threats),

- The person who wants to change things didn't have any independent legal advice, or didn't fully understand the financial position when they agreed things,

- The person who wants to change things (or the children) would suffer really serious financial hardship if the agreement wasn't changed,

- The children's needs would not be met,

- Something unexpected has happened since the agreement was made, and it means that the agreement is now unfair.

If you reach an agreement at court sometimes there is not time to write up a full consent order for you both to sign. If this happens the lawyer for the other side should write down 'heads of agreement', which is a summary of what you have agreed and this should be explained to the Judge. As long as it is sensible the Judge is likely to approve it. At that point, even though it has not yet been converted into a court order, it is binding and neither of you will be allowed to change your mind. This is a *'Rose'* agreement (named after the case of *Rose v Rose* [2002] EWCA Civ 208).

If there later turns out to be a dispute about a *Rose* agreement (what has been agreed or whether there has been an agreement at all) the court may have to hold a special hearing about that to decide:

- if the agreement was reached and

- if so what it was, or

- if no agreement was actually reached the matter will have to go on to a trial for the Judge to decide the appropriate order (see *Xydhias v Xydhias* [1998] EWCA Civ 1966).

The court will have to think about the guidance in the *Radmacher* case.

See also Chapter 25: Challenging Decisions.

14.20 Bankruptcy

Sometimes one party will go bankrupt before the family court can make a decision about sorting out the finances. A bankruptcy can limit the range of orders the court can make. If the family court thinks this is a sham to avoid paying out to an ex it can annul the bankruptcy. The Trustee in Bankruptcy has to be told about the family court case so that they can tell the court what they say about the assets available.

If you think your ex is about to go bankrupt you really should seek urgent legal advice.

15. Finances For Separating Cohabitees

15.1   Introduction

The legal situation for couples who have never been married or civil partners is different from that faced by married couples or civil partners.

Many people think that if they are 'common law man and wife' they will be just as entitled to a share of the assets and income as if they were married. In reality there is no such thing as a common law wife (or husband) and no particular legal protection for one.

A common law wife or husband has no claim for maintenance (regular payments of income), or for a share of income or pension, although they may be able to make a claim for a financial order about a child which, in very limited circumstances, may include maintenance (see below under Schedule 1 heading).

15.2   Tenants

If you live in a property under a council or housing association tenancy which is in both your names or in your ex's name you may be able to make an application under the Family Law Act 1996 for a transfer of tenancy into your name. This is not possible with a private landlord [s53 & Schedule 7 FLA 1996].

If the tenancy is in both of your names, it only takes one of you to bring it to an end, and once it is done the court cannot do anything to get the tenancy back. Although people are rarely silly enough to surrender a tenancy out of spite, the court can make an order stopping either of you from surrendering (giving up) your tenancy before the court has had a chance to sort things out. If you are worried about this you must ask the court to make a 'without notice' order by making an application for transfer of tenancy under the FLA 1996 without telling the other person first. See Chapters 8 and 22 for more information on how 'without notice' applications are made [see also Part 10 FPR].

An application for a transfer of tenancy is made on form D50B and injunctions are dealt with at Rule 20.4, Part 10 and Part 18 FPR (Form FP2).

The court will have to weigh up both of your financial and housing needs and re-sources, and the needs of your children before deciding whether to transfer the tenancy (the law on this is set out in Chapter 21). To do this, the court will probably need witness statements dealing with the each of the legal criteria (tests) set out in the relevant section of the FLA (for example whether either party has somewhere else to go, whether they have any particular housing needs such as a need to stay in a home specially adapted for their disability etc) and there may be a need to attach supporting documents about some of these things (medical evidence, financial information, information from housing office).

Sometimes these cases have to go to court so that the court can make an order, because if you or your ex were to *agree* to transfer the tenancy the Local Authority might say that the person who has agreed to let go of their tenancy is 'intentionally homeless' and that the Local Authority have no duty to rehouse them. This problem does not exist where the court decides for you.

For as long as your name is on a tenancy you are responsible for paying the rent along with anyone else on the tenancy even if you have moved out. Your landlord is entitled to chase you, your partner or both of you for the whole of any rent arrears if you are both on the tenancy. So if you have rehoused yourself elsewhere and don't need to worry about being intentionally homeless, it is a good idea to get your name removed from the tenancy. Speak to your landlord about this - if it is agreed you will not need to go to court to sort it out.

15.3   Owner occupiers

A cohabitee or former cohabitee may have a claim to a share of property (houses or land). Sadly, because cohabiting couples have to rely upon a hotch potch of old and out of date law, the law sometimes doesn't work very fairly, and it can be difficult to assess how good your chances of success are. For married couples it doesn't usually matter too much who owns what, because the court can adjust the assets between the parties to achieve a fair outcome. However, the court's role when dealing with cohabiting couples is limited to identifying who IS the owner of the home or land (although it can adjust assets to a limited extent for the benefit of a child only - see below under Schedule 1 heading).

If you are able to agree between you what your house is worth and how to split the proceeds, so much the better. You can sort this out between you with a little bit of help from a conveyancing solicitor either by selling the property or by leaving one of you in the property and buying the other one out on payment of an agreed figure. You will obviously need to arrange for one name to be taken off the mortgage (get the mortgage company's permission), and for one name to be taken off the title of the property - your conveyancer can help you with this. Remember to make sure that you each share the costs of sale or conveyancing and build in the costs of estate agency fees etc.

Whatever else you do, try and ensure that you keep up to date with any mortgage repayments. If your house is in joint names and you default you will both have difficulty getting a new mortgage and will be at risk of repossession. If your mortgage company repossesses and sells the house, you will not get such a good price and will have to pay additional fees. Try and agree a holding position with your ex about the mortgage until you have sold the house or sorted things out, and if you cannot pay, make sure that you keep in touch with the mortgage company, explain what is happening and ask for time to pay.

If however you can't sort things out there are two main types of legal case that you might need to consider if you are separating and in need of financial support or remedy:

- A claim under the Trusts of Land and Appointment of Trustees Act 1996 (ToLATA for short - if you hear a lawyer or Judge talking about 'T'larter' this is what they mean),

- A claim under Schedule 1 of the Children Act 1989.

15.4 Disputes about ownership of property - ToLATA

If you are in dispute about a house or other land that you own jointly, or that is in one of your names but a share of which you think you might be entitled, you may be able to make a claim under ToLATA to ask the court to:

- decide what proportion of the property you own, and if so

- whether it should be sold in order to release your share of it.

This type of case is not formally recognised by the courts as a family case, but is treated as an ordinary civil claim (see the Civil Procedure Rules on the Justice website). This is important because it means that the court will look at any legal costs differently. If you were to bring (or defend) a claim and did not succeed, you might have to pay some or all of your ex's legal costs. This could be a lot of money, so it is important to be as sure as you can, before you start a claim under this piece of law, that you have a good chance of success, and that you have a reasonable chance of getting enough money out of it to be worth the risk. You should also seriously consider any proposal that is made by your ex to resolve things by agreement, and if necessary ask a lawyer to give you some advice about that. If you press on unreasonably you might have to pay their costs of going to court. It is also important because it means that the court might be a bit less flexible with you about keeping to the rules, and might run things a bit more formally than in most other family cases.

It is a good idea, before you do anything else, to try and agree between you what your house is worth - and even if you can't agree, to get a reasonable idea for yourself what it is worth and how much equity is in it.

This book can only give you very general guidance about how the courts will approach ownership of houses and land for cohabitees. In this area of law it is almost always worth going to see a lawyer for some advice before deciding what to do, even if you decide to make a claim as a litigant in person.

You need to understand a little bit about how you can own property. There are two ways:

- You are the legal owner. This means that it is written down and your name is on the title of the property.

- You have an entitlement to a share in a property that is not visible from the legal documents.

Where someone else other than the legal owner is also entitled to a share in the property, the law says that the legal owner holds the property on trust for the beneficial owner(s). This is what makes this type of law so unpredictable. This type of entitlement that is not written down is called a 'beneficial interest' or 'equitable interest' by lawyers.

Land law tells us that usually everything relating to the ownership of houses and land needs to be in writing to be valid, but sometimes people do or say things that mean they can gain an entitlement even though it is not in writing and even though the title documents do not say they are an owner. There are lots of names for this, but one of them is a constructive trust. In essence a constructive trust is a legal way of saying that the way the parties have behaved in relation to the property means that they have effectively created a shared ownership of the property that should be honoured. The court can decide that you share owner-ship of the property in this way based on the evidence about what you have said to one another ('this is our house'), or sometimes even if it was not said based upon things you have done that show that this was what you both intended (this is called a common intention).

The law about common intention is difficult even for lawyers and where everything hinges on common intention it can be difficult to predict outcomes. You should think seriously about seeing a lawyer if there is likely to be an issue about ownership of a property. This chapter is just a sketch outline; it can all get very technical.

If you are worried that your ex might try and sell the house before your claim has been sorted out, you might be able to register a notice or restriction at the Land Registry to prevent this happening, or at least to warn off potential purchasers so that they can't say they didn't know. The forms and various information leaflets are available on the Land Registry website.

15.5   Both names on the property

If both of your names are on the title of the property the starting point will be that you own the house in equal shares unless you agreed otherwise in writing at the time of the purchase (for example sometimes where one person puts all their divorce settlement into a new home and the other does not contribute very much they might ask their solicitor to record on the Land Registry documents that they do not want to own the house equally but that one should own 60% and the other 40%). If something else has been agreed later on the court may uphold that later agreement. If both of your names are on the title of the property but for some reason you think that you do not own equal shares it is good idea to see a lawyer.

Since 1998 Land Registry forms contain a form called TR1 which is where the parties' common intentions about the shares in which a property is intended to be held are usually recorded. If this has been completed it will be treated as an accurate record of what you intended and therefore of the proportions you own the property in - but unfortunately it isn't mandatory and it is in cases where it hasn't been completed that there may be disagreement about what was intended.

In 2011, in a case called *Kernott v Jones* [2011] UKSC 53 the Supreme Court looked at the law relating to common intention where a property is held in joint names but there is nothing written down or specifically agreed about how big each party's share should be. *Kernott v Jones* tells us that if you own a property in joint names the presumption (or starting point) will be that you intended to own it in equal shares. That presumption will not apply if the evidence shows that this wasn't in fact what the parties both intended - and in those circumstances the court would have to look at the evidence to work out what they must have intended at the time. If the court takes the view that the parties had different intentions from one another, that their intentions changed or that it is impossible to work out what they intended at the time it can 'impute' (assign) an intention in order to work out what shares are fair having looked at everything that has gone on. *Kernott v Jones* tells us that the court can sometimes consider what happened after the separation.

There is a bit more detail about how the court will approach evidence relating to common intention below (15.7).

15.6   Written agreement

If you have a declaration of trust or written cohabitees agreement this will usu-ally be binding. There are some circumstances where it might not be (fraud or mistake).

15.7   Name not on title and no written agreement

If your name is not on the title of the property there is no automatic entitlement to anything. The starting point will be that you have no interest in it and you will have to prove otherwise. Without a written agreement this will be difficult. You might be entitled to a share in the property if:

- you have agreed to share it and can prove that you have said this to each other,

- you have contributed to the deposit,

- you have behaved in a way that persuades the court that you both in-tended to share the property.

The law in this area is difficult and complicated and reliant on an understanding of really complicated case law. Often the court has to decide if there has been an agreement or 'common intention' to own the property jointly and in equal shares, but the court cannot decide that you own the property in this way unless there is *evidence* of an agreement or a common intention. When deciding this the court will look at:

- things that you have said to one another over the years, including prom-ises made and conversations about 'our house',

- how have you treated the property - as your family home, with both helping to maintain and improve it?

- how have you treated your finances and who has paid for what - have your finances been kept separate or pooled together?

You can see that a lot will depend on how much you can remember about what has been said between you in the past, perhaps in casual conversation, and it is really difficult to remember it accurately and to be sure that the court will accept your version of events over your ex's. This makes the outcome in this type of case very unpredictable - before you do anything else go and see a lawyer. You could take a written note with you of your answers to the points above to help your solicitor assess your case.

If you need to ask for an order under ToLATA you will need to start your case in the County Court not the Family Court - this is one of the few categories of case which arises from a family dispute but doesn't fall under the Family Court. If you need to bring a claim which is partly ToLATA and partly Schedule 1 (see below) you should start both cases at the same time but on each application form ask the court to hear them together - think of it as a single Judge wearing both a Family Court 'hat' and a County Court 'hat' at the same time.

The rules that apply to a ToLATA case in the County Court are the Civil Procedure Rules (CPR) not the FPR. In civil proceedings cases are allocated to a track, depending on value and complexity. Your case is likely to be allocated to the Fast Track or Multi Track. If it is allocated to the fast track the legal costs that can be claimed back by a party are limited, so there is less costs risk.

15.8   Schedule 1 Children Act 1989

If you have children you may be able to make a claim under Schedule 1 of the Children Act 1989 for financial provision for the children from their other parent. If you are a non-parent with a child arrangements order saying the child should live with you or special guardianship order in your favour you may make an application for financial provision from one or both of the child's parents.

Schedule 1 CA is treated as a 'family' case and falls under the FPR, Part 10 'Financial Remedies'. The procedure for a Schedule 1 CA application is very similar to the procedure in an application for other financial orders after divorce, so you may find Chapter 14 helpful.

The court is only allowed to deal with maintenance for children in very limited circumstances:

- If the parent who would pay maintenance is earning above the maximum amount of income dealt with by the Child Maintenance Service or CMS (currently £3,000 per week).

- If the other parent is not required for some other reason to pay child support via the CMS, for example because they live abroad, you may be able to make a claim under this piece of law, although there may be practical difficulties in pursuing a claim against someone who does not live here.

- The court may make an order relating to the expenses attributable to the child's disability.

- The only other type of income claim you can make in respect of children is for school fees.

The court can make the following capital orders:

- Payment of a lump sum for the benefit of the children.

- Transfer of a property into the Applicant's name for the benefit of the children, or an order that property should be settled for their benefit (this means they get to use it but it is not held in their name or the Applicant's name).

Where the court makes an order relating to a house under Schedule 1 the property will usually be returned to the other party once the youngest child reaches 18, or possibly when they finish school or university. The parent does not get to keep the property or use it for themselves (obviously they can live in it with the child while they are caring for them!).

When deciding what order to make the court has to consider **all the circumstances** including:

- **the income, earning capacity, property and other financial resources which each parent or Applicant has or is likely to have in the foreseeable future**

- **the financial needs, obligations and responsibilities which each parent or Applicant has or is likely to have in the foreseeable future**

- **the financial needs of the child**

- **the income, earning capacity (if any), property and other financial resources of the child**

- **any physical or mental disability of the child**

- **the manner in which the child was being, or was expected to be, educated or trained.**

You will see that these are similar but not identical to the s25 factors that the court has to consider when dealing with finances on divorce (see Chapter 12).

15.9   Splitting the possessions

It is unfortunate if you end up falling out over who gets the sofa or the washing machine or the double bed, and the court is not a great forum for sorting out these kinds of disputes. It is far better to agree between you how to divide things up, and as long as it works for you it doesn't matter whether it's by drawing lots or by selecting in turns or by who actually paid for the item. You might even agree to sell the lot and split the proceeds, but when selling used goods you obviously won't make enough to replace the items new. The only mechanism through which you can get the court to decide about who owns what item of furniture is through the small claims court. You should really ask yourself whether it is worth the stress and effort to pursue a claim in this way. Unless it's a pretty high value item it is probably better to cut your losses and move on. If you want to talk this through with someone your local CAB or law centre will probably be the best place to go.

PART 4: CHILDREN

16.   The Law Relating To Children

16.1   Introduction

The law relating to children is mainly contained in the Children Act 1989. Because it will be referred to so often I'm going to refer to the Children Act 1989 as the CA for the rest of the chapter. There are a few other pieces of law, which are sometimes relevant, but most readers of this book will need only to look at the CA.

Before we look at the CA however, we need first of all to look at the law on jurisdiction.

16.2   Jurisdiction (or: can the court make an order?)

Jurisdiction is whether or not the court is allowed to deal with a case. The English & Welsh courts have jurisdiction (power) to deal with case where:

- an application has been made by someone the CA permits to make an application;

- the child is habitually resident in England or Wales (the question of habitual residence and whether the courts in this country are allowed to make orders about a child who has a connection abroad is dealt with in Chapter 18).

Judges don't have any power to pull in a case off the street - *someone* has to start a court case, but once a case has been started the court is in charge of the case.

In some cases once a family court is dealing with one issue relating to a child it can make certain other types of order even when nobody has made an application. For example, if the court is already dealing with an application for a child arrangements order it can make a domestic violence injunction (see Chapters 21 and 22) or a prohibited steps order if it thinks that is required (this is called making an order of its own motion).

Once an application about a child has been started it will only conclude when the court makes final orders or when the court permits the application to be withdrawn.

16.3   Who can apply for orders?

Generally speaking a parent will not need permission to make an application for a s8 order (child arrangements, specific issue or prohibited steps), but other people who want an order generally do need permission [s10 CA]. See Chapter 20 for an explanation of when you may need permission to make an application.

16.4 The structure of the Children Act 1989

The structure of the CA is pretty simple. It gives the court the power to make a range of orders about children but does not say exactly when the court should make each order, because every family is different.

The CA says that court must treat the welfare of the child as the most important thing (this is called the 'paramountcy principle' and is set out at s1(1) CA). Trying to put the child's welfare first is sometimes described as doing what is in the 'best interests' of the child.

Whenever the court considers making an order under the CA it must only do so when making an order is better than making none at all (this is called the 'no order principle' [s1(5) CA]).

The court must also work on the basis that delay in the case is likely to harm the welfare of the child [s1(2) CA].

In working out what will best promote the welfare of the child the court has to look at all of the circumstances, but the act gives the court a checklist as a guide [s1(3) CA]. Really what the checklist does is try to focus the Judge's mind on what is right for that particular child in their particular circumstances, and not just look at each parent's rights in respect of their children.

The court will come back to the welfare checklist again and again in making all its decisions, so it is worth setting it out here:

- **The ascertainable wishes and feelings of the child concerned (considered in the light of his age and understanding);**

- **His physical, emotional and educational needs;**

- **The likely effect on him of any change in his circumstances;**

- **His age, sex, background and any characteristics of his which the court considers relevant;**

- **Any harm which he has suffered or is at risk of suffering;**

- **How capable each of his parents, and any other person in relation to** whom the court considers the question to be relevant, is of meeting his needs;

- **The range of powers available to the court under the Act in the proceedings in question.**

The CA says that 'harm' in relation to a child means **ill-treatment or the impairment of health or development, including, for example, impairment suffered from seeing or hearing the ill-treatment of another**. This reflects the fact that experts on children generally agree that children who have been living in violent households can suffer harm even if they were usually in a different room from the violence. In different cases different parts of the welfare checklist will have more relevance or will be more or less important.

16.5 The presumption of parental involvement

In 2014 Parliament amended s1 CA to include a presumption of parental involvement that will amend the CA by adding a new subsection (2A) to s1 CA. A presumption is like a starting point, and is the basis upon which the court operates unless one party proves it shouldn't apply. The presumption that s11 will bring in is that **involvement of the parent in the life of the child will further the child's welfare**.

The CA says that 'involvement' can be any kind of involvement - not necessarily direct and not necessarily any particular division of time. So it isn't a presumption that children should live with both parents or spend equal time with each parent (and nor is it a presumption that they shouldn't).

The presumption of parental involvement only applies if the parent can be involved in the child's life in a way that does not put the child at risk of suffering harm. The court must treat this as being possible unless there is 'some evidence before the court in the particular proceedings' to suggest that involvement in the child's life would put the child at risk of suffering harm whatever the form of the involvement.

The presumption really describes (in quite a complicated way) what was already happening in courts. Judges often say that the starting point is that a child should have contact with both parents. The precise wording of this bit of new law was controversial in Parliament, and if you look at it closely you will see that it is really only a presumption about whether there should be some involvement - even if it is no more than a letter a year - rather than a presumption about how much involvement there should be or what form it should take. It could be said that the presumption of parental involvement is more a message for parents who might try and frustrate a child's relationship with their other parent that this is inappropriate and harmful than it is a message to Judges.

16.6 Orders under The Children Act

The court can make a range of orders under the CA. This book deals mainly with orders the court can make when members of a child's family cannot agree things between themselves. These are called 'private law' orders and they are contained in Parts I and II of the CA.

Orders a parent can ask for (private law orders):

- **Parental responsibility order** [s2-4A CA] (giving a Father, other parent figure or carer legal rights and responsibility for a child - biological mothers automatically have parental responsibility)

- **'Section 8' orders** [s8 CA] - there are three types:

  - Child arrangements order (setting out where a child will live and when, and setting out when a child will see a particular person, usually a parent);

  - Specific issue order (deciding a particular point of dispute about a child's upbringing such as where a child should be schooled or whether he should be circumcised); and

  - Prohibited steps order (a sort of injunction that stops a person doing something to or with a child, for example saying a parent must not remove a child from his school or take them abroad). NB before 22 April 2014 the court made contact and residence orders rather than child arrangements orders, this was amended by the C&FA 2014.

- **Activity directions /conditions and enforcement orders** [s11A-11P]

- **Change of name, removal from jurisdiction** [s13 CA]

- **Family assistance order** [s16 CA]

- **Monitoring order** [s11H CA]

- **'Barring order'** [s91(14)]

- **Financial orders regarding children** [s15 and Schedule 1 CA] - these are dealt with in Chapter 15, but also see Chapter 12.

16.7 Changing terminology

You will notice from the list above that the court does not make 'custody' orders. This rather old-fashioned terminology (which makes children sound like bits of property) was abolished by the CA, and replaced with contact and residence orders. On 22 April 2014 contact and residence orders were abolished and re-placed with child arrangements orders (actually, occasionally the word 'custody' is used in English courts in some international child abduction cases, and this is because 'custody' is still used in European law). If you have an old-style contact or residence order from before 22 April 2014 it will automatically convert to a child arrangements order.

The legal effect of a child arrangements order that says who a child should live with is almost identical to the legal effect of a residence order.

The legal effect of a child arrangements order that says a child should live with different people at different times is almost identical to the legal effect of a shared residence order.

The legal effect of a child arrangements order that says a child should spend time with someone is almost identical to the legal effect of a contact order.

Since child arrangements orders have been brought into force the court's en-forcement powers that used to only apply to contact orders now also apply to orders that say a child should live with different people at different times (what would have been a shared residence order in the old terminology).

16.8 Orders social services might ask for (public law orders)

Where the court is asked by social services to make an order, this is called a 'public law order', because a public body is asking the court to make orders in order to protect a child that it says is at risk, for example orders that allow social workers to remove a child from the care of their parents. Public law orders are set out in Part IV of the CA.

The following is a list of public law orders that the court can make under the CA:

- **Emergency protection order** (very short term orders to take children into care in very urgent cases only)

- **Care order** (gives social services shared parental responsibility for a child. This is what permits social services use to remove a child from her par-ents when the parents do not agree)

- **Supervision order** (gives social services the power to supervise a family, and a duty on them to support and assist the family)

- **Contact with a child in care** (saying what contact social services must provide between a child in care and his family)

- **Secure accommodation order**

- **Education supervision order**

- **Child assessment orders**

As well as giving the court powers to make these orders, the CA also sets out the range of powers and duties that social services have towards children who are in need or who are at risk of harm. These are not dealt with in this book.

The Adoption and Children Act 2002 deals mainly with placement for adoption and adoption. It is structured in a similar way to the CA in that it has a welfare checklist that the court must consider before making orders.

This book does not deal in any detail with public law orders. If social services go to court to get care orders or to remove a child from home the parents are entitled to free legal advice and representation through legal aid. Other family members sometimes want to get involved in these cases but may not be entitled to legal aid. There is a separate chapter for those family members covering the types of things they might need to deal with if they are unable to get a lawyer (see Chapter 20).

This book does not cover the law that relates to adoption (including step-parent adoption) or surrogacy. There is some basic information about arrangements for same sex couples with children, but it is really only a sketch. See Chapters 17 and 20. This book gives detailed information about the range of private law orders that can be made under the CA in Chapter 17.

16.9   Other relevant parts of the Children Act

Under s7 CA the court has the power to order CAFCASS or social services to write a welfare report in order to help it reach a decision. You might hear this being described as a 'Section 7 report'.

If the court is worried that the children might be at risk of significant harm (really serious harm) and thinks that social services perhaps ought to consider whether or not to start care proceedings the court will order a different sort of report under s37 CA, which tells social services to investigate the case and consider whether they should take their own action to protect the children. If the court orders this type of order it can make interim care orders to protect the children until the report has been finished.

Although this book does not cover care proceedings it is useful to understand the basics about when the court can and cannot make care or supervision orders. It is a complicated area of law, but for the purposes of this book we can summarise the law as saying that the court can only make this type of order when a child is suffering or likely to suffer significant harm from the parenting they are receiving, or because they are out of the parents' control. It is only where the courts think things *might* be bad enough to pass this test (called the 'threshold' by lawyers) that a s37 report should be ordered. Sometimes in very difficult contact cases s37 is used as described in Chapter 17.

As well as the CA itself there are lots of authorities which give the court guidance as to how it should approach and weigh up the factors on the welfare checklist, how it should manage delay and what procedure should be followed. Some of these are discussed in Chapter 17, which deals with all the various private law orders, with the exception of Schedule 1 applications for financial orders in respect of children which are covered in Chapter 15.

16.10 The law on taking children abroad or away from their home

Generally you should not take your child out of the UK unless the other parent and anyone else who is named in a child arrangements order as a person with whom the child lives has agreed, or the court has given you permission. If you do you may be guilty of a criminal offence under the Child Abduction Act 1984, even if you have just gone for a holiday.

The situation is slightly different depending on whether there is a child arrangements order saying who the child lives with in place or not.

If there is no child arrangements order saying who the child lives with

Although it isn't a *criminal* offence to take a child abroad without the Father's consent if he does not have parental responsibility (see Chapter 17), this could still count as a 'wrongful removal'. If a child has been wrongfully removed this means it could lead to child abduction proceedings being started under the Hague Convention on International Child Abduction (this only applies if the country they have gone to is a signatory to the convention, but most are. Check the Reunite website for a list). A removal by a mother is likely to be a wrongful removal even if the Father doesn't have parental responsibility, if he has not agreed that the child can go and any of the following apply:

- he is having regular contact, or

- if there is a child arrangements order saying that the child should spend time with him, or

- there are ongoing court proceedings.

The idea of the Hague Convention is that children who have been wrongfully removed are normally returned to their home country quickly, so that a decision to be made about whether or not they should be allowed to be taken to live permanently abroad can be made in the court in the country where they were taken from.

If there is a child arrangements order saying who the child should live with

A person named in the child arrangements order as a person with whom the child should live is allowed to take the child abroad without the consent of anyone else as long as it is for not more than a month (although if the order also says that the child lives with or spends time with another person that order still applies so any trip must be fitted around that or agreed with the other person). If they stay for longer than a month without the agreement of the other parent this would still be a criminal offence *as long as the other parent has parental responsibility*.

If a parent who isn't named as a person with whom the child should live takes the child abroad without the consent of the other parent (and of any other person who is named as the person with whom the child should live) and they do not have the permission of the court either, this is a criminal offence.

In both these cases child abduction proceedings could be started as described above.

If there is an order saying the child should live with one of you some of the time and another person (usually the other parent) some of the time

You will both be entitled to take the child abroad for up to a month, as long as this doesn't cut across the times that the child arrangements order says the child is to live with the other person (it probably will).

Regardless of whether there is a child arrangements order saying where a child is to live, if a parent takes a child abroad in breach of a prohibited steps order (see Chapter 17) or any other court order that says they must not do so this is a criminal offence and again child abduction proceedings could be started. It would also be a contempt of court that the family court could potentially punish you for by fine or imprisonment. It is also probably a criminal offence to take the child abroad over dates that put you in breach of the parts of a child arrangements order relating to the time the child should live or spend with the other parent (lawyers could probably argue either way about this but you don't want to risk it [s1(5A(b) Child Abduction Act 1984]).

If you have tried but been unable to communicate with the other parent about the trip abroad you are not committing an offence. If the child lives with you and the other parent is being unreasonable in refusing to consent, you would not be committing a criminal offence, but it should be obvious that different people might have different views about what is and is not unreasonable and you need to be very careful.

If there is any doubt, the safest course of action is to make an application to the court for permission. Otherwise you could be prevented from going away because the other parent has applied for an urgent order saying you must not remove the child, or you may be forced to come back home as a result of Hague Convention proceedings being started in the country you have gone to. And to cap it all off, when you come back you may find yourself arrested for child abduction.

If you want to take your child abroad for a holiday and the other parent does not agree, or if you cannot agree how you should sort out the disruption in the other parent's time with the child, or if you want to take your child to live abroad with you see Chapters 17 and 18.

If you are worried that your ex may be about to abduct your children or has already done so you should seek legal advice urgently, explaining that it cannot wait. If you cannot get an immediate appointment go to court taking all the information you can and ask for an urgent appointment before a Judge, and ask the Judge to make whatever orders he sees fit.

If one parent moves away with a child to somewhere else in the country and the other parent does not know where they have gone, the court can make orders under the Family Law Act 1986 [FLA 1986] to find out where a child has been taken so that it can then decide what should happen in the long term. The orders are:

- Disclosure of the whereabouts of a child [s33 FLA 1986].

- Recovery of a child [s34 FLA 1986].

Under s33 FLA 1986 the court can make an order telling any person that they must tell the court where the child is, or provide any information that might help work out where the child is.

If taking the child away was a breach of a child arrangements order (for example the child is supposed to be living with the parent left behind) OR if the court has ordered the person to return the child or bring the child to court and they have not done so, the court can make an order to recover the child. You can only ask for an order for recovery of the child if the other parent knows about the order to return the child and has ignored it.

When the court makes an order for recovery this tells the Police or an officer of the court that they can take a child by force if necessary and return them to where they are supposed to be.

17.   Cases Relating To Children

This chapter is the longest chapter in the whole book. It's difficult to separate out the different types of issues relating to arrangements for children into different chapters, and although I have separated the chapter into sections it is sensible to read the whole lot if you are involved in a case concerning your children. Don't skim read it. Read it thoroughly and if you are losing focus take a break and come back to it.

This chapter assumes that the Family Court in England & Wales has jurisdiction (is allowed) to make orders about the children because the family are based here. If your family situation is complicated by a history of one or both parents or the children living abroad or being taken abroad you should check Chapter 18 to ensure that there are no jurisdictional issues.

17.1   Private law orders

This chapter covers the following types of private law orders:

- **Parental responsibility order** (giving a Father or carer legal rights and responsibility for a child - mums automatically have parental responsibility)

- **'Section 8' orders** [s8 CA] - there are three types:

  - Child arrangements order (setting out when a child will see or have contact with a particular person, usually a parent, and / or where a child will live including any shared arrangement)

  - Specific issue order (deciding a particular point of dispute about a child's upbringing such as where a child should be schooled or whether he should be circumcised)

  - Prohibited steps order (a sort of injunction that stops a person doing something to or with a child, for example saying a parent must not remove a child from his school or take them abroad)

- **Activity directions and conditions** [s11A-11P]

- **Family assistance order** [s16 CA]

- **Monitoring order** [s11H CA]

- **Change of name** [s13 CA]

- 'Barring orders' [s91(14)]

The following orders are dealt with in other chapters:

- **Enforcement orders** [s11A-11P] - Chapter 19

- **Removal from the jurisdiction** [s13 CA] and other things to do with moving with children or taking them abroad - Chapter 18

- **Financial orders regarding children** [s15 and Schedule 1 CA] - Chapter 15, but also see Chapter 12 for orders under the MCA.

17.2 Basic procedure

It is a legal requirement for a person starting an application for a private law order about a child to attend a Mediation Information and Assessment Meeting [MIAM] before starting a case [PD 3A]. There are exceptions to this, for example urgency or where there is evidence of domestic violence. Further details of this scheme are set out in Chapter 8, and more information about alternatives to court including mediation is in Chapter 2. You should carefully read that information before attempting to start a case. You cannot skip this stage unless one of the exceptions applies.

Part 12 of the Family Proceedings Rules 2010 (FPR) deals with applications about children, but other parts of the rules are also relevant sometimes. PD 12B (Child Arrangements Programme) and 12J (Child Arrangements and Contact Orders: Domestic Violence and Harm) may also be relevant. PD12B sets out the basic procedure for applications relating to contact and living arrangements.

If you need permission from the court to make an application you must use form C2 and your application will be dealt with under Part 18 FPR (see Chapter 20). Parents usually don't need permission, but see s10 CA and Chapter 20 for more details of where permission is required.

You must fill in form C100 to start an application for an order under s8 CA and form C1 for an application for parental responsibility. Other forms are set out in Practice Direction 5A.

FPR Rule 12.3 tells you who must be a Respondent to the application (who the parties to the case are). Usually this is just the parents, but if the child is living apart from either parent this will usually include whoever they are living with. Anyone with parental responsibility (PR) is entitled to be a party to proceedings about a child where they ask [Rule 12.3(2)] and they should be told about the case so they can decide whether to play any part in it.

Once your application has been issued the court will tell the other party / parties that the application has been issued but you must send a copy of it to them yourself [Rules 12.7 & 12.8 FPR].

The case will then broadly follow the process set out in PD12B, the Child Arrangements Programme (CAP).

Once the court has the application it will ask CAFCASS to carry out basic safeguarding checks with the Police and social services about the Applicant and Respondents and any children (the role of CAFCASS is outlined in Chapter 3 and set out in more detail in the rest of this chapter), and if practical by speaking to each of you by telephone. The purpose of these checks is not to make any recommendations or decisions about the case but simply to establish if there are any particular safety or risk issues that the court will need to consider at the first hearing, so the telephone call is likely to be brief and quite focused rather than an opportunity for you to go through the whole history. CAFCASS will report this information back to the court before the first hearing (unless the first hearing is an urgent one organised at short notice). CAFCASS will usually give you a copy of that information before or at the first hearing, or you can ask the Judge to direct it if they do not [see PD 12B, paragraph 14.13 of the Child Arrangements Programme]. This is usually called a safeguarding letter or 'Schedule 2' letter.

CAFCASS will also carry out a risk assessment if they are worried about anything that comes out of those checks or which comes up later on [s16A CA, PD 12L].

When the case is issued the court will decide by looking at the paperwork what level of Judge should handle the case and whether the case requires any particular directions to be made - for example if the parties haven't been to a MIAM the court might say that they have to do so before the case can proceed. The court will send you a copy of any order made at this stage. There is Guidance on Allocation [see Justice or FLBA Guidance Locator] which sets out what sort of cases should be dealt with by different levels of Judge. Most straightforward cases about child arrangements orders will be dealt with by Lay Justices, but cases involving complexity may be allocated to a more senior Judge. Once allocated the court will try and ensure that the same Judge deals with your case throughout but this is not always possible, and it can sometimes be necessary to reallocate a case (for example where it becomes more complex than is first thought).

If you are the Respondent to an application you will be sent some forms along with the application itself. You must fill in and return those forms within 14 days of receiving them [Rule 12.32 FPR]. If the matter is urgent you may not have time to do this before the first hearing. One form you should be sent is a C1A, and it asks about past harm or abuse to you or the children. It's important that you fill this in fully if it applies to you.

Unless there is an urgent issue that can't wait, the first hearing will be listed about five or six weeks after the application is issued, to allow time for the checks above to be carried out. You should be notified of the date at least ten working days in advance, although sometimes this will be shorter.

The first hearing is called an FHDRA (First Hearing Dispute Resolution Appointment) - if you hear people referring to a 'Federer' they mean a FHDRA rather than a tennis player! At the FHDRA the court will try and work out what the case is really about and will try to find a way of sorting it out by agreement. There is usually a CAFCASS officer at the FHDRA who will try to help you and the court sort the case out by agreement or make suggestions about how it might be sorted out or about what needs to happen next. They might want to talk to you and your partner (together or separately) before you go into court, and this can mean that you will need to be at court for a while. The court will look at whether there is any safety issue arising from the basic checks that CAFCASS have carried out.

One of the things the court will consider at this stage is whether or not there is a significant and important factual dispute about risk or harm that needs to be sorted out before long term decisions can be made. If this is the case the court might want to make directions in preparation for a fact finding hearing (see below).

The court will also consider at this stage whether it needs any further assistance from CAFCASS or social services in the form of a report.

In a standard case the court will make directions for any further evidence to be filed, including reports, and then list the case for a Dispute Resolution Hearing (DRA) to take place once everyone has seen that material. A DRA is another short hearing at which the court will try and resolve matters, but if it cannot be resolved the court will list a Final Hearing, which may be longer because there may need to be some evidence.

Of course, depending on the needs of the case this standard process may need to be varied.

17.3 Other things you need to know about court procedure

If the Respondent does not attend a hearing the court can carry on anyway as long as the court is satisfied that they have had reasonable warning about the hearing and that the case needs to proceed [Rule 12.14(6) FPR].

If the Applicant doesn't attend a hearing the court can refuse the application or go ahead with the hearing (as long as the court thinks it has enough evidence to do this) [Rule 12.14(7) FPR].

If nobody comes to a hearing the court can refuse the application [Rule 12.14(8) FPR].

These rules about going ahead when not everybody is at court don't apply to hearings where the court is going to be considering whether to make enforcement orders or activity directions orders and the evidence is not complete.

The general rule is that you must not file any witness statement or evidence which has not been asked for by the court [Rule 12.19 FPR]. If you want to file anything you must ask the court to direct that you should be allowed.

You must not have your child examined or assessed for the purposes of producing an expert report for the court case unless the court has first given you permission [Rule 12.20 FPR].

The points above relate to particularly to applications about children but there is more about general court procedure in Chapter 8.

17.4   Parental responsibility

When the CA was first created PR was thought of as mainly for biological parents: one mum one dad, but in certain circumstances it can be awarded to other types of parents or to carers and might be held by one, two or more people at the same time.

What actually is PR?

In truth even lawyers struggle to define PR. It is often said to be 'that bundle of rights and responsibilities that go with being a parent', whatever that means!

If you are the Father of a child you are legally *responsible* for a child even if you have no PR and even if you have no contact with them. With very few exceptions, you will be required to pay child maintenance, subject to your income, whether you have PR or not (unless the children live with you of course).

A parent or other person with PR is entitled to be consulted and informed about important life decisions such as:

- significant medical treatment and medical information on request

- choice of school and progress at school and information from school

- where a child lives

- their name

- their religious upbringing

- taking them abroad

PR does not entitle a parent to interfere in the day to day arrangements that the other parent has made for a child whilst they are living with them. This means that PR does not entitle a parent to interfere in things like:

- contents of lunchbox or diet

- daily routine - baths, mealtimes etc

- hygiene and grooming

- arrangements for after school activities

This doesn't mean that parents should not be encouraged to discuss what they think is appropriate and best for their children on a day to day level, or to raise concerns with one another, and it doesn't mean that these are not things that can be raised with the court when it is considering for example an application about child arrangements. But whether or not somebody has PR doesn't make any difference to these things.

On a day to day basis the biggest impact for Fathers of obtaining PR is that the school will be under a duty to keep you informed of how your child is doing at school, invite you to parents evening (possibly a separate time from your ex if necessary), to sports day, plays etc., and send you general information about the school (school reports, tell you about photos etc.). Schools sometimes struggle to understand the legal position, so you may need to write to the school explaining that you have PR and you would like them please to send a copy of everything that goes home to both parents.

A Father with PR will also be able to deal with any medical issues that arise during contact or whilst on holiday, although in practice routine medical matters are not normally obstructed by a lack of PR. Do not forget that any Father with PR must consult with the Mother about any decisions that he is making in the same way that she must consult with him.

If both parents have PR and cannot agree on schools the court will have to decide. Similarly, if both parents have PR and one objects to the other taking the children abroad, the court will have to be asked to decide (although a parent with a child arrangements order that names them as a person with whom the child is to live can take a child abroad for up to a month even without consent [s13 CA]).

PR becomes important where social services are involved with a family because although he should be consulted a Father might get excluded if he has not got PR. He does not technically have a say in decisions being made about children without PR.

Who has it?

- All Mothers have parental responsibility (PR).

- If the Mother was married at the time of birth her husband will have PR whether or not he is on the birth certificate.

- If the parents were unmarried at the time of birth but the child was born on or after 1 December 2003 and the Father's name is on the birth certificate he will have PR.

- If the parents were unmarried and the Father is not on the birth certificate he will not have PR unless the parents both sign a PR agreement and lodge it with the court, or the court grants him PR by making an order.

- If the parents were unmarried at the time of the birth but the child was born before 1 December 2003 the Father will not have PR unless the parents both sign a PR agreement and lodge it with the court, or the court grants him PR by making an order. The court must make a PR order to the Father where it makes a child arrangements order saying that the child should live with him for at least some of the time [s12(4) CA]. Once granted to a Father this PR will continue even if the child arrangements order does not.

- A Father who has been named as a person with whom the child should live in a residence order made before 22 April 2014 will have PR even if the order is no longer in force or has been varied to a child arrangements order [s4 CA].

- A second female parent (i.e. the female partner of a biological mother, where the conception falls under HFEA 2008) will either automatically have PR [s2(1A) CA] or can acquire PR for a child in the same ways as an unmarried father (i.e. through birth certificate, PR agreement with the other parent or by court order) [s4ZA CA]. See Chapter 20 for more on this sort of scenario.

- The civil partner or spouse of a parent with PR (i.e. a step-parent) can obtain PR for a child by agreement of all of the parents with PR or by court order [s4A CA].

- The same sex spouse or civil partner of a parent who for some reason does not qualify under HFEA could acquire PR through the step-parent route, or through a child arrangements order naming them as a person with whom the child should live.

- The same sex partner of a parent who is neither married or in civil partnership, and who for some reason does not qualify under HFEA can only acquire PR through a child arrangements order naming them as a person with whom the child should live (or through adoption). The PR will only last as long as the child arrangements order continues to name them as a person with whom the child should live.

- Where a court makes a child arrangements order that names a person as someone a child should spend time with or have contact with (but not live with) the court has to consider whether it would be appropriate to grant PR under s4 or 4ZA CA, and the court can also grant PR to a non-parent who is named as someone with whom the child should have contact if it thinks that is appropriate. If granted that PR will continue for as long as the child arrangements order continues to name them.

I'm a dad - will the court grant me PR?

Almost certainly. If it is not agreed you may find there is a frustrating delay, but it is almost inevitable in the long run.

Although it can be refused the kinds of cases where this happens are the exception rather than the rule. These are generally the kinds of cases where the court is concerned that you would abuse PR to undermine the Mother caring for the children or behave in an oppressive interfering way.

Before the court will grant PR it must consider the Father's attachment and commitment to the child, and his motivation for the application.

As of 22 April 2014 the court must consider whether to grant a Father PR whenever it makes a child arrangements order which names a Father as someone who is to have contact or spend time with the child (i.e. it can still make a PR order even if you are only having contact).

If the court makes an order saying the child should *live with* the Father it MUST make a parental responsibility order (you should remind the court to actually do this - you don't get the PR automatically, the court must make a separate order saying you have PR for it to be effective).

I'm a mum - and I'm worried about PR being granted to my child's dad

Don't be. Many mums worry about PR being abused, but it is not a licence to interfere in your life. Read the section below on what PR means - you will probably feel better about PR when you understand it.

Be realistic. PR will almost certainly be granted. You may be able to delay it, but probably won't be able to prevent it ultimately.

Can PR be removed?

- A Mother's PR cannot be removed except by adoption.

- A Father who has automatic PR (through marriage) cannot have his PR removed except by adoption.

- A Father who has acquired PR through a PR order, birth certificate or a residence or child arrangements order saying the child should live with him can have his PR revoked by the court. If the residence /child arrangements order is still in force the PR cannot be revoked by the court.

- A person who is not a parent but who has PR through a residence order or child arrangements order saying the child should live with them will only have PR for so long as the residence / child arrangements order remains in place.

- A second female parent who has acquired PR through s4ZA is in the same position as an unmarried father who has acquired PR.

- Step-parent PR under s4A can only be removed by the court.

So, in most cases once granted PR cannot be removed. And even where that is possible, it is very rare. An example is the case of *D (A Child)* [2014] EWCA Civ 315, where PR was removed from a father who had convictions for sexual abused of children. Even though he removed PR, Lord Justice Ryder said in *D (A Child)* [2014] when giving judgment that:

> 'Nothing I have said in this judgment should be construed to
> suggest that it has become or should become easier to remove an
> unmarried father's parental responsibility. I would strongly resist

> *any move in that direction. It is vitally important to encourage the exercise of parental responsibility by fathers. Children have a right to that benefit.'*

Another example of the sort of case where this has happened is when a Father had been guilty of very serious violence against the Mother of the children, leaving her with Post Traumatic Stress Disorder, and was serving a sentence of imprisonment for GBH against her (*A v D (Parental Responsibility)* [2013] EWHC 2963 (Fam)).

There have been only a handful of reported cases of removal of PR since the CA came into force in 1991 including these two, which should give you an idea of how unusual it is for this step to be taken.

A parent's PR will be heavily restricted but not removed if a special guardianship order or care order is in place (see Chapter 20).

17.5 Some important legal points about parental responsibility

In cases where the court has to decide whether it should grant PR the Judge will consider all the circumstances, but is likely to look in particular at:

- The degree of commitment the Father (or other person) has demonstrated,

- The degree of attachment between the Father (or other person) and child,

- The Father's (or other person's) motivation for the application (for example, is it just to control or get at the Mother?).

Conditions can be placed on PR if necessary, but this is quite unusual (*Re D (Contact and PR: Lesbian Mothers and Known Father) (No 2)* [2006] EWHC 2 (Fam)).

PR cannot be suspended by the court, although the court can delay granting PR by adjourning the application (*Re G (Parental Responsibility Order)* [2006] EWCA Civ 745).

Same sex couples

The non-biological female parent of a child of a same sex couple can acquire PR and be recognised as a legal parent in a number of ways, depending on whether the child was conceived by a known or unknown donor, via a clinic or not [s4ZA]. The criteria for a woman in a same sex relationship to be treated as the second parent of the child alongside the biological mother are set out in s43 HFEA.

If the woman is not eligible to be recognised as a full parent for one reason or another they can either adopt the child or can acquire PR via a child arrangements order but this latter option leaves them vulnerable upon separation - if the separation means it is not viable for them both to share residence the order may be discharged leaving them without legal status.

There is more information in Chapter 20 about assisted conception and same sex couples.

17.6   Specific issue orders and prohibited steps orders

These are dealt with next because they are relatively easy to describe.

A specific issue order can deal with any number of things that parents cannot agree about a child's upbringing. Typically though it will be about one of the following things:

- Religious observance and education. For example, should a child be circumcised, be taught Arabic, be christened or go to the synagogue?

- What school they should go to.

- Medical treatment. For example, should the child have the MMR or some other inoculation?

- To return a child's passport to the other parent or their solicitor or to the court.

The court can make a prohibited steps order (a sort of injunction) telling a parent or other person that they must not do something relating to a child. This can cover a number of things but typically it will be about one of the following:

- Not to go to the child's school or the venue for some other regular activity or to hang around outside.

- Not to remove the child from the care or control of the parent they live with or any child-minder or school etc they have been left with.

- Not to approach the child in the street or attempt to pass messages to them.

- Not to apply for a passport for the child.

- Not to remove the child from the jurisdiction of the court.

- Not to permit the child to sleep or reside at a particular address or to change their address without notifying the court.

- Not to permit the child to come into contact with a particular person or to engage in a particular dangerous or inappropriate activity.

You will see from this list that prohibited steps orders are most often used where there is a concern that the child might be taken from their home or school, that they might be abducted or moved to an address where they cannot be found. Generally, a parent is entitled to know where the children are living, but if there are allegations of domestic violence it is common for the victim or alleged victim to keep their address confidential. This is allowed by the court, but the parent must lodge their address with the court and keep the court up to date (form C8). You can ask the court to order this if there is a concern that nobody knows the address and the other parent might move to avoid contact.

If you are asking for a prohibited steps order to be made you should ask the court to attach a penal notice so that it can be enforced straight away if it is broken (see Chapter 23 which explains penal notices and enforcement). The court might say 'No' the first time round, but if there is a breach of the order you must apply back to court, ask the Judge to attach a penal notice and ask the court to make arrangements for the amended order to be served on the other person again.

Prohibited steps orders tend to crop up alongside applications for other s8 orders, so read the information below about child arrangements orders.

17.7 Child arrangements orders

A child arrangements order settles the arrangements for who a child should live with and when, and setting out who they should spend time with (most often the other parent). A child arrangements order can do one or both of these things.

Until 22 April 2014 the court made contact and residence orders instead. If there is a contact or residence order in place relating to your children it will automatically be treated as if it were a child arrangements order in the same terms. You do not need to do anything. The order is still valid.

When the court makes a child arrangements order naming who the child should live with the person who is named will gain PR if they do not already have it [s12 CA]. If the person who gains PR in this way is the Father the court should be specifically asked to make a separate PR order. Although non-parents will only keep PR for as long as the child arrangements order continues to name them a Father who has gained PR in this way keeps it, and the order should make this clear.

What is the difference between child arrangements orders and contact and residence?

There is very little difference in legal terms between the old and new orders - they do largely the same things but have different names.

The idea behind the changes was to send a signal to Judges, lawyers - and parents - that labels and formulas don't matter as much as the arrangements being a good fit for the child in question.

Where the court makes a child arrangements order saying that a child will live partly with one parent and partly with the other the order is likely to say when the child is to live with each parent, but the order does not need to divide a child's time equally or in any particular pattern. Instead the order will set out the arrangements that the court thinks or the parties agree are best for the children. This might be one week with each parent in turn for some families, a three night / four night pattern for another, or a week nights / weekends arrangement for another. The same applies to orders that describe time spent or contact - there is no standard formula, although some arrangements are tried and tested and fit well around a 'standard' school and work life.

Previously some parents spent a lot of time and energy arguing about whether the arrangements for their children should be described as 'shared residence' or residence and contact, or worrying about whether or not their equal status was properly reflected in the division of time between the two parents.

The court can make an order for a child to live with two adults in the same household (for example parent and new partner or both the paternal grandparents). More often than not though a child arrangements order in these circumstances will name only the person who is the blood relative or main carer. There is generally no need for it to name both and the award of PR to a step-parent in this way can be controversial or upsetting for the parent the child does not live with. However, see above for step-parent PR.

How long does a child arrangements order last?

A court can't make a child arrangements order for a child who is already 16 unless there are exceptional circumstances. But if an order is made before a child is 16 how long does it last? Actually, the CA is a bit unclear in this area. A child arrangements order that is just about contact will usually last until a child is 16, whilst one which says where a child will live will usually continue until they are 18. In practice this doesn't matter much in most cases, but sometimes it crops up. See my blog post 'How long does a child arrangements order last?' (and comments) on Pink Tape for a discussion of the technical confusion in this area.

How cases about child arrangements tend to progress - what to expect

Straightforward cases will follow the CAP Child Arrangements Programme in PD12B set out above. The CAP is designed to be flexible though, so your case may not follow the process exactly as described.

Sometimes when cases first come to court money is at the root of the dispute. Often the parent who is looking after the children may be unhappy that they are not receiving any financial help to look after the child. Although many parents often make a link between payment of maintenance and contact the law sees them as totally separate and it is important to recognise this from the start. The court will not be interested in either of you saying 'he can see the child if he pays some maintenance' or 'I'm not paying maintenance unless I see my child'. But if you are a parent seeking contact, common sense says that it will probably help to rebuild bridges if you either explain why you can't pay maintenance, or pay at least some maintenance if you can. Likewise, if you are a parent caring for a child, common sense tells you that you are unlikely to improve your chances of getting some financial support from your ex if you simply stop contact - and the court won't get involved in the child support issue because it is not allowed to deal with things that are the responsibility of the CMS. Don't try and use the court process to air your grievances about money. Save your energy for sorting out the contact dispute.

Applications for contact are rarely sorted out in one go. Often contact may need to be restricted whilst the court gathers evidence or whilst a long enough slot for the Judge to hear all the evidence is obtained. The court can make short term (interim) orders before reaching any final decision [s11 CA].

Commonly, if the allegations or concerns that are being raised can be worked around, the court will be able to make some order, but may need to resolve other more tricky issues at subsequent hearings. For example, if it is said that a Father is a dangerous or disqualified driver and that this puts the children at risk, the court can still order contact as long as the Father confirms that he agrees (or the court orders) that he must use only public transport or get a friend or named person to drive him.

Even though a hearing may be described as a final hearing the court may decide that it cannot resolve everything and the case will need to come back again for another hearing in the future. Although Judges are encouraged to try and re-solve cases as quickly as possible so that the parties do not get stuck in court for years on end, some cases do need a staged approach. Depending on the type of case and the things which are being raised as objections to contact progressing this can be a frustrating process.

17.8 Allegations of domestic violence

Where allegations of domestic violence or abuse of a child are made (typically but not always by the parent with whom the child is living) the court may need to hold a special 'fact finding' hearing when it will listen to the evidence and decide if the allegations are true. This type of hearing is dealt with at Chapter 21 - if there are allegations of this kind in your case you should read that chapter and PD 12J.

During that period whilst allegations are being pursued but before the court has been able to decide whether they are true, the case will be stuck in a sort of limbo - generally contact is likely to tick over but not significantly progress whilst this is outstanding. If contact has stopped it might not be realistic to expect it to start up again until after the fact finding hearing if the allegations are serious. Where allegations of violence are made against the parent with whom the child is living the court is unlikely to move them until it has heard the evidence and made findings unless there is very clear evidence of an immediate risk (see below under 'Arrangements for where the children should live').

The court will not usually order a welfare report (see below) until any finding of fact has been dealt with. This is because it is sometimes impossible to make recommendations without knowing who is telling the truth about things like violence that could affect what is best for the child. A CAFCASS Officer's recommendations, like a Judge's decisions, must be based on evidence and proven facts not assumptions. However, it is becoming more common for a Judge to order a report that makes recommendations on an 'either or' basis. So, if the allegations are found true I recommend x, but if they are not I recommend y. That way it is sometimes possible to avoid a two stage hearing process and get a decision quicker. But it won't work well in all cases and it doesn't allow for any risk assessment taking into account a perpetrator's reaction to findings made against them.

The court might decide a fact finding hearing is not needed if:

- the allegations of violence or abuse wouldn't significantly affect the outcome even if they were true, or

- the bulk of the allegations are admitted (the admissions will need to be recorded, usually on the court order), or

- the person the allegations are about has criminal convictions for domestic violence against the person making the allegations. These convictions can't be challenged in the Family Court so if they are quite similar to the allegations made in the Family Court the Judge might not also need to hear evidence about lots of other detailed allegations.

A party cannot rely upon allegations of domestic violence unless they have been proved by admission, conviction or through a fact finding hearing. There is no half way house - if someone wants to rely on allegations of domestic violence and they are not prepared to go through a fact finding hearing the court will treat the allegations as if they did not happen, or just put them to one side if they aren't relevant to the decision (for example, if the most recent incident was a long time ago before the children were born or where things have moved on since). The only time the court will treat unproven allegations as if they might have happened is whilst the preparations for the fact finding hearing are being made. If an allegation is admitted that can be relied upon - the admission should be recorded clearly on the court order. If there is a conviction there is no need to 'prove' the allegation as the criminal court has done that job already.

If there has been a fact finding hearing the court will progress the case on the basis of what it has decided at that hearing. So, if the Judge finds the allegations were true that is that. And if the Judge has not made the findings the court will proceed on the basis that the things never happened. Neither party is entitled to keep challenging those decisions about the facts except in very limited circumstances (see Chapter 25).

Because the decisions the court makes about factual disputes are once and for all it is important to get the decision right. This means that cases must be properly prepared before the Judge hears the evidence and this means that allegations of domestic violence often cause delay in contact applications.

17.9 Welfare stage

Once the court has dealt with any fact finding exercise it can move on to the welfare stage of the case, and everyone in the case will have a known factual background to work with. Obviously if it hasn't been necessary to hold a fact finding hearing the court will either be able to resolve the matter swiftly at the first hearing or proceed directly to consider welfare much earlier on.

Often the person applying for contact (or for the child to live with them) is the person that is said to have behaved inappropriately in the past. Depending on the nature or degree of any violence that has taken place between parents and depending on the risk that it might happen again (the court will look at things like whether or not a violent parent can take responsibility for what has happened or whether they have undertaken anger management or therapy), a court may decide to order supervised contact, contact where the parents use a third party to avoid coming into contact with each other, or more unusually only indirect contact (letters, cards, emails etc.) or exceptionally no contact at all.

If the court has heard all the evidence and rejected the allegations of violence the case can progress. The court may take a more cynical view in future of attempts to frustrate or slow down the progress of contact coming from a parent who has made unsubstantiated allegations in the past.

Case law and PD 12J all say that the case should continue to be dealt with by the same Judge that heard the fact finding hearing if at all possible.

17.10 What happens if there are admissions or findings?

Depending on how serious the findings are the court might want to ask CAFCASS to report on the case and recommend what is in the best interests of the children or to order a risk assessment. The court could say that the person who has been violent has to go on a course or have some treatment before contact could be considered. In less serious cases it may just be that the findings will affect how handover is organised.

When the court moves on to this second welfare stage of the case it will not only look at the incidents it has decided have taken place, and the conduct of both parents towards each other and towards the child, but will also look at:

(a) the effect of the domestic violence or abuse on the child and on the arrangements for where the child is living;

(b) the effect of the domestic violence or abuse on the child and its effect on the child's relationship with the parents;

(c) whether the applicant parent is motivated by a desire to promote the best interests of the child or is using the process to continue a process of violence, abuse, intimidation or harassment or controlling or coercive behaviour against the other parent;

(d) the likely behaviour during contact of the parent against whom findings are made and its effect on the child;

(e) the capacity of the parents to appreciate the effect of past violence or abuse and the potential for future violence or abuse. [Pa 37 PD 12J]

The court must also consider whether or not the person who has been violent or abusive should be required to obtain advice or treatment prior to the making of any order [pa 33 PD 12J].

The court will often look at the case of *Re L & Others (Contact: Domestic Violence)* [2000] EWCA Civ 194 when thinking about how matters should progress. In *Re L* some very experienced children experts (Dr Sturge and Dr Glaser) made recommendations to the court about how to deal with contact where there is a history of violence and the list above is drawn partly from that guidance. So, if you hear the Judge or lawyers talking about '*Re L*' this is what they mean. You can find it on BAILII.

The court will also look more generally at the welfare checklist in deciding what to do, but it may ask for other professionals to help, by offering their opinion or expertise.

There is a lot of useful information about how the court will deal with things in PD 12J.

17.11 Contact

Almost all cases about children involve some issue around contact so this chapter will spend quite a bit of time on it. Although the court no longer makes 'contact orders' a child arrangements order can say what contact a child should have with their family.

How much contact?

The reality of any divorce or separation is that both parents will probably spend less time with the children than they did before. This is basic maths as a result of the fact that you will most likely not both be spending time with the children *at the same time*. Do not expect things to be the same. Children have the same amount of love and the same amount of time to give to you both but now they have to divvy it up between you.

The important thing is the quality of the contact. Of course if your contact is heavily restricted it will impact on the quality, because you will be limited as to what you can do and how enjoyable you can make it.

For most families it is not practical to divide a child's time so that they are spending exactly or even roughly equal amounts of time with each parent. It might be possible whilst they are of pre-school age, but once kids are at school, and particularly as they get older and begin to fill their weeks with extra-curricular activities, it is quite a conundrum to work out. And although views differ, some people who work with children think that having two homes can be quite difficult for pre-school children to understand and manage.

It is not uncommon for a parent seeking contact to come to court with a detailed analysis of exactly what percentage of the time the children will be spending with each parent, or who has the most number of nights with the children. Please don't do this. The court will not reduce its decision to a mathematical exercise and arguing that having the kids only 40% of time is unfair will simply irritate the Judge and demonstrate that you have missed the points made above. Kids don't care how the percentages work out, they just want to spend time regularly with both of you without having to worry about you arguing or saying negative things about one another. Having fun for 20% of the time is far more valuable than having a miserable 50%. You will still be 100% their parent even if you don't have 50% of their time.

For a significant number of families the natural way to divide things up is for the children to be based with one parent in the school week and for the parents to share the weekends and holidays between them. Unless you live around the corner from one another it can be complicated, unsettling and exhausting to have the kids moving from one home to the other throughout the school week. Looked at from one perspective the parent with whom the children spend the weekdays will get much of the drudgery, whilst the other parent can focus on fun weekend activities. Looked at from another perspective many parents long to be a part of that daily routine of homework and baths and getting up for school, and want to be more than a weekend entertainer or treat giver. It's a balance and there is no one right answer.

What is workable may be significantly affected by finances, the geography of where you live, working hours and other commitments. But probably the most commonplace arrangement that is agreed by parents or ordered by the courts is something along these lines:

- Children have main base with one parent,

- The children spend every other weekend with the other parent, most often from Friday after school to Monday morning at school,

- The children spend a night each week or every other week with the other parent, most often a Wednesday (so there isn't too big a gap between contacts),

- The children spend half the holidays with each parent, usually alternating Christmas, New Years, birthdays etc.,

This last type of arrangement sometimes used to be described as shared residence, although most often it was described as residence and contact. Now that the courts are making child arrangements orders this sort of arrangement is most likely to be described as 'living with' one parent and 'spending time' with the other, but it might be described as 'living with' each of you for specified times (some people say 'shared living with' order, but that doesn't exactly trip off the tongue!). Frankly it makes absolutely no difference (except for as described above for PR, and in cases where there might be foreign travel that you don't agree about - see Chapter 18).

This is not offered as a solution that will necessarily be right for you, but might help you to put into context the needs of your own family. Parents sometimes think this type of arrangement is a standard order that is dished out to all families by the courts - this is not the case. It is just what seems to be the most reasonable and realistic balance for a lot of families, but Judges will be quite prepared to make different orders depending on what is right for your family. For families where both parents live very close together and communication is tolerable much more flexible or creative solutions can work well. And of course, what is right and practical for one family now may change a lot as the children get older, and as schools, jobs and activities change etc.

Restrictions on contact

It is not uncommon for a parent to say that the children should only be able to have contact with the other parent under supervision because there is some risk or concern. This might be because of domestic violence as above, and / or because of drug or alcohol abuse, mental health problems, because the parent has a history of saying inappropriate things to the child or simply because they have little practical experience of things like changing nappies or of managing children's difficult behaviour, or because they are irresponsible or are likely to bring the children into contact with inappropriate adults. Of course it might be that these things are said without justification.

It is rare for the courts to accept that there should be no contact at all for anything other than a very short period of time. The starting point will be that there should be some contact even if it needs to be somehow restricted or monitored. An order refusing all direct contact between parent and child engages Article 8 of the European Convention on Human Rights this means that it can only be made if the order is necessary and proportionate.

A recent example of a case that reiterates that stopping all contact and giving up is really a last resort is *Re W (Direct Contact)* [2012] EWCA Civ 999. In that case the court said that contact should not be stopped unless it is the last resort for the Judge and until the Judge has grappled with all the alternatives that were open to him. The question is whether that evidence is sufficiently cogent to justify such an exceptional outcome. This authority is a really useful one to refer the Judge to in a long running case where the court is considering bringing proceedings to a close.

However, none of this means that the court must or will order *unsafe* contact. Supervision or monitoring can take various forms. It might involve supervision by a professional including in a contact centre, or simply reaching an agreement that a trusted friend or family member will be present throughout and will alert the other parent or stop the contact if there are any problems.

Sometimes a parent will want to restrict where the contact takes place, for example that it will have to be in a contact centre, or in the home of the parent or grandparents, sometimes that it must not be in the home of the other parent if the home is thought to be unsuitable.

Transport, handover and communication

Very often where there are allegations of domestic violence, abuse or harassment (whether they are true or not) it will be sensible to make arrangements for handing the children between the parents that limit the opportunities for conflict or for further allegations to be made, and will protect the children from witnessing arguments or upset. This protects both the children, and both parents, either from abuse or from false allegations.

If there are objections to one parent knowing the other parent's address (see prohibited steps order / specific issue order above) or if a non-molestation or occupation order prevents one parent going to the children's address, handover may need to be away from the home. Alternatively a non-molestation order can be varied to say that the person must not go to the house except for the purposes of contact, but this can get rather messy and confusing and can lead to allegations that the parent has gone to the home when they should not have done.

Common ways to deal with this type of issue are:

- Hand over at a contact centre or public place such as a train station, supermarket or shopping area - anywhere where there are lots of people around. Don't worry too much about whether or not there is CCTV - this can be reassuring for some parents (it protects against bad behaviour and false allegations) but the reality is that if there is an incident or allegation the tapes will be very hard to get hold of and may well have been wiped by the time they are requested for the court.

- Agree a neutral or trusted person that can drop off and collect the children

- Make arrangements for one parent to let the other know when they are outside the house (text, beep horn etc.) and the parent at home can watch the children walk safely to the car from the doorway.

- Communicate by text message (each party will have a record which deters abuse and protects against false allegations).

- Use a communication / contact book. Buy a notebook in which you can record important things such as if a child has been ill, when they last had their medication or what parties or activities they must go to whilst with the other parent, what homework needs to be done, or requests to change dates or arrangements. It can pass between the parents at handovers avoiding the need for awkward or tense conversation. It is obviously better to talk to each other but if you can't do this without tension or confrontation this can be helpful.

- Use email. Operate a policy of sleeping on emails before you send them. If you aren't sure if it will be taken as provocative - don't send it.

There are online services for separated parents to use which combine some of these things electronically.

As a starting point the court will expect you to each share in the transport arrangements and costs of contact. However one parent may have to shoulder the burden of most or all the travel arrangements depending on finances and practicalities (for example if one parent doesn't drive and the buses make the journey longer than is appropriate for the kids). Some parents arrange for one to deliver and one to collect, others agree to meet half way.

A word about contact centres

Contact centres are a safe space which allow parents and children to have contact where otherwise it would not be possible. In some cases it might be said that contact will have to take place in a contact centre for the foreseeable future (although it is far from an ideal long term solution), but in most cases it is a temporary measure whilst the court is gathering evidence to work out whether there is any risk and how contact should proceed in the longer term.

There are broadly two types of contact centre:

- The vast majority of contact centres offer what is called 'supported contact', which is different from 'supervised contact'. There will usually be a number of families in a communal space with a limited number of staff or experienced volunteers. There is an element of supervision in that staff or volunteers will keep an eye on all the families having contact and will intervene or assist if there is a major problem but there will be no individual supervision of each family, of what is being said etc. This type of contact centre will generally not provide a report on how contact has gone, although occasionally they may provide a log of attendance and times. This type of supported contact centre is generally free. They are sometimes in purpose built buildings, but more often in community spaces such as church halls or children's centres.

- A limited number of contact centres offer what can properly be described as 'supervised' contact. There is almost always a charge for this service (which can be quite high), although in some areas CAFCASS or other agencies fund a limited supervised service that they may be able to refer you to. If contact is supervised there will be one member of staff (possibly social work trained but certainly experienced in working with children) who will be monitoring the contact at all times. Usually this will take place in a space without other families present rather than in a communal environment. Where there is supervised contact there will often be a report writing service, although there may be an additional charge for this. Generally speaking a report will be a more or less detailed log of what has happened rather than an assessment per se, but it can be very helpful in trying to see how contact has worked or what areas of concern there may be.

Most contact centres are open only on Saturdays and for limited hours. Quite a few offer contact only on alternate weekends. Most offer no more than two or three hour long slots. A few are open on Sundays or weekdays.

Most will be happy to act as a handover point even if contact doesn't take place inside. Most contact centres will offer a staggered arrival arrangement so parents don't have to come face to face and so that difficult confrontations in front of the child can be avoided. Some have separate waiting rooms for each parent.

Each parent will usually need to fill in a form and attend an initial appointment (sometimes with the child) before the contact centre will accept the family. There is sometimes a wait for a place.

The National Association of Child Contact Centres provides lots of information about contact centres and what centres are available local to you. Their website now offers a facility for parents to self refer where no lawyers are involved.

Nobody wants their contact to be restricted to a contact centre, but it is important to keep contact going (or if it has stopped to get it going again as soon as possible) for three reasons:

- So that the children can maintain a relationship with both parents even if it is in less than ideal circumstances,

- So that if the court decides contact no longer needs to be in a contact centre it can move on more quickly without the need for reintroduction,

- So that the court and the other parent can be reassured that the person having contact can behave appropriately in contact and that it is beneficial to the children (whether by formal assessment or just by passage of time and lack of problems).

I'm applying for contact - what should I expect?

What you have to do if you are a parent wanting contact (you are most likely to be a dad) is park your frustration and be practical and realistic - don't vent your frustration. Work out what you need to demonstrate in order to knock down each barrier between you and the goal you want to achieve and work on a plan to do that. Read the chapter on evidence [Chapter 9] and think how it applies to your case.

Until the Judge has decided whether the allegations being raised are true he has a duty to protect the children just in case they are true. It is very frustrating when false or exaggerated allegations impact on contact which *you* know would be perfectly safe, but there is no point in wasting your energy on trying to alter this reality - until the Judge has heard the evidence he does not know *what* the situation is. Focus on ensuring that the contact you do have is good and make absolutely sure that you do not open yourself up to criticism on any other front. Focus on demonstrating that the allegations or criticisms made are not borne out, by gathering evidence, taking part in any assessment that is recommended and by coming back to court with regular and positive contact since the last hearing under your belt. Your other half may be obstructing the contact that has been ordered but you can't change that other than by raising it at court or by making an application for enforcement (which has its own difficulties - see Chapter 19). Focus on the things you can control - your own behaviour, your own evidence.

Even if false allegations are being made by your ex (especially if false allegations are being made against you) DO NOT try and have it out with them, and absolutely DO NOT do this when the children are around. It WILL be raised at the next hearing and it will be said that you have behaved inappropriately. This creates a bad impression and all you have achieved is a distraction from the strengths of your case. Try and anticipate the consequences of your actions. This goes for criticising your ex to friends, via Facebook, sending text messages or voicemails. It never helps. This is particularly important if the allegations are that you are harassing your ex, that you have been violent or that you have an anger management problem. It is very easy for someone to provoke you into behaving foolishly and then to use it as evidence to prove their point. Don't fall for it.

It is really important to keep up contact. You may have an objection in principle to a contact centre. Swallow your pride and do it anyway. Take the best contact that is available either by agreement or by asking the Judge to make an interim (temporary) order. The more contact you are having at the time the Judge makes a decision and the more stable it has been, the easier it is to progress it and the further on you will be able to get. The court will not expect a child to manage a massive change in routine all in one go, particularly if they are quite little. You want to at least have a rolling start by the time the court makes a decision.

It is tempting to respond to criticism or allegations with criticism and counter allegations. Unless your application is also an application for the children to live with you this is likely to be unhelpful and may even harm your case, because the court will see you as hostile. It is frustrating to be the only parent under the spotlight, but if you are asking for contact that is the way it is. Concentrate on demonstrating why there are no good reasons to restrict your contact, not on showing that your ex is worse than you.

The court will generally restrict the issues and the evidence to those which are relevant to the actual application, so if your application is for contact only, asking for a drug test of the other parent is likely to be knocked back - the court is not making decisions about the standard of their parenting, but about *your* contact. Going on and on about how rubbish the other parent is will just give the court the impression that you are more focused on the adult issues than the needs of the child. Rest assured this will then be used against you by the other party's lawyer. Rule: if the application is your application for contact, focus on showing yourself in a good light, not on showing your ex in a bad light. Make a conscious decision that you will run your case this way (you can say what you like to your close friends or family if you know they will not interfere but don't spread gossip and don't unload on someone who will be unable to stop themselves sticking their oar in). Check in with yourself every so often - are you sticking to this?

If you are the parent who is wanting to restrict or stop contact you also need to give yourself a reality check. It is very rare for the courts to say at the end of the case that there should be no contact at all. If you have genuine and serious reasons for wanting very restricted or no contact between your kids and their other parent you must be prepared for what might be a long haul, because the court will look exhaustively into this before finally concluding that what you propose is the right solution.

The court will take the view in almost all cases that children should have a relationship, including face to face contact with both parents, even if those parents are in some respects pretty hopeless - and the court will persevere to make sure this happens.

If you don't have what the court thinks are good enough reasons you are likely to find that the court makes contact orders in spite of your opposition, and the court can enforce those orders if you don't keep to them. This is dealt with below.

The court will take into account the impact of ongoing contact on you as the parent caring for the child, including any risk that contact will be so stressful for you that it will affect your ability to care for the child or will impact upon the child because you are so distraught. This is quite exceptional however, and there must be strong evidence that this would be the likely outcome of the contact the other parent is asking for.

What else can I do to move my contact on?

Sometimes it can help to offer formal promises, called undertakings, to the court about an issue that has been raised and that is stopping contact moving forwards. For example, you can promise not to drink alcohol for 24 hours prior to or during contact, promise not to drive, promise not to bring anyone to contact, or promise not to take the child to a particular place or do a particular activity.

These might not be long term solutions, but can be a way of making sure that contact can carry on until a longer term solution is found.

You should only give an undertaking to the court if you are sure you understand what you are promising and that you can stick to it. You must make sure that the wording of any promise is clear enough that you know exactly what you can and cannot do - if it is not absolutely clear ask the Judge or the other lawyer to clarify it or to change the wording so that it is clear. This is important because if you break the promise the court can send you to prison for up to two years, or can fine you.

There is more general information about undertakings in the section on Domestic violence (see Chapter 21) because undertakings are often very helpful in that type of case.

17.12 Arrangements for where the children should live (formerly 'residence')

Much of what has been said above under the heading of contact is applicable to applications about where children should live. Most often where there are allegations of domestic violence the child will be living with the parent who is alleging violence, and this means that until the fact finding hearing has been dealt with the only orders the court can really make are child arrangements orders for interim contact, and as previously noted these may need to be pretty restricted. Even where there is effective shared residence there may still need to be careful arrangements for handover and communication.

Even where a child is already living with one parent, and even where there is no current suggestion that this should change the parent with care will often ask the court to make a child arrangements order that confirms that the child should live with them.

The effect of a child arrangements order that sets out who a child should live with will be that although the Police have no automatic powers to enforce it, they are more likely to intervene to ensure that a child is returned home if they are called upon. If there is a risk or threat of child abduction notified by a parent named in a child arrangements order as the person the child lives with the Police can issue a port alert (which tells the authorities at all air and sea ports not to let the child leave the country). In addition it will be a criminal offence for the other parent to take the child out of the UK without the consent of the resident parent or the court. A child arrangements order naming a person as the person with whom the child lives authorises that person to take a child abroad for up to a month without seeking permission, but it does not stop the other parent asking the court to prevent this if they do not agree, so it is usually best to try and get agreement first and leave time for any objections to be raised.

Unlike contact cases (where a series of interim orders are often made) the court rarely makes interim orders in respect of where a child should live, except to confirm the existing position. The court will almost certainly not change residence on a 'without notice' basis, although it may list the case on short notice (perhaps a day or two) in order to quickly decide whether the issues are so serious that there does need to be a short term change to protect the child.

Whilst it is possible to make an application for an interim change of residence the court will only change a child's home if the concerns are very serious and very urgent and if the evidence is really quite strong. This is for two reasons:

- The court wants to avoid disrupting the child twice, once at the start of the case, and once at the end once the matter has been more carefully looked into,

- The Judge should try not make any decisions that pre-judge the final decision

This is commonly referred to as the 'status quo argument' and it really just means it's pretty tough to persuade the court to change where a child lives on an interim basis. When making interim orders the court should make orders to hold the balance so as to cause the least possible harm to the child. Those orders do not necessarily give any indication of what the final outcome will be, although as noted below the disruption to a child of a (further) change of residence will have to be weighed in the balance at the end of the day.

When the court is considering applications about where a child should live from both parents, it will need to look at all the factors in the welfare checklist and is likely to need some input from CAFCASS, particularly about things on that list that it cannot investigate itself. For example, there may be issues about whether or not one or other parent has suitable accommodation, enough space for the children, whether or not they have suitable arrangements for the children to be cared for if they are working, or issues about how appropriate their new partners are. These issues may involve the need for home visits, interviews or background checks.

Where there has been a background of real difficulties with contact, one issue which may feature significantly is the ability of either parent to promote the child's relationship with the other parent. Sometimes a dispute about where the child should live has been part of the case from the start, but in other cases a parent has tried for years to get contact going and to maintain it and has been obstructed at every turn. In this type of intractable contact case sometimes an application for a change of residence to the other parent is an option of last resort.

Where both parents are practically able to care for the children, but one struggles to be at all positive about the other parent or is hostile or obstructive of contact this could be something that would lead to the court recommending the child should live with their other parent because they would be better able to meet the child's emotional needs.

The difficulty with cases where a child is living with a parent who is relentlessly negative about the other parent is that children very often take on the views of the parent they live with and cannot be budged. Children who themselves are irrationally hostile to contact with their other parent are often described by experts as alienated. Some experts describe a child in this state as suffering from Parental Alienation Syndrome (PAS) and view the alienating parent as causing emotional and psychological damage to the child (although alienation itself is very real, PAS is not universally accepted by courts or psychiatrists as a valid condition). Alienation is easy to identify but difficult to tackle because the parent who is alienating the child is either oblivious or extremely determined (and possibly cannot help themselves or needs treatment). It is also worth saying that the fact that one parent is highly critical of the other in a harmful way does not necessarily mean that the criticized parent is not also contributing to the reluctance of a child who does not want to go to contact. Sometimes the child is just caught in the middle of the criticism of each parent by the other and is frozen like a rabbit in the headlights. Cases are rarely black and white - you must continually and consciously refocus yourself on whether anything you are doing is making things worse. Change the things you can change: your own behaviour. Sometimes insisting on what *should* be can make a problem worse - your child *should* be having contact with you but they can't because it is emotionally impossible for them. Sometimes keeping on pushing it can make it even worse and, painful as it is, you have to take a step back for a time until things are better. These extreme situations fortunately won't arise in many cases and this book cannot really help you with the right answers in your case, all I can really say is that you need to continually think long and hard about why things are happening and what impact your own actions are having and will have on your child, and base your actions on how it IS for them not how it ought to be.

There are powers to enforce child arrangements orders set out in Chapter 23, but these are unlikely to be effective in cases of extreme and entrenched hostility. They can make things worse.

If the court was considering a change of residence in a case where the current resident parent is simply not able to support the child's relationship with the other parent (often described as 'implacable hostility'), it would have to also consider the other parts of the welfare checklist, such as how the child would manage the change. In cases where there is this level of hostility the child is likely to be torn between their parents and to find things very difficult whatever the court does, and it can sometimes just be too risky to move a child. The court might order a change of residence even if a child was saying they did not want this, if it is felt that they were being harmed by the process of alienation, but only if the pros outweighed the cons.

Some authorities which apply to intractable contact or implacable hostility cases are:

- *Re A (Children)* [2009] EWCA Civ 1141 where the court made an order transferring residence to the parent seeking contact, but this was over-turned on appeal because it was a weapon of last resort.

- *Warwickshire County Council v TE v SE v S* [2010] EWHC B19 (Fam) where the court initially tried to transfer residence to the Father but failed, and in the end the parents agreed that the residence order should transfer back to the Mother. An earlier decision in the same case is at [2010] EWHC 3721 (Fam)

- *Re M (Intractable Contact Dispute: Interim Care Order)* [2003] EWHC 1024 (Fam) where the court made a s37 CA order directing the local author-ity to investigate the children's circumstances, and subsequently made a residence order in the Father's favour, a supervision order to the local authority and required contact between the children and their Mother to be at the discretion of the local authority.

In other cases courts have been prepared, as a last resort, to make a 'suspend-ed residence order', which is just an order saying that a child will live with one parent as long as they continue to ensure the child attends contact but that if contact is frustrated the child will automatically go to live with the other parent. There is no reason why this sort of order could not be made using the new ter-minology.

Re S (Transfer of Residence) [2010] EWHC 192 (Fam); [2010] 1 FLR 1785 is one ex-ample of the court being prepared to transfer residence in the face of implacable hostility to contact, although ultimately that attempt failed (see *Warwickshire County Council v TE & Ors* [2011] 1 FLR 1789 – it is the same case, but the case name is different because social services had become involved by this stage).

There are some general observations below under the heading of the welfare checklist that will apply to applications for a child to live with you.

What is the financial significance of a child arrangements order that says who a child should live with?

There are three ways in which the arrangements for where a child lives might affect you financially:

- Housing,

- Benefits,

- Child support entitlement / liability.

As a single parent without a child living with you, you will be given less priority for social housing than you would if you were caring for children. The fact that you need a place suitable for them to stay at is unfortunately not going to help bump you up the list. You can't even use a child arrangements order naming both parents as persons with whom a child should live to persuade the local authority that the children need to be provided with two homes (this was tried and failed in a case called *Holmes Moorhouse v LB Richmond Upon Thames* [2009] UKHL 7).

If you are married the court will consider your need for a home for the children to stay in during contact, when working out how to divide the finances, but if there is simply not enough money to provide two homes this will not help.

The person who the children live with will be entitled to claim child benefit, and possibly child tax credits or working tax credits. Their entitlement to housing benefit and council tax benefit will be calculated on the basis that they have dependants. Unfortunately, the law as far as benefits is concerned sees everything in black or white - they either live with one person or the other. There is no system to share the benefits between parents who share the care and the cost of bringing up children even under a child arrangements order that names both of you as people that the child should live with. The right to claim benefits will go to the parent who has 51% or more of the care.

The court can make orders saying that a proportion of the child related benefits should be paid over to the other parent every week or month, but the CA isn't really set up for this. You have to persuade the court to make it a condition of the s8 order [s11(7) CA] but most Judges will refuse to do this because this kind of order would be very difficult to enforce and this is possibly not what this section of the CA was meant for. It would be highly unlikely that a Judge would make an order like this at all unless it was agreed by both parties, and it would be just as effective to put it as a recital. It is also quite difficult to work out what amount should be paid over, since one parent might be entitled to more than the other because their circumstances are different.

If two parents put in competing claims for child benefit or child tax credit often payments to both of them will be automatically suspended for several months in order to prevent fraud and that can cause real hardship for everybody. If there are disputes between you about who should claim what benefit try and sort them out between yourselves to avoid this happening.

As far as Child Support is concerned the system is slightly more responsive to different arrangements. Whilst the CMS can only cope with the idea of children living with one parent or the other, rather than with both, the formula that is used to work out how much child maintenance is payable does build in a reduction based on the number of nights spent with the 'non-resident parent', although it is not a very sophisticated calculation.

17.13 Shared care & labels

Does it matter whether you are named as someone the child 'lives with' as opposed to 'spends time with'? Frankly this is not the big deal that many parents consider it to be. Labels do not matter to children.

Shared residence, as it used to be called, has always been controversial. Legally, the difference between contact and residence has always been slender, but it has been hugely symbolic for parents who feel their role as parent is undervalued - particularly fathers. The aim of the amendments to the CA that abolished residence and contact orders was to put an end to the frequent arguments over labels.

It cannot be emphasized enough that an order that says a child should spend X amount of time with you is almost identical in its consequences to an order that says they should *live with* you for the same period of time, particularly if you already have PR. The only real difference is in relation to holidays abroad - and as set out elsewhere that is a difference that is often insignificant where the order also provides that the child will be with their other parent regularly enough to prevent a trip abroad without agreement.

Under s8 CA the court can name one parent as the person the child will 'live with', and can say the child will spend time with the other, or the court may make an order naming both as people with whom the child will live, going on to set out what time will be spent in each household. This is equivalent to what was previously known as a shared residence order.

A child arrangements order naming both parents does not always divide a child's time equally between two households, in fact more often than not there will be some inequality of division for practical reasons, such as the need to ensure that a child can get to school and back with ease. The detail of how a child's time is split between two homes will depend entirely on what is practical bearing in mind the distance between the two homes, the location of school and other places the child regularly has to go to, and the need to ensure the child does not spend all his time travelling backwards and forwards or ping ponging from one home to another, which can be very tiring and unsettling.

For some parents the label 'shared residence' was more important than the quantity of time or vice versa - it may be that for some parents an order saying the child 'lives with' them will assume the same significance. Parents who consider themselves the primary carer are often reluctant to concede the perceived status of the sole resident parent, whilst those who are struggling to cement or re-establish a relationship with a child they live separately from are desperate for the reassurance that a child arrangements order identifying them as a person with whom the child will share a home will bring (or that they think it will bring).

Shared residence orders no longer exist. But in fact the strict legal significance of a shared residence order was always pretty limited:

> *'Such an order emphasises the fact that both parents are equal in the eyes of the law and that they have equal duties and responsibilities as parents. The order can have the additional advantage of conveying the court's message that neither parent is in control and that the court expects parents to co-operate with each other for the benefit of their children'* [Lord Justice Wall's definition in *Re K (Shared Residence Order)* [2008] EWCA Civ 526].

Most Fathers these days will either have or will be able to acquire parental responsibility, which is the primary mechanism by which a parent's legal status is recognised. See the section above on PR.

Whilst PR entitles the parent holding it to be consulted and involved in significant life decisions and to obtain information about a child, a child arrangements order that names a parent as someone the child lives with permits that parent to make day to day decisions about the care of a child. PR does not entitle a parent who is not named in a child arrangements order as a person with whom the child lives to interfere in the day to day care of a child whilst they are living with their other parent, and neither does an order that does name them. A child arrangements order that says the child will live with both parents means that both parents have the right to make day to day decisions about the care of the child *whilst the child is in their care,* but it does not give them the right to stick their oar into how the other parent manages things during their time. But since the court will not expect a resident parent to interfere in the other parent's contact time in any event, it is worth asking: *What would it really add to have an order that says 'lives with' rather than 'spends time with'? If you are agreed about everything else ask yourself whether the knock on effects of continuing a dispute just on this front is worth more than the name you give the time you spend with the kids?*

One benefit of a child arrangements order that says the child will live with both parents is that both parents can each take the child abroad without the consent of the other, but are restricted from doing so for more than a month unless they have the consent of the other or an order of the court. Where this kind of order is in place this will apply to both parents, but the reality is that, if one parent did wish to take a child abroad, they would almost always need to seek the agreement of the other in any event because any trip abroad is likely to cut across time which the order says should be spent with the parent left behind.

Shared residence orders were said to send a signal to the parties that they are equal in status, but the reality is that they were equal in the eyes of the law in any event. It is often more important to focus your energies on what time will be spent with each parent than what it's called.

'Lives with both' as a stepping stone to 'lives with me'?

It is easy to see why a parent might take the view that they need to gradually build towards their ultimate goal. This is often an anxiety of resident parents, and sometimes it is behind the approach taken by a parent prepared to play the 'long game'. But in reality, if an application is made to change a child's living arrangements further down the line, the court will look at the welfare of the child in the round, and what arrangement is going to best meet his needs. If a shared residence arrangement is in place and has been working the court is unlikely to change it. A parent who is resisting the making of a child arrangements order naming her ex as the person with whom the child lives is unlikely to find that the child's main care is transferred to the other parent if she has been able to promote the co-parenting relationship.

When will the court make an order for shared living arrangements?

The court will only make an order saying a child lives with both parents at different times where it reflects the reality on the ground - it shouldn't be made where a child is not going to live at or visit the home of both parents. But other than this there is no hard and fast rule about what does and does not qualify for this sort of order - there is no magical percentage of the child's time that qualifies a parent for the label 'lives with'. That said, where a child effectively has two homes and spends roughly equal proportions of time with each parent there will usually need to be a very good reason for not saying in the order that the child lives with both parents (*Re K (Shared Residence Order)* [2008] EWCA Civ 526).

For example, in a case where the children stay with you every other weekend and once overnight in the middle of the week and where the holidays are roughly equally shared, the court might be prepared to describe this as 'living with' - or it might not. It will depend on the wider circumstances of the case (such as any issues of control), on the Judge, on any recommendation by CAFCASS, and on the other parent.

The court can still make a 'living with' order in favour of both parents where the relationship between the parents is not good and where they struggle to work with one another (*Re W (Shared Residence Order)* [2009] EWCA Civ 370). This is something that CAFCASS officers or social workers sometimes get wrong.

The court should first of all decide what time should be spent with each parent and then decide if it is appropriate to say that a child should live with both parents is appropriate (*Re K (Shared Residence Order)* [2008] EWCA Civ 526).

17.14 The involvement of professionals

CAFCASS & welfare reports

CAFCASS are involved from the start of cases involving children when they carry out safeguarding checks. Depending on how the case progresses they may continue to be involved or may drop out of the picture.

s7 CA says the court can order a welfare report when it needs some guidance. A report will usually be from CAFCASS, unless social services are currently involved with the family, in which case they will probably be asked to report instead.

In recent years CAFCASS have been overwhelmed with work and the courts have now devised different types of welfare report (under FPR rule 12.6(c) the court can ask CAFCASS for advice without asking for a full report). There is some local variation, but generally the court will be able to ask for different types of report to suit different cases. This helps to ensure that families are not waiting any longer than is necessary for their report. You might hear the following referred to:

- Wishes and feelings report. This will be quicker but will not necessarily deal with all the issues the court needs to think about. It is not always written by a very experienced social worker.

- Single issue report. This could involve, for example, just dealing with the question of whether contact can take place at dad's home or whether mum's new partner can be present at contact. The CAFCASS officer would probably check the home, or meet the new partner (and possibly do some background checks) and would write a short report.

- Full s7 report. This should be a report looking at all the points in the welfare checklist and making recommendations about the outcome or progress of the case, whether that be where the child lives, contact or both.

- Addendum report. The court might need a further report or an update. If there has not been a long gap between the reports this can usually be done relatively quickly, but otherwise the case might have to go to the back of the queue and wait for a CAFCASS officer to be allocated to the case - this might not be the same one.

It is impossible to give very accurate guidelines about how long a report will take as things change all the time and workloads vary from area to area. But a wishes and feelings report might be as quick as four weeks, whilst a full report generally takes around 12 weeks.

Sometimes the CAFCASS officer will say that they cannot make a recommendation until they know whether certain allegations are true or not. This usually means that the report has to be delayed until the court has heard the evidence and made findings about the truth of the allegations. Most often a report will not be ordered at all until after a fact finding hearing, but sometimes the CAFCASS officer might think a fact finding is necessary where previously the court and the parties have thought otherwise. This causes delay. As noted above, it is becoming more common for a judge to order a report that makes recommendations on an 'either or' basis to avoid this potential problem.

Other experts and assessments

Social services may separately be involved with a family and sometimes their assessments find their way into the case papers. Most commonly the court might look at Initial Assessment or, if the Initial Assessment has shown serious concerns, a Single Assessment (sometimes referred to as a Core Assessment). If social services have been involved both parents should be entitled to see the assessment reports.

If the court considers that there might be a risk of significant harm to the children it may ask social services to write a s37 report in which they will have to think about whether or not they should be taking any action to protect the children, for example by starting care proceedings. s37 reports are described in Chapter 16.

Sometimes the CAFCASS officer (or social worker) will say in their report that some other expertise is required. Sometimes the court will identify this at the outset and skip straight to that stage without ordering a welfare report at all. This might be a psychological (or psychiatric) assessment of the child or parents, or some kind of risk assessment. Sometimes there is a recommendation that contact should be supervised and assessed with a report at the end.

If there is a need for this type of assessment and one or both of you is a litigant in person there may be a real problem about how that is paid for. If someone is publicly funded by legal aid they may be able to get it paid for, but the general rule is that the costs should be split equally regardless of funding and so the person with legal aid may only be able to get half paid for. Sometimes the court will appoint a Guardian for the child, and they will get public funding which can pay for some or all of the work that needs to be done (see below on Guardians).

Legal aid can never pay for assessments of contact or for the supervision of contact so unless this type of assessment is available through some other funding mechanism it will be very difficult to get it paid for. Social services will usually not pay. Some local branches of CAFCASS fund supervised / assessed contact which is free to the families where CAFCASS recommend and refer. Working out these practical issues can require a lot of investigation and leg work and there is not always a solution if you do not have funds.

If there are allegations made about your drug or alcohol use it makes sense to agree to undergo a hair strand test (with a blood test also if the allegation is about alcohol) to prove this allegation is untrue.

If you are confident your test would come back clean DO NOT stand on principle and say you don't see why you should have to undergo the test or demand that you both take one just to score points. Whatever the truth of the matter, it will look as if you are hiding something. YOU may know you have not taken drugs, but the Judge will only know that if you show her the clear test results.

These tests can be quite expensive depending on the type of test, whether you are testing for one drug or all sorts of drugs, and how long you want to go back - so it is important to try and get clarity about what drugs are being alleged and when so you can test for the right drugs rather than paying for tests you don't need. You can sometimes justify the other party paying for your hair strand or blood tests on the basis that they are raising the allegation and they should pay for it but if they are funded by legal aid this will probably be unsuccessful. The likelihood is that you will be asked to pay at least half of the costs of a hair strand test, and if you can't do so the court has no magic wand to wave to get it paid for. If there is no other way of funding a drugs test it may be worth approaching your GP to see if they can help, although they may not be prepared to carry out tests which are not medically necessary. If you are a recovering alcoholic or drug user in treatment, your service provider may have a testing service, but again this is usually only available if it is part of your treatment or abstinence programme.

Children's Guardians

Usually in private law cases the children are not parties to the proceedings. Some examples of the types of case where the court will make a child a party and appoint a Guardian for them are:

- Where CAFCASS has recommended this,

- Cases involving high levels of conflict where the child's needs are being drowned out by the dispute between the adults,

- Where there are very serious allegations of physical, sexual or other abuse relating to the child, or allegations of domestic violence which can't be sorted out with the help of a CAFCASS officer,

- Where a teenager has very strongly expressed views that cannot be properly dealt with just by a welfare report or is opposed to a proposed course of action,

- Where there are complex medical or mental health issues,

- Where the case is unusually complex,

- Where there are international complications which might involve a foreign court or foreign authorities (for example immigration difficulties but not child abduction), but the new FPR suggest that the court should consider other things instead of a Guardian.

The Guardian will usually instruct a solicitor for the child (your child will get legal aid to cover the cost of this). If the child strongly disagrees with the views of the Guardian about what is best for them, and the court considers they have sufficient age and understanding, they may be permitted to instruct their own solicitor directly. The Guardian will separately tell the court what they think is best for the child, whilst the solicitor will tell the court what the child wants.

A Guardian is usually but not always appointed by CAFCASS. Sometimes another organisation like the National Youth Advocacy Service can be asked to appoint a Guardian.

A Guardian has a more involved role than a CAFCASS officer who has just been asked to write a report. They will generally be more proactive in asking the court to make directions if they think the case is going off track, and they will also have their own legal advice and representation, along with public funding to pay for any reports or assessments that they think are necessary to get to the bottom of the issues for the benefit of a child (subject to the limits on what public funding can pay for as described elsewhere in this chapter).

People often get anxious when they are told a Guardian is going to be appointed for their child, thinking that someone else is going to be given authority over them or that their parental rights are being passed to someone else. In fact a court Guardian (technically a *Guardian ad litem*) is not the same as a legal Guardian that you might appoint to care for your child if you died [see s5 CA]. A court Guardian has no parental rights or responsibilities over or to your child - their role is limited to representing the child's wishes and best interests to the court and helping the court to reach a decision that is right for the child.

What if I have issues with my child's guardian?

A guardian that sees things from your perspective is a real advantage. But the guardian is there to try and look at things from the perspective of the child - and they may not agree with your take on things. You cannot ask for a guardian to be removed simply because they disagree with you - and in itself the fact that they happen to agree with your ex does not necessarily mean that they are biased. Although it is possible to apply for the guardian to be discharged (FPR 16.25(1)(b)), cases where a guardian is removed are very rare. See *QS v RS (No 2) (Application to Terminate Appointment of Guardian)* [2016] EWHC 1443 (Fam) for a good example of a failed application. The case confirms that the court will rarely order the appointment of a fresh guardian.

Family assistance order

A family assistance order is an order which creates a duty upon CAFCASS or social services to advise, assist and (if appropriate) to befriend the members of the family named in the order (parents and / or children) [s16 CA].

If the family assistance order runs alongside a child arrangements order that contains a contact provision the court can ask the officer from CAFCASS or social services to give advice and help to get contact going, to improve it and to keep it going.

If the order runs alongside any s8 order (child arrangements, prohibited steps or specific issue orders) the court can ask the officer to report on those issues.

A family assistance order can only be made where the parents named consent to it being made, and if the order is directed to social services they must also agree to the order being made.

They can be quite useful in cases which really need to get out of the court arena but which need a guiding hand in order to progress or to ensure things stay on track, but in practice these orders are not used very often. In practice it is usually necessary to have a dedicated individual from social services or CAFCASS who has been working with the family already and who is volunteering to continue their support above and beyond report writing.

A family assistance order will usually run for 12 months, although the court can name a shorter period. It can't last for any more than 12 months.

Activity directions & conditions

Whenever the court is considering making or changing a child arrangements order it can make an activity direction [s11A CA]. This tells the person named (usually one or both parents) that they must take part in an activity. The activities parents can be ordered to attend are:

- Separated parenting information programmes (SPIPs)
- Domestic violence perpetrator programmes
- Mediation advice and information sessions

The SPIP is the most commonly ordered because in many areas there are no available approved domestic violence perpetrator programmes, and because mediation has usually already been considered before the case began.

An activity direction to attend a domestic violence perpetrator programme may follow on from findings of domestic violence, but it is unlikely to be ordered before findings or admissions have been made. The course is free.

The SPIP is free. Normally both parents will be required to attend, although not necessarily both together.

There is information about contact activities and what is available local to you on the CAFCASS website.

An activity direction is not intended to be part of a final order, but is something the court hopes will help the case progress. Rather oddly, when the court makes a final order it can do all the same things but the only difference is that order will be called a contact activity *condition* rather than an activity *direction* [s11C CA].

Monitoring order

The court can make an order directing CAFCASS to monitor child arrangements for up to 12 months [s11H CA] and CAFCASS may be asked to report back to the court if there are problems with compliance. This monitoring order may run for a period after the court case has concluded.

17.15 How the welfare checklist works in practice

Highlighted below are some of the parts of the welfare checklist which most often feature in applications for child arrangements orders.

Children's wishes and feelings

Often parents want the Judge to follow the child's wishes. There are a number of problems with this, which are generally more difficult the younger a child is:

- What children say is not always what children want. And what children want is not always what is best for them.

- Children can be heavily influenced by parents, particularly the parent they live with. They often say one thing to one parent and something quite different to the other. They sometimes take on or repeat the views of the parent they live with.

- They often display upset or anxiety before or after contact but it is difficult to tell whether this is because of the contact itself or because they know that it upsets the parent they live with, or because children sometimes struggle to switch from one compartment of their life to another, where rules and the environment may be very different.

- Children are sometimes unrealistic - sometimes they say that they want to live with the other parent because the one they live with is the one that has to tell them 'no' on a daily basis, whereas the other parent takes them on trips and buys them treats. It is easy for children to imagine their parents as playing good cop bad cop roles (and easy for separated parents to fall into this trap too), and they are unable to appreciate that if they went to live with the other parent things would probably be similar but in reverse.

- Older children are obviously more able to explain what they want, but they are also better able to pick up on the tensions between parents and to be quite manipulative in trying to please everyone or in trying to take the line of least resistance.

- What children say can often be in direct contrast to their behaviour or body language. They may say they are having a good time but it is obvious from observation that this is not so. They may appear to be coping but may then experience difficulties in other areas of their life (for example bed wetting or poor school performance).

In short, what children say is not always the most reliable basis for making decisions about their future, and the court will not necessarily do what a child asks them to do. An example often given by judges is going to the dentist. Sometimes children say they don't want to do something, but a responsible parent whose child was reluctant to go to the dentist would still ensure they went.

The court should always consider the wishes and feelings of a child, and the older they are the more important these will be. But very often where the wishes of a child are very strongly expressed the court will ask for assistance from someone who is expert in understanding children rather than the law - and will order a welfare report, most likely from CAFCASS (see below).

Age

A contact, prohibited steps or specific issue order can only run beyond a child's 16th birthday if the court has decided that the case is exceptional [s9 CA].

Quite apart from the legal limitation on orders about children who are over 16, the court will be increasingly reluctant to make orders about teenagers the older they get. This is because the older they get the more able they are to make their own decisions and act on them. If they want to go and live with one parent there is little the court can do to stop it, and an order that the child is strongly opposed to is difficult if not impossible to enforce. If you think back to the 'no order' principle, you will see that often the courts cannot make an order because it will not achieve anything, and might even make things worse because the child will be upset that their wishes have not been respected by the Judge or the parent who has asked for the order.

The likely effect on a child of any change in his circumstances

Change is most often relevant to the pace of progress with contact and to living arrangements.

Even if the court has decided there are no particular reasons why contact should be restricted it is unlikely to order it to increase massively if contact is not already established or has been erratic, particularly so if the children are young. The court may adopt an approach with reviews to make sure that things are going okay. If they are more confident that it is simply a matter of taking it at a suitable pace for the child, and that things will develop smoothly the court may make a single order that builds in staged increases in contact over a period of time without the need to come back to court. If there is a problem the parties can always ask the court for a hearing, but it gives everyone greater certainty about the future and saves time, cost and emotional energy compared with having a hearing and possible mini-court battle at every point of increase. This is more likely to be the approach since the CAP was introduced, as that guidance discourages multiple review hearings in most cases [see PD12B pa 15.4].

When it comes to changing where a child lives, the status quo argument is a powerful one. In cases where there is a disagreement about where a child should live, the court will usually only subject a child to a change of circumstances if there will be some overall benefit to a child. Often short term disruption will be outweighed by other factors, such as a child being able to live with his siblings, receiving far better care, or living with a parent who can promote contact with the other parent where this is not currently happening.

However, this does mean that where both parents are broadly able to offer appropriate care for a child and matters are relatively evenly balanced, the question of change can be really important. If the court takes the view that the child will be okay in either home the question is; can the disruption caused by such a significant change in circumstances be justified? The answer is probably not.

If a child would have to change school as a result of a change of home the court would need to look closely at the impact this is likely to have on them. For a child who is resilient, well-adjusted and academically able the impact is likely to be manageable, whereas for a child who is unsettled or struggling at school or who has special educational needs or a particularly important bond with school staff it may have a profound effect. On the other hand if a school where the non-resident parent lived was clearly more suitable (perhaps because of particular educational needs) and the parties were both equally able to meet the child's other needs this could outweigh change.

Emotional needs

This can often be overlooked when parents are preparing their case. Things that are likely to impact on a child's emotional needs include:

- Being exposed to violence or arguments or tension either in the home or when the parents meet

- Being exposed to negativity from either parent about the other

- Being separated from a sibling including a step sibling or other relative who they have been close to. The court will be reluctant to separate siblings or step siblings who have been used to living together.

- Being in a high criticism, low praise environment.

17.16 Change of name

Where there is a child arrangements order in place which says where a child should live nobody is allowed to permit a child to go by a surname other than that on his birth certificate unless all those with parental responsibility agree. If a child lives with his Mother and the Father does not have PR there is no such restriction.

If parents cannot agree about the name a child will use or a parent wishes to obtain the court's approval for a change of name the court can make an order under s13 CA.

If there is no child arrangements order in place spelling out where the child should live any application for a change of name is a type of s8 specific issue order (although it doesn't make much practical difference which piece of law it falls under: the court still has to consider the welfare of the child and the 'no order' principle).

These types of application most often happen where a Mother wishes to revert back to her maiden name and wishes to change the child's name to match, or where she remarries and changes her name, wishing the child to take the same surname as hers and as any subsequent siblings. It sometimes arises where a child has never been known in practice by the name on their birth certificate, for example where names fall out of use because they are difficult to spell or pronounce, particularly double barrelled names.

You need to look at case law to get some idea of how the court should approach this type of application.

Dawson v Wearmouth [1999] UKHL 18 tells us that:

- The fact that a Mother's surname is different from the child's is not normally enough on its own to justify a change in name.

- The name the child was registered with at birth is relevant and perhaps important factor in assessing where the balance of advantage for the child's welfare lies. But it is not all-important.

In *Re W, Re A, Re B (Change of Name)* [1999] 2 FLR 930 (not available on BAILII) Lady Justice Butler-Sloss summarised some of the principles as follows:

e) On any application, the welfare of the child is paramount and the Judge must have regard to the s 1(3) criteria [this means the s1 CA Welfare Checklist].

f) Among the factors to which the court should have regard is the registered surname of the child and the reasons for the registration, for instance recognition of the biological link with the child's Father. Registration is always a relevant and an important consideration but is not in itself decisive. The weight to be given to it by the court will depend upon the other relevant factors or valid countervailing reasons which may tip the balance the other way.

g) The relevant considerations should include factors which may arise in the future as well as the present situation.

h) Reasons given for changing or seeking to change a child's name based on the fact that the child's name is or is not the same as the parent making the application do not generally carry much weight.

i) The reasons for an earlier unilateral decision to change a child's name may be relevant.

17.17 Barring orders

At the end of any case about children the court is allowed to make an order preventing a person from making any more applications under the CA unless they have first got permission from the court to do so [s91(14)]. The court can say this applies to all applications under the CA or just a particular sort (e.g. no more applications for child arrangements orders). I'm calling these 'barring orders' because it's less of a mouthful than 'a s91(14) order', but it's not strictly accurate because it's not a complete bar on applications, just an extra hurdle.

The court can make a barring order because one of the parties has applied for one or because the Judge himself has decided it is appropriate. But the court should never make this order unless both parties have been given advance warning and an opportunity to tell the court what they think about the suggestion. It should never be sprung on anybody, particularly if they don't have a lawyer (see for example *In The Matter of G* [2008] EWCA Civ 1468).

In the case of *C (A Child), Re* [2009] EWCA Civ 674 the Court of Appeal gave guidance about the procedure to be followed in these cases. They said:

(1) *'Ideally, such an application should be made in writing on notice in the normal way. The court can then, having heard all relevant submissions, make an order one way or the other.*

(2) *There will, however, be cases in which the question of a section 91(14) order arises either during or at the end of a hearing. It may arise on the application of one of the parties, or on the court's own initiative. One or more of the parties before the court may be un-represented.*

(3) *In the circumstances identified in paragraph (2), the court may make an order under section 91(14). It is, however, of the utmost importance that the party or parties or other persons affected by the order, particularly if they are in person:*

(a) *understand that such an application is being made, or that consideration is being given to making a section 91(14) or-der;*

(b) *understand the meaning and effect of such an order; and*

(c) *have a proper opportunity to make submissions to the court in answer to the application or to the suggestion that a sec-tion 91(14) order be made.*

(4) *Where the parties (and in particular the person affected by the*

section 91(14) order) are unrepresented, it may be possible for the court to deal with the matter in argument without a formal application, although if the representative for the party affected seeks a short adjournment to take instructions, such an application should normally be granted. If there is a substantive objection to the section 91(14) order, then the court should require the application to be made formally on notice in the normal way.

(5) Where the party affected by a proposed section 91(14) order is in person it is particularly important that he or she (a) understands the effect of such an order; and (b) is given a proper opportunity to respond to it. This may mean adjourning the application for it to be made in writing and on notice.

(6) Where the parties are both or all in person, there is a powerful obligation on any court minded to make a section 91(14) order to explain to them the course the court is minded to take. This will involve the court telling the parties in ordinary language what a section 91(14) order is; and what effect it has, together with the duration of the order which the court has in mind to impose. Above all, unrepresented parties must be given the opportunity to make any submissions they wish about the making of such an order, and if there is a substantive objection on which a litigant wishes to seek legal advice the court should either normally not make an order; alternatively it can make an order and give the recipient permission to apply to set it aside within a specified time.

(7) None of this guidance is designed to address the merits of section 91(14) orders, which as my Lord has indicated are exceptional, and in relation to which there is now a substantial jurisprudence.'

I've set that guidance out in full so that you can have it to hand if you are suddenly faced with an application of this sort without warning.

That deals with the process, but you also need to understand what sorts of behaviour / factual background would justify the making of an order. The case of *P (A Child)* [1999] EWCA Civ 1323 gives some useful guidelines, and makes clear that a barring order is very unusual, and is normally only appropriate where there have been repeated and unreasonable applications. If the Judge is thinking about making an order when there has only been one application, you should remind her of this principle, which applies even if the proceedings have been long and difficult. There are cases where a s91(14) bar could be imposed at the end of a first application but this would be very unusual indeed.

The court can make the order against one or both parties, and quite often does make an order telling both parties to go away and take a break from court.

The court must say how long the bar will last for. Although it can say that it will last for an indefinite period this would be very unusual.

The court cannot attach conditions to the bar, in other words it cannot say in the order itself what must be done before another application will be allowed, but the Judge can say in court what should be addressed before the court is likely to agree to let another application proceed (this could be recorded as a recital but it can't be part of the order itself) (see *S (Children)* [2006] EWCA Civ 1190 and *Stringer v Stringer* [2006] EWCA Civ 1617).

If a s91(14) bar is made and you want to bring a new application you must fill in a C2 form asking for permission. You should address all the points that had concerned the Judge when the bar was made and try to demonstrate what has changed. The *S (Children)* case above gives some helpful guidance on the way the court approaches applications for permission. Generally speaking you should not expect to be successful in an application for permission unless a reasonable period of time has passed since the order was made.

18. International Issues, Relocation & Abduction

This chapter deals mainly with situations where a parent wishes to travel or move abroad with children, and briefly with child abduction. However it also includes some information about jurisdiction in cross border cases and about jurisdiction in divorce or financial cases with a foreign element. For convenience, it also covers relocations of children within the UK.

18.1   Jurisdiction (or: can the court make an order?) (Children)

Generally speaking, if a child lives in England or Wales there will be no difficulty in making an application to the Family Court in England & Wales.

What follows is a summary of the law in cases where the situation is a bit different. It is a complicated area, so this is only a rough outline - if you think one of the following applies it is a good indicator you need to check the position with a lawyer.

The first thing to say is that a lot depends on where the child is 'habitually resident', but that habitual residence is very difficult to explain and people often disagree about it. If a child has always lived with his parents in England & Wales he will almost certainly be habitually resident there but habitual residence can change over time. It doesn't necessarily change on the day a person moves from one country to another or after a specific period of time living in a new place. I've explained a bit more about habitual residence below at paragraph 18.4.

The main piece of law in this area is a European Regulation called Brussels II Revised [Brussels IIR]. Brussels IIR remains in place and will remain in place until BREXIT is complete, but it is unclear what it will be replaced with once the UK exits the EU. For most families questions of jurisdiction are a non-issue or the answer will be very obvious, and generally speaking, IF the child is 'habitually resident' in England & Wales the court will have jurisdiction under Brussels IIR. However, this book can't really deal with every scenario, so if there is any doubt you really need to seek some advice - try and find someone with some demonstrable experience of international/jurisdictional issues as not all family lawyers are familiar with this area.

As a rule of thumb:

- If a child is not *present* in England & Wales the court may still deal with an application if the child is *habitually resident* here but temporarily away (including if abducted);

- If a child is neither *present* nor *habitually resident* in the UK the court may not be entitled to make any orders about the child, although there are some exceptions;

- If a child is *present* but not *habitually resident* in the UK (perhaps they have just arrived or are on holiday) the court may be able to make temporary orders. If the child has been abducted from a country that is signed up to the Hague Convention on child abduction to this country the court will deal with the question of return according to the rules set out in that convention (See below at paragraph 18.9 for more on the Hague Convention).

18.2 Enforcement of contact orders between member states of the EU

Where an order about child contact has been in one country in the European Union it is enforceable in any other country in the European Union (Article 41 Brussels II Revised). So, for example, if an order is made in Poland about a child who subsequently moves to England, the Polish order can be enforced through English courts. To make an order enforceable in another member state the court that made it must issue an Article 41 Certificate. The certificate is confirmation that:

- 'If the judgment certified was given in default, the person defaulting had good and sufficient notice so as to arrange a defence or where service did not comply with conditions, the Defendant accepted the decision unconditionally

- All parties were given an opportunity to be heard

- The child was given an opportunity to be heard unless a hearing was considered to be inappropriate having regard to age or maturity.'

Essentially this is confirmation that the process leading to the order was fair.

So, if there is an Article 41 certified order in place relating to children who are present or habitually resident in England or Wales the court can be asked to enforce it.

If the court in England & Wales makes an order about children living here, but where the order may need to be enforced abroad, it is sensible to obtain an Article 41 Certificate at the time it is made, just in case. For example, if the order is for children to return to Poland with one parent, but to have contact with the parent left behind, a certificate would make the contact order applicable and enforceable in Poland.

Legal aid may be available for a parent left behind to enforce an order under Article 41 in the other country.

18.3   Jurisdiction *within* the UK (Children)

England & Wales has a separate legal system from Scotland and Northern Ireland.

If there is a court case ongoing in Scotland or Northern Ireland relating to the child then matters must generally be dealt with there [FLA 1986].

Generally, if a child is habitually resident in Scotland or Northern Ireland the court in that part of the UK must deal with any application unless there are ongoing matrimonial proceedings (a case about divorce / ending a civil partnership) in England & Wales [FLA 1986].

If a child is physically present in England & Wales but habitually resident in another part of the UK the court can make orders in the short term on the basis that the child is in need of protection but then it has to hand the case over to the court where the child is habitually resident [FLA 1986].

If it is unclear where they are habitually resident, perhaps because they used to live abroad but you recently moved here, or because they came to stay here temporarily with the intention of returning back abroad - things may be a little more complicated.

18.4   What is Habitual Residence?

Habitual residence does not have a one-line easy definition and although in most cases it's obvious where a child is habitually resident, in some it isn't at all clear. It depends upon a consideration of the factual circumstances in each case.

In *Re A (Children), (Rev 1)* [2013] UKSC 60 the Supreme Court agreed that the place where a child is habitually resident is 'the place which reflects some degree of integration by the child in a social and family environment in the country concerned. This depends upon numerous factors, including the reasons for the family's stay in the country in question'.

Because an infant or young child is dependent on those who care for him and shares the same social/family environment, it is necessary to assess the integration of his carer(s). This integration of the adults is less important as the child gets older.

18.5 Moving around the country

Often one parent will want to move because they have a new job, new partner or want to move back to where their family is based. Generally speaking there is nothing that requires one parent to live near the other, and if one parent wants to move some distance away there is nothing to stop them doing so. Even where a child arrangements order is in place this does not restrict *where* the parent may live with the child as long as it is in the UK (unless the court has specifically attached a condition to the order, which is unusual). However, if a move is so far away that it is impossible to stick to the order for contact, the parent wanting to move ought to apply to vary the contact order before going.

If the parent who is going to be left behind wishes to prevent such a move they will have to apply to the court for a prohibited steps order or some other order, such as an order saying the child must move to live with the parent left behind or the imposition of a condition on an order for the child to continue living with the parent who wishes to leave.

It used to be thought that the court would not prevent a move unless there were exceptional circumstances, but this is no longer the case. The court considering such an application would have to look at what was in the best interests of the child (looking at the welfare checklist), and in particular what the impact of the move might be on the child, including the impact on their relationship with the left behind parent. If the distance is very great this might be significant (*Re C (Internal Relocation)* [2015] EWCA Civ 1305). In *Re F (Children)* [2010] EWCA Civ 1428 a Mother wanted to relocate to the Orkney Isles. The court refused the application because the move would be so stressful and would involve so much upheaval for the children.

If the court thinks that the reason for the moving is to engineer a reduction in contact to exclude the other parent, or to make an existing shared care arrangement impractical, the court might make orders to prevent a move. An example of this is the case of *Re T (A Child) sub nom ETS v BT sub nom Re L (A Child)* [2009] EWCA Civ 20, where the court decided that the Mother wanted to move from London to Somerset in order to frustrate the shared residence order that was in place. The Mother had previously made an unsuccessful application to move abroad with the child, which the court had decided was motivated by the wish to diminish the Father's relationship with the child and the application to move within the country was part of the same approach. The court did not allow her to go.

If you are planning to move any significant distance it is usually best to let the other parent know well in advance so that you can sort out arrangements for the children spending time with both of you, and so that if there is any dispute one of you can apply to court before you go. This might seem like a nuisance but it is better than finding yourself on the wrong end of an application for a variation of a child arrangements order to say the child should live with the other parent or an application for a prohibited steps order in a court miles away from your new home. Think about how it may look later if you just go without getting either agreement or permission.

If there is an existing child arrangements order in place that will need to change due to travelling times you are likely to end up in breach of that order if you move without agreeing alternate arrangements or making an application to court first. If the move is going to make the existing arrangements unworkable you will need to make an application to vary the existing order.

In some cases the court might expect the child to remain in their existing school until it has made a decision about the relocation, and if you have already moved this might mean them staying mainly with the other parent until it is sorted out or a lot of travel time for you and the child (if this is practical).

If the other parent is proposing to move and you do not agree, you could make an application to the court for a prohibited steps order to stop this happening (see abduction below). If you are a parent who has shared care or who is in a position to take on the main caring role you will need to think about whether you should make an application for the child to live with you. If you are only having quite limited contact with the child or cannot for practical reasons take on their care the real issue is likely to be not whether the other parent is allowed to move, but how contact can best be sorted out.

If a move takes place before the other parent is made aware it is possible to ask the court for an order that they should return back to the local area whilst things are sorted out for the longer term, but such an order will not be automatic - it will depend on what is in the child's best interests (*Re R (A Child)* [2016] EWCA Civ 1016). It will also depend to some extent on what is practically possible - if a parent has already sold their home / given up a tenancy or taken a job it may be impractical to order an immediate return.

18.6 Children taken or moved to unknown addresses

Chapter 16 sets out the powers the court has to order someone to tell it what they know about the location of a child [s33 & s34 FLA 1986].

If there is any possibility that your child may have been taken abroad or may be about to be taken abroad you should contact a solicitor without delay telling them that you need urgent advice about child abduction and if you cannot get an urgent appointment with a solicitor you should contact the International Child Abduction & Contact Unit who can help you make an application for the return of the child.

If however you have simply lost touch with the other parent and need their address in order to re-establish contact or to make an application, or if the other parent has moved away and hasn't told you where, you can apply to the court for an order for 'disclosure of the whereabouts of a child' [s33 FLA 1986, Form C4]. You need to work out who to make the application against. Typically you may need to make an application against one of the following:

- A family member (perhaps a grandparent) who is thought to have helped the parent to move away or who is still in touch with them,

- The Department for Work and Pensions or Her Majesty's Revenue and Customs, because the parent is likely to be claiming Child Benefit, Child Tax Credits or other state benefits and will have had to register a new address, or

- A Local Authority in the area where the parent is likely to have gone to, because the child will be registered at a school.

s33 FLA 1986 does not mean that the information about the child's address will be sent directly to you. Usually the order will say that the information must be given to the court, in case the other parent wants to keep their address secret from you. The court can then send any application to them and if they want to keep their address private from you the other parent can fill in Form C8 asking the court to allow this. The important thing is that the court is kept up to date with the child's address, even if you don't have it.

The court will usually tell you when it receives the information about the child's whereabouts. At that point you should ask for an order that the other parent must not move the child again without telling the court in writing.

If the other parent is living a long way off the application might get transferred to the court nearest to them.

If necessary the court can order the recovery of a child, but this is quite uncommon. It is most likely to happen in cases where a parent has taken a child from the care of the parent who usually cares for him, rather than where the main carer has moved away with the child. If you need to apply for the recovery of a child use Form C3.

If taking the child away was a breach of a child arrangements order (for example the child is supposed to be living with the parent left behind) and if the court has ordered the person to return the child or bring the child to court and they have not done so, the court can make an order to recover the child. You can only ask for an order for recovery of the child if the other parent knows about the order to return the child and has ignored it.

When the court makes an order for recovery this tells the Police or an officer of the court that they can take a child by force if necessary and return them to where they are supposed to be.

18.7   Child abduction

This book does not deal with child abduction in any detail, but if your children are taken abroad without your consent and the other parent is refusing to bring them back, you should contact the International Child Abduction & Contact Unit, who will be able to advise you about what steps need to be taken. The Reunite website is very helpful too. The International Child Abduction & Contact Unit represents parents whose children who have been abducted to foreign countries in court cases abroad to get them brought home. You will be entitled to legal aid for this.

In cases of child abduction it really is important that you act fast and that you get proper legal advice tailored to your circumstances. There is some very basic and general information below about some first steps you might take in an emergency whilst you are sorting out a lawyer, but it is really important that you see a lawyer as soon as possible. Use the Reunite website to find a lawyer who knows about abduction - it is a specialist area.

You should also read PD 12F, which is really helpful and clearly explained. It explains how you can get the Police to issue a 'Port Alert' to all airports and ferry ports in really urgent cases to prevent abduction. You do not need to go to court to get a port alert issued.

If for any reason you cannot get an urgent appointment with a solicitor you should go to the Family Court and explain that you need to make an urgent application to prevent a child abduction and you would like a 'section 9 Judge' to exercise his High Court powers. A 'section 9 Judge' is a Circuit Judge who is allowed to sit as a High Court Judge when necessary, and this kind of Judge can order a port alert, and a range of orders which can be enforced by the Tipstaff. The Tipstaff is an officer of the High Court, who is a little bit like a Police Officer because he has a range of powers to find, locate and recover children. It really is far far better to get a solicitor to do this for you, but if you do have to go to court alone, make sure that the court staff and the Judge are told it is URGENT, that the issue is CHILD ABDUCTION and that you might need HIGH COURT ORDERS. This should give the Judge a reasonable idea of what he can do to help. Not all Family Courts have Judges with these powers.

If you live near a District Registry of the High Court you should make your application directly there.

If the court does make any orders, you should ask the Judge for the court to arrange for service.

18.8 Removal from the jurisdiction - temporary

If you wish to take your children abroad with you for a holiday out of the jurisdiction (in this case this means out of the UK) you must obtain the agreement of their other parent. If you are named in a child arrangements order as a person the child lives with you may take them out of the UK for up to a month, unless another person with PR says no. This doesn't mean you can ignore any part of the child arrangements order that says they should be spending time with or living with another person though.

If you do not have the other parent's consent or a child arrangements order naming you as a person the child lives with, you may be committing a criminal offence under the Child Abduction and Custody Act 1985 [CACA] which can be punished by fine or imprisonment.

If you want to take your children abroad with you but the other parent will not agree you must make an application to the court for its approval (if you are allowed to do so through a child arrangements order as described above you don't have to go to court to get approval). You should make your application promptly because they can take some time to resolve. You should include as much information about your trip, the purpose of it, the accommodation, who will be going, what contact you propose to permit the other parent to have whilst you are gone and how it will be facilitated, along with your return travel tickets and any reservation details. If your application is urgent, for example a family funeral, you need to ensure that the application is marked urgent and that you say on the form why it is urgent and ask for the time for service to be abridged (shortened). Tell court staff it is urgent. If the other parent has a solicitor you may be able to avoid going to court by providing copies of all of this information to them, or by offering to attend court and giving an undertaking (promise) to the Judge that you will return the children by a certain date. See Chapter 21 for an explanation of what an undertaking means.

Even if the other parent does not have PR it is always better to inform them of your plans, try to get their agreement and to go to court for approval if you cannot. If you continue making plans for travel without their consent you may find yourself faced with an application to prevent you from going or an application for the children's return under the Hague Convention, the former meaning you may not be able to go on holiday and your travel costs will be wasted, the latter meaning you may arrive back at the airport with a welcoming party waving court orders at you.

If you are the parent who is concerned about the children going abroad and you are unable to reach an agreement, you may need to make an application to court. If you have a good reason to be concerned that the other parent may not return the children at the end of the holiday (for example they have family abroad and have said they would like to live there or have threatened not to bring them back) or that they might come to some harm abroad, you should consider attending court urgently to ask the court to prevent them from leaving or at least to obtain the reassurances listed above (return flight tickets etc). You should do this 'without notice' to the other parent. The court may make a holding order until the matter can come back to court with both of you present. You should take legal advice if you can about this, but if not you should go to court anyway and ask the Judge to make a prohibited steps order. In some cases it may be appropriate to obtain the kind of orders that only the High Court can make, usually where there is evidence somebody is making deliberate plans to flee the country to somewhere from which it will be difficult to secure their return (see paragraph 18.10 below).

When a court is asked to approve a proposal to take a child abroad for a foreign holiday, the details of where the child is going to be taken and the risks of abduction or any risks associated with the destination or holiday will also be relevant. If there are concerns raised about possible abduction through non-return, the court may be more anxious if the country is not a signatory to the Hague Convention (See *R (A Child)* [2013] EWCA Civ 1115). The court will ask the following questions:

- Is the trip is in the best interests of the child?

- Is there is a risk of abduction and what would the risk be if that actually

239

happened (e.g. how hard would it likely to be to get them back from the country in question)?

- Is the court positively satisfied that the advantages of visiting outweigh the risks of the trip? If not the court will say no.

18.9   Thinking about agreeing to your children going abroad

Generally speaking it is much harder to successfully abduct a child to a country in the EU or which has signed the Hague Convention on child abduction. There is a list of countries who are signatories on the Reunite website. Please be careful if you Google 'the hague convention' - there is more than one relating to family law, but they don't all relate to child abduction!

In summary, the Hague Convention says that where children are 'wrongfully removed' or kept abroad by one parent, the court in the country they have gone to must send them back to this country, so that the courts here can decide if they should be allowed to go to live abroad. There are a few (quite limited) exceptions, but usually the foreign court must send the children back quickly for a decision in the country they have come from (although 'quickly' for a court might not seem very quick to you). Whether a removal is 'wrongful' or not depends on whether you have something called 'custody rights'. This is a European term, and the courts here have said that if you have PR, a child arrangements order naming you, if you are having regular contact, or if there is a court case ongoing about your children you probably do have 'custody rights', and this means that a removal you haven't agreed to might be wrongful (it won't be wrongful if it is permitted because a child arrangements order says the child lives with the person taking them abroad and they are only going for less than a month - it would probably be wrongful if it was in breach of a prohibited steps order or for longer than a month). Hague applications do not always progress as quickly as they ought to and if the children are returned but the parent who abducted the children still wants to go back, the court here will then have to decide on their application for permission to remove them, which may or may not succeed.

18.10 Removal from the jurisdiction - permanent

The CA does not tell the court much about how to deal with these applications, and the Court of Appeal has made clear in a number of recent cases that there is no presumption for or against allowing a parent to move abroad with a child, and the court must look at what is in the best interests of the individual child by reference to the welfare checklist (*Re F (A Child) (International Relocation Cases)* [2015] EWCA Civ 882).

Payne v Payne [2001] EWCA Civ 166 (listed on BAILII as *P v P*)) is a case which is now generally accepted to set out an outdated and rather sexist approach to this sort of case, in contrast to the recent cases which make clear that the welfare checklist should be the main guide for the court - but it still contains some useful guidance which is useful to help you think about the sort of things which the Judge might be interested in.

The following is a summary of the guidelines given in *Payne v Payne* by Dame Elizabeth Butler-Sloss at pa 85-86 (slightly edited for ease of reading):

(a) *The welfare of the child is always paramount.*

(b) *There is no presumption in favour of the applicant parent.*

(c) *The reasonable proposals of the parent with a residence order wishing to live abroad carry great weight.*

(d) *The proposals have to be scrutinised with care and the court needs to be satisfied that there is a genuine motivation for the move and not the intention to bring contact between the child and the other parent to an end.*

(e) *The effect upon the applicant parent and the new family of the child of a refusal of leave is very important.*

(f) *The effect upon the child of the denial of contact with the other parent and in some cases his family is very important.*

(g) *The opportunity for continuing contact between the child and the parent left behind may be very significant.*

These observations were made on the premise that the question of residence is not a live issue. If there is a real dispute as to which parent should be granted a residence order, and the decision as to which parent is the more suitable is finely balanced, the future plans of each parent for the child are clearly relevant. If one parent intends to set up home in another country and remove the child from school, surroundings and the other parent and his family, it may in some cases be an important factor to weigh in the balance. But in a case where the decision as to residence is clear, the plans for removal from the jurisdiction would not be likely to be significant in the decision over residence.

18.11 Divorce and financial cases with a foreign element

You can get divorced in England & Wales if one or both of you are habitually resident there. In fact even if you are no longer both habitually resident in England & Wales the court may still be able to deal with your divorce: the court can deal with your divorce where any of these apply:

(a) both of you are habitually resident in England & Wales;

(b) both of you were last habitually resident in England & Wales and one of you continues to live there;

(c) the Respondent (i.e. the person whose ex is asking for a divorce) is habitually resident in England & Wales;

(d) the Petitioner (i.e. the person asking for a divorce) is habitually resident in England & Wales and has lived there for at least one year immediately before the presentation of the application; or

(e) the Petitioner is domiciled and habitually resident in England & Wales and has resided there for at least six months immediately before the presentation of the application.

The country which deals with the divorce is usually the country which is entitled to deal with the financial aspects.

It is possible that you and/or your ex will be entitled to apply for a divorce in more than one country. It is sometimes thought that there is an advantage to dealing with matters in one country as opposed to another (see for example news headlines about London being the 'divorce capital' as it is seen to be favourable to wives). Different countries do have different approaches to financial arrangements on divorce, and to things like maintenance, but it is impossible for this book to set out all the pros and cons. Whether you would be better off divorcing in this country or another depends on the circumstances of your case, but the important point to remember is that the person whose divorce application is issued first is the person who gets to choose which country deals with it. If you think that it is important you are divorced here (for example for the very practical reason that you have returned home from living abroad and you don't want to have to deal with proceedings abroad in a foreign language), then you need to avoid a situation where your ex issues an application before you in another country.

Although generally the country dealing with the divorce will also deal with the finances, Part III of the Matrimonial and Family Proceedings Act 1984 does allow the English / Welsh court to make financial orders after an overseas divorce in some circumstances. Someone divorced abroad who wants the English / Welsh court to take over dealing with the finances must get permission from the court here. There is a 2 stage test:

- One of you must be domiciled or habitually resident in England & Wales on the date of the application for permission, or the date on which the divorce was obtained; or

- One or both of you must have a beneficial interest (a share) in a property in England or Wales which was at some time during the marriage a matrimonial home.

If one of those applies, the court will consider:

- what connection you each have with England & Wales, with the country where you got divorced, or any other country; and

- any financial benefit which the person applying (or a child of the family) has received, or is likely to receive, in a different country.

If permission is granted your application for financial remedies can proceed just as with any other (see Chapter 14).

19. When Things Go Wrong - Enforcing & Changing Child Arrangements Orders

19.1   Introduction

When orders are not being stuck to or are not working there are two main types of application which will naturally follow:

- Applications to vary by the person who doesn't want to stick to the order,

- Applications to enforce the order by the person who wants the order to stay the same.

Because they often occur together both types of application are dealt with in this chapter.

19.2   Variation applications

If there is a child arrangements order (or an old residence or contact order) which you think needs to change you must make an application to vary it and you must do it straight away, unless you and the other person have agreed things between you. If you just stop doing what the order tells you to do without applying to vary the order you will be in breach of it and the other parent will be entitled to apply for enforcement of it.

Some common reasons for a parent thinking that an order needs to change are:

- The other parent is not sticking to it regularly,

- The child is struggling or unhappy with the arrangements,

- The arrangements have turned out to be or have become impractical (for example because of transport and timing difficulties that cannot be worked out),

- The arrangements are not safe, or

- A combination of the above.

To make an application to vary an order you should fill in Form C100 (the FPR are a bit inconsistent about this, you might be asked to fill in a C2) and follow the instructions in Part 18 of the FPR. The court might not make a final decision straight away as a result of your application, but it might make a temporary order until it can. If the court has not changed the order you must still stick to it or you will be in breach, even if you have made an application.

You should bear in mind that the court will not usually change an order very soon after it has been made unless something has changed or the order has not been able to work as expected so that it is not in the child's best interests for it to carry on as it is. You are unlikely to be successful on an application just because you disagree with it: you will need to produce evidence to show that even though the order was appropriate when it was made, it is not now appropriate. You must say in your application what has happened since the last hearing when the order was made or looked at that means the court should now make a different decision.

19.3 Enforcement generally

Enforcement is the range of things a court can do to make sure people stick to the orders it makes.

The Family Court has the following powers to enforce orders for children:

- Financial compensation order: where a person has broken a child arrangements order and that has resulted in a financial loss to the other person such as travel expenses (this could be either parent and money goes to the parent who has lost out),

- Enforcement order: where a person has broken a child arrangements order. This takes the form of an unpaid work (community service) requirement and could apply to either parent,

- Breach of an enforcement order,

- Committal to prison for contempt of court by breaking an order (including an enforcement order) or an undertaking (up to two years - with no time off on licence as with criminal prison sentences),

- Fine for contempt of court by breaking an order or undertaking (the money goes to the court),

- Order for recovery of a child where an order telling a person to return a child has been breached.

Most applications for enforcement are dealt with under the same part of the rules that covers private law proceedings, including contact [Part 12 FPR]. But if you are applying for enforcement of an order or undertaking by way of committal to prison or fine your application will fall under Part 37 FPR.

All child arrangements orders automatically include something called a 'warning notice' on the bottom of them.

A warning notice says that a child arrangements order must be obeyed or an enforcement or financial compensation order can be made and incorporates a 'penal notice' saying that a breach can be punished by fine or imprisonment.

These notices are what make the order enforceable. Breaking an order without a notice is still a contempt of court, but the court cannot do anything about it if the warning is not on the order [s11K CA], other than by varying the s8 order itself (for example by reducing contact where the parent who is coming for contact keeps on not showing up).

If the warning is not on the order for some reason, the person complaining about the breach must ask the court to attach a warning / penal notice to the order and then wait for another breach before that can be enforced. Recent caselaw tells us that a penal notice must be on the front page of the order to be valid (*Re Newman (An Application By Gloucestershire County Council for the Committal To Prison)* [2014] EWHC 3136 (Fam)). By extension this probably applies to a warning notice too. This is worth checking when you receive an order from the court or if you are at risk of imprisonment for breach.

If the order is not a child arrangements order the court does not automatically attach a penal notice and you will have to ask the court to attach one either at the time the order is made, or when it is first broken, so that the court can take action next time it is broken. You are most likely to need to ask the court to attach a penal notice to a prohibited steps order (see Chapter 17).

To enforce an order it must have been served on the person who has to comply with it, complete with the warning notice / penal notice before any breach.

- For enforcement orders or financial compensation orders, this will be done by the court sending the order out by post.

- Sometimes lawyers write out an order by hand at court - this does not always have the warning notice written on it, as the court staff will add this on when it is typed. Some courts are quite slow at getting orders typed and sent out. If there have been historic problems with contact and you are worried the typed order might not arrive before a special occasion of contact (Christmas for example) you could ask the lawyer drawing up the order or the court to ensure that the warning notice is written out fully on the handwritten order that is given to you at court, or ask the Judge to request that the court staff should type it up straight away so it can be handed to you both before you leave (this is not always possible).

- Where the application is for imprisonment or fine for contempt of court the court must usually be satisfied that the order has been given personally to the person at risk of punishment, but this might not be necessary if the person was at court when the order was made and was told what it said. The penal notice must be clearly set out on the front page of the order.

19.4 Undertakings

If someone has broken a formal promise they have given to the court this can be enforced by fine or imprisonment. The procedure for dealing with a breach of undertaking is set out in Chapter 22.

19.5 Criminal standard

Although these powers of enforcement are powers held by the Family Court, they must generally be proved to the criminal standard because they are so serious. This means that they must be proved beyond reasonable doubt (or to use the more modern phrase, the Judge must be satisfied so that he is sure). So you do need solid evidence in order to prove a breach, including evidence of the order or undertaking that has been breached and service/knowledge of it.

19.6 Enforcement orders

Enforcement orders are dealt with in Section 11J - 11N & Schedule A1 CA.

If a child arrangements order has been broken and the other person wants to make sure it does not happen again one way of dealing with it is to issue an enforcement application [s11J CA]. Until 22 April 2014 enforcement orders were only available to enforce a breach of a contact order. Since the CA has been amended and contact and residence orders abolished enforcement orders are now available to enforce both 'residence' and 'contact' parts of a child arrangements order.

An application for an enforcement order must be made on Form C79. The application must be served personally on the person they are against (post is not good enough). The rules say this must be done by the person who has asked for the enforcement order, but you can ask the court to do it for you if you do not have a lawyer [Rule 12.35(3) FPR]. The Child Arrangements Programme [PD12B] says that the court must try and list your application within 20 working days of it being issued.

Do not assume that an application for an enforcement order is necessarily the best or most effective way to achieve what you want to. Sometimes it can make matters worse, and it can be quite a rigmarole getting through the process described below. For example, sometimes children will pick up on the fact (or will be told directly) that daddy is trying to have mummy sent to prison or to get mummy into trouble with the Judge, and this can cause the contact to break down because the child is angry.

Sometimes it might be better to ask the court to list the matter for a hearing or to write saying that if there is a further breach you will issue an application for enforcement and see if that produces any results.

The court can only make an enforcement order if it is proved beyond reasonable doubt that a person has failed to comply with a child arrangements order. Even if a breach has been proved, the court cannot make an order if the person who has broken it proves that they have a reasonable excuse for not complying with the order. They only have to prove that it is more likely than not that they had a reasonable excuse.

Things that might be a reasonable excuse could be:

- The person who was supposed to be bringing the child to contact could not do so because they were rushed to hospital and nobody else was able to bring the child at short notice,

- The child was too unwell to travel (always get a doctor's note),

- The other parent has been abusive or violent at contact handover and it is not safe to go,

- Unavoidable transport problems (train delays or cancellations, car break down etc - NOT oversleeping and missing the bus).

Things that might not be a reasonable excuse could be:

- A child saying that they do not want to go to contact - a parent is expected to make all reasonable efforts to encourage and persuade a child to go, particularly if they are younger. If the child's reaction is very extreme it might be a reasonable excuse but you should apply to vary urgently if this is happening,

- It is too difficult or inconvenient to transport the child or to fit the contact in with your routine. If the order is not practical you must apply to vary it.

Things that are definitely not a reasonable excuse include:

- You think the order is wrong,

- You've changed your mind about what you agreed to at court,

- The other parent has not paid any maintenance or child support.

The court also has to think about whether an enforcement order is really necessary and proportionate to the seriousness of the breach. The courts will generally try to find a practical solution to make contact work better, and will only be prepared to make enforcement orders when other attempts have failed.

On a practical level, the court can't make an enforcement order if:

- there is no unpaid work available in the local area

- the person in breach of the order is not suitable for unpaid work. This is often the case where the person is a single parent caring for a number of children or if they have work or study hours that would make it impossible to combine with unpaid work.

If the court is thinking about making an enforcement order it must ask CAFCASS to provide information about what work is available and whether or not the person is suitable for unpaid work, and whether or not it is likely to interfere with work, study or conflict with any religious beliefs. This all takes time to arrange as CAFCASS have to liaise with probation who run the unpaid work schemes, and it is not top of CAFCASS' priority list.

If and when the court does make an enforcement order it will have a warning notice attached so that any breach of the enforcement order (for example not turning up for unpaid work) can also be enforced. CAFCASS will be asked to monitor the person's compliance with it.

The maximum unpaid work requirement is 200 hours, and it must be completed within 12 months, although this can be extended.

An enforcement order can be suspended (this means that it won't have immediate effect but will automatically come into action if there is a further breach, and the court might also impose a new enforcement order in relation to the second breach) [s11J(9) CA].

The court can revoke (end) an enforcement order if:

- it decides that no enforcement order should have been made, or

- there has been a change of circumstances that means that it should be revoked, or

- there has been satisfactory compliance with the child arrangements order since and the court considers it would be appropriate for the enforcement order to be revoked. The court has to think about whether or not the person will carry on complying with the order if the enforcement order is ended [Part 4 Schedule A1 CA].

This really means that the courts first priority will be getting contact running well and smoothly rather than to punish for the sake of it. If things can be made to work without the enforcement order being in place, then the order should generally be revoked.

If the enforcement order is broken the court can amend the order to increase the number of hours work that must be done or make a fresh enforcement order as well as or instead of the first one.

- The court can only do this if the breach of the enforcement order is proved beyond reasonable doubt.

- If the person in breach of the order is able to show that it is more likely than not that they had a reasonable excuse for not complying with the enforcement order the court cannot add to the enforcement order or make a new one in this way.

- The court can only make the changes that are necessary in order to make sure that the person sticks to the child arrangements order in future, and that are proportionate with the seriousness of the breaches of the child arrangements order and enforcement order.

If an enforcement order has been broken it might be appropriate to make an application to commit (see below).

Compensation orders are dealt with in sections 11O and 11P CA.

The court can order financial compensation to be paid by the person in breach of a child arrangements order to someone else if they have suffered financial loss because of the breach. The main people who are allowed to ask for financial compensation are the person the child lives with, the person whose contact it is, or the child [s110 CA].

- The amount of compensation will not be more than the amount by which the person is actually out of pocket. This amount must be proved (for example bus or train tickets or fuel receipts).

- The court must consider the financial circumstances of the person paying.

As with enforcement orders the court cannot make a financial compensation order if there is a reasonable excuse for the breach. Unlike enforcement orders the breach only needs to be proved on the balance of probabilities which means more likely than not, rather than beyond reasonable doubt.

As with enforcement orders there must have been a warning notice on the order and it must have been sent to the person in breach before the order was broken.

19.7   Committal for breach of contact or enforcement order

Until the powers to make enforcement and compensation orders were created in recent years the only way the court could enforce a contact order (before they were abolished) was through the threat of committal to prison. This was not very effective because it was almost always counterproductive to send the children's main carer to prison, and did nothing to help relations between the parents or between the children and the parent seeking contact, who were often upset at the thought that daddy was trying to have mummy sent to prison.

These problems still exist. And now that the court has alternatives in the form of enforcement orders the courts are even less likely to use these powers to enforce breach of orders, probably not unless all other options have been tried and failed - for example, an application to commit could be made where an enforcement order has been broken.

The procedure for committal is set out in the general chapter on enforcement (see Chapter 23).

NB: If you are facing an application for your committal you are entitled to legal aid to defend yourself. Unusually this can be granted by the Judge dealing with the case - this is not widely understood by judges or lawyers so if you have any difficulty refer them to the case of *Re Ramet (Application for the Committal to Prison)* [2014] EWHC 56 (Fam) (see in particular paragraphs 33-34).

19.8   Child not returned home

Child arrangements orders can also be enforced through s33 and s34 FLA 1986 as described in Chapter 17.

Where someone is keeping a child in breach of a child arrangements order the court can order them to return the child and if that order was broken could enforce that breach by committal. In order to make the breach enforceable the order would have to be precise about when and where the child was to be returned, it would have to attach a penal notice and it would have to be personally served on the person who was keeping the child before the time had expired for returning the child. Details of how to make an application for committal are set out in Chapter 23.

20. Special Cases - People Other Than Parents, Kinship Care & Assisted Reproduction

20.1 Introduction

There are a number of scenarios in which adults other than parents may be involved in proceedings relating to children, and very often legal aid is not available. I have tried to cover those scenarios which are most likely to come up in this chapter.

The scenarios when someone other than a parent is most likely to become involved with the Family Court but without a lawyer are:

- When a step parent, grandparent or adult sibling is asking to see a child,

- When a member of the extended family or family friend is caring for the child,

- When a member of the extended family or family friend wishes to care for a child who has been taken into care,

- When a child has been badly injured and the injury is not thought to be accidental and there are a number of people who had the opportunity to cause the injury or abuse the child, and the court is going to hear evidence to work out who it was, anyone who it is suggested had the opportunity to cause the injuries may be invited to be involved in this part of the case as an 'intervenor',

- When a child or adult has alleged that the child has been abused by someone other than a parent and the court needs to hear evidence to work out if that is true or not, the person who it is suggested has done this may be involved in this part of the case as an intervenor,

- Where one spouse (or civil partner) is asking the court to give them a share of property you have an interest in or that is held in your name, or where one spouse says a property in your name isn't really yours. You might be invited to intervene,

- Where a child has been conceived through some non-conventional means, for example through gamete (sperm or egg) donation (through a clinic or by informal arrangement) or through surrogacy, and where as a result there is confusion or disagreement about the legal status of the adults involved and what role they should play in the child's life.

This book mainly deals with cases where the dispute is between parents. Lawyers call this type of case 'private law' as the dispute is between private individuals, even though social services might be asked to give a view. Where the state through social services applies to the court to take a child into care, this is called a 'public law' case because a public body is one of the parties to the case. The child is also made a party to this type of case and is given their own Guardian whose job it is to tell the court what is in their best interests and what they want (not the same as a guardian appointed to care for a child whose parents have died).

In public law cases parents are automatically entitled to legal aid and so this book does not need to cover this type of case. When non-parents are asking the court to make orders about contact or in relation to a child living with them, they would normally do this by making a private law application, but if social services have already made their own application, they would need to try and join in the public law case. For that reason this chapter gives a little bit of information about public law proceedings.

This is quite a wide ranging list, so this chapter is a bit of a catch-all.

20.2 Care proceedings

A Local Authority social services department (LA) applies for a care order or supervision order when they are worried that a child has suffered significant harm or that they might do so if they don't do something to protect the child, for example by removing them from their parents. Often the court will make interim (temporary) care or supervision orders whilst it is gathering information about what should happen in the long term.

A care order gives the LA parental responsibility (PR) along with the child's Mother, and Father (if he has PR). A supervision order does not give the LA PR, so whilst the LA can keep an eye on what is happening at home the LA does not have so much control.

If the court makes an interim care order the child will often be removed from home, although sometimes a child can remain at home even with a care order in place (perhaps with regular spot checks), because the care order allows the LA to remove the child if things deteriorate at home (although usually an LA would come back to court as soon as possible if this happened). Before a care order is made the LA will prepare a written care plan that says what the LA plan to do with the child if the order is made - usually but not always the plan is to place the child away from home at least for a short time, until everyone can work out what should happen in the long term.

If the LA think a child needs to be removed from home, they have a duty to try and place the child with a family member if possible. There might be a care or supervision order in place whilst the child is living with the family member, or if the LA is not so worried about retaining the power to control things a child arrangements order saying the child should live with the family member might be enough, sometimes coupled with a supervision order. If a child arrangements order of this sort is made instead of a care order the person named in the order as the person the child will live with will gain parental responsibility, but the LA won't (parental responsibility is explained at Chapter 17).

If a child is in foster care, the priority will probably be to ensure that the child has contact firstly with her parents, or the primary carer if this is someone different. Sometimes this means that other family members get pushed to the back of the queue, particularly with older children who have lots of after school activities to fit in or where transport arrangements make contact difficult or disruptive.

If you are related to a child in care and wish to have contact or want to offer to have them living with you in the short or long term, you need firstly to make contact with the child's social worker to let them know and to ask them to assess you. You should do this as soon as possible and you should try and confirm your request in writing. The social worker should make a decision about contact and should carry out a kinship assessment. This will involve them meeting with you and anybody else who lives in your home, carrying out Police and social services checks, visiting your home and possibly taking up references. Often this is done in two stages - a short viability assessment, and if this is positive a fuller assessment.

Sometimes when a public law case is started there is an urgent need to find somewhere for the child to stay, and they may be allowed to stay with you for a short period whilst the assessment is being carried out. Under Regulation 17-24 of the Care Planning, Placement and Case Review Regulations 2010 the LA can allow a child to stay with a family member for up to ten days whilst their suitability is being assessed. This can be extended for up to 16 weeks to allow a full assessment to be carried out. If you find yourself caring for a relative in this way you should ask immediately for a full assessment of your ability to care in the medium to long term so that this can be done before the ten days runs out. You may not want to make decisions yet about caring for a child long term but if it turns out that the child cannot return home the court will want to move quickly, so it is important to push for an early assessment if there is a chance you would offer your home in those circumstances. You can do this even though your preference would be for the child to go home as long as that is safe. Slightly different regulations apply in Wales [The Care Planning, Placement and Case Review (Wales) Regulations 2015 (Regs 16-21)].

Why the rush? Can't I wait and see?

It is important to understand that this sort of case must now be concluded within six months by law, unless an extension is granted by the court. That is the window for all options for the children's care to be explored - there is no time to wait and see if the parents can pull up their socks and resume care of the child. Anybody who wishes to be considered, even if it is just as a fall-back, must ask to be assessed at the earliest possible moment. This can cause tensions because it can seem as if you are undermining the parents of the child, but the parents will have been advised by their own lawyers from the beginning that this is a necessary part of the process. It is important that family members are assessed as a fall back because if the parents cannot resume care of the children and there is no family member with a positive assessment at the end of the case the court may well be asked to make placement orders, enabling a child to be adopted by strangers.

If your assessment is positive you may need to make an application to the court for a child arrangements order saying the child should live with you, or for a special guardianship order, or the child may be placed with you as an approved foster carer. The difference between these is explained below. You might want to take some legal advice about which is the appropriate arrangement, so sometimes if you cannot get legal aid and cannot afford advice, and the LA is supportive they may well pay for you to obtain some advice from a local solicitor (they have a duty to consider whether they should do this). Websites like Grandparents Alliance, Coram Children's Legal Centre and Family Rights Group have some useful information on them.

If your assessment is not positive and you still want to have contact or to have a chance to care for the child, you may need to try and join in the care case and you may need to ask the court for a reassessment, preferably from someone independent of the LA who have already made their mind up about you. You need to take action as soon as possible and it is a good idea to see if you can get legal aid or afford some legal advice at this stage. If you are caring for a child under a child arrangements order or your son or daughter has delegated PR to you in writing you may be able to obtain legal aid, depending on your finances and the strength of your case. You should ask the social worker for a copy of the assessment they have carried out. If one or both of the parents is supportive of the child living with you, you may find it helpful to make contact with one of their solicitors who may be able to help explain where the case has got to and give you the case number. This basic information is useful so that:

- you can refer to it in your own application,

- you can find out the date for the next hearing,

- you can go along and ask the Judge to hear what you want to say.

You may also be able to make contact with the child's Guardian who may want to find out more about you before making their own recommendations to the court. The Guardian's views are important, and they might disagree with the view of the social worker who assessed you.

If you do need to make an application to court you will need to complete form C2 (assuming you can't get legal aid so a solicitor can do all this for you). You should complete as much of it as you can including the case number, names of the parties and their solicitors / contact details and date of the next hearing if known - if you do not have all the contact details for the other parties you could ask any solicitor that you do know is involved, or you could just explain in your application that you are missing information. You will need to make clear if (for example) you wish to be made a party to the case, and that you want a further assessment, and what all this is for (for example, you want to care for the child). You will need to say briefly why a further assessment is necessary (for example, what is wrong with the existing one?). You will need to either send your application to all the parties or ask the court to serve it on them. Check if you qualify for help with fees.

20.3 Contact

Contact where the child is not in care

This section assumes that you have tried and failed to make arrangements for contact by agreement with one or both parents. You must have attended a Mediation Information and Assessment Meeting (MIAM) before starting a case of this kind [PD 3A]. There are exceptions to this. Further details of this scheme are set out in Chapter 8.

You should read Chapter 16 which tells you about child arrangements orders under s8 Children Act and the welfare checklist. These general principles all apply to contact applications by non-parents and are not repeated here.

Non-parents often need permission to make an application for a child arrangements orders [s10 Children Act 1989]. You will not need permission if:

- you are married to or are the civil partner of one of the child's parents and the child has been treated as a child of your family (step-parent),

- the child has lived with you for three years or more overall (counting any periods between five years ago and ending no more than three months ago),

- you have the agreement of everyone who is named in a child arrangements order as a person the child lives with and who has parental responsibility,

- the child is in care and you have the agreement of social services, or

- everybody who has parental responsibility (usually one or both parents) agrees.

If none of the exceptions above apply you will need to make an application for leave (permission) to apply for a child arrangements order. When deciding whether to give you permission, the court will look at s10(9) of the Children Act 1989 which says that it must consider all the circumstances but focusing on:

- the nature of the application you are asking to make,

- your connection with the child,

- any risk that there might be of the application disrupting the child's life to such an extent that he would be harmed by it,

- if the child is being looked after by social services, their plans for the child's future and the parents' wishes and feelings.

To apply for leave to make your application fill in form C2 (available on the Justice website or at the court office). You may have to pay a fee, although this may not be payable if you are on a low income. Ask at the court office. At the same time as you make the application for leave you should also fill in the main application form for contact.

If there are already private law proceedings up and running between the child's parents C2 is the only form that you will need - say at section 2 of that form that you want:

- leave to apply for a child arrangements order (if necessary),

- to be joined as a party to the existing proceedings,

- to make an application for a child arrangements order within the existing proceedings.

If there are no other proceedings already running, then you must fill in form C100 which is the main contact application form (and form C2 as above if you need permission). In the box for 'Respondent's name' be sure to include the names of both parents (and, if the child is living with somebody else instead of a parent, the name of the person the child is living with), and then give further information in the relevant box. Fill in as much of the form as you can. Both forms should be submitted to the court at the same time. If you are also making an application for a child arrangements order saying the child should live with you this all goes on the same form.

The court will then process your application and it will follow the procedure set out in Part 18. The court may deal with it by listing a hearing. If everybody agrees you should have leave this will usually be straightforward and will not hold things up. Sometimes an application for leave will be dealt with separately and it might not be able to be dealt with at the first hearing, so there may be some delay. It very much depends on what other things are going on within any court case that is already running and within the children's lives as to whether your application is able to be the main focus of the court's work or whether other issues must take priority.

If your application for leave is not agreed you should think about what you would say about each of the points set out above from s10(9) of the CA.

Cases which help explain how the court should apply s10(9) CA include *Re J (A Child) (Leave to issue application for residence order)* [2002] EWCA Civ 1346 and *Re H (Children)* [2003] EWCA Civ 369. This second case is not available on BAILII but in summary the court said that where an Applicant (a grandmother) was the only blood relative who was willing and able to advance a case for care of the child, she should have been granted permission to apply for residence and to be a party to the care proceedings.

Contact where the child is in care

If the child is in care a non-parent cannot make an application for contact unless they have parental responsibility, or the child was living with them under a child arrangements order immediately before the care order was made (or the High Court had ordered the child to live with them immediately before the care order was made - this is very unlikely to apply as it happens very rarely).

If you fall into one of the above categories you may make an application for contact without leave (although you should approach the LA first because they may agree that you should have contact anyway and then you would not need to apply for an order). You should fill in form C2 as set out above, saying at section 2 that you want to join the case and that you want to apply for contact to a child in care (if you are also asking for the child to live with you say this here and also fill in form C100 asking for a child arrangements order). Fill in form C15 (an application for contact to a child in care) and take this into the court at the same time.

An order for contact to a child in care is made under s34 CA, not s8 CA and the enforcement rules are different.

20.4 Child arrangements orders - living arrangements

A child arrangements order that says the child lives with you will entitle you to parental responsibility for as long as that order lasts, but you will still need to consult and seek agreement from the parents of the child about their care and life decisions.

If you are not a parent you may need permission to make an application for this sort of child arrangements order. You won't need permission if you fall into any of these categories:

- you are married to or are the civil partner of one of the child's parents and the child has been treated as a child of your family (step-parent),

- the child has lived with you for three years or more overall (counting any periods between five years ago and ending no more than three months ago),

- you have the agreement of everyone who is named in a child arrangements order as a person the child lives with and who has parental responsibility,

- the child is in care and you have the agreement of social services, or

- everybody who has parental responsibility (usually one or both parents) agrees.

OR

- you are a foster parent or relative the child has lived with for at least a year [s10(5A) & (5B) CA] (this only applies to applications for the child to live with you, these people need leave to apply just for contact). If you are a relative who has been asked to take care of a child around the start of care proceedings the court may make an interim child arrangements order confirming that position whilst the case is worked through. If this happens it won't matter that you haven't applied for permission for an order.

If the court orders that a child that has been in the care of the LA should live with you, even if you were previously been caring for the child as a foster carer the LA may pay you an allowance. This is not something that LAs have to do, but most will have a written policy dealing with allowances paid to foster carers or kinship carers. Many LAs publish their policy online (try the search function on their website) or you could email the LA or ask the social worker for a copy. You will be entitled to child benefit and any other tax credits just like a parent, subject to your circumstances. Often grandparents have savings for their retirement which make it difficult to get legal aid or to qualify for benefits. You can make an application for maintenance to the CSA but if the parents are not working this may not do you much good.

A child arrangements order normally only continues until the child is 16 but for non-parents, if you ask for the child arrangements to last up to age 18 the court can make this order [s12(5) CA]).

20.5 Special guardianship

Special guardianship orders are described at s14A-F CA. A special guardianship order (SGO) places a child or a young person to live with a non-parent long term. An SGO is intended to create a long term secure placement and to give the special guardianship all the powers they need to make decisions about the care of a child on a day to day basis, without interference from the child's parents. When it makes an SGO the court can make a child arrangements order saying that the parents should have contact, although in practice this is quite uncommon.

There are some important differences between an SGO and child arrangements orders or adoption. You can think of an SGO as somewhere between child arrangements and adoption:

- It is different from adoption because it does not sever the link to a child's parents as with adoption, and there is more likely to be contact with the parents,

- Unlike adoption, it can be discharged in the future,

- It is more secure than a child arrangements order because a parent cannot apply to have it discharged (and to have the child back living with them) without the permission of the court,

- It is different from a child arrangements order because the special guardian is entitled to exercise their PR without reference to the parents except in very limited circumstances.

Although a parent's ability to exercise their parental responsibility is very limited, where there is a special guardian they remain entitled to be involved in decisions about change of name, adoption or any long trips abroad (more than 3 months).

The Coram Children's Legal Centre produces a really useful leaflet describing special guardianship.

Before an SGO can be made the LA must consider whether or not there should be a financial or other support package put together. Depending on your means they have a duty to provide a special guardian allowance.

You will be entitled to child benefit and any other tax credits just like a parent, subject to your circumstances.

The SGO allowance is ignored when your tax credits are calculated. You should make sure you have been properly assessed for support and financial assistance before the court makes the SGO.

20.6 Fostering

As a foster carer looking after a child under a care order you will not have parental responsibility for the child, whereas the LA will have parental responsibility. This has two important consequences:

- You will not be able to make decisions about the care of the child without the approval of the LA (through the social worker) and the agreement of the child's parents (if they have parental responsibility).

- The LA will have an ongoing responsibility to ensure that you are looking after the child in a way that they think is appropriate. If they do not think that things are going as they ought to the LA might want to place the child elsewhere. This means that you may be better supported, but you will have to allow social workers into your home and cooperate with them on a regular basis, and you do not have much security about the future.

As a foster carer you may be entitled to foster carers allowances, and if so these should be at the same rate as non-family foster carers. The law can be quite difficult to understand in this area but it can be roughly summarised by saying that if the LA have approached you to arrange accommodation for a child then you are acting as a foster carer for them, and they have to pay you just like any other foster carer. If the arrangement is one reached between you and the parents entirely independently of the LA it is a private fostering arrangement and they don't have to pay you as a foster carer. A case called *SA v KCC* [2010] EWHC 848 (Admin) covers this, but it is really complicated to read.

If you think that the LA is not paying you the right amount of allowances, firstly get a copy of their policy and check it to see if they are complying with it. If they are not, write to them explaining why they are not and asking for it to be remedied and for payments to be backdated (check their complaints policy to make sure you are going about it the right way). Send a copy of your letter to the Guardian's solicitor. If you have tried and failed to resolve the issue by talking to the social worker or by complaining to the LA, you can ask the Local Government Ombudsman to look at it. Websites like Family Rights Group and the Coram Children's Legal Centre may have useful information about these sorts of issues.

You will not be able to claim child tax credits or working tax credits for any child you are caring for as a foster carer (this does not stop you claiming for any of your own children). You might be able to claim working tax credits for your own children even if you were not previously able to, because, as a foster carer, you are likely to be treated as employed full time. You should ask for help from your CAB, local Law Centre or the social worker in assessing the impact on your finances of being a foster carer. You could also look at the Child Poverty Action Group website (click on 'search this site' and type in 'foster carer') which has lots of helpful information.

20.7 Intervenors - non-accidental injury

When it has to decide how a child has suffered injuries the court will try and work out who is in 'the pool of potential perpetrators'. That is likely to be anyone who had sole care of the child or who was left alone with the child in the period when the injury was likely to have been caused, such as parents, grandparents, babysitter or child-minder.

If there are people who are in the pool who are not already involved in the case the court may decide to invite them to be involved in the fact finding part of the case so that it can make a decision based on as much evidence as possible, and so that anybody who might have a finding made against them has an opportunity to defend themselves.

If a finding is made that a person has deliberately injured a child it might not affect them immediately, but it could have very serious consequences in the long run. If the person goes on to have their own child, or to move in with a partner who has children, social services might decide that the children were not safe in the care of the person who has the finding against them and might want to remove the children. So it is important not to ignore an invitation to intervene - the court will have made the order because the allegations are serious and you are at risk.

What to do if you are invited to intervene

If you can get a lawyer do so straight away. Ask the court or one of the lawyers in the case for a set of the papers straight away. Go to any hearing you have been told about even if you have not yet managed to get a lawyer and tell the court you want to be involved but that you are trying to get a lawyer sorted out. Ask for an adjournment to allow you to get a lawyer if necessary.

Read the sections on fact finding in the chapters on domestic violence and children to get an understanding of generally how these hearings operate. The principles will be the same, although with a non-accidental injury there might be lots of complex expert evidence about the injuries, how they were caused and when they were inflicted. This is one of the reasons you might need a lawyer.

20.8 Assisted reproduction

When a couple or individual conceives a child through the use of some form of assisted conception / gamete donation, the question of whether the donor has any entitlement or responsibility depends upon whether or not the conception was carried out so as to comply with the requirements of the Human Fertilisation & Embryology Act 2008 [HFEA]. If the criteria were complied with a donor will have neither any financial liability for the child through child support nor any legal status as a parent, and the partner of the person carrying the child will be entitled to be treated as the father / parent.

The provisions of the HFEA apply to children conceived through assisted conception by a married heterosexual couple, civil partners, a married female couple, or living as partners in an enduring family relationship. They are quite complicated, and the summary below is just intended to give you a rough outline.

Where the child has been conceived by the placing of sperm, eggs or both inside the woman carrying the child, the woman who carries the child is treated as the mother (except in surrogacy cases - see below).

Married heterosexual couple

If a woman carrying the child was married to a man at the time of conception, and the child was conceived by using someone else's sperm through artificial insemination (i.e. not through intercourse) or through the insertion of an egg or embryo, her husband is treated as the father unless it is shown he didn't consent to the insemination / implantation [s35 HFEA].

Unmarried heterosexual couple

Where a woman is carrying a child as a result of treatment (egg / embryo donation or artificial insemination) but where the embryo was not created using the male partner's sperm, the male partner will be treated as the father of any resulting child if the couple have each given written consents to him being treated as the father, and those consents have not been withdrawn [s36-7].

In these cases the donor of the sperm is not to be treated as the father of the child [s41].

The Father will be able to obtain PR in the usual ways, through registration on the birth certificate, PR order or agreement [s4 CA, see Chapter 20 for more about PR].

NB: The above *only applies* if the pregnancy arises 'in the course of treatment services provided in the UK by a person to whom a licence applies' i.e. through a clinic NOT to informal arrangement / home artificial insemination between friends or through the internet.

In cases where three adults make informal arrangements between them the legal parents will be the person whose genetic material led to the pregnancy even if they have agreed something else.

Heterosexual woman - deceased husband

Where a woman who has become pregnant by using her dead husband's sperm and the husband consented to that before his death he may be treated as the father of the child [s39]. If the pregnancy arose from a donated egg implanted after the husband's death the husband may also be treated as the father of that child if he consented (as long as the law doesn't make someone else the father) [s40]. In these cases the woman must take steps to register the husband as the father within 6 weeks of the birth.

In these cases the donor of the sperm is not to be treated as the father of the child [s41].

Female civil partners / married couple

Where a woman is married to or in a civil partnership with another woman and conceives by artificial insemination or egg donation the other woman is treated as a parent of the child unless it is shown she did not consent to the process [s42].

The second female parent automatically has PR [s2 CA, see Chapter 20].

Female partners - not married or in civil partnership

If one woman has given an egg and both she and the woman who is carrying the resulting child have given written consent to her (the woman giving the egg) being treated as a parent, and if those consents have not been withdrawn, then the she is treated as a parent [s43-44].

As with sperm donors, a woman who is a simple egg donor is not to be treated as the parent of the child [s47].

NB: This only applies if the pregnancy arises 'in the course of treatment services provided in the UK by a person to whom a licence applies' i.e. through a clinic NOT to informal sperm donation between friends or through the internet.

In cases where three adults make informal arrangements between them the legal parents will be the person whose genetic material led to the pregnancy even if they have agreed something else.

The second female parent automatically has PR if she has entered into civil partnership / marriage with the mother at any point between conception and birth. Otherwise she can obtain PR by registration on the birth certificate, or by PR order or agreement (as with an unmarried father) [s2 / s4ZA CA, see Chapter 20 for more about PR].

Surrogacy

Under s 54 HFEA a couple can make a joint application to court for a parental order, relating to a child carried by another woman through a surrogacy arrangement. The order confirms that the child is to be treated in law as the child of the couple.

The child must have been conceived by using either the sperm or eggs of one of the couple applying for the order.

The Applicants must be either by husband and wife, civil partners or two persons living as partners in an enduring family relationship (but not close family members). The couple's relationship must be ongoing.

Both partners and the woman who carried the child must have **freely, and with full understanding of what is involved, agreed unconditionally to the making of the order**.

No money can have changed hands other than legitimate expenses of the woman carrying the child.

The child's home must be with the Applicants and one of them must be domiciled in the UK / Channel Islands / Isle of Man at the date of the application in order for the court to be allowed to make the order.

The application must be made within six months of the child's birth but the order cannot be made within six weeks of birth because the woman who carried the child cannot give valid consent for six weeks after delivery.

Although it is beyond the scope of this book to deal in detail with the HFEA it is important to note that the criteria are very specific (and are not set out in full above).

If you are in a same sex relationship and considering some form of assisted conception you need to be very careful about the arrangements that you come to and give them some serious thought in advance. Private or informal arrangements between friends or acquaintances relating to sperm donation that are not carried out through a clinic may have very different legal consequences for the status of both the female and male participants than in cases that fall under the HFEA 2008 - the legal status of a male donor and second female parent could be fundamentally different to what you anticipated or agreed. Similarly, if you are considering donating sperm you need to be sure you understand what your legal rights and responsibilities are. Depending on whether or not the requirements of the HFEA are complied with you may not be treated as the legal father. On the other hand you could find yourself legally responsible for maintaining a child that you never intended to have responsibility for.

It is worth saying that even if a male donor is not legally the father of a child it may be that he will be able later to make a successful application for contact if the child has an established relationship with him or the court thinks it would be in his interests to maintain a link. Agreements between the adults prior to the conception may not be legally binding and the court may override them if it is in the best interests of the child.

It is vitally important that all parties involved have a common understanding of what their role and legal status will be once the child is born. This is best obtained by taking legal advice before conception - do your research and don't just rely on this book.

Problems with parental orders

There have been a significant number of cases in the last few years where something has gone wrong with the process of arranging a surrogacy and the court has had to try and sort things out - if the correct consents are not recorded properly at the time of conception an intended parent can be left without legal status. In a number of cases the clinics who have arranged things have failed to get the right signatures on the right forms, and this has meant that adults involved cannot legally be treated as a parent as planned. It is really important that you use a reputable clinic (check the Human Fertilisation and Embryology Authority (HFEA) website - they have previously audited clinics on this issue and identified quite widespread problems with proper consent forms).

To achieve legal status as parents, a parental order must be applied for before the child is 6 months old - although in some unusual circumstances the courts have extended that this is not something that you should bank on. The gov.uk website covers how to apply at www.gov.uk/become-a-childs-legal-parent.

20.9 Intervening in financial proceedings between spouses or civil partners

If you become aware of a dispute between spouses about whether or not you own a property or about what your share in it is, it is important that you respond to any invitation to intervene in the proceedings promptly, making very clear what your position is. If you ignore the court case having been told about it you could find that the court makes an order saying you don't own the property and you will be bound by it (stuck with it). If you find out about this sort of dispute but haven't been asked to intervene you can ask the court if you can, so that you can have your say, put forward your evidence and explain to the court why you say you own or are entitled to some or all of the property.

PART 5: DOMESTIC VIOLENCE & ABUSE

21.   The Law Relating To Domestic Violence & Abuse

21.1   Introduction

Both the Family Court and the criminal courts deal with domestic violence and abuse, but in different ways. This book does not cover the criminal courts, but there is a little bit of information at the end of this chapter about something called a 'go order'.

When lawyers, Judges and those who work with the victims of domestic violence talk about 'domestic violence' or 'domestic abuse' they mean more than just physical violence or hitting. PD 12J defines it as follows:

> *'The term 'domestic violence' includes any incident or pattern of incidents of controlling, coercive or threatening behaviour, violence or abuse between those aged 16 or over who are or have been intimate partners or family members regardless of gender or sexuality. This can encompass, but is not limited to, psychological, physical, sexual, financial or emotional abuse.*
>
> *'Controlling behaviour' means an act or pattern of acts designed to make a person subordinate and / or dependent by isolating them from sources of support, exploiting their resources and capacities for personal gain, depriving them of the means needed for independence, resistance and escape and regulating their everyday behaviour.*
>
> *'Coercive behaviour' means an act or a pattern of acts of assault, threats, humiliation and intimidation or other abuse that is used to harm, punish or frighten the victim.'*

This definition has been drawn from the Government's cross-departmental definition of domestic violence and abuse. Coercive control has been a criminal offence since 2015.

At the time of writing the definition is likely to be amended to also say:

> *'Harm' means ill-treatment or the impairment of health or development including, for example, impairment suffered from seeing or hearing the ill-treatment of another; 'development' means physical, intellectual, emotional, social or behavioural development; 'health' means physical or mental health; and 'ill-treatment' includes sexual abuse and forms of ill- treatment which are not physical.*

This draws together the definitions of harm and other terms already contained in The CA 1989.

In this chapter I'm going to use the word domestic *abuse* to cover domestic violence and other kinds of abuse.

Harassment is usually described as any behaviour which happens more than once and which the person receiving it finds upsetting and wants to stop. This could be anything from lots of nuisance phone calls, or abusive texts, to repeatedly coming round to a person's house or hanging around where they are likely to be.

If a partner, spouse or ex (or other family member) has been violent, abusive, threatening or harassing the person on the receiving end will often seek protection from the Family Courts through an injunction, called a non-molestation order (often shortened by lawyers to 'non-mol') or an order stopping the abusive person from returning to the family home (an occupation order). The power to make a non-mol or occupation order comes from Part IV of The Family Law Act 1996 (FLA) (Note: there is also an FLA 1986, which is different). They can also go to the Police, which may lead to a criminal prosecution. You may have heard the phrase 'restraining orders'; this is a term used in the USA and which you may have heard on television dramas or seen in newspapers. A restraining order in England & Wales is similar to a non-molestation order, but it is usually made in non-family 'stalking' type cases or in Criminal Courts (Protection from Harassment Act 1997 or PHA). This book deals with non-mols, but does not deal with restraining orders. Non-mols are dealt with in more detail below.

Even if there is no application for an injunction or occupation order, Family Courts also have to consider allegations of domestic violence when they are dealing with cases concerning children. If a parent says that the other parent should not have contact, or should have restricted contact because they have been violent and the other parent does not agree that allegations of abuse are true or accurate, the court may have to hear evidence about the allegations of abuse and decide what did and did not happen. This is called 'fact finding' and is often carried out at a special hearing just for that purpose. Lawyers call this a fact finding hearing, or a *'Re L'* hearing (*Re L & Others (Contact: Domestic Violence)* [2000] EWCA Civ 194). *Re L* is a case which gives guidance to the courts about how to deal with allegations of domestic abuse and it tells the courts that if the violence or abuse that is alleged to have taken place is so serious that it would affect the court's decision on contact, the court must first decide what has actually taken place (make findings) before going any further. Once any fact finding has taken place the court will decide how its findings impact on the question of contact. This second stage of the process is called the 'welfare stage'.

More information about how domestic abuse is likely to be handled in cases involving children is contained in Chapter 22 (which looks at the practical side of domestic abuse cases) and in PD 12J.

21.2   Non-molestation orders

In the words of the FLA, a non-molestation order is an order **prohibiting** (stopping) a person (the Respondent) from **molesting another person** who is **associated** with them [s42]. An order that stops someone doing something is called an injunction, so a non-mol is a kind of injunction.

First of all you need to work out if the person asking for the order and the person who is stopped from doing something by the order are 'associated', because the court can only make an order if they are.

You are associated if you have been engaged (but only for three years after your engagement ended), married, civil partners, lived together (as partners rather than lodgers etc) or have a child together or if you are related (this does not include very distant relatives - if you are not sure if you are associated because you are related check s63 FLA 1996 for a list).

Even if none of the above apply, you are also associated if you have had an intimate relationship for a significant duration (intimate probably means sexual or at least romantic. A brief fling probably doesn't count, but a serious and established relationship that has been going for a while would.)

You are associated if you are both parties to other family proceedings

There are a few other situations in which you might be 'associated' but they are unusual.

Occasionally people find that they cannot fit into any of the categories that make them associated and they cannot get an order under the FLA 1996. If this is the case the court has similar powers to make an injunction under the PHA (often called a restraining order). The PHA is not dealt with in this book.

Molestation in this context doesn't just mean inappropriate physical touching, which is probably what it might mean to most people. You can think of molestation as a sort of old fashioned term which really means harassment. If an order is made it will usually not say 'you must not molest' or even 'you must not harass' because it is difficult to understand exactly what that means. Usually an order will set out a list of things that would be molestation, for example sending text messages or attending a particular address.

When can the court make a non-molestation order?

The court can make an order protecting the person asking for the order (the Applicant) or any **relevant children** (or both). A 'relevant child' is generally a child living with or who might reasonably be expected to live with either of you.

Normally an application has to be made in writing on the correct form, but even where there is no application, a Judge dealing with Family Court proceedings in that area already started between you can decide to make an order if he thinks that it is necessary [s42(2)(b) FLA]. This doesn't happen very often, perhaps most often if one person is very threatening or abusive in court and in front of the Judge.

The court has to consider all the circumstances when it decides whether to make an order, but the FLA tells the Judge to look in particular at the health, safety and wellbeing of the person asking for the order and any relevant child.

There is no fixed length for an order. It is up to the court how long to make the order for. Most often it is made for a year.

What if it's urgent or it is unsafe to let the other person know you are going to court for an order?

Often the person asking for the order needs the order to protect them immediately, or they need the order to be in place before the other person finds out they have come to court in case they react badly. In cases like this the court will arrange a short hearing the day the application is issued and will make a temporary order to protect the person until a hearing can be arranged once the other person knows what has happened (Lawyers call a temporary order an 'interim order'). This type of hearing where only one party knows and attends is called a 'without notice' hearing and the order that is made is called a 'without notice' order (Lawyers and Judges often call this *'ex parte'* which means the same thing - the FLA itself describes these orders as *'ex parte'*).

The court can make a 'without notice' order **where it considers it just and convenient to do so** [s45 FLA]. The court again has to look at all the circumstances, but s45 of the FLA mentions in particular:

- **Any risk of significant harm** to the person asking for the order (or any relevant child) caused by the other person if the order is not made straight away

- Whether the person asking for the order is likely to be put off applying if the order is not made straight away

- Whether the other person probably knows that the person is trying to get an order but is avoiding being served with papers to stop this happening, and if keeping on trying to serve the papers is going to cause very serious problems.

If the court makes an order before the other person has been told, it should usually fix another hearing after the other person has been told so that they have a chance to say whether or not they object to the order continuing. This is sometimes called a return date hearing.

21.3 Breach of non-molestation orders

If a person who is told not to do something by a non-mol breaks the order this is called a breach.

Any breach of a non-mol is a criminal offence. The maximum penalty is five years in prison.

Any breach of a non-mol is an arrestable offence, even if it is not something that would otherwise be something the Police could arrest someone for. This means the Police are *allowed* to arrest, but doesn't mean they *have* to arrest.

The Family Court does still have the power to punish a person for breach of a non-mol, but this is rarely used. It might be used where the Police keep on failing to act on breaches of the order. In order to get the Family Court to punish for breach an application has to be made to the Family Court for a warrant of arrest. This is a document that tells the Police to arrest the person breaking the order and to bring him to court [s47(8) FLA].

21.4 Undertakings

An undertaking is a solemn promise given to the court. Where someone asks for a non-mol order the court can accept an undertaking instead, promising not to do the things that would have been prevented by an order. Because breaking an undertaking is not a criminal offence, the court can only accept an undertaking where it is happy that the risk of a criminal prosecution is not needed to stop the person from behaving badly.

If an undertaking is broken (breached) the person who has broken their promise can be punished by the Family Court, because breaking a promise to the court is a contempt of court. This can only happen if an application is made by the person who was asking for the order and if the breach is admitted or proved (just like a criminal case it must be proved 'beyond reasonable doubt'). The court can fine the person or send them to prison, although they won't get a criminal record. The longest they can be sent to prison is two years (but you can think of this as roughly equivalent to a four year criminal sentence, because there is no early release on licence like in criminal cases). Quite often the court will suspend the sentence if this is the first breach, and a first breach would not usually receive a sentence of anything near two years unless it was very serious.

An undertaking is between the court and the parties to the case. It does not give the Police any particular powers.

21.5 Occupation orders

An occupation order is an order making rules about who can live in a house, how they must behave in the house and which parts of it they can use. It can tell a person they must leave a house, must not go to a house or must not go within a certain distance of it, or down the street it is on.

An occupation order telling somebody they must leave their home is not usually made unless there are very good reasons, and unlike non-mols (which are often made without notice and on an urgent basis) occupation orders are usually only made after the person who might be asked to leave has had a chance to say why this shouldn't happen at a court hearing.

Depending on the circumstances, an occupation order can be made under any one of sections 33-38 FLA. Each of them is slightly different so it is important to work out which applies to you:

(a) If the person wanting an occupation order is **entitled to occupy** the property they want the order about, the application comes under s33 FLA, which gives the court the greatest powers. This includes people who own their home, are named on the tenancy of their home or whose spouse or civil partner owns the home or is named on the tenancy, as long as the property has been their home together (or was intended to be).

An occupation order under this section can be addressed to any associated person (see above) who lives or has lived in the house or was going to live in the house.

Most cases fall under this section, so you only need to read about the other sections if the person asking for an order is not entitled to occupy.

The court has to consider all the circumstances including [s33(6) FLA]:

- **The housing needs and housing resources** of both parties and relevant children

- **The financial resources** of each party

- The likely effect of any order or of a decision not to make one on the health, safety and wellbeing of the parties and any relevant child

- The conduct of the parties

As well as looking at the factors above, the court has to decide where the 'balance of harm' lies. s33(7) describes the way the court must make its decision. It's quite tricky to explain, but in a nutshell where it is worried that the consequences of either course of action are very serious, the court has to work out the least risky option. It says, that if the court thinks that the person asking for the order (or any relevant child) is **likely to suffer significant harm** from the other person without the order being made, then the court MUST make the order UNLESS the other person (or relevant child) is likely to suffer equally bad or worse significant harm themselves if an order IS made.

There is no restriction on how long an order under this section can last for.

(b) Where you are divorced or ex-civil partners and one of you has no right to occupy you will fall under s35 FLA. (Unless the court has made an order before your divorce / dissolution was finalised you will only have the right to occupy if your name is on the tenancy or if the house is owned in your name or joint names. See Home Rights below.)

The person without the right to occupy can apply for an order against the person who is entitled to occupy. The person with the right to occupy would apply under s33.

The type of orders that can be made under s35 are very similar to s33.

The things the court has to think about before deciding whether to make an order (the criteria) are slightly different to s33. As well as the things described above under s33 (housing needs, financial resources, effect of an order, conduct etc) the court must also think about:

- the length of time since you lived together,

- how long it is since you were divorced / your civil partnership was dissolved, and

- whether there are still financial proceedings running arising from your divorce or dissolution that concern a house, or any proceedings concerning financial provision for a child (see Chapter 15 on Schedule 1 Children Act 1989).

The court can make an order telling the person without rights they can stay or come back, and telling the other person not to stop them, as long as it has considered all the circumstances (including the list above).

If the court thinks that the unentitled person (or relevant child) might suffer **significant harm** from the entitled person if it does not also make an order which tells the entitled person to leave or which tells them how they must behave in the home then it *has* to make that extra order, *unless* the person entitled to occupy (or relevant child) might suffer as much or more harm as a result. This is the balance of harm test again.

Orders under this section can be made for a maximum of six months only and can be extended more than once for six months at a time.

(c) Where you are or were living together as a couple (but not married or civil partners) and one of you has no right to occupy you are covered by s36 FLA, for example if the house or tenancy is in one of your names only.

The person without the right to occupy can apply for an order against the person who is entitled to occupy. The person with the right to occupy would apply under s33.

The type of orders that can be made under s36 are very similar to s33.

Again, the things the court has to think about before deciding whether to make an order are slightly different to s33. As well as the things described above under s33 (housing needs, financial resources, effect of an order, conduct etc) the court must also think about:

- the nature of your relationship and how much commitment was involved

- how long you cohabited for

- whether there are any children of both of you or who you have both had parental responsibility for

- the length of time since you lived together, and

- whether there are any financial proceedings running concerning a house or financial provision for a child (see Chapter 15 on Schedule 1 Children Act 1989).

The court can make an order telling the person without rights they can stay (or come back), and telling the other person not to stop them as long as it has considered all the circumstances (including the list above). But if the court is being asked to make an order which tells the person who is entitled to occupy to leave or which tells them how they must behave in the home it must think about whether or not the person asking for the order (or relevant child) is likely to suffer significant harm from the other person without that type of order, and whether the harm suffered by the other person might be as bad or worse. Unlike the sections dealt with so far the law does not tell the Judge he MUST make an order - it is up to the Judge to make a decision once he has thought about all these things.

Orders under this section can be made for a maximum of six months only and can be extended once only for a period of up to six months.

(d) Where you are or have been married / civil partners but neither of you are entitled to occupy (for example you are lodgers, illegal subtenants, squatters or licensees) you are covered by s37 FLA.

To apply for an order under this section BOTH of you must still be living in the house which was your home together when you were married / civil partners. Either of you can apply for an order.

The court has to bear in mind the same things as under s33(6) and (7) (housing needs and resource, finances, effect of order, conduct and the balance of harm test where there is a risk of significant harm).

Orders under this section can be made for a maximum of six months only and can be extended more than once for six months at a time.

(e) Where you are or were living together (not married / civil partners) but neither of you are entitled to occupy, you are covered by s38 FLA.

To apply for an order under this section BOTH of you must still be living in the house which was your home together when you were a couple. Either of you can apply for an order.

The court has to bear in mind the same things as under s33(6) (housing needs and resource, finances, effect of order, conduct) and it has to consider the risk of significant harm, but it does not have to carry out the balance of harm test, and the law does not tell the court it MUST make an order.

Orders under this section can be made for a maximum of six months only and can be extended once only for a period of up to six months.

21.6 Breach of occupation orders

Unlike a non-mol, a breach of an occupation order is not a criminal offence. It can be punished by the Family Court in the same way that a breach of undertaking can be punished (see above).

When a court makes an occupation order it usually attaches something called a 'power of arrest', which tells the Police that they can arrest the person if the order is breached. If the court thinks that the person the order is about has used or threatened violence against the person asking for the order (or against a relevant child) it MUST attach this power of arrest unless it is satisfied that it is not needed to protect the Applicant and children. Because occupation orders are usually only made where the court thinks that there has been actual or threatened violence and because it is important that there is no risk of a repeat the power of arrest is almost always attached.

When the Police arrest a person under this kind of power of arrest they are not being arrested for committing a crime (although they might also have committed a crime), but for contempt of court, and they have to be brought by the Police to the Family Court to be dealt with. This must be within 24 hours of arrest or they have to be released. When this happens the court can go on to punish the person for the breach (if it is admitted or proved) without a written application being made by the person who has asked for the order. It is important to establish what piece of law the person has been arrested under - if the arrest has been under criminal powers they cannot be brought to the Family Court in this way.

21.7 Other powers under the Family Law Act 1996

Home rights

If you are both named on the tenancy you are both entitled to occupy the property. This means that you are not allowed to just change the locks.

Married couples and civil partners have something called home rights, which means they are both entitled to occupy the home they share together (or planned to share together) even if the house or tenancy is not in their name (it has to be in the name of one of the partners though). These rights carry on even after separation (and again this means you are not entitled just to change the locks), but once your divorce or your civil partnership dissolution is finalised (or once the other partner dies) these rights end and you will only be entitled to occupy a property that you own or are a tenant of.

The court can make an order extending your home rights but this must be done before the divorce / dissolution is final [s33(5) FLA 1996].

Upkeep and maintenance of property

When it makes an occupation order (under s33, s35 or s36 FLA 1996 only) the court also has the power to make orders about who should pay the mortgage, rent or utilities, and that the person who stays in the home must look after the furniture in it [s40 FLA 1996]. The court doesn't very often make these orders, because usually (at least if you are married or civil partners) this type of thing will be dealt with in the divorce and related financial proceedings, and this type of order is probably only meant to be used as a holding position rather than a long term solution [s40 FLA 1996].

Transfer of tenancies

The court also has the power to make an order transferring certain tenancies (broadly Local Authority or Housing Association tenancies) to one or other party [s53 & Schedule 7 FLA 1996].

The court can make an order at any time if you are cohabitees, but oddly if you are married or civil partners it can only make an order transferring a tenancy once a conditional or final matrimonial order (ending the civil partnership or marriage) has been made.

The court has to consider all the circumstances including:

- the circumstances in which the tenancy was granted,

- the suitability of both of you as tenants and

- the housing needs and resources of both of you and any relevant children,

- both of your financial resources,

- what effect making an order or not making an order is likely to have on the health, safety and wellbeing of any of you.

When making a decision about transferring a tenancy the court doesn't particularly have to think about how you have behaved towards one another (your conduct).

There is more on transferring of tenancies in Chapter 15.

'Go notices' and 'go orders'

Since 2014 the Police have had powers to help protect people they think are victims of domestic violence [Crime & Security Act 2010]. This is because often when they are called out to a domestic dispute, perhaps by neighbours who hear a ruckus, the victim is too frightened to make a complaint for fear of further violence later on.

When the Police attend a call and think that someone is a victim of domestic violence they can issue a Domestic Violence Protection Notice (A go notice or DVPN) which tells the other person to leave and to leave the suspected victim alone. If the person the go notice relates to does something it says they must not do they can be arrested and brought back to court.

Once a go notice has been issued the Police must make an application for a domestic violence protection order (A go order or DVPO) and there must be a hearing at a Magistrate's court within 48 hours.

At the hearing the Magistrates can make a go order if it is satisfied on the balance of probabilities that there has been violence or a threat of violence and that the order is necessary to protect the person from violence or threats. The court can make the order if the person who is to be protected doesn't agree, but it does have to consider their views. The order can last for between two and four weeks. After that it ends. It is intended to give the victim thinking and planning time.

If the person the go order relates to does something it says they must not do they can be arrested and brought back to court.

22. Cases Involving Domestic Violence & Abuse

22.1 Introduction

The law relating to domestic violence and abuse is set out at Chapter 21. In this chapter I'm going to use the word domestic abuse to cover domestic violence *and* other kinds of abuse.

22.2 Non-molestation and occupation orders

An application for a non-molestation order (non-mol) often starts off with a hearing at which the person who is said to have been violent is not present. This is called a 'without notice' hearing because it takes place without both parties knowing (lawyers will sometimes say '*ex parte*' instead). At a without notice hearing the court will treat the evidence temporarily as if it were true and will therefore usually make a temporary (interim) non-molestation order to protect the Applicant until both parties can come back to court for a short hearing, typically within a week or so. This second hearing, when the case returns before the court is called a '*return date*'.

At the return date the court can consider whether the order should continue or what else might need to be done to finally decide the case. There are generally four possible outcomes to this type of return date hearing:

- Respondent offers undertakings instead of orders - if accepted by the Applicant and the court the undertakings will be formally recorded and will replace the temporary non-mol and this will be the end of the matter. Sometimes both parties will give the same undertakings about their behaviour towards one another (these are called cross undertakings). Undertakings are described in detail below;

- If the Respondent agrees to the order continuing the order will run for whatever period is agreed (and approved by the Judge) and there will be no more hearings;

- If the Respondent disputes the allegations or makes counter allegations or says that the order is not necessary or appropriate (for example because the Applicant is abusing the order by initiating contact or inviting the Respondent around), the matter will be listed for a trial with a longer time slot, probably a ½ day or a day rather than the 30 minutes allocated to a return date;

- If the Respondent doesn't turn up the order is likely to continue.

If the matter is not sorted out by agreement and has to be listed for another hearing, the temporary order will usually remain in place until that longer hearing can happen. Just because the court makes a temporary order does not mean that the court is saying the person who is bound by it is guilty of all the things that have been said about them - this will be decided later by the court when all the evidence is available and when both parties have had time to prepare and present their version of events.

If the court has to hear evidence about domestic abuse it will say that anything the Judge considers was 'more likely than not' to have happened is 'found' i.e. it happened and anything that is not 'more likely than not' to have happened is 'not found' i.e. it didn't happen. This is the 'civil standard of proof' or the 'balance of probabilities' and it means that it is easier for the Judge in a family case to decide you have been violent than it would be for the Criminal Courts to convict you for the same thing.

You should bear this in mind when thinking about whether or not you want to ask the court to hold a trial - you might be confident of a 'not guilty' if the case was a criminal one, but the Family Courts deal with things differently. For a victim of domestic abuse concerned about the consequences of a failed prosecution or a decision not to proceed by the police, it is still possible to secure protection from Family Courts where the criminal law cannot help or where the police are not interested.

If the person against whom allegations are being made agrees to the order continuing there will be no need for the court to hear evidence or to make findings of fact (unless this needs to be done anyway in order to sort out a dispute about the children). This is a good idea in some cases as it removes the risk that the Judge will believe all the allegations and decide you are responsible for the abuse.

If you are faced with an application for a non-mol and decide to agree to an order against you being made or continuing but the court has not heard any evidence or made any findings you should ask the Judge to record at the top of the order that the order is made 'without hearing evidence or making findings' (this is called a 'recital'). This is so that it cannot be said in future that the order was made on the basis of findings that you have been violent. You should not agree to an order being made unless you have read the information below about the consequences of breaking an order and are happy that you understand what the order tells you not to do, and that you will not break the order. If you are not clear about what the order means you must ask the Judge or your ex's lawyer to explain it to you. The lawyer has a duty to explain it to you. If the wording is confusing or unclear ask for it to be reworded before you sign up.

Typically, a non-mol will prevent a person from being violent or threatening, or from harassing or pestering the other person, and may ban some or all communication between the parties except through solicitors. The terms of an order may have a knock on effect on contact and arrangements for handing over any children. If a temporary order is made final it will most often run for a year from the date of the first temporary order, but the court can decide how long this should be and can extend or change the order if necessary.

Another type of injunction that the court can often make is an occupation order (sometimes called an 'ouster' by lawyers). As the name suggests this is an order which deals with who can go to or live in the family home. Even if a person owns or is a tenant of a house or flat the court can order somebody to leave it or order them not to return to it, if it thinks this is necessary to protect the Applicant or any children. Usually this type of order will not be made without notice (unless they have already left and have somewhere else appropriate to stay), because removing someone from their home is a very serious matter. If appropriate the court can 'regulate' the occupation of the property by saying that different parts of the property can be used by each party or that common areas such as the bathroom and kitchen can be used at particular times, but this type of arrangement is not very common.

Because it is easier to obtain an order saying 'don't come back' than it is to obtain an order saying 'you must leave', many solicitors advise their clients not to leave the property voluntarily. This is often, but not always, the right approach: it is harder to persuade the court to let you back in than to let you stay. Both parties remaining in the family home after a relationship has broken down in some kind of stand-off is not generally a pleasant experience and it can be very upsetting and stressful for both parents and any children. It can also create an environment ripe for further dispute and allegations (true or false) of violence, abuse or harassment.

In broad terms, if you cannot agree who should leave, the parent who is primarily responsible for caring for the children is likely to be permitted by the court to stay in the family home. This might not be the case if there are other special circumstances, such as disability or if the person leaving would suffer particular financial hardship or homelessness. The court cannot, however, order someone to leave their home just because the parties have split up and things are very unpleasant. The court only has the power to make an order ousting someone from their home if certain tests are passed. These legal tests and rules are set out in Chapter 21.

Ultimately though, applications for occupation orders are often hotly contested, as both parties may have limited alternative housing available to them - you will have to weigh up all the pros and cons and decide if you want to stay in the home and dig in until it is over, or if it is better and safer for you to leave.

22.3 Making an application for a non-molestation or occupation order

If you are *applying* for a non-molestation order you may be able to obtain legal aid, depending on your income. If you obtain an order against your ex, or the application leads to an undertaking being given instead (see below) you may then be eligible for legal aid in any court case involving that person regarding your children or your finances, if that court case starts within two years of the order or undertaking. The person responding will not be eligible for legal aid unless they are also asking for an order, or sometimes if they would be made homeless by the application. There is more information about legal aid in Chapter 4.

The rules on making applications are at Rule 10 FPR.

You must fill in form FL401 and attach a witness statement. The witness statement must explain the behaviour that has led you to make the application, and if you are asking the court to make the order without notice to the person you want the order to cover you **must** say why. This is usually because you are fearful of their reaction if they find out you are going to ask for an order and you want the order to be in place before they find out [see Rule 10.2 FPR & s45 FLA].

Unless your application is without notice the other person must be given at least two days notice of the hearing from when they are served with the papers. Two days notice means two full days *between* the day they get the papers and the day of the hearing itself.

You are not allowed to serve the application or order yourself (and you probably wouldn't want to anyway!) so you must ask the Judge to direct that the court should serve the application and order on the Respondent and the Police for you [Rule 10.6 FPR].

If your application is for an occupation order or transfer of tenancy order you must also serve the application, and later the order, on the mortgage company or landlord (you cannot ask the court to do this for you).

If you are so unsafe you cannot wait for the two days notice you can ask the court to make an order 'without notice' or with only a shorter period of notice. Your witness statement must explain the urgency.

If you are worried about how the other person will react to your application you may need the order to be in place before they find out, you will need to apply for a 'without notice' order. Your witness statement must explain why you need the order to be made this way.

However, it is not automatic that the court will make an order before the other person is told or without the full period of notice - the Judge has to ask 'Why should I make the order?', not 'Why not?' (*R v R (Family Court: Procedural Fairness)* [2014] EWFC 48). If the Judge thinks it can wait they will hold off from making an order until both of you can be at court. If an order is made any order will usually only be until a further hearing date, or will be reviewed at a further hearing where both of you are able to be present.

The legal test that the Judge has to look at when someone makes a without notice application is set out at s45 FLA 1996 (see Chapter 21).

22.4 Responding to an application

More often than not an application will be made '*without notice*' to you and a temporary order will be in place before you find out about it. If your ex makes a without notice application, you will be served with any order and the application and a witness statement shortly after the hearing.

If a lawyer was present at the hearing, they must give you a written note of what was said and what took place at the hearing if you ask for it. They often won't volunteer this, so you should ask. This might be important if you think the court has been misled.

You may well find there is not time to get legal advice or representation set up in time for the return date hearing, and legal aid is unavailable to respond to non-mol applications anyway. You might qualify for legal aid if you need to cross apply for orders to protect yourself or if the Applicant is asking for orders which would make you homeless.

Before the court hearing read everything you are given carefully, and calmly make a note of which bits are accurate and which are not. Consider if anybody has witnessed what actually happened and whether they might be able to confirm that to the court through a witness statement.

Consider the information in this chapter about undertakings and admissions and decide what your approach will be at the return date hearing. Will you offer an undertaking or will you fully challenge the application.

There is no need to produce a full witness statement in response before the first hearing. If you are going to be challenging the application and the allegations in the witness statement you can ask for time to produce a considered response rather than rushing in before all the evidence is available and before you have had time to think things through. Any temporary order will probably stay in place whilst this happens but it is important not to rush the preparation of your evidence.

If there is something in the detail of the temporary order that causes you a particular difficulty, for example the order says you must not go down a street you need to go down to get to work or prevents you from going to the pharmacy where you collect your medication or effectively stops you from collecting the children - you can ask the just to tweak the order so that it strikes a better balance, or perhaps ask for an alternative handover arrangement to be put in in place.

If the temporary order stops you from communicating with your ex at all you might try and clarify at the hearing what you should do about necessary communications regarding the children, medical emergencies etc. For example sometimes there might be a third party you can communicate through. Don't worry too much about your feelings that this is not necessary, the priority at this stage should be just getting something in place that works even if it is cumbersome or you feel it is unnecessary.

If for some reason the court has not listed a return date hearing and you do not agree with the order, you can ask the court to list one. You are entitled to have your say if you do not think the order should have been made or if you think it should be altered in some way. The order should tell you how to do that, but if not contact the court office (the address will be at the bottom of the order).

22.5 Directions the court will often make

If the matter cannot be sorted out at the return date hearing and the application is challenged by the Respondent the court will usually make directions for a trial of the application. Whilst this is all being done the court will usually keep any temporary non-mol orders in place, perhaps slightly amending the wording if they inadvertently cause a practical problem. The sorts of direction that are commonly made are:

- That there should be disclosure of Police records (usually allowing them 28 days to respond). The court might say that a solicitor acting for a represented party should request this from the Police first, before making an order (there is a working agreement between the courts and the Police about how disclosure will be dealt with and this is part of the agreement);

- That there should be disclosure of social services or hospital records (where they have been involved in call outs), or GP records where they have been involved or notified of injuries (usually allowing them 28 days to respond);

- That any phone records that are relied on should be provided (e.g. where there are text messages or repeat calls);

- The court is likely to direct that there should be witness statements filed, probably in sequence, including those from any other witness apart from the parties themselves. Sometimes the person applying has had to apply in a rush and will want to produce a second, fuller witness statement as well as the one they used to start the case. This will usually happen first, so that the person responding can see all the evidence against them before responding with their own witness statement. If either party wants to rely on the evidence of anyone apart from themselves they must file a witness statement from any other witness at the same time as their own;

- That the Applicant should produce a Scott Schedule that the Respondent should respond to (see below - this is a table itemising each allegation of abuse);

- That there should be a hearing after all that material has been gathered together. If there are directions for disclosure from the Police or social services someone will need to notify the correct person at that organisation of the order made and send them a copy. If you are the Applicant ask the court to direct that the other party's solicitor does this - it will be much more straightforward for them to handle this.

- That there should be 'special measures' put in place to allow the alleged victim to give their evidence without intimidation (screen in court, video link etc). If you think you need special measures it is a good idea to say so on your original application or at the first hearing / return date hearing. Applications for special measures need to be dealt with in advance so the court can book a court room that has the right facilities and things can be got ready. It is possible to object to the grant of special measures to your ex, and sometimes people do object because it looks a bit like prejudging the very issue in dispute - but judges are well aware that the allegations have not yet been tested and may not prove to be accurate.

Special measures may also protect you from allegations that you have attempted to intimidate your ex.

It is important that the evidence is organised to come in the correct order, so that both parties can see the independent evidence (Police, medical etc) before setting out their own position. If there is an application for an occupation order or transfer of tenancy the court will probably expect slightly more focused evidence in the form of witness statements dealing with each of the legal criteria set out in the relevant section of the FLA (for example whether either party has somewhere else to go, whether they have any particular housing needs such as a need to stay in a home specially adapted for their disability etc) and there may be a need to attach supporting documents about some of these things (medical evidence, financial information or information from the housing office). Transfer of tenancy is dealt with in more detail in Chapter 15.

22.6 Fact finding in children proceedings

Where there are children involved, the court can decide whether to deal with both matters together or separately. It usually makes sense for the court to deal with all matters together. Sometimes, therefore, the decision about whether a non-mol should continue will be made after a fact finding hearing has taken place. The court will only hear evidence about the allegations of abuse once and any findings made will be the basis for making both decisions about the children and the Non-Mol.

A fact finding hearing is not necessary or appropriate in all cases. If the majority of the allegations are accepted or if the abusive parent has been convicted of some of the abuse, it is likely that the court will not need to devote a whole hearing to deciding which of the finer points of detail are proved or not. This is because the fine detail is unlikely to affect the main decision: what contact should take place and what arrangements are required for handover. If the parties broadly agree what has happened in the past or if convictions give the court a proven factual base, the court can move on to look at the risks of future abuse, the impact that has or might have on the children and more generally what contact is in their best interests (see PD 12J). A fact finding hearing is only likely to be necessary if the abuse (if proven) would change the order the court would make.

It is important to understand the significance of fact finding. A fact finding hearing forms the factual platform upon which all future decisions of the Family Court will be based. Once the court has ruled on which allegations are proved or not, as far as the court is concerned that is a final decision on what happened.

Once made, findings cannot be overturned or changed except in very exceptional circumstances (see Chapter 25 on challenging decisions). Therefore, it is important that fact finding hearings are taken seriously, properly prepared for and dealt with thoroughly.

Fact finding hearings can hold cases up. A parent on the end of allegations of domestic abuse can find that their contact is in limbo until the Judge has dealt with the fact finding. The court has to operate on the basis that the allegations may be true until it is able to hear the evidence, so often contact has to be restricted whilst this is being sorted out.

The making of findings by the Family Court is not the same as a criminal conviction. The Family Court operates quite differently to a Criminal Court. In the Family Court the standard of proof is lower. In a criminal case a jury must be 'satisfied so that they are sure' before a case is proved (often described as 'beyond reasonable doubt'). But in the Family Courts, if the person making an allegation can persuade the Judge that it was more likely than not to have happened the allegation will be proved and a finding made (this is known as the 'balance of probabilities'). This means that it is easier to prove domestic violence or abuse in the Family Court than it would be in criminal matters, and that things the Crown Prosecution Service might not have pursued, or which have resulted in a Not Guilty verdict can be reconsidered by the court and a finding could still be made. The Family Court does use the 'beyond reasonable doubt' standard in cases where there is a risk of someone going to prison (for example where it is dealing with a breach of a non-mol or undertaking).

It is important to understand that a criminal conviction will stand as proof of guilt in the Family Court, but a not guilty verdict (or a decision by the Police or Crown Prosecution Service) to take no further action (NFA) or drop a case just means that the case hasn't been proved. This is not the same as proof of innocence.

It is important to ensure that all police records of any incidents are obtained. This is important even if you are the person who is on the receiving end of the allegations if you want to make the point that the Police have not been called to each incident, in order to identify inconsistencies between what is alleged in the case and what was said at the time, or in order to demonstrate why the case was NFA'd. It is best to seek this early so that it does not hold things up. If your ex has a solicitor, ask them to sort this out or ask the court to order them to handle the administration of this. If there are any significant injuries alleged, there should be an order for disclosure of medical, GP or hospital records as well.

Most police forces have an agreed procedure for disclosure by the Police of material needed for family court cases, called a Police Disclosure Protocol. It is likely to say that generally the Police should be asked in writing by the parties for voluntary disclosure, and that the court should only make an order saying the Police must provide the documents if that has not been complied with. This can hold things up, and in any event the Police often provide information later than the court has ordered. Do not be afraid to ask for an adjournment or longer to file your statement if important evidence that was due to come in before your statement has not yet been received - it is important to see both helpful and unhelpful evidence before you file your own evidence.

If there are more than a very few incidents of alleged abuse the court will most likely ask the parent making the allegations to produce a 'Scott Schedule' setting out each separate allegation they make. This is essentially a table breaking down the allegations into numbered and dated allegations, with a column for a brief description of the allegation (e.g. on 20 June 2010 the Respondent punched the Applicant to the left cheek), and a column for a brief response (e.g. admitted or denied or the Respondent admitted that he struck the Applicant in self defence etc). When the Judge comes to make a decision he will go through each allegation stating whether it is 'found' or 'not found'. There is a sample Scott Schedule in Part 7 of this book.

The Practice Direction relating to domestic violence and abuse (PD12J) suggests that it may be appropriate for the Judge to ask questions on behalf of one or both parties.

The Family Court also considers questions of domestic abuse in the context of care proceedings. Sometimes where there has been prolonged domestic abuse between parents, or where a parent has a history of becoming involved in abusive relationships, the Local Authority may want to remove the children who have been exposed to it in order to protect them. In this type of case the court may also have to look at questions of what abuse has or has not taken place. Parents in care cases will receive legal aid, so litigants in person involved in cases of this kind are most likely to be grandparents or extended family members putting themselves forward to care for a child. For them the focus should be on demonstrating an understanding of the significance of the abusive behaviour as harmful to children exposed to it (by seeing, hearing or being caught up in it), and an ability to protect the children from further conflict in future (for example managing contact handovers with parents or conflict between parents in the presence of the children), and being able to accept any findings made.

There is more information about applications concerning children in Chapters

16 to 20.

22.7 What happens if an order is broken?

Doing something that is banned by a non-molestation order (breaching the order) is an arrestable criminal offence. This means that if you do anything the order says you should not (even if it is something that would not normally be an offence, such as talking to your ex when the order says you must not communicate at all), the Police can immediately arrest you and can charge you with a criminal offence of breaching a non-molestation order, which can carry a sentence of up to five years in prison.

Doing something that is banned by an occupation order (e.g. going back to the home or going into the home or refusing to leave) is still something you can be punished for, but only by the Family Court, and is not a criminal offence. Attached to the occupation order is something called a 'power of arrest' which means that the Police can arrest for a breach of the order if they think it's appropriate. If arrested by the Police for this sort of breach, the Police must bring the person in breach to the Family Court (not the Criminal Court) within 24 hours of arrest or s/he must be released. The Family Court will then deal with the breach as a contempt of court, and the maximum sentence for a breach of this kind of order is two years. When a Family Court imposes a prison sentence for contempt of court there is no time off for good behaviour or early release on licence, and so a sentence of two years means two years served. When the court deals with a contempt of court it can only find you 'guilty' of contempt if the facts are proved to the criminal standard (i.e. the Judge must be satisfied so that he is sure). This is because the consequences of a finding are potentially so serious.

Both types of orders (non-mol and occupation) will usually be made at the same time and on the same document. It is important to make sure that you understand and the order is clear which bits of its order are non-molestation orders and which are occupation orders because the different types of orders have different consequences as described above. Judges are not always clear about this and sometimes describe things as non-molestation orders when really they should be occupation orders. You need to check which bits of the order say they are an arrestable offence and clarify with the Judge if you are not sure. Something that says you must not go back to your home or within a certain distance of it is really an occupation order and you should point this out, reminding the Judge that it's important because the court should not put you at risk of a criminal offence where this is not justified or permitted by the law.

There is more about what happens when an occupation order (or undertaking

- see below) is breached in Chapter 23 on Enforcement.

22.8 Undertakings

Sometimes an injunction can be avoided by making a solemn promise to the court not to do the things that would go in the order (not to be violent, not to go to a particular address etc). This sort of promise is called an undertaking and the person who has given an undertaking can be punished by the Family Court by a sentence of up to two years in prison as a 'contempt of court' if it is broken. The advantage of an undertaking for the person giving it is that a breach of the undertaking is not a criminal offence, it does not give the Police a power of arrest (unless what you are doing is an arrestable offence anyway), so if the other party wants you to be punished for breach they have to make an application to the court before this can happen. Also, if undertakings are accepted, a fact finding exercise may be avoided. It should be obvious that what is preferable to the person wanting to give an undertaking to avoid an order being made will be less attractive to the person asking for protection, for example because it will not have such sharp 'teeth' or give additional powers to the Police. But if the type of behaviour that you want protection from doesn't require such an urgent response or you are confident the person will stick to promises, this can be a way of avoiding having to give evidence, which can be upsetting. There is little advantage to this however, if the same issues will need to be considered in proceedings about the children (if the behaviour is likely to be put forward by you as a reason for preventing or limiting contact).

22.9 Pros and cons of undertakings

Especially where there are children there are benefits to an agreed solution which avoids the need for a trial. Resolving things by undertaking can take the heat out of the situation and allow both parties to feel reassured that they are protected from further bad behaviour on the one hand or from prosecution arising from malicious allegations on the other.

If both parties are making similar types of allegations against each other it can be sensible for both of you to promise to behave sensibly towards each other by each giving the same undertaking. This means both of you have an incentive to keep the peace in order to avoid complaints that you have broken your promise and should be punished. However, since a change to the rules on legal aid in 2013 an Applicant for a non-mol or occupation order may have difficulty qualifying for legal aid for any related case about the children if they give a cross undertaking, so if your ex is the one who has applied for a non-mol and you have children that the court is likely to need to consider, your ex is unlikely to be in a position to give an undertaking.

Whenever somebody offers an undertaking in this way the court should be asked to record at the top of the order the words 'UPON the Respondent having made no admissions and the court having made no findings of fact' (unless of course there have been admissions or findings).

Reasons to offer an undertaking

Breaching an undertaking is not a criminal offence but can still be punished by up to two years in prison (contempt of court). This may be particularly important for individuals who are at risk of a prison sentence because they already have a history of offending.

There will be no power of arrest. The Police can still arrest you for a breach if what you are doing is an arrestable offence anyway, but an undertaking doesn't give the Police any more powers than they already have.

It avoids findings being made. You might feel the urge to clear your name, but it can sometimes be better tactically to avoid a trial of allegations of domestic abuse if at all possible, for example if you have children and contact may be an issue, or if there is evidence to support the allegations being made.

Reasons to think twice before offering an undertaking

- Where there is a history of false allegations or a pattern of break up and reconciliation and you think you may end up getting back together. You can end up in difficulty if your ex asks you back and then you fall out again. It might be said that you have breached the undertaking.

- Where you think you might not be able to stick to the promises being asked of you. For example, don't promise not to go down a particular street if you have to go that way to collect your benefits each week, and don't promise not to communicate at all if you know that you will have to exchange messages about something very urgent in the near future.

- Where you are not sure what you are promising. Do ask for an explanation of any undertaking drawn up for you by a lawyer. Standard forms of words are contained at the end of the book in the Forms, Templates & Useful Documents section in the Toolkit & Resources.

Reasons not to accept an undertaking

Essentially these are the same as the reasons for offering an undertaking, but in reverse;

- There is no risk of criminal sanction if there is a breach of the order, so the order may not be such an effective deterrent

- There is no power of arrest so there may not be such immediate protection in case of a breach. However, much of the kind of behaviour that would require an immediate response in the form of arrest is probably something they could be arrested for anyway.

Reasons to accept an undertaking

- It avoids a trial where you will have to give evidence

- It is offered voluntarily so is probably more likely to be stuck to

- It is less likely to heighten tensions between you

- It is still punishable by up to two years in prison if broken. You have to make an application to make this happen, but for some people who have had a poor experience from their local Police who are not prepared to act on minor breaches of orders this can have its attractions - it is within your control whether to pursue a breach.

- If the kind of behaviour you are asking to be protected from can be adequately dealt with by a non-urgent response this is probably as good a solution as an order (for example, unpleasant texts or emails as opposed to banging on the door at 3am which may require an urgent Police call-out). Remember, you can still return to court and ask for an order later if there are further problems, although this may mean making a fresh application.

What an undertaking or order might look like

There are certain standard forms of wording which are often used or adapted for non-molestation orders. See the Forms, Templates & Useful Documents section in the Toolkit & Resources.

PART 6: AFTER JUDGMENT

23. Enforcement

23.1 Introduction

Sadly, getting an order is only half the battle in some cases. There are always a few people who make an art form out of ignoring or avoiding court orders. Just as you think you have reached the top of the hill, another mountain range comes into view. Enforcing your order can be a real slog. And to make things worse the rules are complicated and contained in a number of different places.

There are different ways to enforce orders depending on whether they relate to orders to pay money, other orders about the financial part of your divorce, children or breach of a domestic violence injunction.

- Enforcement in relation to orders about children is dealt with at Chapters 17 and 19.

- Some information about enforcing broken injunctions or undertakings is found in Chapter 21.

Orders to pay money might include things like orders made after a divorce or dissolution of civil partnership or orders under Schedule 1 CA 1989 for payment of maintenance or lump sum, and costs orders.

23.2 Court orders

Before describing the various different ways to go about enforcing an order, you need to understand how court orders work. A court order can be broken down into two main parts:

- The preamble or recitals; and

- The order itself.

The preamble is a section at the top of an order which describes the background to how an order came to be made and any things that one or both parties have agreed but which cannot go into the main part of the order, or which do not need to go into the main part of the order. The things that the parties agree should be recorded in this way are called recitals. You can recognise the pre-amble because it is the section above the words 'IT IS ORDERED', and because each line will begin with 'UPON' or 'AND UPON'. Some examples of recitals are included in the Forms, Templates & Useful Documents section in the Toolkit & Resources at the back of the book.

The purpose of recitals is so that if the court or the parties have to reconsider an order or how it came to be made they are able to understand a little bit about what was in the parties' minds at the time. And because there are some things that are an important part of an agreement but which the court doesn't have the power to order, it is important to record that the agreement was only reached because these additional bits were also agreed.

When somebody gives an undertaking in place of an order this will be recorded in the recital. Although the court might look again at the whole order if an agreement contained in a recital is broken (see 'set aside' in Chapter 25), the court cannot force a person to stick to an agreement in a recital. The only thing the court can do is to enforce an undertaking that has been broken by committal to prison.

The main part of the order can be enforced through various methods, depending on the type of order.

- The Family Court can enforce any breach of its own order by committing the person who has broken it to prison, as long as:

  - the terms of the order are clear, including a clear time and date for a thing to be done by;

  - the order has a 'penal notice' on the front page (*Re Newman, An Application By Gloucestershire County Council for the Committal To Prison* [2014] EWHC 3136 (Fam)). A penal notice is a warning telling the person the order tells to do (or not do) something that if they don't stick to the order they can be sent to prison or fined;

  - the person who the order tells to do or not do something knows about the order and what it says (usually because they have been handed a copy of it).

- Orders telling somebody they have to come to court at a particular time, or to provide disclosure / produce a document that are ignored can be enforced through committal (but it may be necessary to ask the court to add a penal notice to the order and set a new time for compliance first as these don't routinely have a penal notice on them).

- Child arrangements orders can be enforced in the following ways:

  - Enforcement of child arrangements orders through the powers given by the CA (dealt with in Chapter 19).

- Enforcement of child arrangements orders by committal to prison is rare, but if appropriate you can follow the procedure for committal set out below.

- Section 34 FLA 1986 can be used to enforce a child arrangements order (see Chapter 17).

• Most breaches of non-molestation orders will be dealt with in the Criminal Courts, but the Family Courts do still retain the power to enforce by committal, which they might exercise if for some reason the Police or Crown Prosecution Service kept failing to act.

• Occupation orders are only enforceable by the Family Courts through committal. Committal for breach of an occupation order or non-molestation orders should be dealt with through the procedure set out below.

• Undertakings can be enforced just as if they were an order of the court, so all of these remedies apply in the same way to broken undertakings as to broken orders. In respect of undertakings for the payment of money this can be more difficult. A number of cases do confirm however that undertakings for payment of money can be successfully enforced by judgment summons (none available on BAILII however, but see *Symmons v Symmons* [1993] 1FLR 317, *M v M (Enforcement: Judgment Summons)* [1993] Fam Law 469).

• Orders to pay money can be enforced by the following methods:

- Judgment summons (a type of committal process in relation to orders to pay money)

- Civil Debt remedies

- Liberty to apply

- Power to execute documents

- Bankruptcy.

23.3 Committal applications (including fine)

The full name of this application is an application to commit a person to prison for contempt of court. The application is based on the fact that when someone knows about a court order but ignores or disobeys it, or has made a promise but has ignored or disobeys that, they are disrespecting the authority of the court.

Because it is a little bit like a criminal trial a committal hearing will usually be dealt with in open court (i.e. not in private) and barristers have to wear wig and gown (although the Judge often permits them to take them off as soon as they get into court!). And just like a criminal trial the person accused can't be made to give evidence that might incriminate him.

To be enforceable in this way the order must be precise and clear about what must or must not be done, and when it must be done by or how long the order lasts.

Usually the order must have been served personally on the person who is now said to be in breach before the breach took place and before the time ran out for them to do anything the order tells them to do (served personally means handed directly to them rather than just posted). This is because in order to prove a contempt of court you have to prove beyond reasonable doubt that the person who has broken the order knew about it. You must then prove that they went on and broke the order (or undertaking) anyway.

The court's approach in dealing with contempt of court is an odd mix of wanting to punish someone for disrespecting the authority of the court so that people know that court orders are something to take seriously (punitive) and just wanting to make sure that in future the order is stuck to (compliance).

Part 37 FPR contains the rules relating to committals.

An application for committal must be begun by following the procedure set out in Part 18 of the FPR, and rule 37.10 tells you what you need to include on the application form. The application must be served personally on the person who has broken the order unless the court says it is not necessary.

It is really important that when you complete the application form you set out each separate breach, giving each a date and a number, a bit like a Scott Schedule (see Toolkit & Resources). For example:

- On 18 July 2010 His Honour Judge X ordered that the Respondent should not go within 100 metres of 20 The Meadows, Bristol (paragraph 1) and that he should not loiter in The Meadows or within 100 metres of any place he knows the Applicant to be.

- On 20 January 2011 in breach of paragraph 1 of the order of 18 July 2010 the Respondent Mr Smith attended at 20 The Meadows, Bristol.

- On or around 21 January 2011 in breach of paragraph 2 of the order of 18

July 2010 Mr Smith followed the Applicant home and drove up and down The Meadows in his car, beeping the horn.

Because the consequences of this kind of application are very serious the court will want to be sure that the procedure has been properly followed. However, the court can remedy any procedural problem if injustice has not been done (*Nicholls v Nicholls* [1996] EWCA Civ 1271, *Devjee v Patel* [2006] EWCA Civ 1211).

The person who makes the application has to prove the breach beyond reasonable doubt. This can be quite difficult if there is no independent witness. Sometimes, with things like silent phone calls, it can be impossible.

The court also has to be satisfied beyond reasonable doubt that the person who broke the order knew that it was a breach of it and that the behaviour in question actually was a breach. This means that if the wording of the undertaking or order is unclear the court will probably not be able to punish the person, but they will probably make the order clearer for the future. This is why the courts now try to avoid using words like 'harass' or 'molest', because they mean different things to different people.

If the contempt is found proved the person who is due to be punished (the contemnor) is allowed to explain the reasons why the sentence for the breach should be less (this is called mitigation) and the person who has proved the breach can say what made the breach more serious (aggravating factors).

The actions the court can take when a breach is proved include:

- Imposing a prison sentence of up to two years, although this is quite rare and would almost never happen on a first breach. It can suspend the sentence on certain conditions and for a period of time, and this power is used more often than in criminal cases where it is now quite rare (*Hale v Tanner* [2000] 2 FLR 879).

- Imposing a fine instead of a prison sentence.

- Imposing no penalty but recording the fact that there has been a breach so that if the person breaks the order again they will not be treated as if this is the first breach.

- Adjourning sentencing for a period of time to see if the order is stuck to.

23.4 Committal on arrest

Most committals will be started with the person who wants to complain about the breach issuing an application. In a case where an occupation order has been broken the Police have a power to arrest the person in breach and to bring him to the Family Court for immediate punishment.

In this kind of committal the Police must bring the person in breach before the Judge within 24 hours of arrest (excluding Sundays and bank holidays). If they don't the person has to be released, but the breach can still be dealt with at a later date if an application is issued in the normal way.

If they are brought to court within 24 hours the Judge might be able to deal with the case there and then (perhaps if the breach is admitted and it is quite straightforward), but is quite likely to have to adjourn the case until a later date, particularly if the person brought to court wants a lawyer and doesn't have one.

The court can remand the person arrested in custody for a short period of time (no more than 8 days) or can allow them to be released on bail with conditions. The person can only be released into the custody of the Police for no more than three days so if the remand is for more than that they will be sent to prison rather than back to the station. The rules for this are set out in Schedule 5 of the FLA 1996.

There can be a remanded in custody for up to three weeks if a medical report is needed.

If there are other breaches which need to be dealt with, but which were not the subject of the arrest an application will need to be made with a request for the court to deal with all of them together.

Otherwise the procedure remains the same as for committal on application.

Important points if an application to commit you to prison is made

- You will be entitled to legal aid if this sort of application is made against you. It can be difficult to find a solicitor to take the case on - you may need to approach criminal and family legal aid solicitors. You might want to refer them to the case of *Re Ramet* [2014] EWHC 56 (Fam), which makes clear legal aid IS available for this - some solicitors seem to think it isn't.

- You do not have to give evidence if you do not want to. It is up to the other person to prove beyond reasonable doubt that you breached the order. In some cases it may be better not to give evidence.

- You do not need permission to appeal a committal order (see Chapter 19).

23.5 Judgment summons

Judgment summons is a form of committal which can be used to enforce an order for the payment of money. It can't be used to enforce arrears of maintenance which are more than 12 months old, or to enforce orders about the finances in general, only orders that say a particular sum of money must be paid).

Rule 33.9 -33.17 FPR deals with this type of application.

- The application may be made in the Designated Family Judge Area most convenient to the person making it.

- The application must be made on a notice of application accompanied by a statement setting out how much is due and under what order (with a breakdown of the figures). It must contain all the evidence you are going to rely on and must attach a copy of the order.

- Once the application has been made the court will issue the judgment summons, and the person making the application must personally serve the application and evidence along with the summons on the person who owes the money no less than two weeks before the hearing. They must also offer to pay a reasonably sufficient amount of money to cover the travel expenses to and from the court [Rule 33.11 FPR].

The court can go on to make an order committing the person to prison if

- the person fails to attend the hearing, or if

- the person who is owed money proves that since the date of the order the person owing the money has had the money to make payment but has refused or neglected to pay it.

The court can suspend the committal order.

Alternatively, where the order that has not been paid is for a lump sum, costs or maintenance order the court can make a new order adding the costs of the judgment summons on top, and re-fixing the date or saying the money should be paid in instalments.

23.6 Civil debt remedies

You can enforce financial orders in family cases using the same tools as in civil courts. Some of the rules are in the FPR, but FPR 33.2 also applies parts of the Civil Procedure Rules [CPR] to family cases. You can locate the CPR on the Justice website. The methods you can use include:

- An order to obtain information from a debtor [see FPR 33.23 and CPR Part 71]

- A third party debt order (ordering someone who owes the non-payer money, like a bank, to pay the money owed directly to the person making the application) [FPR 33.24 / CPR Part 72]

- A charging order, stop order or stop notice (securing a debt onto a property and stopping funds or assets being dealt with) [FPR 33.25 / FPR Part 40]

- An attachment of earnings order [FPR 33.19 and Part 39].

Rule 33.3 FPR says you must make an application on a notice of application accompanied by a statement setting out how much is due and under what order (with a breakdown of the figures). If the application is for 'such method of enforcement as the court may consider appropriate' under FPR 33.3(2)(b) (i.e. if you ask for whatever type of enforcement the Judge is prepared to assist you with rather than specifying just one) the court will order the person who owes the money to attend court and to bring with them any documents the court thinks are necessary. If they do not attend court or bring the documents the court could commit them to prison.

23.7 Liberty to apply

If there are problems with getting compliance with an order made at the end of financial proceedings you can refer the case back to the court to ask for directions about how to implement it. The court cannot reopen the order itself, but where there are practical obstacles stopping the order becoming a reality the court will try to help. This can be useful where, for example, one party is obstructing the sale of a property, or the parties cannot agree about whether or not to accept an offer below the asking price or if there is a dispute about the amount of the agent's fees. It is of course far better to resolve these matters of detail without coming back to court if at all possible.

One useful power that the court has in cases where one party is being obstructive or just ignoring an order, is the power to execute a transfer document. If there has been an order that one person transfers all his estate and interest in a property to the other but they have refused or avoided doing it the court can firstly make an order specifically ordering them to execute (sign and complete) the transfer document and then, if they do not, you can ask the Judge to execute the document himself.

The power to do this is contained in s39 Senior Courts Act 1981 (power of High Court to execute documents) and s31E Matrimonial & Family Proceedings Act 1984 (which says the Family Court has the same powers).

In a case of this kind you are likely to have two main practical problems as a litigant in person:

- Serving the person with the series of orders and applications that will be necessary

- Obtaining and preparing a transfer document ready for the Judge to sign - you will probably need to see a conveyancer about this.

There is nothing about this kind of application in the FPR so you will probably need to fill in an application notice FP1 and proceed under Part 19 FPR.

23.8 Bankruptcy

It is possible to petition for someone's bankruptcy if they have not complied with an order to pay you money. The person must owe you a minimum of £5,000 before you can issue a petition and the costs of issuing a petition are usually prohibitively high. You have to serve a statutory demand before you can issue a petition. Sometimes this will result in payment. It is beyond the scope of this book to give detailed information about bankruptcy petitions, but it is unlikely to be the most effective way to obtain monies owing to you, not least because you may have to share any money received with other creditors.

24. Costs

24.1 Introduction

In many non-family cases the person who wins can expect to recover their own costs from the other side and the loser will be left footing the bill for both sides.

Things operate rather differently in family cases where the 'loser pays' rule does not apply. This is in part because there is not very often one clear 'winner' in a family case.

Costs orders are relatively unusual in family cases, particularly in cases about children, where they are very rarely made. You should work on the basis that any legal or other costs you incur will not be recoverable from your ex.

You can be relatively confident that you will not have to pay your ex's costs, but be warned that if you conduct your case in a really unreasonable way or do things that make the legal costs increase significantly the court might order you to pay some or all of the costs. So it *is* possible for you to end up paying legal costs even when you don't have a lawyer.

This chapter is about circumstances where one party might be made to pay the other person's legal expenses *after* the costs have been incurred. There is information about ways to fund your own legal advice or representation in Chapter 4.

24.2 Costs orders

Costs orders are almost never made in children cases. They are not often made in financial cases, but the rules in relation to financial cases give slightly more scope for the court to order costs be paid by one party or the other. Costs orders can be made on appeal.

For example, in *Re G (Children)* [2013] EWCA Civ 1017 the Court of Appeal approved a costs order in a children case against a father where it had not been necessary for him to launch the case, where the proceedings had been used as a vehicle to get at the mother and to make her feel insecure and where the Father's arguments had been absolutely hopeless. That amounted to unreasonableness on the Father's part and he was ordered to pay the costs, even though a costs order might be 'devastating' for him.

What this means in practice is that you should only begin a court case where you have made genuine efforts to resolve your dispute beforehand, for example by considering mediation, and once a case is up and running you must be alive to whether or not any step you take in the case serves any useful purpose, whether or not any application has any realistic prospect of success and whether there is a more efficient way of doing things. *You* may not be incurring legal costs but every action has an equal and opposite reaction, and whenever you send a letter or make an application your ex's lawyer will have to read the new paperwork and so charge for the extra work. The court will be mindful of the fact that you are doing your best without a lawyer, but in certain circumstances might expect you to pay some of the legal costs you have caused, particularly if the court takes the view that you are deliberately making more work for your ex's solicitor as a tactic to try and exhaust their funds for legal advice.

The costs rules are at Part 28 FPR, and in PD 28A. The court has to think about a number of things when deciding whether to make a costs order and if so, how much, such as:

- how the parties have conducted their case overall and on any particular issue

- any failure to comply with a rule or practice direction or order

- what open offers to settle have been made and how reasonable they have been (this does not include without prejudice offers to settle - see Chapter 8)

- the financial impact on the parties of any costs order

If somebody is going to ask the Judge to order that the other person should pay their legal costs they have to give advance notice of that - before the day of the hearing [PD 28A]. You can object if you are not given advance warning and breakdown of how the amount given has been reached (but the trouble is if it isn't dealt with on the day more costs are possibly incurred coming back again so there is a risk of an even bigger bill if you lose). You are entitled to disagree with the court making any costs order, or to say that the court should only award a portion of the costs, and to object to the amount of costs that are being sought (for example because they are excessive or for unnecessary work or for something that you shouldn't have to pay for).

IMPORTANT: If your case is a Trusts of Land and Appointment of Trustees Act 1996 case (see Chapter 15) the costs rules are very different - the court will treat this as a non-family claim and the person who loses is likely to have to pay the costs of the person who wins. This means that a ToLATA claim is much more financially risky than a claim for married people or civil partners, even where you are saving costs by not instructing a lawyer.

How much?

Costs can rise in a case very quickly. If you do end up paying the other party's costs this could run into several thousands of pounds depending on whether you are paying all the costs of the case or just a portion of them. In financial cases you will be able to keep a check on this because at each hearing the lawyers should produce a costs estimate of how much has been spent. This does not happen in children cases.

The court can order that someone should pay all the costs of the whole case, a certain amount, a certain percentage, or the costs of a particular part - so, for example if a really silly application has been made within a case the court could order the costs of that application to be paid, or if everyone attends court for a particular hearing but has not been able to go ahead because of something someone has done or not done, the costs of that hearing could be paid by the person who has caused costs to be wasted.

24.3 Other types of costs orders

Expenses as a litigant in person

The 'costs' that I am talking about in this chapter are the fees that any lawyer involved in the case has charged their client, including by passing on court fees they have had to pay when issuing an application.

Technically the court can make an order relating to some costs of a litigant in person (or those of another person if they are a litigant in person too) but the same rules apply as above, so it is pretty unlikely.

The costs that the court could make an order about are things like court fees you have paid out and the financial loss to you, for example arising from carrying out research for your case and attending the hearing. You have to prove financial loss, for example that you have a loss of earnings because you have had to take time off work, and you can only recover up to 2/3 of what it would have cost for a lawyer to do the same things for you.

You cannot recover the fees of a paid-for Mckenzie friend, although it is just possible that if they have been granted rights of audience or a right to conduct litigation by the court you could claim.

In all these examples though you still have to justify the court making an order for costs in the first place. You must provide evidence of your loss BEFORE the day of the hearing at which you want to ask for costs. You cannot just raise it at the end of the hearing.

The rules about costs of a litigant in person are set out in Civil Procedure Rules 46.5 and CPR PD46. FPR r28.2 says this rule applies to family cases (you may need to remind the court about this because these sorts of applications are new and quite uncommon).

Wasted costs

This is a relatively unusual type of costs order where the court orders that a lawyer who has done something to cause costs to be wasted (perhaps because they haven't prepared or don't file documents or don't turn up and the hearing has to be adjourned) should pay the costs wasted *personally*. This book does not deal with that type of order.

Witness expenses

Professional witnesses will expect their attendance at court to be paid for by the party who has instructed them or by the party who has asked them to attend.

Unfortunately any family members or friends who come to court to give evidence will be unable to claim their travel expenses or loss of earnings if they come voluntarily. If they are summoned to court the party who has issued the summons must pay them 'conduct money' but this is nominal and is really intended to cover their travel only.

Expenses arising from breach of child arrangements order

If you are a parent whose child arrangements order has been breached and you have wasted money on things like getting to a handover that did not take place, or on buying travel tickets for contact that didn't happen you might be able to claim compensation under s11O and s11P of the CA. See Chapter 19 which deals with enforcement in respect of children.

24.4 Enforcing costs orders

Readers of this book are more likely to be on the wrong end of a costs order than to be the person trying to recover them from the other side.

Unless the court orders otherwise a costs order must be paid within 14 days. Sometimes the court will make a costs order but say 'not to be enforced without leave' - this is unusual nowadays but if this is the case the person wanting their costs paid must return to court and ask for leave to enforce the costs. Chapter 23 tells you how you can enforce a costs order.

25. Challenging Decisions

25.1 Introduction

This chapter deals with:

- what to do if you want a new Judge,

- how to appeal, and

- when you can ask to set aside an order.

(Chapter 19 deals with varying child arrangements orders).

25.2 Getting a new Judge

It is understandable that when a Judge makes a decision that one party is not happy with, they will want to have a different Judge next time around. However, this can be quite difficult to achieve.

In financial proceedings a Judge is expected to come off the fence and give a clear view at an FDR (see Chapter 14), so after that has happened he will automatically be disqualified from dealing with the case again.

Sometimes when a Judge has given a very clear view in other types of cases (lawyers call this an indication) before hearing all the evidence, the Judge will volunteer to step away from the case. This is called recusal. If a Judge has given a firm indication of what his view is *before* he has heard all the evidence you may be able to ask him to recuse himself. You should explain politely to the Judge that he has given a clear indication of his view and this creates an *impression of bias*. If the Judge (or Lay Justices) has said or done something inappropriate and refuses to recuse himself, you will need to ask for a copy of the court recording or Legal Adviser's note if you are in a court which does not use audio recording for any appeal.

In family cases, the general rule is that the courts try wherever possible to keep the same Judge on a case as much as possible (this is called Judicial Continuity). A case can be reallocated to a different level of Judge if it becomes complex (see Allocation Guidance on Judiciary website Family Court Guide) but where a Judge has heard evidence and made a decision or findings of fact, there is guidance which the court must follow that says that normally the same Judge must continue to deal with the case, because he knows the case well and has seen the witnesses give evidence, which gives him an advantage over other Judges. This means that when a Judge who has heard evidence has made a decision that you do not like it can be really difficult to get them removed from the case, because the very reason you want them removed is the very reason that the guidance tells the Judge that he must keep the case. Usually, the only way a new Judge will become involved is if the original Judge is simply unavailable - this is one of the few occasions when the fact that the courts have more work than they can handle can operate in your favour. Even if you are lucky enough to get a new Judge, he will probably have details of the findings made by the first Judge and will be bound by them, although they may take a different view about what to do next.

A case called *F v (1) M (2) D (3) N* [2007] EWHC 2543 (Fam) tells us that the test for a Judge deciding whether or not to recuse himself is whether or not in all the circumstances:

- **a fair minded and informed observer** adopting a **balanced approach**

- would conclude that there was a **real possibility** that the Judge (or Lay Justices) was **biased**.

So whilst you do not have to show that the Judge was actually biased you do have to show that there is an *appearance of bias*.

Of course it is a tricky thing to suggest to a Judge that he is biased, and probably not much less tricky to suggest he just *looks* biased - think carefully before you make any application of this kind. If you are unsuccessful you will be stuck with a Judge who you have openly criticised. If you disagree with a decision of a Judge to recuse himself you will need to appeal the decision (see below) but if you are unsuccessful you will achieve nothing but delay and a potentially an even more difficult relationship with the Judge.

I have heard it suggested on parents' forums that if a Judge recuses him or herself, then any orders which he or she has made in the case become void. That is not correct, so please don't make an application for recusal in the hope that any order that has been made will be wiped out. If you want to get rid of an order you don't like you need to appeal it. If an appeal succeeds on grounds that the Judge was biased the order may then be set aside, but just getting the Judge to step down won't make the order void.

25.3 Appeals

Although in some areas of family law things are clear cut and there is a single right or a single wrong answer, this is not always so. As has been seen with the welfare checklist and s25 criteria, family law relies heavily on the Judge forming his own view about what is the best thing to do. The law provides the framework and reminds the Judge what she has to think about and how she has to reach a decision, but it doesn't always say what the right order is. Family law allows for there to be more than one right answer.

The court dealing with any appeal will generally accept any findings of fact that have been made unless something has gone very obviously wrong with the process that led to the findings. This is because the original Judge heard the evidence and saw the witnesses and is in a much better position to Judge the facts than an appeal court.

If you are going to challenge a decision through an appeal you have to be able to demonstrate that something serious has gone wrong with the procedure followed so that the decision is unjust, or that the Judge has gone beyond making one of several possible right decisions and made a wrong one.

It is particularly difficult to appeal a case management decision, i.e. a decision made by a court about how the case should be prepared for a final decision such as directions for filing evidence or obtaining expert reports. This is because such decisions are really matters for the Judge who is responsible to deal with using her first-hand knowledge of what is happening on the ground, and there is rarely a single 'right' or a 'wrong' approach.

25.4 Rules for appeals

The parties will still have to do what the order says unless and until the appeal is successful. If the person appealing wants the order to be put on hold until the appeal is dealt with they have to apply for a stay on the order.

25.5 Permission

In many cases you need permission from the court in order to appeal. You can get this from the Judge who made the decision by asking for permission to appeal at court as soon as the judgment is given, or by asking the court or Judge that you need to appeal *to* (in your notice of appeal).

The following cases do not require permission:

- Appeals against committal orders (for contempt of court)

- Appeals from Lay Justices

Basically, you need to seek permission to appeal against any order made by a Judge. If you are going to appeal a decision made in the Family Court you will need a transcript of the judgment and any relevant evidence, or at least an approved and accurate note of it.

Practice Direction 30A says that if you don't have a lawyer any other lawyer present at the hearing must give you a copy of their note of the judgment if you ask for it. You can ask them to do this and to send their note to the Judge for them to confirm it is accurate. Then you can send this to the appeal court. This is easier (and cheaper) than getting a transcript, and probably quicker. If you do need to get a transcript (perhaps because there wasn't any lawyer involved) you should ask the Judge to order a transcript at public expense, otherwise you will have to pay for this (see 5.33 & 5.34 PD 30A for when this will be allowed).

If you are going to appeal a decision of the Lay Justices you will need a copy of the Legal Adviser's notes of evidence (if relevant) and the Lay Justices' written 'Facts and reasons'. You should ask for the Legal Adviser's notes to be provided at the end of the hearing when the decision is given. If you forget you must write to the court as soon as possible asking for them.

Lay Justices are allowed to give you short reasons at the end of a hearing and give you their fuller written reasons within the next 72 hours. If this happens in your case you should wait for the full reasons before appealing and send those to the appeal court.

25.6 Where to appeal

Check rule 30.3 and PD 30A to make sure you are appealing to the right Judge / court, but generally:

- An appeal from the Lay Justices is to a Circuit Judge in the Family Court.

- An appeal from a District Judge in the Family Court is to a Circuit Judge in the same court.

- An appeal from a Circuit Judge or Recorder is to a High Court Judge in most cases except care and adoption cases, which go to the Court of Appeal.

- An appeal from a High Court Judge is to the Court of Appeal.

Slightly different rules apply to appeals from cases heard in the Principal Registry in London. See the table at paragraph 2.1 of PD30A.

Appeals to the Court of Appeal are covered by a different set of rules (Civil Procedure Rules 1998 Part 52, available on the Justice Website). The procedure described below is set out in the FPR and applies to all appeals to the High Court and Family Court.

Appeals heard in the Family Court or High Court

The procedure here is set out in the FPR and applies to all appeals to the High Court and Family Court. You must appeal a final decision within **21 days** of the decision unless the court sets another date [FPR r30.4(2)]. BUT if you are appealing a 'case management decision' (a decision about how the case should proceed) you must appeal within **seven days** of the decision [FPR r30.4(3)]. If you are not sure if the decision you want to appeal is a case management decision or not, err on the side of caution and appeal within seven days - or ask the court to clarify and extend time. If you cannot meet this deadline you must apply for an extension of time BEFORE the time runs out, and you must make this application to the Appeal Judge / Court [Rule 30.7 FPR].

If the court refuses you permission to appeal without a hearing you can ask for a hearing, but you have to ask in writing within seven days of finding out that permission was refused.

If a High Court Judge or Designated Family Judge refuses permission to appeal without a hearing and they think that your appeal is 'totally without merit' (hopeless), they can order that you are not allowed to try again at a permission hearing.

The court will only give you permission where the appeal would have a **real prospect of success** OR there is **some other compelling reason** why the appeal should be heard. The court can grant you permission on some points and refuse it on others.

You make an appeal using form N161 Appellant's Notice. The notes that go with N161 (N161A) and Practice Direction 30A tell you what you need to attach to your appeal notice (see from paragraph 5.8 and 5.9 - be careful, there are slightly different lists depending on whether or not the appeal is in the Family Court or High Court). One very important thing is that you must include a copy of the order made and either a note or transcript of the judgment (Judge) or written reasons (Lay Justices). If any of the documents are missing when you need to file your appeal documents say so on the appeal form, explain why and send them in as soon as they become available - do not wait for them. These documents must all be served on the other party to the case including any representative of the children.

Your appeal notice should set out all the grounds (reasons) for your appeal. If it does not you may not be allowed to rely on other things you have thought of later, for example that the Judge has failed to consider an important piece of information, or has attached too much importance to one thing and not enough to another, or that the Judge has got the law wrong (you will need to say what the law is and what the Judge has got wrong). You are encouraged to produce a 'skeleton argument' explaining your case, but if you are not represented this is optional.

The other party to the appeal is the Respondent (this can be confusing because they might have been the Applicant originally). They will not have to do anything unless permission is given, but then they will have a chance to fill in a Respondent's notice (N162 and notes N162A) saying if they object or agree to the appeal. If you are a Respondent to an appeal, you are encouraged to produce a skeleton argument explaining your position on the appeal, but if you are not represented this is optional.

If the court gives you permission the appeal will be listed for a hearing. Sometimes the court will list a hearing for 'permission with appeal to follow', meaning that if you get permission they will hear the appeal immediately in the same hearing. Normally the court will not hear any oral evidence and it will only look at papers that were in front of the court at the date of the original hearing. The court does have the power to allow fresh evidence, but will only do this if there is a very good reason why the evidence wasn't produced before and only if it is really important evidence.

If a court allows an appeal it can set aside the order or part of it and order a rehearing before another Judge or panel of Lay Justices, or substitute its own decision for the decision of the court below.

Appealing consent orders

You can appeal a consent order (PD30 pa 14.1) but you must include with your notice of appeal a statement setting out the change in circumstances since the order was agreed or other circumstances justifying a review or re-hearing.

It is not really clear when you should use this route, as in most cases a set aside application is likely to be more appropriate.

Appeals to the Court of Appeal

In most respects appeals to the Court of Appeal work exactly the same as I've set out above. But there are a few differences. The rules are in Civil Procedure Rules (CPR) Pt 52 and PD52C.

- PD52C tells you what documents you need to include with your appeal. In the Court of Appeal a skeleton argument is not optional!

- The test for permission is the same (real prospects of success OR some other compelling reason). BUT see below if your appeal is a second appeal.

- Rule 52.14 deals with the costs of transcripts at public expense.

25.7 Second appeals

If you appeal an order and your appeal is unsuccessful (or if the other party has successfully appealed) you might be able to make a second appeal against the decision of the appeal court.

A second appeal will be to the next tier up from the appeal Judge: an appeal from a Circuit Judge goes to the Court of Appeal, and an appeal from the Court of Appeal goes to the Supreme Court.

Appeals to the Court of Appeal are covered by Part 52 of the Civil Procedure Rules 1998 (see Justice website).

You would need to seek permission to appeal from the Judge dealing with the first appeal or from the court you are going to appeal to in a similar way to the process on first appeal.

You would need to file an appellants notice within 21 days of the decision you are appealing unless the court has set a different time.

The remaining procedure can be found in Part 52 CPR. The important difference to be aware of is that on a second appeal the court will only give permission if the appeal would raise an important point of principle or practice OR there is some other compelling reason for the Court of Appeal to hear it. This really means it will be pretty difficult to persuade the Court of Appeal to hear the appeal.

25.8 Responding to an appeal

If the other person involved in your case appeals you can do one of four things:

- Do nothing. If you are happy with the order you can leave it up to the court to decide whether to allow the appeal.

- If the appeal is to the Court of Appeal, you may file a short skeleton argument (3 pages max) saying why you don't think they should get permission to appeal (see CPR PD52C paragraph 19).

- If you want to make arguments in support of the existing order at the appeal hearing you can file a skeleton argument before the hearing (required in the Court of Appeal).

- File a Respondents notice. If you also wish to challenge the order (perhaps a different part of it or for different reasons) you need to say so and say why. If you don't do this you may not be allowed to make your points at any appeal hearing. The FPR / CPR (depending on which court it is) tell you what to do and when.

25.9 Set aside

There are a number of specific circumstances when the FPR allow someone to apply to set aside an order, for example an order that has been made in the absence of one party or an order that has been made without a hearing. This type of application is not dealt with here - see Chapter 8. Applications to vary child arrangements orders are dealt with in Chapter 19 (an order about a child can be varied where it is no longer appropriate - this chapter is about orders which weren't appropriate in the first place!).

The rules in this area have recently changed. In financial remedy cases rule 9.9A FPR and PD 9.9A now apply.

You can ask for your financial remedy order to be set aside on the following grounds :

- fraud

- material non-disclosure

- certain limited types of mistake

- a subsequent event, unforeseen and unforeseeable at the time the order was made, which invalidates the basis on which the order was made

- there might be other reasons not listed here, but these are the main grounds as set out in the PD.

The application is made to the court that made the original order.

In cases of non-disclosure in financial proceedings, the court would have to first consider evidence of non-disclosure of the situation as it was *at the time of the trial*, and find as a fact that there had been material non-disclosure before the court could consider whether the original order should be set aside. The fact that there may have been later changes in circumstances or information that would not have been available at the trial is not relevant to this sort of application. A successful set aside application in financial remedy proceedings enables the court to go back to square one and start again OR to impose an alternative order if that is appropriate. There are no guarantees the outcome will be any better next time around.

In children matters, if there have been findings of fact made against a person and new evidence later emerges that demonstrates the findings were wrongly made the correct application is probably an application to set aside the findings to the original Judge that made the findings. The evidence would normally have to be significant and material that was not available first time around.

It is extremely important that you act as promptly as possible in cases of this kind.

Set aside applications are quite rare and quite tricky and if at all possible you should seek urgent legal advice about this type of application.

Note: At the time of writing the justice.gov.uk website doesn't seem to have been updated to include rule 9.9A on set asides. This is an administrative error. Until it is fixed you can find the rule by searching legislation.gov.uk for Family Procedure (Amendment No 2) Rules 2016.

25.10 Complaints against professionals

If you wish to complain about the court facilities, court staff or management your local court will have complaints forms and a complaints policy.

If you wish to complain about the Judge (for example about how he has behaved rather than the decision he has made) you may write to the Office for Judicial Complaints.

If you wish to correct factual inaccuracies in a CAFCASS report you should contact the CAFCASS Officer to do so. If you wish to complain about the conduct of a CAFCASS officer CAFCASS have a complaints procedure, available on their website under policies.

If you wish to complain about an individual lawyer you should complain to their firm (solicitor, legal executive) or chambers (barrister) in the first instance.

Local Authorities have their own complaints procedure which is usually published on their website. If you wish to complain about a social worker who has written a report about your children you should follow that procedure.

26. Postscript - The Future

Since the first edition of this book was published in 2011 a lot has changed, and a large number of revisions to this book have been necessary for this third edition. The book is as up to date as possible as at 13 June 2017.

Things that are on the horizon include:

- Changes to how vulnerable witnesses are dealt with by the family court, including the participation of children.

- Brexit may mean there is a change *in time* (not yet) in the way in which cases involving cross border families are dealt. At the moment decisions about which country's court should deal with a case with an international (European) element are usually dealt with under European regulations.

- Before the 2017 snap election was called Parliament was considering a change to the law that would mean that if you are accused of domestic abuse and do not have a lawyer, you will not be allowed to question your accuser yourself, and the court may appoint a lawyer to ask questions for you, at the court's expense. This would not be the same as being fully represented, as the lawyer would only be involved in the questioning of that witness, and you would still have to represent yourself through the other parts of the case. At the time of writing it is unclear whether similar legislation will be put before the new Parliament. Even if it is, this is just an outline of the proposed change to the law, as the detail might change as it goes through Parliament, or it might not get passed at all.

- In February 2017 there were reports that the five year cut off for evidence of domestic abuse required to qualify for legal aid was going to be scrapped. These changes have not yet been made.

- At the time of writing there are increasing calls for divorce law reform, with many groups calling for 'no fault' divorce, after the Court of Appeal ruled that a wife could not obtain a divorce from her husband as she had not proved that his behaviour meant it was unreasonable to expect her to continue living with him (*Owens v Owens*). That case is due to be dealt with by The Supreme Court, and it is possible that this case will prompt Parliament to change the law.

- It is expected that the court service will launch a platform allowing spouses and civil partners to apply for a divorce / dissolution online from

Autumn 2017, and the aim is for it to be possible to complete the whole divorce process online by 2019. There are also changes to the way in which financial remedy applications are managed administratively – as of June 2017 they will be dealt with separately from the divorce itself, with the divorce being dealt with in a 'Regional Divorce Centre' and the financial aspects of any financial application that aren't agreed being dealt with at the local court. At the time when we went to print the changes were just being announced, so the details are unclear and may be subject to change.

- A new Pensions Advisory Group was recently created. They are aiming to publish guidance about pensions on divorce which may be helpful.

If you are worried that things might have changed since this book was published you can check the website that accompanies this book - www.nofamilylawyer. co.uk, where we will try to publish details of any major developments, or say if anything is up and coming. You could also check on the Family Law Week or the Justice websites.

PART 7: TOOLKIT & RESOURCES

Key To Abbreviations & Symbols

This book does not always regurgitate the precise wording of the law because it is meant to be a manageable and easy to use guide for non-lawyers. Often the law is paraphrased or rephrased or summarised. Where we have used an exact phrase or term that comes directly from the law this is in **bold**. References to the piece of law that is being described are at the end of the sentence in question [in square brackets like this] so that if that particular piece of law comes up in your case you can look up the exact wording using the internet (you might not always need to do this).

Any forms referred to are available for download via the justice.gov.uk website (or collection from your local court office) unless otherwise stated. They can usually be completed on your computer but not saved. It is better to fill in a draft by hand and only type in your final answers when you are sure you are ready to finalise and print. Always print 3 of everything.

This book tries not to use too much legal jargon. Any legal words or abbreviations are explained in the glossary.

Abbreviations

A particular section of a law is referred to as s2 or s3.

The Acts most commonly referred to are abbreviated in this book as follows:

Children Act 1989	CA
Family Law Act 1996	FLA 1996
Family Law Act 1986	FLA 1986
Matrimonial Causes Act 1973	MCA
Civil Partnership Act 2004	CPA
Trusts of Land and Appointment of Trustees Act 1996	ToLATA
Human Rights Act 1998	HRA

Also, we have abbreviated the European Convention on Human Rights to ECHR.

The rules applicable to family cases (Family Procedure Rules 2010) are abbreviated to FPR. The FPR are divided into Parts e.g. Pt 4, Chapters e.g. Ch 3 and Rules e.g. r4.5. Different parts of the FPR have additional guidance called Practice Directions attached to them e.g. PD12A.

Other abbreviations

First Directions Appointment	FDA
Financial Dispute Resolution	FDR
First Hearing Dispute Resolution Appointment	FHDRA
Dispute Resolution Appointment	DRA
Non-molestation order	Non-Mol
Prohibited steps order	PSO
Parental responsibility	PR
Child Support Agency	CSA
Children & Family Court Advisory & Support Service	CAFCASS
Local Authority	LA

Although not all of them are used in this book, lawyers often use letters to identify individuals or parties lawyers. Some of these are set out below.

Mother	M
Father	F
Husband	H
Wife	W
Applicant	A
Respondent	R
Maternal GrandMother	MGM
Maternal Grandparents	MGPs
Paternal GrandFather	PGF
Paternal Step-GrandFather	PSGF (Etc)
Maternal Aunt	MA
Paternal Uncle	PU (Etc)
Maternal Great GrandMother	MGGM (Etc)
Guardian	G
Social worker	s/w

District Judge	DJ
His / Her Honour Judge (a Circuit Judge or recorder)	HHJ
Family Proceedings Court	FPC
Lord Justice	LJ
High Court Judge (Mr(s) Justice X)	J

Case citations

FLR	Family Law Reports
EWFC	England & Wales Family Court
EWHC (Fam)	England & Wales High Court (Family Division)
EWCA (Civ)	England & Wales Court of Appeal (Civil Division)
SC	Supreme Court

Jargon Buster

WORD/PHRASE	DEFINITION
Advocate	Someone who is entitled to speak on your behalf and represent you in court.
Affidavit	A formal sworn statement of fact. Like a witness statement but sworn on oath (or by solemn promise for the non-religious) in front of someone who is authorised to take oaths (solicitors will do this for a small fee but you can do it for free at your local court office). Affidavits are rarely required. Witness statements are far more common. One exception is the Form E in financial proceedings which is a specific type of affidavit and must be sworn.
Applicant	The person (party) who starts the case by making an application. A person who didn't start the case but who later makes an application for a direction in the course of that case is sometimes called the Applicant when that application is being dealt with, which can be a bit confusing. And where both parties make similar applications (called cross applications) they are both Applicants. Usually where this happens the person who got their application in first is called the Applicant. See also Claimant and Respondent.
Authority	An authority is the written judgment of a court containing a legal principle, which was decided in another case, which can be applied to other similar cases. If it is a judgment of a more senior Judge than the one in your case the court has to follow it. See Binding.

Jargon Buster

WORD/PHRASE	DEFINITION
Beneficial Interest	A type of entitlement to land or a house which is not written down. For example, you may have an entitlement to a share in a property which cannot be seen from the legal documents. Someone who is the legal owner of a property (the person whose name is on the land registry documents) is often also the beneficial owner, but sometimes they are different - a legal owner can hold a property or part of a property 'on trust' for another person, for example sometimes when a couple buy a house together but only put it in one name.
Binding	An authority is binding upon all courts below it. This means it has to be followed by less senior courts. If it can be distinguished (that is, be shown to be about different circumstances to the current case and therefore not applicable) it does not have to be followed.
Black letter law	A phrase used to describe the sort of law that is formally written down in primary or secondary legislation made by Parliament, rather than the common law as explained by judges through case law.

Jargon Buster

WORD/PHRASE	DEFINITION
Bundle	This is the organised set of papers that everybody works from in a case. They are structured in a set way into different sections, with page numbers and an index so that everything is easy to find and everybody knows what document is being referred to. The solicitor for the person making the application usually has to prepare them (or the solicitor for the Respondent if the Applicant has no solicitor). Usually the bundle is agreed. If parties cannot agree about the inclusion of certain documents these might be put in a small supplemental bundle and the Judge will have to decide whether to include them in the case. There should usually be no objection to a document that has previously been filed with the court being included in the bundle, unless the court has asked for a smaller bundle of the essential documents only.
Capacity	When somebody is suffering from a mental illness or learning disability this can sometimes make it difficult for them to understand the case or make proper decisions about it or give instructions to a lawyer. If this is the case they may lack capacity and someone else may have to run the case and make decisions for them - this person is called a litigation friend.
Care proceedings	When social services start a case asking for an order that gives them the power to make decisions about a child (a care order) including to remove a child from its parents.
Case summary	A short document that summarises the basic facts in a case, what has happened so far and the things which are coming up for the court to deal with. See also Position statement.

Jargon Buster

WORD/PHRASE	DEFINITION
Child arrangements order	An order setting out arrangements for where a child should live and when, and / or arrangements for who else they should spend time with. Replaced contact and residence orders from 22 April 2014.
Child Maintenance	See Child Support.
Child support	Child maintenance. Paid by the parent who does not live with a child to the other parent for the child's needs and expenses. The amount payable is fixed by law and can be paid voluntarily or via the Child Support Agency.
Citation	A citation is the string of letters and numbers that identifies a particular case and tells you where to find it. This book uses neutral citations. See Chapter 10.
Civil	Civil refers to any kind of law or case apart from criminal. Family is a type of civil law, but sometimes it can be used to mean all types of non-criminal law apart from family.
Claimant	See Applicant and Defendant. The person who starts the case by making a claim. In most family cases this person is called the Applicant but occasionally they are called Claimant.
Collaborative Law	A dispute resolution process for separating couples that aims to help couples sort things out without going to court.
Committal	When a family Judge sends somebody to prison for breaching an order, undertaking or rule of court, they are committed to prison.
Common Law Wife	There is no such thing as a common law wife.

Jargon Buster

WORD/PHRASE	DEFINITION
Competent	A child is competent (sometimes also known as *Gillick Competent*) when they are of an age and maturity and understanding to be able to give proper instructions to their lawyer.
Conciliation Appointment	A type of dispute resolution, sometimes available at court in cases about children, early on in the case. Conciliation means getting you to agree not getting you back together (that's reconciliation!).
Conference	A meeting with your lawyer (at court or in their office) is called a conference.
Consent	Agree.
Consent order	An order that everyone in the case has agreed and the court has approved.
Contact	Time spent with a child and the parent that they don't live with. See also Staying Contact, Visiting Contact, Supervised Contact and Supported Contact.
Contempt of court	When a court order or undertaking is broken, this disrespect for the court's authority is known as contempt of court. The court can punish the person for their behaviour by committal or fine. Contempt in the face of the court (e.g. behaving very disruptively and abusively in court) is not necessarily a breach of an order, but is very bad behaviour that takes place in the presence of the Judge.
Contested	Not agreed. A contested hearing is one that has been set up in the knowledge that a particular issue will have to be decided, and with a long enough time estimate to allow that to happen.

Jargon Buster

WORD/PHRASE	DEFINITION
Cross allegation	Or counter allegation. An allegation made in response to an allegation made by the other party (for example where both parties allege that the other was the aggressor in a particular incident between them).
Cross application	Where two opposing parties each make the same type of application, each asking for the same order in their favour (for example both parents apply for the children to live with them).
Cross examination	Questions asked by the other side's lawyers of your witnesses, or by you of the other party's witnesses designed to test the evidence and show up its weaknesses. See Leading questions and Examination in chief.
Counsel	A barrister
Counter Schedule	A schedule (table) setting out the allegations made in response to initial allegations (for example where both parties allege domestic violence by the other on different occasions). See Scott Schedule.
Custody	1. Someone who is in prison is 'in custody'.
	2. Often used in newspapers to refer to residence, but there has been no such thing as 'custody' of a child since the CA 1989 (except in international child abduction cases because the term is still used by other countries).
Deputy	A Judge who has the word Deputy in their title is not less senior but part time. They might be semi-retired or still work as a lawyer some of the time.
Directions hearing	A short hearing to make plans and manage the case before a final decision can be taken. See Review.

Jargon Buster

WORD/PHRASE	DEFINITION
Disclosure	Showing and providing copies of documents you want to rely on to the other party and their lawyer, and to the court.
Discretion	When the court is allowed to do something but has to decide whether or not it should.
Disputed	Things that are not agreed are disputed or 'in dispute'.
Duty	Something the court or some person must do. See Power / discretion.
Enforceable	Something is enforceable if the court has power to make it happen or to punish if an order saying it must be done is not stuck to.
Equity	Equity is the bit of your house you actually own, when you've taken into account what you owe on it. You can think of your equity as what is left after you have sold the house, paid off the mortgage or any other debts secured against it and paid the estate agents and conveyancing solicitors' fees.
Evidence in chief	The main evidence of a witness, which includes the contents of any witness statements and any oral evidence given prior to cross examination via examination in chief or, if there is no lawyer, by initial oral evidence.
Ex Parte	See Without notice.
Examination in chief	See Evidence in chief. Questions asked by the lawyer or person calling a witness to get further evidence in chief from a witness. Must be Open questions only.

Jargon Buster

WORD/PHRASE	DEFINITION
Expert witness	A person who has been asked to produce a report for the case because they have some kind of expertise the court needs in order to decide the case, for example a psychologist, psychiatrist or independent social worker.
Extempore	When a Judge gives his judgment as soon as the evidence and the legal submissions have finished. See Reserved.
Fact finding	The process by which the court decides whether allegations are true or not. In the Family Court, if the court thinks a fact is more likely than not to be true it is 'found' i.e. true and if the court thinks it is more likely than not to be untrue it is 'not found' and treated as not having happened.
File	When you provide copies of documents to the court you are filing them. Usually, whatever you file should also be served. See Serve.
Financial Dispute Resolution Hearing (FDR)	A special type of hearing in financial cases where the Judge actively tries to help the parties reach an agreement. What is said at that hearing is Without prejudice and can't be referred to at the final hearing.
First Directions Appointment (FDA)	The first hearing in financial cases where the main aim is to make sure all the necessary information has been provided, and to work out what else needs to be done before the case can progress. If possible the court will also conduct a Financial Dispute Resolution Hearing at the same time.

Jargon Buster

WORD/PHRASE	DEFINITION
Guardian	1. The person responsible for trying to ensure that the children's welfare is promoted through the court process and that their wishes are explored and made known, and who has a duty to report and make recommendations about what should happen and what the outcome should be. Usually a CAFCASS officer (see Chapter 17).
	2. Where a parent with parental responsibility appoints another person to be the child's guardian if they die [s5 CA].
Habitual residence	This has slightly different meanings in different contexts but roughly means the place where a person is settled or rooted.
His / Her / Your Honour	What you call a Circuit Judge or Recorder.
Injunction	An injunction is a general name for any type of order that tells somebody they must not do something. There are lots of different types, for example, a non-molestation order, occupation order, avoidance of disposition (freezing) order, or a prohibited steps order.
Interim	Temporary, whilst a case is ongoing.
Intervenor	Someone who gets involved in the case because of a specific issue (for example because it is said they have caused injury to a child or because they say they own part of a property which is part of a divorce case).

Jargon Buster

WORD/PHRASE	DEFINITION
Issue	1. When an application, petition or claim is formally started it is issued. You can tell something is issued because it has the court (seal) stamp on it. 2. Something is 'an issue' in a case if it is disputed. Things that are agreed are not issues in the case.
Judge	The person who makes the decisions. A Judge will be a qualified and experienced lawyer (sometimes a barrister and sometimes a solicitor).
Judgment	The reasons and decision of a Judge. Can be spoken or in writing. It will be recorded in the County Court on tape. In cases heard by Lay Justices you will receive written facts and reasons instead.
Jurisdiction	The legal power to do something.
Justices	Magistrates, also referred to as Lay Justices, a Bench or Panel.
Lay	A person who is not legally qualified is a lay person. When a solicitor instructs a barrister on behalf of their client they are called the 'professional client', and the original person is called the 'lay client'. A Lay Justice or Magistrate is a lay person because they are not legally qualified (this is why they have a legal adviser in court with them).
Leading question	See also Open questions. A closed question, or a question which suggests a particular answer or puts a proposition (You did x or y didn't you? Do you agree that x? Can you confirm...?). Used to test or challenge the evidence of the other sides witnesses in cross examination (you said x and y so x must be true). You cannot ask leading questions of your own witnesses.

Jargon Buster

WORD/PHRASE	DEFINITION
Leave	Permission.
Magistrates	See Justices.
Mediation	A voluntary and private process where a trained and impartial mediator tries to help parties find their own solutions to disputes.
My friend	What lawyers call other solicitors in court (quite old-fashioned).
My learned friend	What lawyers call barristers in court (quite old-fashioned).
Notice	Giving someone advance warning of something (usually an application) by sending them the documents.
Official Solicitor (the)	Will act on behalf of an adult who is unable to give instructions to their lawyer because they are mentally unwell. They give instructions based on what they think is best for the person who is unwell.
Open questions	A non-leading question, in other words, a question that introduces a topic but does not suggest a particular answer (what, when, why, how, who). Compare to Leading questions.
Oral Evidence	When a person gives evidence as a witness by answering questions in court. A witness giving evidence will tell the Judge what has happened and what their position is. Contrast with submissions (Think about it as: evidence = what, submissions = why).
Parental responsibility	The legal rights and responsibilities that a parent has. Automatic for Mothers and married Fathers and most Fathers whose name is on birth certificate. Usually granted on application to Fathers who don't hold it.

Jargon Buster

WORD/PHRASE	DEFINITION
Part-heard	When a Judge starts to hear evidence but runs out of time and has to finish the evidence on another day, the case is 'part-heard' until the evidence has been finished and judgment given. The same Judge and advocates must deal with the case until the evidence is finished and the judgment given. When a case is part-heard the court and the advocates have to give it priority in their diaries so that the evidence can be finished as soon as possible.
Party	A person who is formally involved in a case because they have made an application for an order or because they are responding to an application for an order. A person with parental responsibility for a child should always be a party to a case involving the child, even though they may not wish to take part, and a Father is entitled to become a party even if he doesn't have parental responsibility. Sometimes other people are parties to a case, for example if they have applied for an order in respect of a grandchild or if somebody is asking for an order that directly affects them. A child is not usually a party to a case which is about them but they will be a party if a Guardian has been appointed for them. Sometimes a Local Authority can be a party, but only where they are asking for an order such as a care order. In family cases it is usually only parties who can come into court. Witnesses can usually only come into court whilst they are giving evidence (apart from professional witnesses and parties).
PD	Practice Direction (guidance that supplements the rules of court).
Penal notice	A warning on the front of a court order explaining that if the order is broken the person who has broken it could be punished by fine or imprisonment. See also Warning notice.

Jargon Buster

WORD/PHRASE	DEFINITION
Periodical payments	See Spousal maintenance.
Permission	Also called Leave. You have to get permission to make some sorts of applications.
Position statement	A short document which summarises the position of one party at the time of a particular hearing. See also Case summary.
Power	Means that the court can do something, not that it has to. See Duty / discretion.
Power of arrest	Means the Police are allowed to arrest somebody if they break the order that has the power of arrest attached to it (usually an occupation order). The Police have to bring the person to the Family Court for punishment, not the Criminal Court.
Precedent	The judgment of a case decided by a senior court, and which sets out a legal principle that has to be followed by other courts.
Proceedings	A court case.
Professional witness	A witness who is involved in the case as part of their job (social worker, CAFCASS Officer, Psychologist etc).
Prohibited steps order	An order telling a person they must not do certain things in relation to a child.
Put to proof	When a party does not accept the other party's version of events they put them to proof, meaning that they require them to prove the fact in court by providing evidence.

Jargon Buster

WORD/PHRASE	DEFINITION
Recital	A recital is something that is recorded at the top of a court order, but which is not actually part of the order itself. It is usually used to record background information which will later explain why the order was made, or to record agreements that the parties have reached, which go hand in hand with the bits that the court is ordering.
Recusal	When a Judge stands down from a case before hearing it because of a conflict of interests or bias.
Reporting officer	A CAFCASS Officer who will write a report making recommendations about the applications.
Reserved	When a Judge goes away to think about his judgment before giving it. See Extempore.
Residence	Where a child lives. A court cannot make a residence order anymore and all existing residence orders have been automatically converted to child arrangements orders. See Child arrangements order.
Respondent	The person who is responding to an application started by someone else (the Applicant).
Return date hearing	A hearing to give the other person a chance to say whether or not they object to an order continuing if the court had made the order before the other person was told about it.
Review hearing	A hearing to review the progress of a case, and to update or tweak the arrangements if necessary. See Directions hearing and Contested.

345

Jargon Buster

WORD/PHRASE	DEFINITION
Scott Schedule	A numbered table setting out each allegation of domestic violence or abuse that a party is asking the Judge to find proved in date order, with page references. See also Counter schedule.
Serve	To provide a copy of a document to the other parties in the case (or someone else if directed to do so by the Judge).
s9 Judge	A Judge who is allowed to sit as a High Court Judge.
Shared residence	An arrangement where the children split their time between two home bases. Shared residence orders no longer exist but a child arrangements order can set out these sorts of arrangements (and an old shared residence order will have automatically converted to a child arrangements order in the same terms).
Skeleton argument	A written outline of what law is relevant and how it applies to the case or hearing. Sometimes prepared before a hearing, sometimes not until the evidence has been concluded. See Submissions.
Spousal Maintenance	Regular income payments from husband to wife or vice versa. Not the same as child maintenance. Also known as periodical payments or PPs.
Staying Contact	Contact which includes an overnight stay. See also Contact and Visiting Contact.

Jargon Buster

WORD/PHRASE	DEFINITION
Submissions	At a directions hearing or at the end of a longer hearing after the evidence has been given each party has an opportunity to explain to the Judge what they say should happen and why, and to tell the Judge why the evidence that has been given and the law support their argument. These are submissions. Compare with (Think of it as: evidence = what, submissions = why). Occasionally submissions are dealt with in writing. See also Skeleton argument.
Supervised Contact	'Supervised' contact is generally used to refer to contact where one or more individuals are nominated to oversee contact throughout to ensure it is safe and appropriate. In a contact centre this would usually entail the parent and children being supervised individually by a staff member, separate from other families. Very few contact centres offer this and the costs are often prohibitive. Most contact centres offer Supported Contact. See also Supported Contact. Supervised contact can also refer to contact outside a contact centre where another trusted family member or friend agrees to be present at all times to ensure it is safe and appropriate.
Supported Contact	Supported contact is the arrangement commonly in place in most contact centres. It means that whilst staff or experienced volunteers will be present and generally keeping an eye on the various families present they will not be supervising each family separately or monitoring what is being said. In this scenario families usually have contact in a larger room (such as a church hall) with other families and children can interact with one another. See also Supervised Contact.
Third Party	Someone other than the parties in the case.

Jargon Buster

WORD/PHRASE	DEFINITION
Threshold	The test for deciding whether or not the court is allowed to make a care or supervision order. If the threshold is proved the court can make an order (although it doesn't have to) but if it is not the court cannot. The threshold is about whether a child has suffered, is suffering or is likely to suffer significant harm.
Undertaking	A solemn promise given voluntarily to the court not to do something. Can be punished by the court if broken. See also committal.
Visiting Contact	Contact limited to the daytime i.e. no overnight stay. See also Contact and Staying Contact.
Warning notice	A type of penal notice that relates to Child Arrangement Orders. It warns that if the order is broken the person who has broken it could be subject to an enforcement order or might have to pay financial compensation. See also Penal notice.
Without Notice	When someone goes to court to ask for an order without telling the other party they are going, usually because it is urgent or in cases where the order needs to be in place before the other person finds out (also sometimes called ex parte).
Without Prejudice	Correspondence or communication between parties that is privileged (private between them) and not to be seen by the Judge, in order to try and settle a case. Usually in the form of an offer letter. Discussions at an FDR are without prejudice.
Witness statement	A written document containing the evidence a witness will give at court. It must have a signed statement of truth at the bottom of it.

Internet Resources

All the resources referred to below are free to access, although some sites may also have additional subscription only services.

All the website addresses were checked at the time of publication, but things do change quickly on the internet. Although the websites I have suggested are all sites I think are reliable and balanced, you do need to use the internet wisely and form your own view about the reliability of the information you obtain.

Table of internet resources

NAME	DESCRIPTION	WEBSITE ADDRESS
Advicenow		www.advicenow.org.uk
Alcoholics Anonymous		www.alcoholics-anonymous.org.uk
BAILII (British & Irish Legal Information Institute)	Publishes judgments in family and other courts, where permission to report has been given.	www.bailii.org
Bar Council	Information about barristers including how to instruct one directly through public access.	www.barcouncil.org.uk
Bar Standards Board	Independent organisation regulating barristers.	www.barstandardsboard.org.uk
CAFCASS	Children & Families Court Advisory Service.	www.cafcass.gov.uk
CAFCASS Cymru	Children & Families Court Advisory Service (Wales)	www.wales.gov.uk/cafcass-cymru
CB7 form	Guide for separated parents children and the family courts.	https://formfinder.hmcts-formfinder.justice.gov.uk/cb007-eng.pdf
Chartered Institute of Legal Executives (CILEX)		www.cilex.org.uk

Table of internet resources

NAME	DESCRIPTION	WEBSITE ADDRESS
Child Maintenance Options	Information on child maintenance and how you can sort it out by agreement between you.	www.cmoptions.org
Child Maintenance Service	Statutory service working out how much should be paid, and collecting payments.	www.gov.uk/child-maintenance
Child Poverty Action Group (CPAG)	Information about welfare benefits and tax credits.	www.cpag.org.uk
Child Protection Resource	Blog containing information and views about child protection matters.	www.childprotectionresource.co.uk
Citizen's Advice Bureau		www.adviceguide.org.uk
Civil Legal Advice	Get free and confidential legal advice in England and Wales if you're eligible for legal aid.	www.gov.uk/civil-legal-advice
Coram Children's Legal Centre	Really useful information about family law, on special guardianship in particular.	www.childrenslegalcentre.com
The Couple Connection	Relationship advice and support. See also the Parenting Connection and One Plus One.	https://thecouple connection.net
Court and Tribunal Finder	Find out which is your local court or divorce unit.	https://courttribunalfinder.service.gov.uk/search/

Table of internet resources

NAME	DESCRIPTION	WEBSITE ADDRESS
Dad Info	Service providing separated parents with suggestions about the most successful way to communicate, negotiate and solve problems after family breakdown.	http://dadinfo.splittin-gup-putkidsfirst.org.uk/home
Department for Education (formerly DCSF)		www.gov.uk/government/organisations/depart-ment-for-education
Direct.Gov	A range of government information.	www.gov.uk
Direct Access Portal	Official Bar Council portal listing qualified Direct Access barristers, mediators and arbitrators.	www.directaccessportal.co.uk
Expert templates	The Law Society has developed a suite of templates to use when instructing experts in family proceedings.	www.lawsociety.org.uk/support-services/fami-ly-court-resources/fami-ly-law--templates-for-in-structing-experts//
Families Need Fathers	Charity concerned with maintaining a child's relationship with both parents during and after family breakdown.	www.fnf.org.uk
Family Court Guide	Includes Judicial Guidance and Practice Directions and other useful information. Not always promptly updated at time of going to print.	www.judiciary.gov.uk/re-lated-offices-and-bodies/advisory-bodies/fjc/guid-ance/familycourtguide/

Table of internet resources

NAME	DESCRIPTION	WEBSITE ADDRESS
Familycourtinfo	Basic information for court users, designed for court users local to Bristol but some info helpful for others.	www.familycourtinfo.org.uk
Family Justice Council	About the Family Justice Council.	www.judiciary.gov.uk/related-offices-and-bodies/advisory-bodies/fjc/
Family Law Bar Association	Representative body for family barristers, publishes At A Glance Book.	www.flba.co.uk
Family Law Bar Association Guidance Locator	Links to guidance in family law.	http://flba.co.uk/blog/2016/01/01/guidance-locator/
Family Law Week	Judgments and commentary on family cases.	www.familylawweek.co.uk
Family Mediation Council	Family mediation body.	www.familymediation-council.org.uk
Family Orders Project	An ongoing project by the judiciary to produce standard form orders.	www.judiciary.gov.uk/publications/family-orders-project/
Family Rights Group	Advises parents and other family members whose children are involved with or require children's social care services because of welfare needs or concerns.	www.frg.org.uk
Find a barrister	Directory of public access barrister (barristers who accept instructions directly). See also Bar Council website.	www.barcouncil.org.uk/using-a-barrister/find-a-barrister/ and www.barcouncil.org.uk/using-a-barrister/how-to-instruct-a-barrister/

Table of internet resources

NAME	DESCRIPTION	WEBSITE ADDRESS
Freedom Pro-gramme	A 12 week programme pro-viding information to men and women about domestic violence.	www.freedom programme.co.uk
Gamblers Anony-mous		www.gamblers anonymous.org.uk
Grandparents Plus		www.grandparentsplus. org.uk/
Government Legis-lation Website	Statutes (largely revised) and Statutory Instruments (in original form). Court rules on Ministry of Justice site.	www.legislation.gov.uk
Guidelines for Judges meeting children	Produced by the Family Justice Council.	www.judiciary.gov.uk/ wp-content/uploads/ JCO/Documents/FJC/voc/ Guidelines_+Judges_see-ing_+Children.pdf
Help with court fees	Apply online for fee remis-sion if on low income.	www.gov.uk/help-with-court-fees
Hidden Hurt	Information and support for both male and female vic-tims of domestic violence.	www.hidden hurt.co.uk
House of commons briefing papers	A range of useful reports summarising aspects of family law (select Type - Commons briefing papers, Topic - Crime, civil law, justice and rights; sub topic: family law; years: all).	http://researchbriefings. parliament.uk
House of Lords	Archive of judgments before formation of the Supreme Court in July 2009.	www.publications. parliament.uk/pa/ld/ ldjudgmt.htm

Table of internet resources

NAME	DESCRIPTION	WEBSITE ADDRESS
Intelligent Divorce	Fixed fee service which supports couples (together or separately) to gather all the financial information they will need for advice from a barrister about the likely outcome at court, which they can use to help reach an agreement.	www.intelligentdivorce.co.uk
International Child Abduction & Contact Unit	See also Reunite. Tel: 020 7911 7045/7047 Out of hours emergency (Reunite advice line) 0116 2556 234.	https://www.gov.uk/government/publications/international-child-abduction-and-contact-unit-application-form
Judicial Conduct Investigations Office	How to make a complaint about the judiciary.	https://judicialconduct.judiciary.gov.uk
Judiciary of England & Wales	Judgments (all judgments on this site will also be on BAILII which is easier to search) and Practice Directions (links to Justice website at www.justice.gov.uk, but this is the easiest way to locate the right page).	www.judiciary.gov.uk
Justice website	Contains rules, practice directions, court forms and guidance, and information about courts (addresses, maps and contact details).	www.justice.gov.uk
Land Registry	See in particular Land Registry Public Guide 20: Applications Under the Family Law Act 1996.	www.landregistry.gov.uk

Table of internet resources

NAME	DESCRIPTION	WEBSITE ADDRESS
Law Society	Information about solicitors including how to find one.	www.lawsociety.org.uk
LawWorks	Solicitors Pro Bono Group.	www.lawworks.org.uk
Legal Aid	Check if you can get legal aid.	www.gov.uk/check-legal-aid
Legal Aid Finder	Directory of legal advisers and family mediators who do legal aid work.	https://find-legal-advice.justice.gov.uk
Legal Choices	Just the facts about lawyers and legal problems - impartial and unbiased.	www.legalchoices.org.uk
Legal Services Board	Independent body overseeing the regulation of all types of lawyers.	www.legalservicesboard.org.uk
Legal Ombudsman	Body dealing with consumer complaints about lawyers.	www.legalombudsman.org.uk
Lexis Nexis	Various resources - all Practice Directions to the Family Procedure Rules can be found here under 'Practice Guidance'.	www.familylaw.co.uk
Local Government Ombudsman	Deals with complaints about Local Authorities (Councils). Advice Line: 0300 061 0614.	www.lgo.org.uk
Marilyn Stowe	Family Law and Divorce Blog.	www.marilynstowe.co.uk
Match	Charity offering support and information to mothers apart from their children.	www.matchmothers.org

Table of internet resources

NAME	DESCRIPTION	WEBSITE ADDRESS
MIND	For better mental health. Helpline: 0300 123 3393.	www.mind.org.uk
Ministry of Justice	See in particular Civil and Family Procedure Rules, Practice Directions and Court Forms.	www.justice.gov.uk
MoJ videos	Videos produced by the MoJ (search for 'family court').	www.youtube.com/user/ MinistryofJusticeUK
Money Advice Service	Information about financial issues, including sections on divorce and separation.	www.moneyadvice service.org.uk
Narcotics Anonymous		www.ukna.org
National Association of Child Contact Centres (NACCC)	Search facility for contact centres by location and type of service. Range of information for families. Helpline: 0800 4500 280 (9.00-1.00, Mon-Fri).	www.naccc.org.uk
National Family Mediation	NFM videos promoting family mediation.	www.nfm.org.uk/index. php/about-nfm/nation-al-family-mediation-me-dia-centre/videos
National Youth Advocacy Service (NYAS)	Provide information and advice to children. Act as children's guardians in difficult private law cases.	www.nyas.net
No Family Lawyer	Three YouTube videos about what happens in court.	www.nofamilylawyer.co.uk/ going-to-court-videos. html

Table of internet resources

NAME	DESCRIPTION	WEBSITE ADDRESS
One Plus One	A charity whose aim is to enhance understanding of how family relationships contribute to the well-being of adults and children. See also The Parent Connection and The Couple Connection.	www.oneplusone.org.uk
Only Dads	Advice and support for single dads.	www.onlydads.org
Only Mums	Advice and support for mums going through separation and divorce.	www.onlymums.org
Parliament	Text of Bills currently passing through Parliament.	www.parliament.uk
The Parent Connection	Supports parents through separation and co-parenting difficulties. It can also be used by parents who are just worried about their relationship. See also the Couple Connection and One Plus One.	https://theparentconnection.org.uk
Personal Support Unit	Voluntary service helping litigants in person.	www.thepsu.org
Pink Tape	The blog run by the author of this book.	www.pinktape.co.uk
Public Law Project	Information about exceptional funding under the Legal Aid, Sentencing and Punishment of Offenders Act 2012. Helpline: 0207 843 1260.	www.publiclawproject.org.uk/exceptional-funding-project

Table of internet resources

NAME	DESCRIPTION	WEBSITE ADDRESS
Refuge	Support and information about domestic violence.	www.refuge.org.uk
Resolution	Family Solicitors' Organisation. Information about the ethos you should expect from a good family lawyer. Details of collaborative lawyers. Search facility for Independent Financial Advisers.	www.resolution.org.uk
Respect	Domestic Violence Perpetrator Programmes.	www.respect.uk.net
Rethink	Advice and helplines for people with issues relating to mental illness.	www.rethink.org
Reunite International	UK charity specialising in international parental child abduction. (click on 'resources' for a list of signatories to the Hague Convention).	www.reunite.org
Rights Info	Human Rights News, Views and Info.	www.rightsinfo.org
Rights of Women	Women's charity to help women through the law.	rightsofwomen.org.uk
Royal Courts of Justice Advice Bureau	Citizen's Advice Bureau providing free advice to litigants in person, including family law. Able to refer to Bar Pro Bono Unit where appropriate. Appointments line: 0203 475 4373.	www.rcjadvice.org.uk

Table of internet resources

NAME	DESCRIPTION	WEBSITE ADDRESS
Samaritans	Confidential non-judgemental emotional support for people experiencing feelings of distress or despair.	www.samaritans.org
Shelter	The housing and homelessness charity.	www.shelter.org.uk
Solicitors Regulation Authority (SRA)	Independent body regulating solicitors.	www.sra.org.uk
Sorting Out Separation	Government run support service for people going through family breakdown.	www.sortingoutseparation. org.uk
Suesspiciousminds	Blog written by child protection solicitor.	www.suesspiciousminds. com
Supreme Court	Judgments of the Supreme Court since its formation in July 2009.	www.supremecourt.uk/ decided-cases/index.html
Surviving Safeguarding	Blog written by parent who has been through the care system.	www.survivingsafeguarding.co.uk
The Transparency Project	Educational charity helping to make family law and the work of the family courts clearer. It does not provide legal advice.	www.transparencyproject. org.uk
Wikivorce	Advice and support on divorce.	www.wikivorce.com
Women's Aid	Support and information about domestic violence.	www.womensaid.org.uk
Your Rights	Liberty guide to human rights. Tells you how a conviction becomes spent.	https://www.liberty-human-rights.org.uk/human-rights/privacy/criminal-records

Table of Cases

Table of Cases

Table of Cases

Forms, Templates & Useful Documents

Court Forms

Court forms can be downloaded from the Justice website or collected from your local court.

I have tried to tell you what form to use as each type of application is described. The main forms are as follows:

Mediation	FM1
Confidential address	C8
Statement of Service (children)	C9
Children applications	C1 (PR)
	C100 (s8 applications)
	C1A (supplemental information form) or C2 (permission or an application once a case is started)
	C79 (enforcement of contact order).
Divorce / Civil Partnership	D8 (application)
	D84 (application for conditional order)
Finances	Form A (to start it)
	Form E (financial disclosure)
	D81 (consent order application)
Non-molestation / occupation	FL401

If you are unsure of which form to use Practice Direction 5A provides a list - but the easiest thing to do is to ask at your local court.

You can complete your form on your computer but be aware you cannot save the text you type in. It is usually best to print it out and fill in a draft by hand first, and then type it in when you are sure what you want to say.

Templates and checklists

Words in [Square brackets] need to be checked and adapted as appropriate

- they may offer you a selection of words, or point you towards what information you need to include.

XXXX means you need to fill in the blanks.

Words in italics are notes for reference and should not be included in your document.

The format for the heading of the witness statement can be used for any document you prepare for court: you just need to swap the title 'WITNESS STATEMENT' for the correct title.

List of sample documents/templates

- Witness statement
- Questionnaire
- Schedule of Assets
- Statement of Issues
- Common phrases used in children act orders
- Scott Schedule
- Common phrases used in financial orders
- Common wording for non-molestation orders and undertakings

Other documents

These days most things can be found on the internet. A few things are more difficult to access and so are contained in this section. Court forms are not reproduced as they can be downloaded from the Justice website or collected from your local court, but I have listed the most commonly used forms and what they should be used for.

Although I have not set out all the relevant law in this book there are one or two things which come up time and time again and which it is helpful to keep handy. These are reproduced in this section.

Key law

(See the Key Law section in this part for the full text):

- FPR Parts 1 & 4

- s1 Children Act 1989

- s25 Matrimonial Causes Act 1973

- ss33, 42, 45, & 46 Family Law Act 1996

- Schedule 7 Family Law Act 1996

- ss33 & 34 Family Law Act 1986

- Practice Guidance: McKenzie Friends

Witness Statement

Practice Direction 22A sets out what your witness statement must look like. The template provided is based on the Practice Direction. Use numbered paragraphs and space your text so it is not hard to read. Put page numbers on the bottom. Spell out numbers (e.g. fifty not 50). Don't use both sides of the page.

You must say where you don't have direct knowledge of something, for example if someone has told you something or if you have found it out from some other source (I know this because...).

Beyond that, the important thing is the substance of the statement. It is up to you to fill in the substance in some kind of logical order.

If you are responding to the other party's witness statement you could respond to each paragraph in the order that they have set out theirs. Or you can deal with things chronologically, or issue by issue with headings. There are pros and cons to each approach - it can be very confusing and irritating to read a witness statement that refers back to another document all the time. Ideally you want your witness statement to make sense as a standalone document. On the other hand it is important to be sure that somewhere within your witness statement you respond to all the points raised against you, and this can get forgotten if you don't respond to each paragraph. My personal preference is to deal in chronological or issue order and to check after you've done a first draft that each paragraph in the other party's witness statement or each point made against you is covered somewhere. This is what the Practice Direction suggests.

The witness must sign the Statement of Truth at the bottom of the statement and also sign each exhibit. If the court decides that a false statement has been deliberately made it does have the power to punish the person who made it as a contempt of court, so it is important to be clear and accurate.

Suggestions for Children Act statements

You might want to include a section in your statement which deals with any particularly relevant factors in the welfare checklist, perhaps including a paragraph for each. Particularly in respect of contact applications it can often be helpful to set out how you think the order you are asking for (or the order the other parent is asking for) will affect the child under the heading of 'Likely effect of any change in circumstances' (s1(3)(c) Children Act 1989).

Suggestions for statements about removal from the jurisdiction

If you are applying to remove a child from this jurisdiction it is important to exhibit as much well researched information as you can about where you are going and what the arrangements for accommodation, working, healthcare and schooling will be. You must also set out clear proposals for contact, how you envisage it happening (skype, phone, face to face etc) and what contributions you can make to the costs of that contact. If it is part of your case that your care of the child will be affected if you are forced to stay somewhere where you would be very unhappy, you must explain why this is, and if possible attach supporting evidence.

Suggestions for witness statements in domestic violence cases

It is generally important to set out a separate response to each allegation. Sometimes all you can say is 'I simply do not know what the Applicant is talking about. This did not happen', but in many cases you can explain that the version of events given is inaccurate and give your own, accurate, account. Just saying 'I deny all of the allegations' is unhelpful to everyone.

If there is no Scott Schedule deal with the allegations in chronological order, with a heading for each (e.g. 'Alleged incident on DATE').

If there is a Scott Schedule (see Chapters 22 and 23), deal with each allegation in the order they appear on the schedule, with a heading that corresponds to the date and schedule number.

Suggestions for occupation order / Transfer of tenancy cases

Use the criteria from the relevant part of the FLA 1996 to structure your statement. Make sure you have covered each one of the things that are listed. See Chapter 21, The Law Relating to Domestic Violence & Abuse.

Remember that if your witness statement is in support of an application you are making without telling the other party you must say why it has to be dealt with without them being told (e.g. you are fearful of their reaction).

Witness Statement Template

[NAME OF PARTY *You*]

[INITIALS & SURNAME OF PERSON MAKING STATEMENT]

[WHETHER THIS IS THE PERSON'S FIRST / SECOND / THIRD [ETC] STATEMENT]

[NUMBER & INITIALS OF ALL EXHIBITS]

[DATE OF STATEMENT]

IN THE FAMILY COURT (SITTING AT [XXXX])

CASE NO: [XXXX]

B E T W E E N:

[NAME OF THE PERSON APPLYING FOR AN ORDER]

APPLICANT

-AND-

[NAME OF THE OTHER PARTY]

[1ST] RESPONDENT

[-AND-

NAME OF ANY OTHER PARTY E.G. THE CHILD

2nd RESPONDENT

(only if the child has been joined as a party or there is some other party)]

[1ST / 2ND ETC] WITNESS STATEMENT OF THE [APPLICANT / RESPONDENT ETC] [NAME]

I, [NAME], of [SET OUT ADDRESS *or say* 'AN ADDRESS WHICH I WISH TO KEEP CONFIDENTIAL' *if appropriate*], make this statement pursuant to the order dated [DATE] and [in response to [OTHER PARTY'S NAME]'s application for [FINANCIAL REMEDY / CHILD ARRANGEMENTS ORDER ETC] *or* in support of my application for [FINANCIAL REMEDY / CHILD ARRANGEMENTS ORDER ETC]].

I am the [XXXX *state your relationship to the child and other party*]. *If this is your*

367

first statement it is usually helpful to identify each of the children and their ages and to state when you got together, when you separated and where each of you is living.

All matters contained in this statement are within my own knowledge unless otherwise stated.

Set out your evidence here, using a separate paragraph for each issue or topic.

If you need to attach a document do it like this:

There is now shown to me marked [XXXX *insert exhibit no, which is your initials and a number, starting with 01 for the first exhibit, 02 for the second etc] [then say what the exhibit is e.g. a letter from my GP dated XXXX]. Attach each exhibit to the end of the statement with its own cover sheet - template below].*

I believe that the facts stated in this statement are true.

This is a statement of truth and you should use this wording whenever you have to file a document which has a signed statement of truth.

Signature

NAME

DATE

Exhibit Cover Sheet

[NAME OF PARTY *You*]

[INITIALS & SURNAME OF PERSON MAKING STATEMENT]

[WHETHER THIS IS THE PERSON'S FIRST / SECOND / THIRD [ETC] STATEMENT]

[EXHIBIT NO]

DATE OF STATEMENT

IN THE FAMILY COURT (SITTING AT [XXXX])

CASE NO: [XXXX]

B E T W E E N:

[NAME OF THE PERSON APPLYING FOR AN ORDER]

APPLICANT

-AND-

[NAME OF THE OTHER PARTY]

[1ST] RESPONDENT

[-AND-

NAME OF ANY OTHER PARTY E.G. THE CHILD

2nd RESPONDENT

(only if the child has been joined as a party or there is some other party)]

THIS IS EXHIBIT NO. [XXXX] TO THE [1ST / 2nd] STATEMENT OF [NAME]

Signature

NAME   DATE

Common phrases used in Children Act orders
Recitals

> AND UPON the [Applicant / Respondent] [agreeing / undertaking] to...

> ...Use his best endeavours to arrive at contact on time

> ...to [contribute £[x] to the costs/pay half the costs] of transporting the children to and from contact

> ...to pay a sum equivalent to [x%] of the [Child Benefit / Child Tax Credit] to the [Applicant / Respondent] each week (*in cases of shared care this resolves the problem that only one parent can claim benefits for the children – however if you have two children you can agree that each can claim child benefit for one of them*)

> ...not to remove the children from the care and control of the [Applicant / Respondent] save for the purposes of contact as described below [or as otherwise agreed]

> ...not to attend at [other party's address] save for the purposes of handover in respect of contact as described below [or as otherwise agreed]

> AND UPON the parties [agreeing / undertaking] ...

> ...not to make negative remarks about one another in the presence or earshot of the children

> ...to use a communication book to inform one another of matters relating to the children

> ...to give one another [x days / weeks] advance warning of any proposed change in the contact arrangements or in respect of the dates of holiday contact as described in Paragraph [X] below

> ...to notify the other immediately if the children become unwell whilst in their care

> ...to notify the other by text at the earliest possible opportunity if for any reason they or the children are unable to attend contact

> ...not to discuss the case with the children or in the presence of the children and not to question the children about their wishes and feelings

AND UPON the [Applicant / Respondent] undertaking in the terms annexed hereto (usually this is in the form of a non-molestation order which is described below)

AND UPON the [Applicant / Respondent] having made no admissions and the court having heard no evidence and having made no findings of fact (*this is often used where you are agreeing to certain standards of behaviour but without admitting any inappropriate behaviour in the past*)

Orders

The [Applicant / Respondent] Mother shall make the child available for contact as follows:

(a) [Once per month on] [on every] [alternate/fourth] [day] from [time] to [time], collection from [location] and return to [location]

(b) By telephone on [Day(s)] at [time] [Applicant / Respondent] to ring [in / out] on the [Name]s [mobile / landline]

(c) For [half - or as agreed] of each school holiday (including half terms) dates and times to be agreed between the parties

(d) Such further and alternative contact as the parties may agree

Note the phrase '*make the child available*' is used, which is not the same as making a child go. Sometimes courts are now using the phrase '*shall allow*'.

Since 22 April 2014 there are a set of standard templates for court orders used by the court in CAP cases, which can be adapted to suit the needs of the case by the court. At the time this book was published these are available on the FLBA website and are linked to from www.nofamilylawyer.co.uk. They are likely to be available on the Judiciary or Justice website in due course. The above phrases can be added into the templates as appropriate.

Scott Schedule

A Scott Schedule is a table used to help the court and the parties see clearly what allegations are being made and what the response is to each. This helps the court to analyse whether a fact finding hearing is actually necessary and ensures that if it is the evidence is focused on the issues that are actually in dispute, and that the judgment covers all the necessary points.

The person making the allegations starts by breaking down their allegations into separate numbered allegations, giving a date for each (or an estimation of the date if unsure) and a short summary of what it is said happened. The fuller account will be contained in the witness statement.

The person responding responds by writing next to each allegation 'admitted' or 'denied' or by giving a summary of the alternative version of events.

If the response involves making allegations against the other party (cross allegations) or if there are totally separate cross allegations (i.e. ones that are not simply alternate versions of the original allegations but which are not referred to at all in the allegations so far listed) these should be included in a counter schedule, which the person making the original allegations will need to respond to.

Bundle page references should be included if possible, but if not the witness statement should be identified by date and paragraph number given.

IN THE FAMILY COURT(SITTING AT [XXXX])

CASE NO: XXXX

BETWEEN:

NAOMI SMITH — APPLICANT

AND

JOHN SMITH — RESPONDENT

APPLICANT'S SCHEDULE OF FINDINGS SOUGHT

	DATE	Applicant's allegations	Reference	Respondent's response	Reference	Findings
1	20/06/17	R punched A in the face, causing bruising.	A's statement 30/06/17 pa 6. Bundle C25.	Denied.	R's statement 07/07/17 pa 3.	
2	21/06/17	R locked A in the bathroom and refused to let her out.	A's statement 30/06/17 pa 7.	Admitted.	R's statement 07/07/17 pa 4.	
3	22/06/17	R was abusive to A and called her a slag.	A's statement 30/06/17 pa 7	Denied. A was abusive to R and pushed him. See counter schedule.	R's statement 07/07/17 pa 4.	
4	23/06/17	R harassed A by telephoning her and coming to the house.	A's statement 30/06/17 pa 7.	Denied. R accepts that he telephoned A and visited the house but at her instigation and invitation.	R's statement 07/07/17 pa 4.	

Signature

Name

Date

373

IN THE FAMILY COURT (SITTING AT [XXXX])

CASE NO: XXXX

BETWEEN:

NAOMI SMITH

APPLICANT

AND

JOHN SMITH

RESPONDENT

RESPONDENT'S COUNTER SCHEDULE OF FINDINGS SOUGHT

	DATE	Respondent's allegations	Reference	Applicant's response	Reference	Findings
1	19/06/17	When drunk, A kicked R repeatedly and scratched his face, causing bleeding.	R's statement 07/07/17 pa 1.	Denied.	A's 2nd statement 20/08/17 pa 2.	
2	22/06/17	R locked A in the bathroom. A was verbally abusive to R and pushed him.	R's statement 07/07/17 pa 4.	A admits she pushed R but only in order to get away from him.	A's 2nd statement 20/08/17 pa 3.	

Signature .... Name .... Date ....

Income Needs

There are items that you should list on your income needs in a case about finances. Some of the items below may not be relevant to you but this checklist should help make sure you don't forget anything and underestimate your income needs.

- Mortgage / Rent
- Council tax
- Water rates
- Electricity / Gas or other fuel (e.g. coal or logs)
- Landline and broadband
- Mobile
- TV subscription
- TV license
- Life insurance
- Buildings insurance
- Contents insurance
- Car insurance
- Car tax
- Petrol
- Car maintenance
- Boiler maintenance
- House maintenance
- Window cleaning / Gardening
- White goods extended warranty payments / repairs

- Glasses, lenses, dental, prescriptions
- Hairdressing
- Food
- Toiletries

- Clothes

- Social
- Cigarettes

- Subscriptions (Magazines / papers / memberships etc)

- Birthday presents for kids
- Xmas presents for kids
- Holidays

- Pension contribution
- Income protection policy
- Credit card or loan repayment
- Health insurance

- Child maintenance
- Children's food, clothing (including uniforms and kits), haircuts etc (as above)
- Extra-curricular activities - fees for sports or clubs
- School trips
- School fees / childcare costs
- Costs of any pets including vets bills
- Gym / swimming etc

Chronology for use in financial proceedings

[NAME OF PARTY *You*]

[INITIALS & SURNAME OF PERSON MAKING STATEMENT]

[WHETHER THIS IS THE PERSON'S FIRST / SECOND / THIRD [ETC] STATEMENT]

[NUMBER & INITIALS OF ALL EXHIBITS]

DATE OF STATEMENT

IN THE FAMILY COURT (SITTING AT [XXXX])

CASE NO: [XXXX]

B E T W E E N:

[NAME OF THE PERSON APPLYING FOR AN ORDER]

APPLICANT

-AND-

[NAME OF THE OTHER PARTY]

[1ST] RESPONDENT

[-AND-

NAME OF ANY OTHER PARTY E.G. THE CHILD

2nd RESPONDENT

(only if the child has been joined as a party or there is some other party)]

[APPLICANT'S / RESPONDENT'S] CHRONOLOGY

FOR [FDA / FDR / FINAL HEARING] ON [DATE]

DATE	EVENT
XXXX	H born ([Age now])
XXXX	W born ([Age now])
XXXX	Parties cohabited

XXXX	**Child [X] born ([Age now])**
XXXX	**Parties married /civil partnership**
XXXX	**Child [Y] born ([Age now])**
XXXX	[H/W] inherits £[x]
XXXX	FMH purchased [joint names / in H/W's sole name]
XXXX	[H/W] made redundant. Redundancy payment of £[x]
XXXX	**Date of separation**
XXXX	**Date of Petition**
XXXX	[H/W transfers / sells X property]
XXXX	**Form A**
XXXX	**H Form E**
XXXX	[Non molestation / occupation] order in favour of [H/W]
XXXX	FMH sold
XXXX	**W Form E**
XXXX	**Conditional Matrimonial Order / Decree Nisi**
XXXX	FDA adjourned because [X]
XXXX	**Date of [FDA/FDR etc]**
XXXX	**Final Matrimonial Order / Decree Absolute**

Signature

NAME   DATE

Note: you can use H and W for Husband and Wife as above or use A and R for Applicant and Respondent. FMH is useful shorthand for Former Matrimonial Home.

The items in bold are dates you should always include - the other items are examples of the types of things that might be included.

Schedule of assets template for use in financial proceedings

[NAME] v [NAME] CASE NO: XXXX SCHEDULE OF ASSETS FOR [FDA/FDR/FH]

	H	W	JOINT	TOTAL	NOTE
HOME					
50 Acacia Ave			£200,000		Value [Not] agreed
Less mortgage (Halifax)			£100,000		
Less redemption penalty			£2,000		If sold before XXXX
Less costs of sale			£6,000		Estimated @ 3% of price
Net equity			£92,000		
OTHER PROPERTIES					
XXXX	[Complete as above]				
Total property				£92,000	
OTHER ASSETS					
X Ltd (business)	£100,000				
Premium Bonds	£2,500				
Total other assets	**£102,500**	£0	£0	**£102,500**	
POLICIES					
Axa Life Insurance [1]	£0	£0	£0	£0	
BANK ACCOUNTS					
HSBC 01234567	-£300				H replies [date]
Lloyds TSB 01234568	£4,000				H Form E [date]
Lloyds TSB 23567896		-£200			W form E [date]
Total Bank Accounts	**£3,600**	**-£200**	**£0**	**£3,400**	
Total assets (excluding pensions)	**£106,100**	**-£200**	**£92,000**	**£197,900**	

	H	W	JOINT	TOTAL	NOTE
LIABILITIES					
Visa Credit Card 98765432	£3,400				Minimum re-payment about £102 p/m
Egg Credit Card 87654321	£2,500				Minimum repay-ment about £90 p/m
Barclays Personal Loan	£9,000				Minimum repay-ment £150 p/m
Total liabilities	£14,900	£0	£0	£14,900	
Total net assets (exclud-ing pensions)	£91,200	-£200	£92,000	£183,000	
PENSIONS					
XXXX Pension	£80,000	£0			CEV [2] [date]
Total pensions	£80,000	£0		£80,000	

50% of total net assets = £91,500

Signature

NAME   DATE

Notes on the schedule of assets

[1] Life Insurance policies need to be included in the schedule even if they have a nil value.

[2] CEV means the Cash Equivalent Value.

You do not have to do a schedule of assets, but it can be a very helpful exercise for you and can help you explain your case to the court. If your ex has a lawyer they will probably produce a document that looks a bit like this.

H / W refers to Husband / Wife but you can use A / R for Applicant / Respondent or some other abbreviation.

Wherever possible include account or policy numbers and state in the NOTES column where the figure comes from (their Form E, your Form E etc) and the date. If a figure is not agreed say so in the NOTES column, and include the alternative figure put forward.

The numbers in this document are made up, but hopefully give you some idea of how to complete the document.

Statement of Issues template for use in financial proceedings

Include the same heading as used for the witness statement, but identifying the document as '[APPLICANT / RESPONDENT]'s STATEMENT OF ISSUES FOR HEAR-ING ON [DATE]' in between the tramlines.

The following issues are examples only, to give you an idea of what sort of things should be included - they are unlikely to all be applicable to you.

(1) What is the value of the former matrimonial home? Should it be sold and the proceeds divided or retained as a home for H/W or the children of the family?

(2) What are the parties' real earning capacities? Is it reasonable to expect the W to obtain part time work now or when the children start school in [Year]?

(3) What are the parties' mortgage capacities?

(4) Has the H disclosed the true extent of his assets and income? Should the court draw adverse inferences from any non-disclosure?

(5) Do the H's parents have a beneficial interest in the property? Do they need to be joined as intervenors?

(6) Has the [Applicant / Respondent] disposed of capital or income in order to defeat the [Respondent / Applicant's] claim?

(7) Can there / should there be a clean break in this case?

(8) Should the sale / disposal of [X] by the [Applicant / Respondent] on [Date] be set aside?

Signature

NAME

DATE

Sample questions for Questionnaire in financial proceedings

As a rule of thumb it's a good idea to conclude every question that doesn't ask for a specific document with the phrase 'Please provide documentary evidence of the same' or 'Please provide documentary evidence of the same including X, Y, Z'.

(1) Please state the [Applicant / Respondent]'s qualifications and experience and estimated earning capacity. Please explain when the [Applicant / Respondent] proposes to return to work and give details of any attempts to find work, and the nature of work sought.

(2) The [Applicant/Respondent] believes that the [Respondent / Applicant] is likely to be eligible for [Child Tax Credit / Income Support / Disability Living Allowance etc]. Please provide documentary evidence of the amount of any such benefit award.

(3) The [Applicant / Respondent] cannot identify from the statements disclosed payments relating to [Child Benefit]. Does the [Applicant / Respondent] have another account into which this is paid? If so please provide details and 12 months statements for any such account.

(4) Please provide copies of credit card statements from [Date] (*usually 12 months prior to Form E*) to [Date] for each credit card in the [Applicant / Respondent]'s name or which [s/he] has use of.

(5) Please provide an up to date mortgage redemption statement / pension valuation.

(6) Please provide sample property particulars that the [Applicant / Respondent] considers suitable for [him/her] self to live in.

(7) Please explain all cash withdrawals or transfers on the bank statements for [Bank or credit card] Account No [XXXX] for any sum greater than £200.

(8) Please explain the transaction on [Date] on bank statement number [X] for the [X] account, for the sum of £[X]. Please provide documentary evidence of the [Destination / source] of the funds.

(9) Please can the [Applicant / Respondent] confirm that he has an account with [X] Bank, or if closed please provide documentary evidence of the closure and whereabouts of any closing balance, and statements for 12 months prior to closure if closed after [Date].

(10) Please can the [Applicant / Respondent] provide bank statements for 12 months for the [X] account referred to on Page [X] of the statements for account number [XXXX] which show a transfer to that account.

(11) Please can the [Applicant / Respondent] provide payslips for the last [3/6] months and [his/her] most recent P60 and documentary evidence of the amount of [his / her] Christmas bonus.

(12) Please can the [Applicant / Respondent] provide documentary evidence of the redundancy payment received in [Date] and state the whereabouts of those funds, with documentary evidence in support.

(13) The [Applicant / Respondent]'s bank statements appear to show a trip to [X] in [date range] (e.g. flight tickets, currency exchange, hotel fees, restaurants). Please can the [Applicant / Respondent] identify the source of funds [s/he] used to pay for this trip.

(14) The [Applicant / Respondent]'s bank statements do not appear to show any expenditure on [e.g. utilities, food, petrol]. Does the [Applicant / Respondent] have another bank account? If so provide 12 months statements for the same.

(15) If not, please explain (with documentary evidence) how [s/he] pays for such items and the source of those funds.

(16) The [Applicant / Respondent]'s bank statements appear to show [him/her] spending £X on [Y] each month. Please explain how this is possible given the [Applicant / Respondent]'s disclosed income of only £[X]. Does the [Applicant / Respondent] earn money in cash?

(17) Please provide a copy of the [Applicant / Respondent]'s tax return / accounts for the tax years ending [09/10, 10/11 etc].

(18) Please provide documentary evidence of the loan referred to in Form E and the terms of that loan, including payment amounts and term.

(19) Please provide an up to date valuation for the [car, jewellery, furniture] referred to in the [Applicant / Respondent]'s Form E (*only if thought to be of significant value*).

Signature

NAME   DATE

Common phrases used in financial orders
Recitals

AND UPON the parties agreeing that the terms of this order are accepted in full and final settlement of all claims that each may have against the other arising out of their marriage (*this means that you have agreed that everything is contained in the order and the order is final - neither of you can come back if you have forgotten something or changed your mind (except for things that can be varied after a final order like maintenance)*)

AND UPON the parties agreeing to divide the contents of the Former Matrimonial Home as described in the schedule annexed hereto (*you would then have a list saying who keeps what.*)

AND UPON the parties agreeing that save as set out below [or as set out in the schedule attached] all property held by either party shall remain the absolute property of the person in whose possession it now is (*That is, if you've got it you keep it. This does mean you must be careful to remember anything you need to get back and put it in the order or on the list*).

AND UPON the parties agreeing to promptly take the necessary steps to close the joint bank account with [Bank] Account number [XXXX], and to each be responsible for half of the overdraft outstanding on it as at [Date].

AND UPON the [Applicant / Respondent] undertaking to use his best endeavours to secure the release of the [Respondent / Applicant] from the mortgage in favour of [Mortgage Company] (*if your house is in joint names and one party is going to stay in the home and have it transferred to them, the mortgage company will have to agree to let that person be responsible for the mortgage. They will only do this if they are happy that the person staying has enough income to keep up the mortgage*).

Orders

The [Applicant / Respondent / Parties] shall by [Date *usually 28 days*] file and serve replies to the [Respondent / Applicant / other]'s questionnaire.

The parties shall by [Date] file and serve property particulars of properties they consider suitable for themselves and the other party and information in respect of their mortgage capacity.

The parties shall by [Date] agree the value of the Former Matrimonial

Home [Address] or in default shall by [Date] obtain a joint valuation [which may be by way of market appraisal]. The identity of any valuer is to be [agreed between the parties or in default to be nominated by the court] [nominated by the Applicant / Respondent from a list provided by the Respondent / Applicant]. The costs of such valuation shall be shared equally in the first instance.

A market appraisal is a free valuation provided by your local estate agent. A full valuation by a Chartered Surveyor will cost several hundred pounds. Depending on the likely value of the property, the extent of dispute about value or your ability to fund a valuation a market appraisal may be a perfectly sensible solution.

The [Applicant / Respondent] shall by [Date] pay or cause to be paid to the [Respondent / Applicant] a lump sum of £X.

The [Applicant / Respondent] shall by [Date] transfer all her/his legal and beneficial interest in the Former Matrimonial Home at [Address] to the [Respondent / Applicant].

The Former Matrimonial Home at [Address] shall be sold forthwith for the best price reasonably obtainable on the open market. [X Solicitors *can be one of the parties' solicitors or someone completely fresh*] shall conduct the conveyancing and the parties shall have joint conduct of the sale.

UPON sale of the Former Matrimonial Home at [Address] as provided for at paragraph [X] above the proceeds of sale shall be divided as follows:

(a) To discharge the mortgage in favour of [Bank]

(b) To discharge the charge in favour of [Bank, credit company or person *if applicable*]

(c) In payment of the conveyancing solicitor's reasonable conveyancing fees

(d) In payment of the estate agent's reasonable fees

(e) To discharge the parties' joint debt to [XXXX *e.g. overdraft, overpayment of child tax credits, credit card*]

(f) The first £X to the [Applicant / Respondent] and the balance to the Respondent / Applicant]

Or more usually

> (a) The balance to be divided equally to the parties
>
> *Or*
>
> (b) [40]% of the balance to the [Applicant / Respondent] and [60]% to the [Respondent / Applicant]
>
> The [Applicant / Respondent] shall pay or cause to be paid to the [Respondent / Applicant] periodical payments in the sum of £[X] payable on [the first day of each calendar month] until [Date] or the [Applicant / Respondent]'s cohabitation for a continuous period of six months, re-marriage or [Date] whichever is sooner. (*Note that if this is said to be for a sum like £1 per year this is called 'nominal maintenance'.*)
>
> UPON compliance with Paragraphs X, Y and Z above there shall be a clean break and the parties' claims against each other for financial relief including capital income and pensions shall stand dismissed and the parties shall not be entitled to make any claim against the other's estate in the event of their death. (*This is known as a clean break in life and death and it means you can't apply to inherit anything from your ex's estate if they die.*)

There are lots of other things that might be included in an order for financial relief, but these are the most common. The wording you see might not be exactly the same - if you are looking at an order drafted by another lawyer ask them to explain what it means. Failing that ask the Judge.

Common wording for non-molestation orders and undertakings

The [Applicant / Respondent] is forbidden to use or threaten violence against the [Applicant / Respondent] or to instruct, encourage or in any way suggest any other person should do so.

The [Applicant / Respondent] is forbidden to intimidate harass or pester the [Applicant / Respondent] or to instruct encourage or in any way suggest any other person should do so. *(The phrase 'forbidden to intimidate harass or pester' is not often used because it is difficult to be exact about what it does and does not include. Instead, courts these days prefer to use very specific wording like that below if possible.)*

The [Applicant / Respondent] is forbidden to communicate in any with the [Applicant / Respondent] including by sending [Him / Her] text messages save through [His / Her] solicitors.

The [Applicant / Respondent] is forbidden from going within 100 metres of [Address] or from approaching or gesturing at the [Applicant / Respondent].

Any of these phrases can be converted into an undertaking, for example:

On [Date] [Applicant / Respondent] appeared in person and gave an undertaking not to use or threaten violence against the [Applicant / Respondent] and to be bound by those promises until [Date].

Key Law & Guidance

Family Procedure Rules

Part 1: Overriding Objective

The overriding objective

1.1. - (1) These rules are a new procedural code with the overriding objective of enabling the court to deal with cases justly, having regard to any welfare issues involved.

(2) Dealing with a case justly includes, so far as is practicable -

> (a) ensuring that it is dealt with expeditiously and fairly;

> (b) dealing with the case in ways which are proportionate to the nature, importance and complexity of the issues;

> (c) ensuring that the parties are on an equal footing;

> (d) saving expense; and

> (e) allotting to it an appropriate share of the court's resources, while taking into account the need to allot resources to other cases.

Application by the court of the overriding objective

1.2. The court must seek to give effect to the overriding objective when it -

> (a) exercises any power given to it by these rules; or

> (b) interprets any rule.

Duty of the parties

1.3. The parties are required to help the Court to further the overriding objective.

Court's duty to manage cases

1.4. - (1) The court must further the overriding objective by actively managing cases.

(2) Active case management includes -

> (a) setting timetables or otherwise controlling the progress of the case;

> (b) identifying at an early stage -

(i) the issues; and

(ii) who should be a party to the proceedings;

(c) deciding promptly -

(i) which issues need full investigation and hearing and which do not; and

(ii) the procedure to be followed in the case;

(d) deciding the order in which issues are to be resolved;

(e) controlling the use of expert evidence;

(f) encouraging the parties to use a non-court dispute resolution procedure if the court considers that appropriate and facilitating the use of such procedure;

(g) helping the parties to settle the whole or part of the case;

(h) encouraging the parties to co-operate with each other in the conduct of the proceedings;

(i) considering whether the likely benefits of taking a particular step justify the cost of taking it;

(j) dealing with as many aspects of the case as it can on the same occasion;

(k) dealing with the case without the parties needing to attend at court;

(l) making use of technology; and

(m) giving directions to ensure that the case proceeds quickly and efficiently.

Part 4: General Case Management Powers

The court's general powers of management

4.1. - (1) In this Part, 'statement of case' means the whole or part of, an application form or answer.

(2) The list of powers in this rule is in addition to any powers given to the court by any other rule or practice direction or by any other enactment or any powers it may otherwise have.

(3) Except where these rules provide otherwise, the court may -

    (a) extend or shorten the time for compliance with any rule, practice direction or court order (even if an application for extension is made after the time for compliance has expired);

    (b) make such order for disclosure and inspection, including specific disclosure of documents, as it thinks fit;

    (c) adjourn or bring forward a hearing;

    (d) require a party or a party's legal representative to attend the court;

    (e) hold a hearing and receive evidence by telephone or by using any other method of direct oral communication;

    (f) direct that part of any proceedings be dealt with as separate proceedings;

    (g) stay the whole or part of any proceedings or judgment either generally or until a specified date or event;

    (h) consolidate proceedings;

    (i) hear two or more applications on the same occasion;

    (j) direct a separate hearing of any issue;

    (k) decide the order in which issues are to be heard;

    (l) exclude an issue from consideration;

    (m) dismiss or give a decision on an application after a decision on a preliminary issue;

    (n) direct any party to file and serve an estimate of costs; and

    (o) take any other step or make any other order for the purpose of managing the case and furthering the overriding objective.

(Rule 21.1 explains what is meant by disclosure and inspection.)

(4) When the court makes an order, it may -

    (a) make it subject to conditions, including a condition to pay a sum of money into court; and

(b) specify the consequence of failure to comply with the order or a condition.

(5) Where the court gives directions it will take into account whether or not a party has complied with any relevant pre-action protocol.

(6) A power of the court under these rules to make an order includes a power to vary or revoke the order.

(7) Any provision in these rules -

(a) requiring or permitting directions to be given by the court is to be taken as including provision for such directions to be varied or revoked; and

(b) requiring or permitting a date to be set is to be taken as including provision for that date to be changed or cancelled.

(8) The court may not extend the period within which an application for a section 89 order must be made.

Court officer's power to refer to the court

4.2. - Where a step is to be taken by a court officer -

(a) the court officer may consult the court before taking that step;

(b) the step may be taken by the court instead of the court officer.

Court's power to make order of its own initiative

4.3. - (1) Except where an enactment provides otherwise, the court may exercise its powers on an application or of its own initiative.

(Part 18 sets out the procedure for making an application.)

(2) Subject to rule 29.17, where the court proposes to make an order of its own initiative -

(a) it may give any person likely to be affected by the order an opportunity to make representations; and

(b) where it does so it must specify the time by and the manner in which the representations must be made.

(3) Where the court proposes -

(a) to make an order of its own initiative; and

(b) to hold a hearing to decide whether to make the order,

it must give each party likely to be affected by the order at least 5 days' notice of the hearing.

(4) The court may make an order of its own initiative without hearing the parties or giving them an opportunity to make representations.

(5) Where the court has made an order under paragraph (4) -

(a) a party affected by the order may apply to have it set aside, varied or stayed; and

(b) the order must contain a statement of the right to make such an application.

(6) An application under paragraph (5)(a) must be made -

(a) within such period as may be specified by the court; or

(b) if the court does not specify a period, within 7 days beginning with the date on which the order was served on the party making the application.

(7) If the court of its own initiative strikes out a statement of case or dismisses an application (including an application for permission to appeal) and it considers that the application is totally without merit -

(a) the court's order must record that fact; and

(b) the court must at the same time consider whether it is appropriate to make a civil restraint order.

Power to strike out a statement of case

4.4. - (1) Except in proceedings to which Parts 12 to 14 apply, the court may strike out a statement of case if it appears to the court -

(a) that the statement of case discloses no reasonable grounds for bringing or defending the application;

(b) that the statement of case is an abuse of the court's process or is otherwise likely to obstruct the just disposal of the proceedings;

(c) that there has been a failure to comply with a rule, practice direction or court order; or

(d) in relation to applications for matrimonial and civil partnership orders and answers to such applications, that the parties to the proceedings consent.

(2) When the court strikes out a statement of case it may make any consequential order it considers appropriate.

(3) Where -

(a) the court has struck out an Applicant's statement of case;

(b) the Applicant has been ordered to pay costs to the Respondent; and

(c) before paying those costs, the Applicant starts another application against the same Respondent, arising out of facts which are the same or substantially the same as those relating to the application in which the statement of case was struck out,

the court may, on the application of the Respondent, stay that other application until the costs of the first application have been paid.

(4) Paragraph (1) does not limit any other power of the court to strike out a statement of case.

(5) If the court strikes out an Applicant's statement of case and it considers that the application is totally without merit -

(a) the court's order must record that fact; and

(b) the court must at the same time consider whether it is appropriate to make a civil restraint order.

Sanctions have effect unless defaulting party obtains relief

4.5. - (1) Where a party has failed to comply with a rule, practice direction or court order, any sanction for failure to comply imposed by the rule, practice direction or court order has effect unless the party in default applies for and obtains relief from the sanction.

(Rule 4.6 sets out the circumstances which the court may consider on an application to grant relief from a sanction.)

(2) Where the sanction is the payment of costs, the party in default may only

obtain relief by appealing against the order for costs.

(3) Where a rule, practice direction or court order -

   (a) requires a party to do something within a specified time; and

   (b) specifies the consequence of failure to comply,

the time for doing the act in question may not be extended by agreement between the parties.

Relief from sanctions

4.6. - (1) On an application for relief from any sanction imposed for a failure to comply with any rule, practice direction or court order the court will consider all the circumstances including -

   (a) the interests of the administration of justice;

   (b) whether the application for relief has been made promptly;

   (c) whether the failure to comply was intentional;

   (d) whether there is a good explanation for the failure;

   (e) the extent to which the party in default has complied with other rules, practice directions, court orders and any relevant pre-action protocol;

   (f) whether the failure to comply was caused by the party or the party's legal representative;

   (g) whether the hearing date or the likely hearing date can still be met if relief is granted;

   (h) the effect which the failure to comply had on each party; and

   (i) the effect which the granting of relief would have on each party or a child whose interest the court considers relevant.

(2) An application for relief must be supported by evidence.

General power of the court to rectify matters where there has been an error of procedure

4.7. Where there has been an error of procedure such as a failure to comply with a rule or practice direction -

(a) the error does not invalidate any step taken in the proceedings unless the court so orders; and

(b) the court may make an order to remedy the error.

Power of the court to make civil restraint orders

4.8. Practice Direction 4B sets out -

(a) the circumstances in which the court has the power to make a civil restraint order against a party to proceedings;

(b) the procedure where a party applies for a civil restraint order against another party; and

(c) the consequences of the court making a civil restraint order.

Children Act 1989

s1 Welfare of the child

(1) When a court determines any question with respect to—

(a) the upbringing of a child; or

(b) the administration of a child's property or the application of any income arising from it,

the child's welfare shall be the court's paramount consideration.

(2) In any proceedings in which any question with respect to the upbringing of a child arises, the court shall have regard to the general principle that any delay in determining the question is likely to prejudice the welfare of the child.

(2A) A court, in the circumstances mentioned in subsection (4)(a) or (7), is as respects each parent within subsection (6)(a) to presume, unless the contrary is shown, that involvement of that parent in the life of the child concerned with further the child's welfare.

(2B) In subsection (2A) 'involvement' means involvement of some kind, either direct or indirect, but not any particular division of a child's time.

(3) In the circumstances mentioned in subsection (4), a court shall have regard in particular to—

(a) the ascertainable wishes and feelings of the child concerned (considered in the light of his age and understanding);

(b) his physical, emotional and educational needs;

(c) the likely effect on him of any change in his circumstances;

(d) his age, sex, background and any characteristics of his which the court considers relevant;

(e) any harm which he has suffered or is at risk of suffering;

(f) how capable each of his parents, and any other person in relation to whom the court considers the question to be relevant, is of meeting his needs;

(g) the range of powers available to the court under this Act in the proceedings in question.

(4) The circumstances are that—

(a) the court is considering whether to make, vary or discharge a section 8 order, and the making, variation or discharge of the order is opposed by any party to the proceedings; or

(b) the court is considering whether to make, vary or discharge a special guardianship order or an order under Part IV.

(5) Where a court is considering whether or not to make one or more orders under this Act with respect to a child, it shall not make the order or any of the orders unless it considers that doing so would be better for the child than making no order at all.

(6) In subsection (2A) 'parent' means parent of the child concerned; and, for the purposes of that subsection, a parent of the child concerned-

(a) is within this paragraph if that parent can be involved in the child's life in a way that does not put the child at risk of suffering harm; and

(b) is to be treated as being within paragraph (a) unless there is some evidence before the court in the particular proceedings to suggest that involvement of that parent in the child's life would put the child at risk of suffering harm whatever the form of the involvement.

(7) The circumstances referred to are that the court is considering whether to make an order under section 4(1)(c) or 4ZA(1)(c) or (5) (parental responsibility of

parent other than mother).

Matrimonial Causes Act 1973

s25 Matters to which court is to have regard in deciding how to exercise its powers under ss. 23, 24 and 24A

(1) It shall be the duty of the court in deciding whether to exercise its powers under section 23, 24 above and, if so, in what manner, to have regard to all the circumstances of the case, first consideration being given to the welfare while a minor of any child of the family who has not attained the age of eighteen.

(2) As regards the exercise of the powers of the court under section 23(1)(a), (b) or (c), 24 above in relation to a party to the marriage, the court shall in particular have regard to the following matters—

    (a) the income, earning capacity, property and other financial resources which each of the parties to the marriage has or is likely to have in the foreseeable future, including in the case of earning capacity any increase in that capacity which it would in the opinion of the court be reasonable to expect a party to the marriage to take steps to acquire;

    (b) the financial needs, obligations and responsibilities which each of the parties to the marriage has or is likely to have in the foreseeable future;

    (c) the standard of living enjoyed by the family before the breakdown of the marriage;

    (d) the age of each party to the marriage and the duration of the marriage;

    (e) any physical or mental disability of either of the parties to the marriage;

    (f) the contributions which each of the parties has made or is likely in the foreseeable future to make to the welfare of the family, including any contribution by looking after the home or caring for the family;

    (g) the conduct of each of the parties, if that conduct is such that it would in the opinion of the court be inequitable to disregard it;

    (h) in the case of proceedings for divorce or nullity of marriage, the value to each of the parties to the marriage of any benefit . . . which, by reason of the dissolution or annulment of the marriage, that party will lose the chance of acquiring.

(3) As regards the exercise of the powers of the court under section 23(1)(d), (e) or (f), (2) or (4), 24 or 24A above in relation to a child of the family, the court shall in particular have regard to the following matters—

- (a) the financial needs of the child;

- (b) the income, earning capacity (if any), property and other financial resources of the child;

- (c) any physical or mental disability of the child;

- (d) the manner in which he was being and in which the parties to the marriage expected him to be educated or trained;

- (e) the considerations mentioned in relation to the parties to the marriage in paragraphs (a), (b), (c) and (e) of subsection (2) above.

(4) As regards the exercise of the powers of the court under section 23(1)(d), (e) or (f), (2) or (4), 24 or 24A above against a party to a marriage in favour of a child of the family who is not the child of that party, the court shall also have regard—

- (a) to whether that party assumed any responsibility for the child's maintenance, and, if so, to the extent to which, and the basis upon which, that party assumed such responsibility and to the length of time for which that party discharged such responsibility;

- (b) to whether in assuming and discharging such responsibility that party did so knowing that the child was not his or her own;(c) to the liability of any other person to maintain the child.

Family Law Act 1996

s33

Read Chapter 21 to make sure that s33 applies to your case. ss34-38 are not set out here for reasons of space.

Occupation orders where applicant has estate or interest etc. or has home rights

(1) If—

(a) a person ('the person entitled')—

(i) is entitled to occupy a dwelling-house by virtue of a beneficial estate or interest or contract or by virtue of any enactment giving him the right to remain in occupation, or

(ii) has home rights in relation to a dwelling-house, and

(b) the dwelling-house—

(i) is or at any time has been the home of the person entitled and of another person with whom he is associated, or

(ii) was at any time intended by the person entitled and any such other person to be their home,

the person entitled may apply to the court for an order containing any of the provisions specified in subsections (3), (4) and (5).

(2) If an agreement to marry is terminated, no application under this section may be made by virtue of section 62(3)(e) by reference to that agreement after the end of the period of three years beginning with the day on which it is terminated.

(2A) If a civil partnership agreement (as defined by section 73 of the Civil Partnership Act 2004) is terminated, no application under this section may be made by virtue of section 62(3)(eza) by reference to that agreement after the end of the period of three years beginning with the day on which it is terminated.

(3) An order under this section may—

(a) enforce the applicant's entitlement to remain in occupation as against the other person ('the Respondent');

(b) require the Respondent to permit the applicant to enter and remain in the dwelling-house or part of the dwelling-house;

(c) regulate the occupation of the dwelling-house by either or both parties;

(d) if the Respondent is entitled as mentioned in subsection (1)(a)(i), prohibit, suspend or restrict the exercise by him of his right to occupy the dwelling-house;

(e) if the Respondent has home rights in relation to the dwelling-house and the applicant is the other spouse or civil partner, restrict or terminate those rights;

(f) require the Respondent to leave the dwelling-house or part of the dwelling-house; or

(g) exclude the Respondent from a defined area in which the dwelling-house is included.

(4) An order under this section may declare that the applicant is entitled as mentioned in subsection (1)(a)(i) or has home rights.

(5) If the applicant has home rights and the Respondent is the other spouse or civil partner, an order under this section made during the marriage or civil partnership may provide that those rights are not brought to an end by—

(a) the death of the other spouse or civil partner; or

(b) the termination (otherwise than by death) of the marriage or civil partnership.

(6) In deciding whether to exercise its powers under subsection (3) and (if so) in what manner, the court shall have regard to all the circumstances including—

(a) the housing needs and housing resources of each of the parties and of any relevant child;

(b) the financial resources of each of the parties;

(c) the likely effect of any order, or of any decision by the court not to exercise its powers under subsection (3), on the health, safety or well-being of the parties and of any relevant child; and

(d) the conduct of the parties in relation to each other and otherwise.

(7) If it appears to the court that the applicant or any relevant child is likely to suffer significant harm attributable to conduct of the respondent if an order under this section containing one or more of the provisions mentioned in subsection (3) is not made, the court shall make the order unless it appears to it that—

(a) the respondent or any relevant child is likely to suffer significant harm if the order is made; and

(b) the harm likely to be suffered by the respondent or child in that event is as great as, or greater than, the harm attributable to conduct of the respondent which is likely to be suffered by the applicant or child if the order is not made.

(8) The court may exercise its powers under subsection (5) in any case where it considers that in all the circumstances it is just and reasonable to do so.

(9) An order under this section—

>   (a) may not be made after the death of either of the parties mentioned in subsection (1); and

>   (b) except in the case of an order made by virtue of subsection (5)(a), ceases to have effect on the death of either party.

(10) An order under this section may, in so far as it has continuing effect, be made for a specified period, until the occurrence of a specified event or until further order.

s42 Non-molestation orders

(1) In this Part a 'non-molestation order' means an order containing either or both of the following provisions—

>   (a) provision prohibiting a person ('the respondent') from molesting another person who is associated with the respondent;

>   (b) provision prohibiting the respondent from molesting a relevant child.

(2) The court may make a non-molestation order—

>   (a) if an application for the order has been made (whether in other family proceedings or without any other family proceedings being instituted) by a person who is associated with the respondent; or

>   (b) if in any family proceedings to which the respondent is a party the Court considers that the order should be made for the benefit of any other party to the proceedings or any relevant child even though no such application has been made.

(3) In subsection (2) 'family proceedings' includes proceedings in which the court has made an emergency protection order under section 44 of the Children Act 1989 which includes an exclusion requirement (as defined in section 44A(3) of that Act).

(4) Where an agreement to marry is terminated, no application under subsection (2)(a) may be made by virtue of section 62(3)(e) by reference to that agreement

after the end of the period of three years beginning with the day on which it is terminated.

(4ZA) If a civil partnership agreement (as defined by section 73 of the Civil Partnership Act 2004) is terminated, no application under this section may be made by virtue of section 62(3)(eza) by reference to that agreement after the end of the period of three years beginning with the day on which it is terminated.

(4A) A court considering whether to make an occupation order shall also consider whether to exercise the power conferred by subsection (2)(b).

(4B) In this Part 'the applicant', in relation to a Non-Molestation order, includes (where the context permits) the person for whose benefit such an order would be or is made in exercise of the power conferred by subsection (2)(b)

(5) In deciding whether to exercise its powers under this section and, if so, in what manner, the court shall have regard to all the circumstances including the need to secure the health, safety and well-being—

(a) of the applicant or, in a case falling within subsection (2)(b), the person for whose benefit the order would be made; and

(b) of any relevant child.

(6) A Non-Molestation order may be expressed so as to refer to molestation in general, to particular acts of molestation, or to both.

(7) A Non-Molestation order may be made for a specified period or until further order.

(8) A Non-Molestation order which is made in other family proceedings ceases to have effect if those proceedings are withdrawn or dismissed.

s45 Ex parte orders

(1) The court may, in any case where it considers that it is just and convenient to do so, make an occupation order or a Non-Molestation order even though the respondent has not been given such notice of the proceedings as would otherwise be required by rules of court.

(2) In determining whether to exercise its powers under subsection (1), the court shall have regard to all the circumstances including—

(a) any risk of significant harm to the applicant or a relevant child, attributable to conduct of the respondent, if the order is not made immediately;

(b) whether it is likely that the applicant will be deterred or prevented from pursuing the application if an order is not made immediately; and

(c) whether there is reason to believe that the respondent is aware of the proceedings but is deliberately evading service and that the applicant or a relevant child will be seriously prejudiced by the delay involved in effecting substituted service.

(3) If the court makes an order by virtue of subsection (1) it must afford the respondent an opportunity to make representations relating to the order as soon as just and convenient at a full hearing.

(4) If, at a full hearing, the court makes an occupation order ('the full order'), then—

(a) for the purposes of calculating the maximum period for which the full order may be made to have effect, the relevant section is to apply as if the period for which the full order will have effect began on the date on which the initial order first had effect; and

(b) the provisions of section 36(10) or 38(6) as to the extension of orders are to apply as if the full order and the initial order were a single order.

(5) In this section—

- 'full hearing' means a hearing of which notice has been given to all the parties in accordance with rules of court;

- 'initial order' means an occupation order made by virtue of subsection (1); and

- 'relevant section' means section 33(10), 35(10), 36(10), 37(5) or 38(6).

s46 Undertakings

(1) In any case where the court has power to make an occupation order or non-molestation order, the court may accept an undertaking from any party to the proceedings.

(2) No power of arrest may be attached to any undertaking given under subsection (1).

(3) The court shall not accept an undertaking under subsection (1) in any case where apart from this section a power of arrest would be attached to the order.

(3A) The court shall not accept an undertaking under subsection (1) instead of making a non-molestation order in any case where it appears to the court that--

> (a) the respondent has used or threatened violence against the applicant or a relevant child; and

> (b) for the protection of the applicant or child it is necessary to make a non-molestation order so that any breach may be punishable under section 42A.

(4) An undertaking given to a court under subsection (1) is enforceable as if the court had made an occupation order or a non-molestation order in terms corresponding to those of the undertaking.

(5) This section has effect without prejudice to the powers of the High Court and the Family Court apart from this section.

Schedule 7 Family Law Act 1996

Section 53. Transfer of certain tenancies on divorce etc. or on separation of cohabitants

Part 1 General

Interpretation

1
In this Schedule—

> 'civil partner', except in paragraph 2, includes (where the context requires) former civil partner;

> 'cohabitant', except in paragraph 3, includes (where the context requires) former cohabitant;

> 'the Court' means the High Court or the Family Court,

> 'landlord' includes—

> (a) any person from time to time deriving title under the original landlord; and

> (b) in relation to any dwelling-house, any person other than the tenant

who is, or (but for Part VII of the Rent Act 1977 or Part II of the Rent (Agriculture) Act 1976) would be, entitled to possession of the dwelling-house;

'Part II order' means an order under Part II of this Schedule;

'a relevant tenancy' means—

(a) a protected tenancy or statutory tenancy within the meaning of the Rent Act 1977;

(b) a statutory tenancy within the meaning of the Rent (Agriculture) Act 1976;

(c) a secure tenancy within the meaning of section 79 of the Housing Act 1985; . . .

(d) an assured tenancy or assured agricultural occupancy within the meaning of Part I of the Housing Act 1988; or

(e) an introductory tenancy within the meaning of Chapter I of Part V of the Housing Act 1996;

'spouse', except in paragraph 2, includes (where the context requires) former spouse; and

'tenancy' includes sub-tenancy.

Cases in which the court may make an order

2
(1) This paragraph applies if one spouse or civil partner is entitled, either in his own right or jointly with the other spouse or civil partner, to occupy a dwelling-house by virtue of a relevant tenancy.

(2) The court may make a Part II order--

(a) on granting a decree of divorce, a decree of nullity of marriage or a decree of judicial separation or at any time thereafter (whether, in the case of a decree of divorce or nullity of marriage, before or after the decree is made absolute), or

(b) at any time when it has power to make a property adjustment order under Part 2 of Schedule 5 to the Civil Partnership Act 2004 with respect to the civil partnership.

3

(1) This paragraph applies if one cohabitant is entitled, either in his own right or jointly with the other cohabitant, to occupy a dwelling-house by virtue of a relevant tenancy.

(2) If the cohabitants cease to cohabit, the court may make a Part II order.

4

The court shall not make a Part II order unless the dwelling-house is or was—

    (a)   in the case of spouses, a matrimonial home;

    (aa) in the case of civil partners, a civil partnership home; or

    (b)   in the case of cohabitants, a home in which they cohabited.

Matters to which the court must have regard

5

In determining whether to exercise its powers under Part II of this Schedule and, if so, in what manner, the court shall have regard to all the circumstances of the case including—

    (a) the circumstances in which the tenancy was granted to either or both of the spouses, civil partners or cohabitants or, as the case requires, the circumstances in which either or both of them became tenant under the tenancy;

    (b) the matters mentioned in section 33(6)(a), (b) and (c) and, where the parties are cohabitants and only one of them is entitled to occupy the dwelling-house by virtue of the relevant tenancy, the further matters mentioned in section 36(6)(e), (f), (g) and (h); and

    (c) the suitability of the parties as tenants.

Family Law Act 1986

s33 Power to order disclosure of child's whereabouts

(1) Where in proceedings for or relating to a Part I order [*a Part 1 order includes a s8 CA order*] in respect of a child there is not available to the court adequate information as to where the child is, the court may order any person who it has reason to believe may have relevant information to disclose it to the court.

(2) A person shall not be excused from complying with an order under subsection

(1) above by reason that to do so may incriminate him or his spouse or civil partner of an offence; but a statement or admission made in compliance with such an order shall not be admissible in evidence against either of them in proceedings for any offence other than perjury.

(3) A court in Scotland before which proceedings are pending for the enforcement of an order relating to parental responsibilities or parental rights in relation to a child made outside the United Kingdom which is recognised in Scotland shall have the same powers as it would have under subsection (1) above if the order were its own.

s34 Power to order recovery of child

(1) Where—

    (a) a person is required by a Part I order, or an order for the enforcement of a Part I order, to give up a child to another person ('the person concerned'), and

    (b) the court which made the order imposing the requirement is satisfied that the child has not been given up in accordance with the order,

the court may make an order authorising an officer of the court or a constable to take charge of the child and deliver him to the person concerned.

(2) The authority conferred by subsection (1) above includes authority—

    (a) to enter and search any premises where the person acting in pursuance of the order has reason to believe the child may be found, and

    (b) to use such force as may be necessary to give effect to the purpose of the order.

(3) Where by virtue of—

    (a) section 14 of the Children Act 1989

    (b) Article 14 (enforcement of residence orders) of the Children (Northern Ireland) Order 1995,

a Part I order (or a provision of a Part I order) may be enforced as if it were an order requiring a person to give up a child to another person, subsection (1) above shall apply as if the Part I order had included such a requirement.

(4) This section is without prejudice to any power conferred on a court by or

under any other enactment or rule of law.

Practice Guidance: McKenzie Friends (Civil and Family Courts)

[NB: This guidance was issued before the Family Court was created in April 2014, so it refers to the County Court - it applies to the Family Court too.]

1) This Guidance applies to civil and family proceedings in the Court of Appeal (Civil Division), the High Court of Justice, the County Courts and the Family Proceedings Court in the Magistrates' Courts[1]. It is issued as guidance (not as a Practice Direction) by the Master of the Rolls, as Head of Civil Justice, and the President of the Family Division, as Head of Family Justice. It is intended to remind courts and litigants of the principles set out in the authorities and supersedes the guidance contained in *Practice Note (Family Courts: McKenzie Friends) (No 2)* [2008] 1 WLR 2757, which is now withdrawn[2]. It is issued in light of the increase in litigants-in-person (litigants) in all levels of the civil and Family Courts.

The Right to Reasonable Assistance

2) Litigants have the right to have reasonable assistance from a layperson, sometimes called a McKenzie Friend (MF). Litigants assisted by MFs remain litigants-in-person. MFs have no independent right to provide assistance. They have no right to act as advocates or to carry out the conduct of litigation.

What McKenzie Friends may do

3) MFs may: i) provide moral support for litigants; ii) take notes; iii) help with case papers; iii) quietly give advice on any aspect of the conduct of the case.

What McKenzie Friends may not do

4) MFs may not: i) act as the litigants' agent in relation to the proceedings; ii) manage litigants' cases outside court, for example by signing court documents; or iii) address the Court, make oral submissions or examine witnesses.

Exercising the Right to Reasonable Assistance

5) While litigants ordinarily have a right to receive reasonable assistance from MFs the Court retains the power to refuse to permit such assistance. The court may do so where it is satisfied that, in that case, the interests of justice and fairness do not require the litigant to receive such assistance.

6) A litigant who wishes to exercise this right should inform the Judge as soon as possible indicating who the MF will be. The proposed MF should produce a short curriculum vitae or other statement setting out relevant experience, confirming that he or she has no interest in the case and understands the MF's role and the duty of confidentiality.

7) If the court considers that there might be grounds for circumscribing the right to receive such assistance, or a party objects to the presence of, or assistance given by a MF, it is not for the litigant to justify the exercise of the right. It is for the court or the objecting party to provide sufficient reasons why the litigant should not receive such assistance.

8) When considering whether to circumscribe the right to assistance or refuse a MF permission to attend the right to a fair trial is engaged. The matter should be considered carefully. The litigant should be given a reasonable opportunity to argue the point. The proposed MF should not be excluded from that hearing and should normally be allowed to help the litigant.

9) Where proceedings are in *closed* court, i.e. the hearing is in chambers, is in private, or the proceedings relate to a child, the litigant is required to justify the MF's presence in court. The presumption in favour of permitting a MF to attend such hearings, and thereby enable litigants to exercise the right to assistance, is a strong one.

10) The court may refuse to allow a litigant to exercise the right to receive assistance at the start of a hearing. The court can also circumscribe the right during the course of a hearing. It may be refused at the start of a hearing or later circumscribed where the court forms the view that a MF may give, has given, or is giving, assistance which impedes the efficient administration of justice. However, the court should also consider whether a firm and unequivocal warning to the litigant and/or MF might suffice in the first instance.

11) A decision by the court not to curtail assistance from a MF should be regarded as final, save on the ground of subsequent misconduct by the MF or on the ground that the MF's continuing presence will impede the efficient administration of justice. In such event the court should give a short judgment setting out the reasons why it has curtailed the right to assistance. Litigants may appeal such decisions. MFs have no standing to do so.

12) The following factors should not be taken to justify the court refusing to permit a litigant receiving such assistance:

(i) The case or application is simple or straightforward, or is, for instance, a directions or case management hearing;

(ii) The litigant appears capable of conducting the case without assistance;

(iii) The litigant is unrepresented through choice;

(iv) The other party is not represented;

(v) The proposed MF belongs to an organisation that promotes a particular cause;

(vi) The proceedings are confidential and the court papers contain sensitive information relating to a family's affairs

13) A litigant may be denied the assistance of a MF because its provision might undermine or has undermined the efficient administration of justice. Examples of circumstances where this might arise are: i) the assistance is being provided for an improper purpose; ii) the assistance is unreasonable in nature or degree; iii) the MF is subject to a civil proceedings order or a civil restraint order; iv) the MF is using the litigant as a puppet; v) the MF is directly or indirectly conducting the litigation; vi) the court is not satisfied that the MF fully understands the duty of confidentiality.

14) Where a litigant is receiving assistance from a MF in care proceedings, the court should consider the MF's attendance at any advocates' meetings directed by the court, and, with regard to cases commenced after 1.4.08, consider directions in accordance with paragraph 13.2 of the Practice Direction Guide to Case Management in Public Law Proceedings.

15) Litigants are permitted to communicate any information, including filed evidence, relating to the proceedings to MFs for the purpose of obtaining advice or assistance in relation to the proceedings.

16) Legal representatives should ensure that documents are served on litigants in good time to enable them to seek assistance regarding their content from MFs in advance of any hearing or advocates' meeting.

17) The High Court can, under its inherent jurisdiction, impose a civil restraint order on MFs who repeatedly act in ways that undermine the efficient administration of justice.

Rights of audience and rights to conduct litigation

18) MFs do **not** have a right of audience or a right to conduct litigation. It is a criminal offence to exercise rights of audience or to conduct litigation unless properly qualified and authorised to do so by an appropriate regulatory body or, in the case of an otherwise unqualified or unauthorised individual (i.e., a lay individual including a MF), the Court grants such rights on a case-by-case basis[3].

19) Courts should be slow to grant any application from a litigant for a right of

audience or a right to conduct litigation to any lay person, including a MF. This is because a person exercising such rights must ordinarily be properly trained, be under professional discipline (including an obligation to insure against liability for negligence) and be subject to an overriding duty to the court. These requirements are necessary for the protection of all parties to litigation and are essential to the proper administration of justice.

20) Any application for a right of audience or a right to conduct litigation to be granted to any lay person should therefore be considered very carefully. The court should only be prepared to grant such rights where there is good reason to do so taking into account all the circumstances of the case, which are likely to vary greatly. Such grants should not be extended to lay persons automatically or without due consideration. They should not be granted for mere convenience.

21) Examples of the type of special circumstances which have been held to justify the grant of a right of audience to a lay person, including a MF, are: i) that person is a close relative of the litigant; ii) health problems preclude the litigant from addressing the court, or conducting litigation, and the litigant cannot afford to pay for a qualified legal representative; iii) the litigant is relatively inarticulate and prompting by that person may unnecessarily prolong the proceedings.

22) It is for the litigant to persuade the court that the circumstances of the case are such that it is in the interests of justice for the court to grant a lay person a right of audience or a right to conduct litigation.

23) The grant of a right of audience or a right to conduct litigation to lay persons who hold themselves out as professional advocates or professional MFs or who seek to exercise such rights on a regular basis, whether for reward or not, will however only be granted in exceptional circumstances. To do otherwise would tend to subvert the will of Parliament.

24) If a litigant wants a lay person to be granted a right of audience, an application must be made at the start of the hearing. If a right to conduct litigation is sought such an application must be made at the earliest possible time and must be made, in any event, before the lay person does anything which amounts to the conduct of litigation. It is for litigants to persuade the court, on a case-by-case basis, that the grant of such rights is justified.

25) Rights of audience and the right to conduct litigation are separate rights. The grant of one right to a lay person does not mean that a grant of the other right has been made. If both rights are sought their grant must be applied for individually and justified separately.

26) Having granted either a right of audience or a right to conduct litigation, the court has the power to remove either right. The grant of such rights in one set of proceedings cannot be relied on as a precedent supporting their grant in future proceedings.

Remuneration

27) Litigants can enter into lawful agreements to pay fees to MFs for the provision of reasonable assistance in court or out of court by, for instance, carrying out clerical or mechanical activities, such as photocopying documents, preparing bundles, delivering documents to opposing parties or the court, or the provision of legal advice in connection with court proceedings. Such fees cannot be lawfully recovered from the opposing party.

28) Fees said to be incurred by MFs for carrying out the conduct of litigation, where the court has not granted such a right, cannot lawfully be recovered from either the litigant for whom they carry out such work or the opposing party.

29) Fees said to be incurred by MFs for carrying out the conduct of litigation after the court has granted such a right are in principle recoverable from the litigant for whom the work is carried out. Such fees cannot be lawfully recovered from the opposing party.

30) Fees said to be incurred by MFs for exercising a right of audience following the grant of such a right by the court are in principle recoverable from the litigant on whose behalf the right is exercised. Such fees are also recoverable, in principle, from the opposing party as a recoverable disbursement: CPR 48.6(2) and 48(6)(3)(ii).

Personal Support Unit & Citizen's Advice Bureau

31) Litigants should also be aware of the services provided by local Personal Support Units and Citizens' Advice Bureaux. The PSU at the Royal Courts of Justice in London can be contacted on 020 7947 7701, by email at cbps@bello.co.uk or at the enquiry desk. The CAB at the Royal Courts of Justice in London can be contacted on 020 7947 6564 or at the enquiry desk.

Lord Neuberger of Abbotsbury, Master of the Rolls
Sir Nicholas Wall, President of the Family Division

12 July 2010

Notes

[1] References to the Judge or court should be read where proceedings are taking place under the Family Proceedings Courts (Matrimonial Proceedings etc) Rules 1991, as a reference to a justices' clerk or assistant justices' clerk who is specifically authorised by a justices' clerk to exercise the functions of the Court at the relevant hearing. Where they are taking place under the Family Proceedings Courts (Children Act 1989) Rules 1991 they should be read consistently with the provisions of those Rules, specifically rule 16A(5A).

[2] *R v Leicester City Justices, ex parte Barrow* [1991] 260, *Chauhan v Chauhan* [1997] FCR 206, *R v Bow County Court, ex parte Pelling* [1999] 1 WLR 1807, *Attorney-General v Purvis* [2003] EWHC 3190 (Admin), *Clarkson v Gilbert* [2000] CP Rep 58, *United Building and Plumbing Contractors v Kajla* [2002] EWCA Civ 628, *Re O (Children) (Hearing in Private: Assistance)* [2005] 3 WLR 1191, *Westland Helicopters Ltd v Sheikh Salah Al-Hejailan (No 2)* [2004] 2 Lloyd's Rep 535. *Agassi v Robinson (Inspector of Taxes) (No 2)* [2006] 1 WLR 2126, *Re N (A Child) (McKenzie Friend: Rights of Audience) Practice Note* [2008] 1 WLR 2743.

[3] Legal Services Act 2007 s12 - 19 and Schedule 3.

Index

W